PROFESSIONAL
IPHONE PROGRAMMING WITH
MONOTOUCH AND .NET/C#

CW00601507

PROFESSIONAL

iPhone® Programming with MonoTouch and .NET/C#

PROFESSIONAL

iPhone® Programming with MonoTouch and .NET/C#

Wallace B. McClure
Martin Bowling
Craig Dunn
Chris Hardy
Rory Blyth

WILEY

Wiley Publishing, Inc.

Professional iPhone® Programming with MonoTouch and .NET/C#

Published by
Wiley Publishing, Inc.
10475 Crosspoint Boulevard
Indianapolis, IN 46256
www.wiley.com

Published by Wiley Publishing, Inc., Indianapolis, Indiana

Published simultaneously in Canada

ISBN: 978-0-470-63782-1
ISBN: 978-0-470-90808-2 (ebk)
ISBN: 978-0-470-90859-4 (ebk)
ISBN: 978-0-470-90860-0 (ebk)

Manufactured in the United States of America

10 9 8 7 6 5 4 3 2 1

For general information on our other products and services please contact our Customer Care Department within the United States at (877) 762-2974, outside the United States at (317) 572-3993 or fax (317) 572-4002.

Wiley also publishes its books in a variety of electronic formats. Some content that appears in print may not be available in electronic books.

Library of Congress Control Number: 2010926847

ABOUT THE AUTHORS

 WALLACE B. (WALLY) MCCLURE graduated from the Georgia Institute of Technology (Georgia Tech) in 1990 with a Bachelor of Science degree in electrical engineering. He continued his education there, receiving a master's degree in the same field in 1991. Since that time, he has done consulting and development for such companies as The United States Department of Education, Coca-Cola, Bechtel National, Magnatron, and Lucent Technologies, among others. Products and services have included work with ASP, ADO, XML, and SQL Server, as well as numerous applications in the Microsoft .NET Framework. Wally has authored books on architecture, ADO.NET and SQL Server, AJAX, and iPhone Programming with Mono/MonoTouch. Wally specializes in building applications that have large numbers of users and large amounts of data. He is a Microsoft MVP and an ASPInsider, and a partner in Scalable Development, Inc. You can read Wally's blog at www.morewally.com. Wally is married and has two children. When not writing software, he plays golf, exercises, and hangs out with his family.

 MARTIN BOWLING is the Founder/President of 27 Creative, a Charleston, West Virginia, based Internet marketing and mobile development consulting firm. Martin has been recognized for his Internet Marketing talents, providing consulting for many Fortune 500 companies and some of the top educational institutions in America. Martin is in demand as a speaker, seminar leader, and consultant in various topics ranging from social media marketing to application development. He is currently focusing on several projects that bring his many passions together, working with a leading social media marketing and SEO firm Search & Social to build a platform to provide scalable SEO and social media marketing to small and medium-sized businesses. His project Tweetcaching.com takes mobile development, social media, and the outdoors and combines it into one great project to allow Geocachers to easily share their finds with their friends and family while they are on the go. Martin continues to find new ways to mash up social media with mobile development to provide a rich experience to users and maximum ROI for the companies he works with. He lives with his wife in Charleston, West Virginia. His black lab, Brewski, keeps him company while he codes. Martin loves a great meal and craft brewing. He can be reached at www.martinbowling.com where he occasionally blogs. For a more up close and personal look at Martin follow him on Twitter at http://twitter.com/MartinBowling.

 CRAIG DUNN has been developing with the .NET Framework since 2001 in both Australia and Canada, on projects ranging from Internet banking to warehouse automation systems (and including a stint building multilingual web sites). He has been involved with MonoTouch since the early betas in August 2009, blogging tutorials at http://conceptdev.blogspot.com and producing the MIX10 iPhone conference schedule application (in conjunction with Chris Hardy) for Microsoft's 2010 MIX conference in Las Vegas. Craig was also 15th in line for an iPad.

CHRIS HARDY, a Microsoft ASPInsider, works for a digital agency called Great Fridays in Manchester, United Kingdom, developing ASP.NET solutions for clients such as Peter Gabriel and Emma Watson. Ever since MonoTouch was in beta, Chris has been developing and evangelizing MonoTouch and was one of the first users to get a MonoTouch application on to the App Store. Speaking at conferences around the world on the subject, Chris has been a key part of the community and is extending this by contributing to the MonoTouch book.

RORY BLYTH has worked in the software development industry for nearly a decade. He began as an independent contractor, then went on to co-host the popular .Net Rocks podcast, work as a public speaker for Microsoft, join Microsoft's Channel9, and deliver many talks for other companies/conferences on diverse subjects including iPhone development using both Objective-C and MonoTouch. He learned iPhone development during a year working at Spotlight Mobile — a development firm where popular iPhone apps such as Style.com and the Barnes and Noble Bookstore were produced.

ABOUT THE TECHNICAL EDITORS

ALEX YORK is a graduate of the University of Manchester in England, where he studied computing science. He has been developing software solutions ever since — almost exclusively with C# and the .NET Framework. After graduating, Alex worked in Manchester for a mobile gaming company, using ASP.NET and WCF on a daily basis. He moved to Norway in 2008 and started working for Bennett, building customer solutions using C# and ASP.NET for recognizable Norwegian brands. In his spare time he was an early adopter of iPhone development with MonoTouch and an active member of the community. He currently works as a technology consultant for Capgemini, in Trondheim.

JOHN MANDIA grew up in London and has been developing since 1999 when he switched from working in marketing to development. During that time he's worked for a value-added reseller (VAR), a .com company, a portal, a design agency, a consultancy and he is currently working for a leading global investment bank. He's been working with .NET since it was in beta, and for a number of years he was a major contributor to an open source project known as Rainbow Portal (2002–2005) which has had over 130,000 downloads. One of his current interests is mobile development, and he's been following MonoTouch since it was in beta when he set up the MonoTouch community site http://monotouch.info and twitter account @monotouchinfo to help others who have decided to take their .NET skills and apply it to iPhone/iPad development.

JIM ZIMMERMAN is an ASP.NET MVP and CTO of Thuzi and TeamZoneSports in Tampa, Florida. He decided to learn Objective-C last year in order to learn how to create iPhone apps for his four kids and for his companies. He has since been convinced that MonoTouch is the way to go allowing him to bring his C# skills with him, giving him a much more rapid development experience. He looks forward to the day when he can have at least 90 percent of the same code running on all relevant mobile devices.

CREDITS

EXECUTIVE EDITOR
Bob Elliott

SENIOR PROJECT EDITOR
Kevin Kent

DEVELOPMENT EDITOR
Jeff Riley

TECHNICAL EDITORS
Alex York
John Mandia
Jim Zimmerman

SENIOR PRODUCTION EDITOR
Debra Banninger

COPY EDITOR
Kim Cofer

EDITORIAL DIRECTOR
Robyn B. Siesky

EDITORIAL MANAGER
Mary Beth Wakefield

MARKETING MANAGER
Ashley Zurcher

PRODUCTION MANAGER
Tim Tate

**VICE PRESIDENT AND EXECUTIVE GROUP
PUBLISHER**
Richard Swadley

VICE PRESIDENT AND EXECUTIVE PUBLISHER
Barry Pruett

ASSOCIATE PUBLISHER
Jim Minatel

PROJECT COORDINATOR, COVER
Lynsey Stanford

COMPOSITOR
Jeffrey Lytle, Happenstance Type-O-Rama

PROOFREADER
Nancy Carrasco

INDEXER
Robert Swanson

COVER DESIGNER
Michael E. Trent

COVER IMAGE
©Marilyn Nieves/istockphoto

ACKNOWLEDGMENTS

I'VE ALWAYS BEEN INTERESTED in mobile development. It wasn't until the summer of 2009 that Wrox and I were able to agree on creating a mobile development/iPhone project. That project, part of the Wrox Blox series, was the first version of this book; it published in November 2009. Two weeks after the release of that project, Associate Publisher Jim Minatel was happy with the sales of the ebook and was wondering about a bigger print book on MonoTouch. Due to my schedule, I needed to get several other authors. I initially thought of Craig Dunn, Chris Hardy, and Martin Bowling. I had spoken with each during the writing of my first book, so it made sense to talk with them about co-authoring the print book. I spoke with Joseph Hill at Novell one afternoon, and he suggested them as well. With some level setting in my initial choices, I talked with each one and they all accepted. I was ecstatic. Rory Blyth joined us a short way into our book. Thanks to Jim Minatel for allowing me to start writing on MonoTouch. Thanks to Bob Elliott for keeping us on target, and a big thanks to Kevin Kent for doing the dirty work of keeping us on task.

Given that my co-authors were on separate continents and hemispheres, I want to thank them for their great work. Craig and Chris did a great job, were very attentive to detail, and were always on top of what was going on.

I want to thank my family. They did a great job allowing me to work on the book and to work for customers as well. I owe them a huge "Thank You."

Finally, I want to thank you for purchasing this book. We hope you enjoy this book as much as we have enjoyed writing it.

—WALLACE B. MCCLURE

SPECIAL THANKS TO my wonderful wife Mandi Rae. Without her I don't know where I would be. Thanks to my mom, CK, Sarah, and all those who have supported me over the years. And thanks to Brewski Firkin for keeping me company while I code.

—MARTIN BOWLING

THANKS TO Karl, Mike, and Chris for inspiration, and to Mum for everything. To Jack, Lilliana, Will, Sam, and Marcus — always do your best.

—CRAIG DUNN

THANKS TO my wife, Cara, for putting up with the long nights and to my parents, Hazel and Bob.

—CHRIS HARDY

CONTENTS

FOREWORD

MonoTouch is a blend of two fascinating and incredibly enjoyable worlds: the C# language and the iPhone. We designed MonoTouch to blend those two universes together, and we did this by tapping into years of experience designing and implementing languages, APIs, and bindings.

Our passion for the iPhone is very simple to explain: Like everyone else we were smitten by the beautiful user interfaces, the well thought out design and a powerful development platform. This combination was hard to resist.

Our love for C# goes back to the year 2000 when Microsoft unveiled their new language to the world. And just like C# rocked the Windows world, it rocked our world. By the year 2000 we had been working on the GNOME Desktop and the Evolution mail client for Linux for a few years, and we had learned our share of lessons in developing desktop applications.

We were developing software in a competitive space, and we needed to produce software faster, with fewer developers. One option was to work harder and work more hours. Instead we had chosen to raise the programming level: We kept performance sensitive code written in C and produced bindings for high-level languages that developers could exploit.

When Microsoft announced C# and the .NET Framework, the language was an immediate improvement that raised the programming level. The .NET language on the other hand ensured that our hands would not be tied to a single language, but also ensured that we could continue to reuse any existing code that we had written in C or C++. C# made us and the world more productive.

Mono over the years grew in every possible direction. It left the desktop comfort zone where it originated and was used on everything from embedded controllers, to mp3 players, to servers, video games, and industrial control.

Mono on the iPhone was created out of our user's demand. Our mono@novell.com e-mail address was bombarded during 2008 and 2009 with requests to bring Mono to the iPhone, and by the summer of 2009 we had a full stack offering that we released in September.

The authors of this book are among the early beta testers of MonoTouch: They were there on the first days of MonoTouch launching, they were there to explore with us the original API design, they were there to help us shape the final product, and they continue to help us prioritize what matters most to developers targeting the iPhone.

You might know some of the authors already. Wally put out the first e-book for MonoTouch in record time, and it helped hundreds of programmers get up and running with MonoTouch within months of the product release.

Chris and Rory are both well known in the Windows/ASP.NET world and are very active members of the MonoTouch community: On our IRC chat room, on Stackoverflow, and on our forums they have answered questions from new developers and helped developers make better applications.

Chris jumped into MonoTouch with the passion that only a rocker from Manchester can exhibit and started the open source Scott Hanselman "Hanselminutes" MonoTouch iPhone application.

Rory has a unique view of the world; he has worked extensively with both .NET and with Objective-C. He is a celebrity in the .NET world, but he is also behind the Barnes and Noble iPhone application, and it is this battle-tested knowledge that he has brought into the MonoTouch community. You could not ask for a better spiritual mentor in this trip.

And you probably know Craig from his excellent series of blogs that have not only served newcomers to get started with MonoTouch, but have also become a reference that I turn to when I need to solve a problem in my own iPhone app. Craig came up with one of the most useful ideas for iPhone applications: the conference application. He used his blog for a while to explore ideas on what would make a useful conference application and produced two open source conference applications: the MonoSpace app and the PDC app.

By the time of the Mix 2010 conference, Craig and Chris produced the MIX2010 application that was available to the MIX attendees. You knew it was a great idea when you would see people using the application on their phones before each session.

Martin has been an early adopter of MonoTouch since its launch. He launched the first iPhone application for social web site DailyBooth and is a contributor to various open-source MonoTouch projects.

Building applications with C# and the iPhone is the best of both worlds. You get to use a strongly typed, type safe, garbage collected language with the hottest APIs for mobile applications, and you get to use both the best libraries created for the iPhone in Objective-C and the best libraries created for C# in .NET.

I leave you in the good hands of Wally, Martin, Craig, Chris, and Rory.

—Miguel de Icaza
VP Developer Platform
Novell

INTRODUCTION

THE IPHONE IS THE MOST EXCITING SMARTPHONE currently in the mobile device marketplace. In the space of 3 years, it has gone from an installed base of zero to an installed base of 80 million devices. Accompanying that growth is a growth in the interest in writing applications that run natively on the device. When Apple originally shipped the iPhone, it had no capabilities to allow custom written applications on the device. Apple listened to the developer marketplace and added the ability to run native applications on the device. Initially, these applications were written in Objective-C. Over time, additional frameworks have been created to allow developers not fluent in Objective-C to target the iPhone.

Since the release of the .NET Framework in January 2002, its growth has been impressive. Currently, the .NET Framework is the most popular development framework in use today. Due to the popularity of the .NET Framework, Ximian, later purchased by Novell, announced the Mono Project. The Mono Project has built an implementation of the .NET Framework that runs on several non-Windows platforms. In the summer of 2009, Novell announced MonoTouch. MonoTouch allows .NET developers, primarily those writing C# applications, to create applications that run natively on the iPhone.

To .NET developers, the ability to write applications that natively run on the iPhone is an amazing and exciting thing as it opens the iPhone to them and their skills. .NET developers are not required to invest the time and effort in learning Objective-C. We're excited by the ability to write native applications for the iPhone with .NET/C#. It opens a whole new world for many developers.

WHO THIS BOOK IS FOR

This book is for .NET developers that are interested in creating native iPhone applications written in .NET/C#. These developers want to use their existing knowledge. While .NET developers are always interested in learning, they also recognize that learning Objective-C and the specifics of the iPhone can be overwhelming. Those developers interested in MonoTouch will recognize that the cost of MonoTouch is easily made up by the ability to quickly target the iPhone using a language that they are already familiar with.

This book is designed for .NET developers that want to target the iPhone. It is designed to help you get up to speed with the iPhone, not to really teach you about the .NET Framework or C# language, which we assume you already know.

This book is designed with introductory material in Chapters 1 thru 4. You should read Chapters 1 thru 4 sequentially. These chapters introduce the MonoTouch product, the basics of developing with MonoTouch and MonoDevelop, and finally, the basics of presenting data to a user with screen and data controls and how to develop a user interface for the iPhone. Once you are comfortable with these concepts, you can typically move from one chapter to another and not necessarily have to read the chapters sequentially.

WHAT THIS BOOK COVERS

This book covers .NET/C# development with MonoTouch. MonoTouch targets the iPhone, the iPod touch, and the iPad. The iPhone and iPod touch coverage is the same except where specifically noted. The iPad is covered specifically in Chapter 13.

HOW THIS BOOK IS STRUCTURED

As we previously indicated, this book is essentially divided into two parts. The first part of the book comprises Chapters 1 thru 4. This part is an introduction to the development experience on the iPhone and the MonoDevelop IDE. This part makes sense to read from beginning to end. Once you feel comfortable with the first part, you can move on to the second part of the book, containing discrete chapters that you can pick and choose from.

WHAT YOU NEED TO USE THIS BOOK

Readers of this book need several things to effectively use this book. These are:

- ➤ An iPhone, iPod, or iPad.
- ➤ **Apple Macintosh:** You need an Apple Macintosh to build and deploy an application on your iPhone device.
- ➤ **Apple iPhone SDK:** You need to download and install the Apple iPhone SDK. The iPhone SDK only runs on the Apple Macintosh.
- ➤ **Mono Framework:** You need to download and install the Mono Framework for the Apple Macintosh. The Mono Framework can be downloaded from the Mono web site at www.mono-project.com/.
- ➤ **MonoTouch:** MonoTouch can be downloaded from the MonoTouch web site at http://monotouch.net/. The free version of MonoTouch allows for a developer to create an application, build the application, and run the application in the simulator. To deploy to the device, the developer must purchase a copy of the Professional or Enterprise version of MonoTouch.
- ➤ **MonoDevelop:** The MonoDevelop IDE can be downloaded from the MonoDevelop web site at http://monodevelop.com/.

 Note that this book uses MonoTouch to develop applications under the terms of the iPhone SDK 3.X license for deploying to the App Store and in the enterprise. iPhone SDK 4 apps developed with MonoTouch can be deployed in the enterprise. Deploying MonoTouch applications under SDK 4 to the App Store may be restricted by Apple's Developer Program License Agreement.

CONVENTIONS

To help you get the most from the text and keep track of what's happening, we've used a number of conventions throughout the book.

 Boxes with a warning icon like this one hold important, not-to-be-forgotten information that is directly relevant to the surrounding text.

 The pencil icon indicates notes, tips, hints, tricks, and asides to the current discussion.

As for styles in the text:

➤ We *highlight* new terms and important words when we introduce them.

➤ We show keyboard strokes like this: Ctrl+A.

➤ We show filenames, URLs, and code within the text like so: `persistence.properties`.

➤ We present code in two different ways:

```
We use a monofont type with no highlighting for most code examples.
```

We use bold to emphasize code that is particularly important in the present context or to show changes from a previous code snippet.

SOURCE CODE

As you work through the examples in this book, you may choose either to type in all the code manually, or to use the source code files that accompany the book. All the source code used in this book is available for download at `www.wrox.com`. When at the site, simply locate the book's title (use the Search box or one of the title lists) and click the Download Code link on the book's detail page to obtain all the source code for the book. Code that is included on the web site is highlighted by the following icon:

Available for download on Wrox.com

Listings often include the filename in the title. If the filename isn't in the listing title or the code is just a code snippet, you'll find the filename in a code note such as this:

Code snippet filename

Because many books have similar titles, you may find it easiest to search by ISBN; this book's ISBN is 978-0-470-63782-1.

Once you download the code, just decompress it with your favorite compression tool. Alternately, you can go to the main Wrox code download page at www.wrox.com/dynamic/books/download.aspx to see the code available for this book and all other Wrox books.

ERRATA

We make every effort to ensure that there are no errors in the text or in the code. However, no one is perfect, and mistakes do occur. If you find an error in one of our books, like a spelling mistake or faulty piece of code, we would be very grateful for your feedback. By sending in errata, you may save another reader hours of frustration, and at the same time, you will be helping us provide even higher quality information.

To find the errata page for this book, go to www.wrox.com and locate the title using the Search box or one of the title lists. Then, on the book details page, click the Book Errata link. On this page, you can view all errata that has been submitted for this book and posted by Wrox editors. A complete book list, including links to each book's errata, is also available at www.wrox.com/misc-pages/booklist.shtml.

If you don't spot "your" error on the Book Errata page, go to www.wrox.com/contact/techsupport .shtml and complete the form there to send us the error you have found. We'll check the information and, if appropriate, post a message to the book's errata page and fix the problem in subsequent editions of the book.

P2P.WROX.COM

For author and peer discussion, join the P2P forums at p2p.wrox.com. The forums are a Web-based system for you to post messages relating to Wrox books and related technologies and interact with other readers and technology users. The forums offer a subscription feature to e-mail you topics of interest of your choosing when new posts are made to the forums. Wrox authors, editors, other industry experts, and your fellow readers are present on these forums.

At http://p2p.wrox.com, you will find a number of different forums that will help you, not only as you read this book, but also as you develop your own applications. To join the forums, just follow these steps:

1. Go to p2p.wrox.com and click the Register link.

2. Read the terms of use and click Agree.

3.   Complete the required information to join, as well as any optional information you wish to provide, and click Submit.

4.   You will receive an e-mail with information describing how to verify your account and complete the joining process.

 You can read messages in the forums without joining P2P, but in order to post your own messages, you must join.

Once you join, you can post new messages and respond to messages other users post. You can read messages at any time on the Web. If you would like to have new messages from a particular forum e-mailed to you, click the Subscribe to this Forum icon by the forum name in the forum listing.

For more information about how to use the Wrox P2P, be sure to read the P2P FAQs for answers to questions about how the forum software works, as well as many common questions specific to P2P and Wrox books. To read the FAQs, click the FAQ link on any P2P page.

1

Introduction to iPhone Development with MonoTouch for C# Developers

WHAT'S IN THIS CHAPTER?

➤ The history of the iPhone and its mindshare

➤ A short history of Mono and its relationship to the .NET Framework

➤ How MonoTouch opens the iPhone to .NET Developers

➤ Why MonoTouch is so attractive to developers

The past several years have seen an amazing growth in the use of smartphones, and *USA Today* recently reported how smartphones have become an indispensable part of people's lives.

Although Windows-based computers running 32-bit x86 or 64-bit x64 processors dominate the desktop computer marketplace, and the .NET Framework is the dominant development environment for the Windows platform, no single vendor or platform dominates the mobile device marketplace; devices based on Symbian, Research in Motion (Blackberry), Windows Mobile, Android, and other platforms are available. In addition, devices may run the same operating system and be presented to the user in separate form factors. This fracture in the marketplace is problematic for developers — how can they take a development framework, or tool, that they already know and use that knowledge in a device that has a large and growing market share?

This chapter looks at how the largest segment of developers can target the smartphone with the highest mindshare, and that the smartphone is growing faster in marketshare than any other device.

PRODUCT COMPARISON

This section takes a quick look at .NET Framework, Mono and MonoTouch — three products that have allowed the largest segment of developers to target the iPhone, the most exciting mobile platform currently in the marketplace.

.NET Framework

In the late 1990s, Microsoft began work on the .NET Framework. The first version of the framework shipped in 2002. Microsoft proceeded to introduce subsequent versions of the .NET Framework and has recently introduced the .NET Framework 4. The .NET Framework comes in various versions, including 32-bit versions, 64-bit versions, a version for the XBOX gaming platform, and a version for Microsoft's mobile devices referred to as the Compact Framework (CF). A few facts about .NET Framework:

➤ Microsoft released a development tool, *Visual Studio .NET*, with the Framework. This tool is the Integrated Development Environment for .NET.

➤ It's based on a virtual machine that executes software written for the framework. This virtual machine environment is referred to as the *Common Language Runtime (CLR)*, and it is responsible for security, memory management, program execution, and exception handling.

➤ Applications written in the .NET Framework are initially compiled from source code, such as Visual Basic or C#, to an intermediate language, called MSIL. The initial compilation is performed by calling the language specific command line compiler, Visual Studio, or some other build tool. A second compilation set is typically done when an application is executed. This second compilation takes the intermediate language and compiles it into executable code that can be run on the operating system. This second compilation is referred to as *just-in-time compilation*.

➤ It's language independent, and numerous languages are available for the Framework. In the Visual Studio, Microsoft has shipped various languages including Visual Basic, F#, C++, and C#.

➤ It has a series of libraries that provide consistent functionality across the various languages. These libraries are referred to as the *Base Class Libraries*.

➤ Microsoft has submitted various parts of the .NET Framework to various standard organizations. Some of these are the C# language, the Common Language Infrastructure, Common Type System (CTS), Common Language Specification (CLS), and Virtual Execution System (VES).

➤ It has the largest number of developers for any development framework out there. As a result, more developers are familiar with the .NET Framework than any other development framework.

➤ A disadvantage of the .NET Framework is that it is not available for non-Microsoft platforms.

Mono

Mono is an open source project that provides a C# compiler and Common Language Runtime on non-Windows operating systems. Mono is currently licensed under GPL version 2, LGPL version 2, the MIT, and dual licenses. Mono runs on Mac, Linux, BSD, and other operating systems.

Mono was officially announced in 2001 and is the brainchild of Miguel de Icaza. Mono version 1.0 shipped in 2004, and currently Mono is at Version 2.6. Mono continues to be led by Miguel de Icaza and is under the general leadership and support of Novell.

As much as there is the desire to match the .NET Framework's features, this is not possible due to the fact that Microsoft has more resources and a head start in the development of those features. At the same time, the Mono project has parity with a large number of .NET Framework features.

Along with Mono, there is an open source IDE called *MonoDevelop*, which started as a port of the SharpDevelop IDE. MonoDevelop began as a project to allow for Mono development on Linux, but with the release of MonoDevelop 2.2, the ability to develop with Mono expanded to the Mac, Windows, and several other non-Linux UNIX platforms.

Though the .NET Framework is very popular, two issues make it unsuitable for running on the iPhone:

➤ At some level Apple and Microsoft are competitors and are likely not too excited to work together.

➤ The .NET Framework fundamentally is dynamically compiled at runtime. This is the just-in-time compilation of the .NET Framework. This is a violation of the Apple license and the operating principles of the iPhone OS.

Given that code running on the Microsoft .NET Framework is compiled to machine code at run-time using the just-in-time compilation, one would expect that applications written for Mono would have the same behavior and thus not be suitable for running on the iPhone. However, Mono has a technology that allows for applications to be compiled ahead of time, referred to as *AOT technology*.

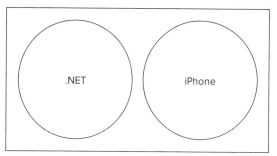

A disadvantage of .NET/Mono and the iPhone is that .NET/Mono developers cannot take their .NET/Mono/C# knowledge and apply it to the iPhone platform. As illustrated in Figure 1-1, you see that the reason .NET/Mono developers can't target the iPhone is because they're two separate entities.

FIGURE 1-1

MonoTouch

In 2009, Novell announced and shipped MonoTouch, which allows .NET developers to create native iPhone applications in C#. With MonoTouch, applications are compiled into executable code that runs on the iPhone. The significance of this should not be understated: .NET/Mono developers can target the iPhone through MonoTouch. This is illustrated in Figure 1-2.

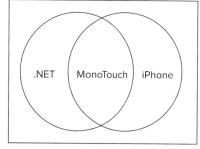

How does MonoTouch accomplish this? Does it somehow allow Windows Forms applications to be translated or recompiled and deployed on the iPhone? MonoTouch provides a

FIGURE 1-2

.NET layer over the native iPhone programming layer present on the iPhone OS, referred to as *Cocoa Touch*. Cocoa Touch is based on the Cocoa layer in the Mac OS X and is available on the iPhone, iPod Touch, and the iPad. MonoTouch does not provide a mechanism to cross-compile Windows Forms applications, but allows developers to build applications that run natively on the iPhone.

Overall, the application programming interface (API) exposed by the MonoTouch SDK is a combination of the .NET 2.0 Framework's core features, the Silverlight 2.0 API, and the APIs on the iPhone. MonoTouch provides a bridge (interop) between the iPhone's native APIs based on Objective-C and C-based APIs to the .NET world that C# developers are accustomed to.

MonoTouch Components

MonoTouch is made up of the following four components:

➤ The `Monotouch.dll` is a C# assembly that provides a binding API into the iPhone's native APIs.

➤ A command-line tool that compiles C# and Common Intermediate Language (CIL) code. This compiled code can then be run in the simulator or an actual iPhone.

➤ An add-in to MonoDevelop that allows for iPhone development and for Interface Builder to create graphical applications.

➤ A commercial license of the Mono runtime, which allows for the static linking of the Mono runtime with the code developed.

Namespaces and Classes

MonoTouch provides a rich set of namespaces and classes to support building applications for the iPhone. Some of the most popular namespaces and classes are:

➤ **MonoTouch.ObjCRuntime:** This namespace provides the interop/bridge between the .NET/C# world and the Objective-C world of the iPhone.

➤ **MonoTouch.Foundation:** This namespace provides support for the data types necessary to communicate with the Objective-C world of the iPhone. Most types are directly mapped. For example, the `NSObject` Objective-C base class is mapped to the `MonoTouch.Foundation .NSObject` class in C#. Some classes are not directly mapped and are instead mapped to their native .NET types. For example, `NSString` maps to the basic string type and `NSArray` maps to a strongly typed array.

➤ **MonoTouch.UIKit:** This namespace provides a direct mapping between the UI components within Cocoa Touch. The mapping is done by providing .NET classes for each UI component, and this is the namespace that developers will likely spend most of their time working with. For .NET developers, Cocoa Touch is an abstraction layer or API for building programs that run in the iPhone. Cocoa Touch is based on the Cocoa API used in building programs that run on the Mac OS X operating system. Cocoa Touch can be thought of as Cocoa tuned for the touch-based iPhone operating system.

➤ **OpenTK:** This namespace is a modified version of the OpenTK API. OpenTK is an object-oriented binding for OpenGL, which stands for the Open Graphics Library. OpenGL is an API for using three-dimensional graphics. OpenTK is a library for performing OpenGL, OpenAL, and OpenCL. It is written in C# and runs on Windows, Mac OS X, and Linux. The OpenTK implementation on the iPhone has been updated to use CoreGraphics and to only expose the functionality available on the iPhone.

In addition, MonoTouch provides a set of additional namespaces that may be important to you. These are:

➤ `MonoTouch.AddressBook`

➤ `MonoTouch.CoreGraphics`

➤ `MonoTouch.AddressBookUI`

➤ `MonoTouch.AudioToolbox`

➤ `MonoTouch.MapKit`

➤ `MonoTouch.MediaPlayer`

➤ `MonoTouch.AVFoundation`

➤ `MonoTouch.MediaPlayer`

➤ `MonoTouch.CoreAnimation`

➤ `MonoTouch.SystemConfiguration`

These namespaces are fairly self-explanatory in their functionalities and are specific to the iPhone.

MonoDevelop

MonoDevelop is a free IDE used for developing with Mono and is an early branch of the SharpDevelop IDE. Originally, MonoDevelop ran only on Linux, but with version 2.2, MonoDevelop began running on the Mac. MonoDevelop on the Mac allows for the creation and management of iPhone projects as well as debugging and deployment to the simulator and devices for testing.

iPhone

There's no doubt that Apple has changed the mobile device marketplace since the introduction of the original iPod in 2001. Although the iPod was not the first device to play mp3 files, it was the first product that played mp3 files, made it easy to use, and provided an easy-to-use marketplace to purchase audio files. The iPod really caused the mp3 device marketplace to explode.

In January 2007, Apple turned the smartphone upside down when it officially announced the first-generation iPhone. The iPhone was designed to be a smartphone that provided web browsing, e-mail, and multimedia capabilities. The first-generation iPhone connected to a wireless network and applications were delivered to the user over the mobile version of Safari.

Writing a web-based application for the iPhone is fairly simple. The Safari web browser is a great tool — it does an excellent job of scaling web-based applications to run an iPhone-sized screen. It also does well running applications that are highly dependent on JavaScript. Upgrading an iPhone web-based application is also a simple matter of deploying a new version of the application to a web server. Many applications have taken this approach.

 Unfortunately, web applications are not suitable for all applications — applications that require some background processing, access to local resources, must work when a network connection is unavailable, and some other application types don't work well in this model.

So, the question becomes how does one write an application that fits into the iPhone?

The first-generation iPhone did not have support for users to load applications on the device. For a few users, this was not acceptable, and they began *jailbreaking* their iPhones, which is the process where users run software on their devices that Apple has not approved.

Jailbreaking has several problems:

➤ **Technical Issues:** Jailbreaking requires the iPhone's owner to perform the operation, and many iPhone users are not technically proficient enough to do this.

➤ **Legality:** The legality of jailbreaking is unclear at the time of this writing. It is not clear where jailbreaking falls within the Digital Millennium Copyright Act. The Electronic Frontier Foundation has asked the United States Copyright Office to recognize an exception to the DMCA that allows iPhone owners to jailbreak their devices. Apple has argued in response that jailbreaking an iPhone is a copyright violation.

➤ **Unknowns:** It comes with a series of unknowns. How well can a jailbroken iPhone be upgraded to new versions of the iPhone operating system (OS)? Will jailbreaking an iPhone open it up to security issues?

In 2008, Apple introduced the second generation of the iPhone, referred to as the iPhone 3G. With this generation and the new version of the iPhone OS, Apple released a number of enhancements, including the ability to run applications natively on the device. In addition to this, Apple has put together an ecosystem whereby users can find and install applications on their iPhone device called the App Store.

These native applications are a great improvement over web-based applications, which are limited in what they can do on a device. Fundamentally, they have to be loaded over the Web and are not able to access all device features. Native applications tend to have more support for device features like the accelerometer, file system, camera, cross-domain web services, and other features that are outside of features available in HTML and JavaScript. In addition, native applications do not depend on the wireless network to be loaded, whereas a web application is dependent on the wireless network for loading.

In 2009, Apple introduced the iPhone 3GS and version 3 of the iPhone operating system. The iPhone 3GS, a refinement of the iPhone 3G, supports higher data rates than the iPhone 3G, an improved camera, an updated CPU, and voice control.

In 2010, Apple announced and shipped the iPad. The iPad is a tablet device, and it has a larger screen than the iPhone. Also significant is that it shipped with the iPhone operating system that is fundamentally different than the iPhone.

Along with the release of each new iPhone, Apple has introduced a new iPod touch. The iPod touch can be thought of as an iPhone without the phone, camera, and support for the 3G data services; however, the iPod touch does have support for wireless networking using WiFi.

Since its availability three years ago, Apple has shipped more than 60 million units of the iPhone. The iPad is estimated to ship several million units of the iPad in its first year of availability, and this will likely result in the iPad being the most popular tablet in 2010.

Unfortunately, for developers, three issues must be considered when running on the device:

- ➤ The iPhone operating system does not allow for software code that is interpreted or dynamically compiled in any way.

- ➤ Apple's licensing for the SDK and developing with the iPhone does not allow for applications to have interpreted or dynamically compiled code.

- ➤ Apple has an extensive validation process for iPhone applications. Some of the automated tests for an application will check for dynamically compiled and interpreted code.

These issues and licensing are something that developers need to be knowledgeable of, and somewhat limit the choices that a developer has for writing applications that run on the iPhone.

MOBILE DEVELOPMENT

There are a few things developers need to know when building applications on the iPhone with MonoTouch:

- ➤ The iPhone has a startup timer. If an application takes longer than 20 seconds to start up, the iPhone OS kills it.

- ➤ The iPhone OS will kill any application that is unresponsive for longer than 20 seconds while the application is running. To work around this, you need to perform some type of asynchronous operation.

- ➤ The time spent processing the `FinishedLaunching()` event counts against the startup timer. As a result, you do not want any long-term synchronous processing in the `FinishedLaunching()` event.

- ➤ The iPhone simulator is good for initial testing; however, it is not necessarily accurate for all testing. Just because something works in the simulator doesn't mean it will run in the iPhone in the same way. Final testing should be completed in the iPhone.

➤ With .NET, executables are fairly small. Every application shares the .NET Framework, so the applications don't have their own copy of the framework. MonoTouch is not built into the iPhone and its applications must have their own copy of the framework; MonoTouch is compiled into your application. The result is that MonoTouch applications are larger on disk than a comparable Objective-C application.

Although MonoTouch is a commercially licensed product, it is still a product that is under continual development, and MonoTouch may not have support for a specific namespace or assembly. You have two options for this situation:

➤ Wait on the implementation of that assembly from the MonoTouch product.

➤ Pull the necessary code or assembly into to your project. This is fairly common if the application needs to use code within the `System.Web.*` namespaces.

In addition to the technical issues of building an application for the iPhone, some design issues that developers should be aware of include:

➤ Don't design an application for a desktop environment and think that it can be scaled down to an iPhone, or any mobile device. An iPhone does not have the display, hardware, or storage of a desktop computer. iPhone and mobile device applications are really good for simple, limited-purpose functions, but they should not do everything that a desktop application does.

➤ The iPhone simulator is a fine tool, but don't limit testing to the iPhone simulator. A simulator is just a simulator. There is a keyboard and a mouse associated with the iPhone simulator. To really test a complicated design, the application must be tested from a physical iPhone.

APPLE IPHONE SDK TOOLS

When the iPhone originally shipped, you could not run third-party native applications directly on the device — until March 6, 2008, when Apple released the first beta of the SDK. The iPhone SDK allows third parties to write applications and run them natively on the device. Since that date, there have been a steady stream of updated beta and released versions of the iPhone SDK. Originally, the iPhone SDK supported both the iPhone and the iPod Touch. With the beta release of the iPhone SDK Version 3.2, Apple added support for the iPad tablet device.

Tools

The Apple SDK contains a number of tools that are important to the MonoTouch developer. These tools are:

➤ **Xcode:** A suite of tools for development in an Apple environment, the main tool being the IDE. Although MonoTouch does not directly use the Xcode IDE, it can help you create a simple app to deploy to a device. You can also use it to verify that the certificates and provisioning information on the associated devices are working properly.

➤ **Interface Builder:** Interface Builder (IB) allows for the graphical creation of a user interface. The MonoDevelop IDE integrates with IB and converts the interface created within IB into a user interface callable by MonoTouch.

➤ **Simulator:** Allows for emulating the iPhone, iPod Touch, and the iPad. Note that the simulator does not run ARM code. It runs x86 code.

➤ **Libraries necessary to target the device:** This includes libraries for Cocoa Touch, audio, video, networking, SQLite, threads, power management, and the general OS X Kernel.

Licensing

The SDK is a free download. Unfortunately, to release software for the iPhone, a developer must join the iPhone Development Program. At the time of this writing, the cost to join is $99 (U.S. dollars) a year. The cost of joining varies from country to country. The ability to distribute applications to devices is dependent on having the necessary development certificates. These are available through the Apple Developer site once a developer joins the iPhone Developer Program.

SUMMARY

This chapter looked at the following items in the marketplace:

➤ The iPhone, its licensing, and its operating system

➤ The .NET Framework and Mono

➤ MonoTouch, which allows .NET developers to target the iPhone

➤ MonoDevelop, which allows developers to have a good IDE to write code with MonoTouch

You should now be familiar with which tools are needed to build a native application with .NET/C# for the iPhone. The next chapter explores the specifics of building a MonoTouch application with MonoDevelop. Chapters 3 and 4 describe how to work with the user controls for user input and for presenting data to a user in a standard form factor. Other chapters in the book will explore specific parts of the iPhone, such as maps, acceleration, and the iPad.

Introduction to MonoTouch

WHAT'S IN THIS CHAPTER?

➤ Getting started with MonoTouch

➤ Using MonoDevelop with MonoTouch

➤ MonoTouch and Interface Builder

➤ Debugging and deploying

What is MonoTouch? If you've bought this book, you probably at least have some basic idea, but this chapter is all about giving you the essential answers to this question so that you have a firm foundation from which to try your hand at and apply your development skills to iPhone application development.

Simply put, MonoTouch is a set of tools that allows developers to build iPhone and iPod Touch applications on a Mac using existing knowledge of the .NET Framework. The MonoTouch application programming interface (API) provides a combination of the core .NET 3.5 Framework features and the core APIs that are provided by the iPhone SDK. To allow this to happen, the .NET Framework is compiled down into ARM code so that it will run on the iPhone device, whereas the iPhone native APIs, those written in Objective-C and C, are exposed via an interop between C# and the native APIs themselves. This allows developers to code against these foreign APIs in a familiar fashion and in a way that they are comfortable with from their knowledge of C#.

BEFORE YOU BEGIN DEVELOPING

I'm going to make an assumption right from the get go and that assumption is that you have an Intel Mac. The reason behind this is that the Apple iPhone SDK only supports these types of machines for development. Because MonoTouch uses the iPhone SDK, you'll also need to adhere to the development restrictions Apple imposes. To get your first MonoTouch application up and running, you need to do a few things:

1. Make sure you have your Intel Mac running at least version 10.5.7.

2. Download and install the Mono framework: www.go-mono.com/mono-downloads/download.html.

3. Download and install MonoTouch: http://monotouch.net/.

4. Download and install MonoDevelop: http://monodevelop.com/Download.

5. Download and install the iPhone SDK: www.apple.com/downloads/macosx/development_tools/iphonesdk.html.

 Order of installation is important since MonoTouch and MonoDevelop depend on the Mono framework. Make sure you install these items in the order stated in the preceding numbered list.

Now that you have all of the components installed, you're ready to delve into MonoTouch. First, we want you to take a look at what MonoTouch contains.

THE COMPONENTS OF MONOTOUCH

The four components of MonoTouch are as follows:

➤   monotouch.dll, which is a C# assembly that provides a binding API into the iPhone's native APIs. (A full list of the APIs that are bound can be found later in the chapter in Table 2-2.)

➤   mtouch, which is a command-line SDK that will compile into C# and Common Intermediate Language (CIL) code. This compiled code can then be run in the simulator or in an actual iPhone.

➤   An add-in to MonoDevelop that allows for iPhone development, which allows MonoDevelop to use the command-line tool mtouch and allows for integration with Interface Builder and the iPhone simulator. It also enables deploying to the device and building for distribution to the App Store and ad-hoc releases.

➤   A commercial license of the Mono runtime, which allows for the static linking of the Mono runtime with the code developed to be sold in the App Store.

What Is Mono?

At the core of MonoTouch is Mono. Mono (which is Spanish for *monkey*) is an open-source implementation of the .NET Framework. It has been created by Novell to enable a cross-platform version of the .NET Framework. This means that the framework can be run on many different platforms such as Apple OS X, Linux, Nintendo's Wii, Sony PlayStation 3, and many others, including

Windows. Because Mono is open source, this enables anyone to use and modify the framework to their own needs, which is useful if you want to target restrictive platforms. With this in mind, MonoTouch uses a modified version of the Mono framework to develop against and then runs a linker on the application code (and the framework) to cut down the size of the overall code in your application. The linker concept is explained further in the "Understanding the Linker" section later in this chapter.

Namespaces and Classes of MonoTouch

The section discusses further the core namespaces and classes that are included within MonoTouch. MonoTouch uses a superset of the Silverlight .NET assemblies, meaning that additional functionality has been added to the Silverlight .NET assemblies within MonoTouch. Table 2-1 shows a list of the .NET assemblies that are available.

TABLE 2-1: Available .NET Assemblies in MonoTouch

ASSEMBLY	API COMPATIBILITY
Mono.CompilerServices.SymbolWriter.dll	For compiler writers
Mono.Data.Sqlite.dll	ADO.NET provider for SQLite; some limitations due to the iPhone OS SQLite version
Mono.Data.Tds.dll	TDS Protocol support; used for System.Data.SqlClient support within System.Data
Mono.Security.dll	Cryptographic APIs
mscorlib.dll	Silverlight
System.dll	Silverlight, plus types from the following namespaces: System.Collections.Specialized System.ComponentModel System.ComponentModel.Design System.Diagnostics System.IO.Compression System.Net System.Net.Cache System.Net.NET.Mail System.Net.Mime System.Net.NetworkInformation System.Net.Security System.Net.Sockets System.Security.Authentication System.Security.Cryptography System.Timers
System.Core.dll	Silverlight

continues

TABLE 2-1 *(continued)*

ASSEMBLY	API COMPATIBILITY
System.Data.dll	.NET 3.5 with functionality such as System.CodeDom, XML config support, OleDb, Odbc removed
System.Json.dll	Silverlight
System.ServiceModel.dll	WCF stack as present in Silverlight.
System.Transactions.dll	.NET 3.5; part of System.Data support
System.Web.Services.dll	Basic web services from the .NET 3.5 profile, with the server features removed
System.Xml.dll	.NET 3.5
System.Xml.Linq.dll	.NET 3.5
System.Linq	.NET 3.5

Taken from www.MonoTouch.Net/Documentation/Assemblies

The MonoTouch product is growing with every release, so chances are that extra functionality will be included since the time of this writing. It will be worth checking the source of the table for any additional changes and updates.

In addition to the .NET assemblies, MonoTouch provides the monotouch.dll assembly, which contains APIs that are bound against the Objective-C and C-based APIs. The key namespaces in this assembly are as follows:

➤ MonoTouch.ObjCRuntime: This namespace provides the interop/bridge between the .NET/C# world and the Objective-C world of the iPhone. This is discussed further in Chapter 11.

➤ MonoTouch.Foundation: This namespace provides support for the data types necessary to communicate with the Objective-C world of the iPhone. Most types are directly mapped. For example, the NSObject Objective-C base class is mapped to the MonoTouch.Foundation.NSObject class in C#. Some classes aren't directly mapped to their Objective-C class name like NSArray. Instead, an NSArray maps to a strongly typed array like UIViewController[] if the array has a collection of UIViewControllers.

➤ MonoTouch.UIKit: This namespace provides a direct binding between the UIKit components within Cocoa Touch. This binding is done by providing .NET classes for each of the UIKit components available. This is the namespace that developers spend most of their time working with.

 For .NET developers, Cocoa Touch is an abstraction layer or API for building programs that run on the iPhone. Cocoa is the API used for building programs that run on the Mac OS X operating system. Cocoa Touch can be thought of as Cocoa tuned for the touch-based iPhone operating system. Read more about Cocoa in Chapter 14.

➤ OpenTK: This namespace is a modified version of the OpenTK API. OpenTK is an object-oriented binding for OpenGL, which stands for the Open Graphics Library. OpenGL is an API for using three-dimensional graphics. OpenTK is a library for performing OpenGL, OpenAL, and OpenCL. It is written in C# and runs on Windows, Mac OS X, and Linux. The OpenTK implementation on the iPhone has been updated to use Core Graphics and to expose only the functionality available on the iPhone.

The other namespaces that are bound from Objective-C in the `monotouch.dll` are listed in Table 2-2. You will notice the exclusion of `MonoTouch.CoreData`, which should be bound from the Objective-C `CoreData` class. This is left out due to the tight coupling it has with the Objective-C way of doing things and tools that go with it for working with persistent storage. Instead, `Mono.Data.Sqlite` should be used as an alternative.

TABLE 2-2: .NET Assemblies Bound from Objective-C

NAMESPACE	DESCRIPTION
MonoTouch.AddressBook	Provides access to the iPhone's Address Book
MonoTouch.AddressBookUI	User interface components for accessing the iPhone's Address Book
MonoTouch.AudioToolbox	Contains low-level audio functionality for custom playback and recording
MonoTouch.AVFoundation	General-purpose audio playback and recording
MonoTouch.CoreAnimation	Provides the ability to make animations
MonoTouch.CoreFoundation	Bindings for low-level C API in Cocoa Touch
MonoTouch.CoreGraphics	Binding to the Quartz 2D Graphics API
MonoTouch.CoreLocation	Provides location facilities
MonoTouch.GameKit	Allows providing game functionality such as P2P communication
MonoTouch.MapKit	APIs to provide rich mapping functionality
MonoTouch.MediaPlayer	Provides audio and video capabilities and linking to the iPod library
MonoTouch.MessageUI	User interface components for sending mail messages in-app
MonoTouch.OpenGLES	Provides the ability to embed Open GL into your application
MonoTouch.StoreKit	Contains APIs to handle in application payments
MonoTouch.SystemConfiguration	Provides network reachability functionality

WORKING WITH MONODEVELOP

MonoDevelop is an open source Integrated Development Environment (IDE) and throughout the book you will be using this tool to write and develop your sample applications. MonoDevelop is a cross-platform IDE, which means it can run on Linux, Mac, and Windows platforms. The IDE has a lot of similarities with Visual Studio, which is available only to Windows users. This being the case, MonoDevelop allows for the development of desktop applications, web applications (in ASP.NET), and Moonlight (the Mono implementation of Silverlight) among many others on Windows, Mac OS X, and Linux machines. With this in mind, it's worth learning about MonoDevelop before you jump into code and worth understanding how a MonoDevelop MonoTouch project is structured.

When you first start up MonoDevelop, you are greeted with a screen that looks very similar to the one that comes up when you open up Visual Studio. See Figure 2-1 for a screenshot of the home screen. The screen is useful because it lists all your recent projects, which is very handy for jumping between projects.

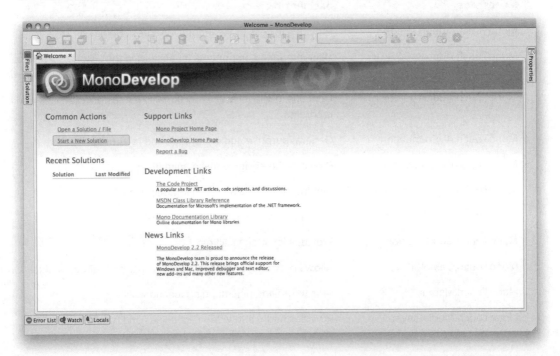

FIGURE 2-1

To create a new MonoTouch project, you can either click File ⇨ New ⇨ Solution from the menu bar at the top of the screen or you can simply click the Start a New Solution button on the home screen under Common Actions. This takes you to a New Solution file dialog as shown in Figure 2-2.

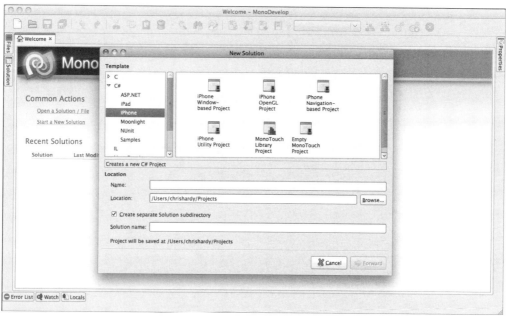

FIGURE 2-2

Table 2-3 lists the different project types you can create.

TABLE 2-3: MonoTouch Project Type Templates

PROJECT TYPE	DESCRIPTION
iPhone Window-based Project	Creates a window for you to start loading your views and other boilerplate code onto.
iPhone OpenGL Project	Creates Open GL boilerplate code for a spinning square.
iPhone Navigation-based Project	Creates a project that is set up with a navigation view by default.
iPhone Utility Project	The utility project is a simple two-view–based project where you can flip the view to reveal "about" information.
MonoTouch Library Project	A project to encapsulate library code for use in MonoTouch.
Empty MonoTouch Project	A completely empty MonoTouch project.

For this example, you simply choose the iPhone Window-based project because this is the most common layout for a MonoTouch project. Give the project a name and click Forward.

The next screen you see is a Project Features screen, shown in Figure 2-3. You won't need to use any of these features because they are more for other types of Mono projects such as desktop applications, so you can skip the screen and just click OK.

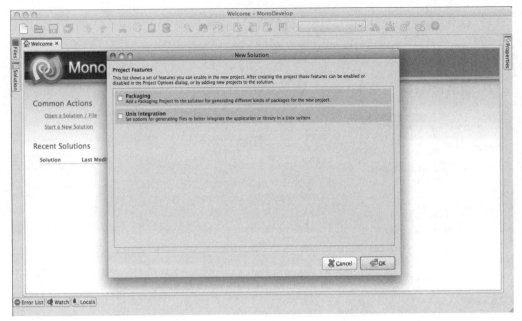

FIGURE 2-3

Taking a deeper look at the MonoTouch project layout you notice a few different things. Figure 2-4 shows the project structure from the default Windows-based project. Your solution file contains one project — a MonoTouch project. Any additional library projects used also need to be MonoTouch projects.

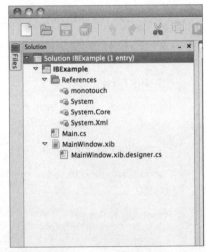

➤ The References folder will be a familiar sight; however notice that the `monotouch.dll` is automatically included as a reference.

➤ The `.cs` file named `Main.cs` is the default startup template used by MonoTouch, and it has the `Main` method within it. The `Main` method is the starting point for an iPhone application, which also starts the application's event loop for handling interaction between the iPhone and the application.

FIGURE 2-4

➤ An XIB file (an XML-based Interface Builder file) called `MainWindow.xib` is the file that contains the user interface for the application. This file is typically modified by using Interface Builder. Interface Builder has some interesting concepts that are explored in the following section.

➤ The `MainWindow.xib.designer.cs` file contains definitions of the views, controls, outlets, and actions that exist within the user interface. (Views, outlets, and actions will be explained later in this chapter.) This file is updated each time that the user interface is updated through Interface Builder. It should not be updated manually.

Now that you've come to grips with the basics of MonoDevelop and MonoTouch projects, you can dive into using Interface Builder and start to create a "Hello World" application.

USING INTERFACE BUILDER

The Interface Builder tool is provided in the iPhone SDK. The tool is commonly used in Mac OS X development and in iPhone application development. Interface Builder provides a drag-and-drop surface for a developer to lay out controls on a screen. Using Interface Builder is very much a love/hate thing, especially for those coming from a Visual Studio background; it has lots of similarities to the designer within Visual Studio, but the way it works and allows controls to be set up is very different.

 Using Interface Builder is completely optional and all controls can be used straight from code, but it is a useful tool for creating layouts.

Interface Builder is integrated straight into MonoDevelop, and double-clicking any `.xib` file automatically opens up Interface Builder for you with the selected `.xib` file.

When you open up Interface Builder, you are presented with a few different windows as shown in Figure 2-5.

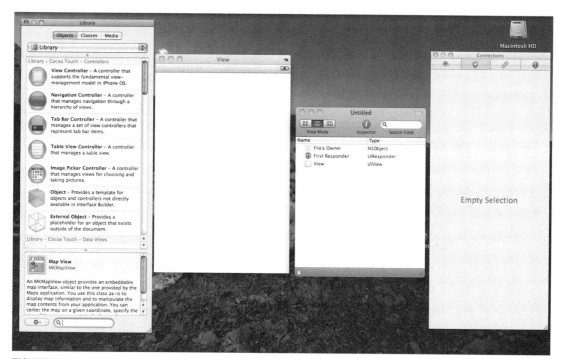

FIGURE 2-5

➤ **Library:** This window contains the Objects, Classes, and Media tabs. These contain the controls that you can click and drag onto the view.

➤ **View:** This window is the view that you can click and drag different controls on to. This enables you to layout your user interface in a WYSIWYG way.

➤ **Connections:** This tab is where you set up connections between your controls and enable them to be modified programmatically. As you can see, this is one of three other tabs. The other three tabs are Attributes, Size, and Identity, which all modify the controls details. Collectively, this window is known as the Inspector.

➤ The fourth window, Untitled in Figure 2-5, is the Main Menu of Interface Builder. This provides a hierarchical view of all the controls on a view.

The next few sections discuss what sort of controls that you have at your disposal with both Interface Builder and just using controls in code.

Working with Library Controls

The Library window contains a bunch of controls that are usable within Interface Builder. These controls are also available in code; the brackets represent the class for the control.

➤ **Controllers** (`UIViewController`): The Controllers are a family of controllers that control some type of activity.

➤ **Data Views:** The Data Views typically present some type of information to the user. The controls presented are:

    ➤ **Table View** (`UITableView`): A Table View presents data to a user in a table list format. Users are able to scroll through the data. Typically, a single cell in a Table View is an entire row (known as a Table View Cell).

    ➤ **Table View Cell** (`UITableViewCell`): The Table View Cell allows for custom look and feel, attributes, and behaviors of cells to be defined and applied within a Table View.

    ➤ **Image View** (`UIImageView`): The Image View displays an image or animation to a user. In the case of an animation, this is defined as an array of `UIImages`.

    ➤ **Web View** (`UIWebView`): The Web View displays web content to a user within an application.

    ➤ **Map View** (`MKMapView`): The Map View displays map content to a user within an application.

    ➤ **Text View** (`UITextView`): The Text View displays multiple lines of editable text.

    ➤ **Scroll View** (`UIScrollView`): The Scroll View provides a way for content to be displayed that does not entirely fit within a single window view.

> ➤ **Picker View** (`UIPickerView`): The Picker View displays a slot-machine–style spinning wheel. For .NET developers new to MonoTouch, this control is similar in concept to a drop-down list box.

> ➤ **Date Picker** (`UIDatePicker`): The Date Picker is a set of rotating wheels that allows for dates and times to be selected.

➤ **Inputs & Values:** The Inputs & Values provide a set of UI controls that are designed for user input. These controls are:

> ➤ **Segmented Control** (`UISegmentedControl`): The Segmented Control can be thought of as a button where different segments/parts of the button function as individual controls.

> ➤ **Label** (`UILabel`): The Label is a control to display text.

> ➤ **Round Rect Button** (`UIButton`): The Round Rect Button control implements touch events. A touch event is like a "click" event in .NET. This is equivalent to a button in .NET.

> ➤ **Text Field** (`UITextField`): The Text Field control allows for users to add text or data through the virtual keyboard.

> ➤ **Switch** (`UISwitch`): The Switch control allows users to toggle values in a user interface. Conceptually, this control is similar to a checkbox.

> ➤ **Slider** (`UISlider`): The Slider control allows users to input a single value from a range of values.

> ➤ **Progress View** (`UIProgressView`): The Progress View control allows for the display of the progress of a running task. Typically, the Progress View is used for long-running tasks to provide feedback to the user.

> ➤ **Activity Indicator View** (`UIActivityIndicatorView`): The Activity Indicator View control provides feedback that a task is currently running. There is no indication of the state of the task, merely one that the task is running.

> ➤ **Page Control** (`UIPageControl`): The Page Control provides the user with information that there are additional pages in the application.

➤ **Windows, Views, & Bars:** These are the windows, views, and bars available in Interface Builder and code.

> ➤ **Window** (`UIWindow`): A window contains multiple views and is the first to be displayed on screen. Since all views will be in a window, you can only ever have one instance of a window.

> ➤ **View** (`UIView`): The View control is a rectangular region for placing controls and handling events.

➤ **Search Bar** (`UISearchBar`): The Search Bar control is a text field with round edges and a search icon. Its UI look is designed to show the user that the field will be used for searching.

➤ **Search Bar and Search Display Controller** (`UISearchDisplayController`): The Search Bar and Search Display Controllers are the Search Bar control, Bookmark button, Cancel button, and a Table View that displays the results of a search.

➤ **Navigation Bar** (`UINavigationBar`): The Navigation Bar is a UI control that supports navigation of content in a hierarchical way.

➤ **Navigation Item** (`UINavigationItem`): The Navigation Item control contains information about a navigation item contained within a Navigation Bar.

➤ **Toolbar** (`UIToolbar`): The Toolbar control displays a toolbar at the bottom of the screen. It supports toolbar items within the toolbar.

➤ **Bar Button Item** (`UIBarButtonItem`): The Bar Button Item control represents an item within a Toolbar control or Navigation Bar.

➤ **Flexible Space Bar Button** (`UIBarButtonItem`): The Flexible Space Bar Button control represents the amount of space within a toolbar.

➤ **Tab Bar** (`UITabBar`): The Tab Bar control allows for a tab bar to be displayed at the bottom of the screen. The Tab Bar control allows for the selection of tab bar items.

➤ **Tab Bar Item** (`UITabBarItem`): The Tab Bar Item control is an item within a Tab Bar control.

Setting Up Outlets

To enable the use of the controls you have dropped onto Interface Builder view, you need to create an outlet for each control. In MonoTouch, *outlets* are instance variables on the class you assign a control to that you define within Interface Builder. The instance variable gives you programmatic access to the control. To demonstrate this, you are going to use an iPhone Window-based project and open the `MainWindow.xib` file in Interface Builder.

 Most of the time you will not want to use controls directly on a window, but rather you use a view added as a sub-view to the window to hook up your controls. This is because in a real application you will be just using the window to add views to and not to display controls.

1. To start off, drag a Rounded Rect Button from the Library Objects tab onto your window. You can set the text of the button by double-clicking the middle of the button and typing in the text. You should have something that looks like Figure 2-6.

2. Even though the button control is on your window, you can't use this control in code without creating an outlet for it. In the library, select the Classes tab and then select `AppDelegate` (this is the class that you want to have access to your newly created button).

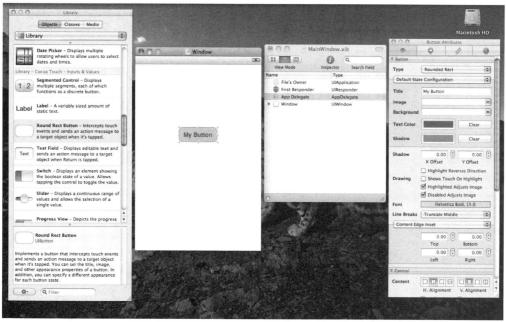

FIGURE 2-6

3. At the bottom of the Library window now is a list of four tabs: Inheritance, Definitions, Outlets, and Actions. For now, you want to select the Outlets tab and click the + button to add in a new outlet. Call the outlet myButton and click Enter to save. You can optionally enter in a type, but you can just leave this type as "id". You should have something that looks like Figure 2-7.

4. You may have noticed that you have not told your outlet which button it needs to be associated with. To do this, you use the Inspector (the far right window in Figure 2-8) to create a connection from the AppDelegate class outlet to the actual button on your window. First select the AppDelegate from the main Interface Builder window (third window in from the left). Then, select the Connections tab in the Inspector (the tab with the blue icon with a white arrow). Your outlet is shown here; you then need to click and drag (to create a connection) from the Inspector outlet to the actual button on your window. Figure 2-8 shows this in action.

Now that you have created this connection, the outlet is set up and is available to be used in code. See the "Hello World with Interface Builder" section later in this chapter to see how this works.

FIGURE 2-7

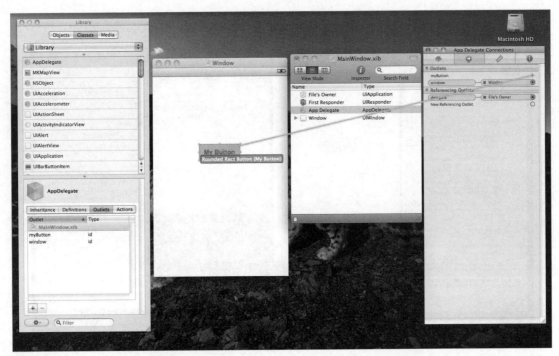

FIGURE 2-8

Setting Up Actions

An *action* is a message that is fired off when a certain event occurs. This is a very similar concept to events within .NET. What MonoTouch does is expose these actions as strongly typed partial methods from the control that fires off the event. You can read more on this in the next section.

Actions are set up in a similar way to how outlets are set up by using the library classes section to create a new action and then connecting this action up to a method on a button.

1. Just like you did to create an outlet, you create a new action and give it a name.

2. Again, doing this the same way as an outlet, you select the Actions tab and click the + button to add in a new action. You should call this action `buttonPressed` to follow with the example images. Interface Builder automatically adds a colon to the end of the method. This is used to denote that it is a method in Objective-C but it does no harm in leaving it in when using MonoTouch.

3. You should notice in the `AppDelegate` Inspector Connections tab a new section called Received Actions, which contains the new action. Click and drag this new action over to the

button. This time, when you let go you should notice a list of available actions pop up for the button. See Figure 2-9 for an example.

The action you probably want to associate with a button is the `TouchUpInside` method. This means that a user has touched a button and has just let go of it.

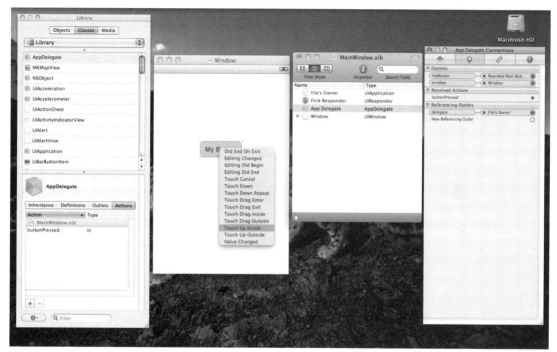

FIGURE 2-9

That's all you need to do associate an action in Interface Builder. See the next section on how you can work with this.

HELLO WORLD WITH INTERFACE BUILDER

Now that you have a good understanding of what outlets and actions are all about, this section shows how you can now use these outlets and actions in MonoTouch to do something simple, such as changing the button text when someone clicks the button. If you haven't followed through the outlets and actions sections, I suggest you do so because this section explains how to use them in MonoTouch.

Once you have saved the `MainWindow.xib` file you created earlier, open up the `MainWindow .xib.designer.cs` file and see what is automatically created. Your designer file should look like Listing 2-1.

LISTING 2-1: MonoTouch generated AppDelegate designer file

```
[MonoTouch.Foundation.Register("AppDelegate")]
public partial class AppDelegate {

    private MonoTouch.UIKit.UIWindow __mt_window;
    private MonoTouch.UIKit.UIButton __mt_myButton;

    #pragma warning disable 0169
    [MonoTouch.Foundation.Export("buttonPressed:")]
    partial void buttonPressed (MonoTouch.UIKit.UIButton sender);

    [MonoTouch.Foundation.Connect("window")]
    private MonoTouch.UIKit.UIWindow window {
        get {
            this.__mt_window =
                ((MonoTouch.UIKit.UIWindow)(this.GetNativeField("window")));
            return this.__mt_window;
        }
        set {
            this.__mt_window = value;
            this.SetNativeField("window", value);
        }
    }

    [MonoTouch.Foundation.Connect("myButton")]
    private MonoTouch.UIKit.UIButton myButton {
        get {
            this.__mt_myButton =
                ((MonoTouch.UIKit.UIButton)(this.GetNativeField("myButton")));
            return this.__mt_myButton;
        }
        set {
            this.__mt_myButton = value;
            this.SetNativeField("myButton", value);
        }
    }
}
```

What you can see from this designer file is that it has created a partial class to go with your
`AppDelegate` class in the `Main.cs` file. You can also see that there is a partial method called
`buttonPressed`, which represents the action that you created. You also have an instance variable
`myButton`, which represents the outlet that you created for the button.

 *You should not edit the designer file because this file is automatically generated
every time the `.xib` is edited in Interface Builder.*

If you go over to the `Main.cs` file where the other partial `AppDelegate` class is you can start coding against the `myButton` variable. You get full IntelliSense since you know it is of type `UIButton`. Because you added the button through Interface Builder, you don't need to add any extra code to initialize the button — this is done automatically.

To pick up the fact that a button has been pressed, you want to create a partial `buttonPressed` method and handle the action by running some of your own code. For this example just change the button's text to say Clicked by using the `SetTitle` method, where you pass in the title of the button and the control state it should be shown for — just use `Normal` for this example. You should end up with your `Main.cs` looking like Listing 2-2.

LISTING 2-2: Using Interface Builder controls

```
// The name AppDelegate is referenced in the MainWindow.xib file.
public partial class AppDelegate : UIApplicationDelegate
{
    public override bool FinishedLaunching (UIApplication app,
                                            NSDictionary options)
    {
        // If you have defined a view, add it here:
        // window.AddSubview (navigationController.View);

        window.MakeKeyAndVisible ();

        return true;
    }

    partial void buttonPressed (UIButton sender)
    {
        myButton.SetTitle("Clicked", UIControlState.Normal);
    }

    // This method is required in iPhoneOS 3.0
    public override void OnActivated (UIApplication application)
    {
    }
}
```

To run the code, you can simply click the cogs icon in MonoDevelop (as shown in Figure 2-10). Keyboard shortcut fans can use Alt+Cmd+Enter to do the same action. This will compile your application, automatically open up the iPhone simulator, install your application on the simulator, and start your application.

FIGURE 2-10

If all has gone successfully, you should see a screen that looks like Figure 2-11. When you click the button, the text should change to Clicked and the application will end up looking like Figure 2-12.

FIGURE 2-11

FIGURE 2-12

HELLO WORLD IN CODE

Because developing with Interface Builder is completely optional, this section shows how to use code to build the same application as in the preceding section.

To start off, you again create a new iPhone Window-based project. This automatically creates the `MainWindow.xib` and designer file, but you won't be using them this time around. Instead, you'll be coding everything in your `FinishedLaunching` method.

> *If the* `FinishedLaunching` *method is not returned in 10 seconds, the iPhone OS kills your application. The best way to manage this is to create a new view as a sub-view of the main window and add in any tasks to be carried out in this view rather than directly on the* `FinishedLaunching` *method. Because this is a simple example, this will not matter.*

First, create a new button to go on the screen. To do this you simply create a new instance of a button by calling the static method `FromType` on the `UIButton` class. Use the button type of `RoundedRect` from the `UIButtonType` enumeration so that it matches the button you used on the previous example.

Because the button is created programmatically, its position within the `UIWindow` must also be set programmatically. To do this you need to set the Frame of the button. You can create a new `System.Drawing.RectangleF` rectangle and pass that to the button's frame property. To make the examples match a little more, you also want to use the `SetTitle` method to set the initial text of the button to My Button.

If you decided to run the code straight away, you wouldn't actually see the button displayed at all. This is because you need to add it to the window. You can do this simply by calling the `AddSubview` on your window and passing in the button you just created. The code to programmatically add a button should look like Listing 2-3 and should be in the `FinishedLaunching` method.

LISTING 2-3: Adding a button programmatically

```
var button = UIButton.FromType(UIButtonType.RoundedRect);
var frame = new System.Drawing.RectangleF(35f, 30f, 250f, 40f);
button.Frame = frame;
button.SetTitle("My Button", UIControlState.Normal);
window.AddSubview(button);
```

When you run the app now, the button appears, but when someone clicks the button, nothing happens. This is where you want to handle the `TouchUpInside` event. Luckily you don't have to dive into any actions to get this to work; you can simply handle the event as you would in .NET. The button instance exposes all the events available to the button that you saw earlier while using Interface Builder. When you add the event for `TouchUpInside`, your code should look similar to Listing 2-4. Obviously this depends on how you have implemented the event, but you should get the same results whichever way you do. This example uses a lambda to create the anonymous delegate.

LISTING 2-4: Adding a touch event to a button programmatically

```
var button = UIButton.FromType(UIButtonType.RoundedRect);
var frame = new System.Drawing.RectangleF(35f, 30f, 250f, 40f);
button.Frame = frame;
button.SetTitle("My Button", UIControlState.Normal);

button.TouchUpInside += (sender, e) => {
   button.SetTitle("Clicked", UIControlState.Normal);
};

window.AddSubview(button);
```

Notice how little code you need to write using Interface Builder comparatively. However, you can see it's much more explicit using code to create the new objects than it is letting .xib files do this for you.

DEBUGGING

MonoTouch supports both debugging in the iPhone simulator and debugging on the device. As you might expect, the debugging story is very similar to debugging through Visual Studio and supports debugging with breakpoints, catchpoints, inspection, watches, an immediate/expression evaluator, a call stack and stepping through code.

On the Simulator

You may have noticed a similar icon right next to the "Run" cog in MonoDevelop; however, this one contains a green bug icon over the top (see Figure 2-13). This is the icon you use to run your application in debug mode. If you want to use the keyboard to do this, you can hit Cmd+Enter.

FIGURE 2-13

You set breakpoints through MonoDevelop the same way you would in Visual Studio — by clicking to the left of the line you want to debug. When your application is running, it hits the breakpoint and highlights the line in yellow. You can then hover over the variables, as you would expect to be able to do in debugging, to inspect individual properties. You can see this in Figure 2-14.

```
45        button.Frame = frame;
46        button.SetTitle("My Button", UIControlState.Normal);
47
48        button.TouchUpInside += (sender, e) => {
49            button.SetTitle("Clicked", UIControlState.Normal);
50        };
51
52
53                }
54
55
56            }
57    }
58
```

button	{MonoTouch.UIKit.UIButton}	MonoTouch.UIKit.UIButton
base	{MonoTouch.UIKit.UIControl}	MonoTouch.UIKit.UIControl
AdjustsImageWhenDisabled	true	bool
AdjustsImageWhenHighlighted	true	bool
ButtonType	RoundedRect	MonoTouch.UIKit.UIButtonType
ClassHandle	0x31a604e0	System.IntPtr
ContentEdgeInsets	{MonoTouch.UIKit.UIEdgeInsets}	MonoTouch.UIKit.UIEdgeInsets
CurrentBackgroundImage	null	object
CurrentImage	null	object
CurrentTitle	"My Button"	string
CurrentTitleColor	{MonoTouch.UIKit.UIColor}	MonoTouch.UIKit.UIColor
CurrentTitleShadowColor	{MonoTouch.UIKit.UIColor}	MonoTouch.UIKit.UIColor
Font	{MonoTouch.UIKit.UIFont}	MonoTouch.UIKit.UIFont
ImageEdgeInsets	{MonoTouch.UIKit.UIEdgeInsets}	MonoTouch.UIKit.UIEdgeInsets
ImageView	{MonoTouch.UIKit.UIImageView}	MonoTouch.UIKit.UIImageView
LineBreakMode	MiddleTruncation	MonoTouch.UIKit.UILineBreakMode

Application Output | Build Output
ild successful.

FIGURE 2-14

On the Device

Debugging on the device is similar to debugging on the simulator. When you select the Debug|iPhone profile within MonoDevelop (shown in Figure 2-15), you will be left with only the debug icon that is clickable. When you click this, the application compiles in debug mode and uploads to the device that is plugged in. It pops open a debugging window (shown in Figure 2-16) to say what IP address and port the device should be pointing at. This is because you will be debugging the device over Wi-Fi, so you want to make sure the device is on the same network as your machine.

FIGURE 2-15

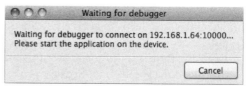

FIGURE 2-16

Applications that are debugging-enabled have extra settings enabled in the configuration. You can view these settings by tapping on Settings and then the name of your application. You should see a screen that looks like Figure 2-17. You want to make sure that the IP address that popped up in the debugging window on your computer and the IP address shown in the device's debug settings match up.

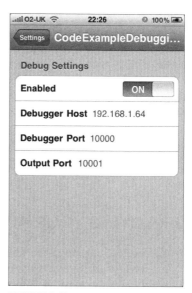

The device may vibrate when the application is in debug mode. This is a way for MonoTouch to tell you that there is a problem, and the problem depends on how many vibrations you get:

➤ **One vibration:** The application could not connect to the machine waiting for the device to connect.

➤ **Two vibrations:** The application could not parse the host address that was configured.

➤ **Three vibrations:** Standard streams (stdout and stderr) could not be set up.

FIGURE 2-17

 To enable debugging on a device, you need to have the full version of MonoTouch and the correct certificates installed. See "Deploying Your Application" later in this chapter for more information.

UNDERSTANDING THE LINKER

Because you can't re-use libraries on the iPhone, every time you put a version of a MonoTouch application on to a device or the App Store, you're also installing the Mono framework. You are probably thinking that having the same Mono framework on the device for every application is a waste, and it would be if this were the case. MonoTouch actually uses a linker tool to go through the Mono framework assemblies and remove the code that isn't being used in your application. This means that each application uses its own unique and stripped-down version of the Mono framework, so when a new version of MonoTouch comes out, you don't have to upgrade every application using

MonoTouch to support the latest version or test for any regressions that might have cropped up. Each application will continue running its own version of the framework.

The linker also helps to get the size of your application down, which is important, especially on a mobile device. If your application is under 20 megabytes, Apple allows you to download this over Edge/3G; if the application is over this limit you need to be connected to a WiFi connection to download the application. Because you're not including the whole base class library and core components of the Mono framework if you are not using it in your application, you are not using up space in your application with unused code.

The linker is integrated into MonoTouch and MonoDevelop, so there is no extra work to enable it. By default MonoDevelop will set up the iPhone simulator profiles (`Debug|iPhone Simulator` and `Release|iPhone Simulator`) to not user the linker, and on device profiles (`Debug|iPhone` and `Release|iPhone`), it chooses the "Link SDK assemblies only" configuration. This means that linker goes through the SDK and removes code that isn't being used, but it does not link the assembly you create. The other configuration is "Link all assemblies", which goes through both the SDK and the assemblies you create. This can commonly cause problems with code involving things such as web services, reflection, or serialization if they are not being statically called in your code. You will want to use the `[Preserve]` attribute on members that may be removed by the linker or `[Preserve (AllMembers=true)]` on types defining these members.

DEPLOYING YOUR APPLICATION

You've got your Hello World application completed, and now it's time to show the world how amazing the application is (or just how awesome MonoTouch is) by deploying the application to your iPhone. Follow these steps to allow you to upload your application to a device:

1. You will need to become a member of the Apple iPhone Developer Program. The cost of this program at time of writing is $99 per year. The location to sign up can be found in the bulleted list at the end of this section.

2. Request and install the Developer Certificate that is obtained from Apple through the iPhone Developer Program membership. This certificate should be visible within the development Mac's Keychain Access utility, which can be found in `/Applications/Utilities/ Keychain Access.app`.

3. Request and install the Deployment Certificate that is obtained from Apple through the iPhone Developer Program membership. This certificate should be visible within the development Mac's Keychain security utility.

4. The iPhone must be properly provisioned. This means that the iPhone is enabled to run debug or test applications that are not downloaded from the App Store. Luckily, Apple supplies a wizard utility through its developer web site that helps in the setup and provisioning of the iPhone.

5. Once the development system is set up, the MonoDevelop project must be set up to deploy the application to the iPhone when the developer selects the option to deploy to the device. This is accomplished by setting the project's options. To get to this screen you right-click on the iPhone project and select options. When the project window opens up, you select iPhone Bundle Signing. By default it uses the first developer certificate that it finds. See Figure 2-18.

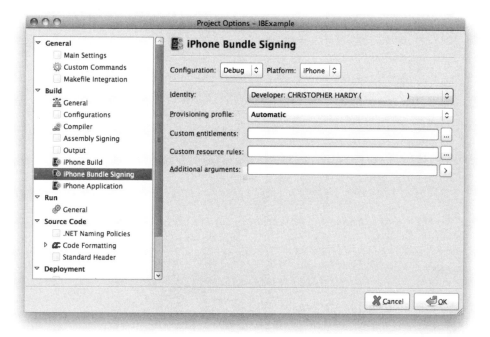

FIGURE 2-18

Apple has several great resources for setting up the keys and for deployment setup for Mac developers. To access these resources, you need to be a member of the Apple iPhone Developer Program (and to view the last two resources, you need to be logged in):

➤ **The iPhone Developer Program web site:** `http://developer.apple.com/iphone/program`

➤ **The iPhone Developer Program's provisioning web site:** `http://developer.apple.com/iphone/manage/overview/index.action`

➤ **An Apple PDF document that describes the certificate process in minute detail:** `http://developer.apple.com/iphone/download.action?path=/iphone/iphone_developer_program_user_guide/iphone_developer_program_user_guide__standard_program_v2.5__final.pdf`

SUMMARY

This chapter showed you how to get set up with MonoTouch and MonoDevelop and showed that using MonoTouch is pretty straightforward and can get you writing iPhone applications rather quickly. MonoDevelop integrates nicely with existing Apple tools and is a familiar look and feel to using Visual Studio, allowing you to pick up the development tools quickly.

3

Planning Your App's UI: Exploring the Screen Controls

WHAT'S IN THIS CHAPTER?

➤ Creating iPhone(y) UI

➤ Exploring the Input & Value objects in Interface Builder

In this chapter you learn about creating your application's UI and specifically how the UI on the iPhone can differ from UIs that you might have created before. You also explore the Input & Value objects from the Interface Builder Objects Library.

Figure 3-1 shows the Input & Value objects in Interface Builder. We discuss those objects later in this chapter. First, however, you need to become familiar with how an iPhone UI generally looks and what patterns for interaction it usually follows.

CREATING IPHONE(Y) UI AND APPLICATION INTERACTION PATTERNS

One of the most important aspects of application development for an iPhone app is the user interface. This is because to most users, the interface *is* the application. Designers and developers spend a lot of time deciding how common interface elements should look and how interaction should occur. The great thing is that the MonoTouch team has ported

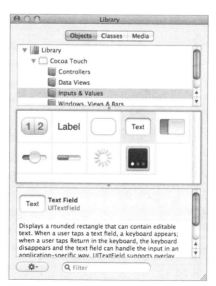

FIGURE 3-1

all of the CocoaTouch classes for making your apps look and feel just like CocoaTouch apps. In addition to exploring these classes, the author urges you to take a look at Apple's *Human Interface Guidelines*; it provides developers with descriptions of interaction patterns for common problems.

Apple provides the *View Controller Programming Guide* for iPhone OS in the iPhone SDK documentation. This document explores several high-level design patterns for user interaction. Apple has created semantics for describing the overall style of interaction for a given screen or set of screens in an application — almost all applications implement designs that can be described according to this vocabulary. With an understanding of these common patterns, you can plan your user interfaces according to your user needs.

Command Interfaces

A command interface is one in which you present your users with a toolbar containing one or more buttons that represent actions for them to take. Command interfaces typically don't use view controllers, but instead wire actions for buttons to other objects directly. You add a `UIToolbar` to your application to implement a command interface.

A command interface might be right for your application if:

➤   You have a very small, limited section of actions that your user can perform.

➤   You are presenting the user with an editable view, maybe something like a drawing surface, and you want to provide a set of tools or actions.

➤   You have one main screen from which the user performs all the actions of your application.

Figure 3-2 shows examples of command interfaces.

FIGURE 3-2

Radio Interfaces

Radio interfaces present a set of buttons that switch between views when a user taps them. These buttons are displayed on a tab bar at the bottom of the window, and each tap swaps to a different view without animating between the views. This type of interface works well for displaying non-hierarchical data. You can use a `UITabBar` to create a radio interface.

A radio interface might be right for your application if:

➤ You have a set of related but disparate screens. If your screens aren't related in nature, you should consider building multiple applications to adhere to the concept of cooperative single-tasking.

➤ Your views are siblings. That is, they don't represent different levels of a hierarchy of data, but rather various views into data that may or may not overlap.

➤ You have a small set of closely related subsets of functionality that can be accessed in any order. Essentially, each view requires a separate main view controller, so the partitioning functionality should consider the architecture.

Figure 3-3 shows examples of radio interfaces.

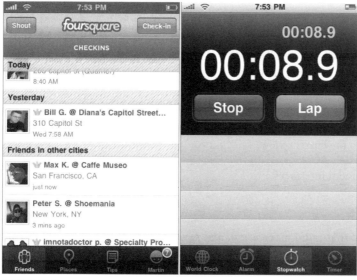

FIGURE 3-3

Navigation Interfaces

Navigation interfaces display a hierarchy of objects. Users tap controls to move toward greater specificity. The `UINavigationController` class is typically used to navigate a hierarchy of `UIViewController` instances. Changing between views animates the more specific view in from the right, whereas the less specific view moves out toward the left. Moving back up the hierarchy animates the views in the other direction.

A navigation interface might be right for your application if you have a set of hierarchical data or functionality that you'd like to allow users to traverse. If your data fits any tree-like data structure, a navigation interface is likely appropriate, and follows standards established by Apple as part of the Cocoa Touch platform.

Figure 3-4 shows examples of navigation interfaces.

Modal Interfaces

A modal interface presents a supplemental view on top of a view. This is most useful when presenting secondary screens, such as an editing screen. Modal interfaces are similar to navigation interfaces in that they animate transitions between views. Navigation interfaces transition through a stack of `UIViewControllers` by animating them horizontally. Modal interfaces differ by transitioning new views onto the top of the stack by animating them vertically. A great example of a modal interface that is mixed in with lots of different types of interfaces is the `UIAlertView`.

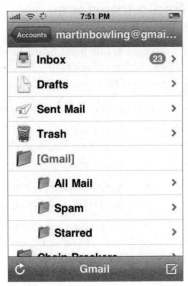

FIGURE 3-4

A model interface might be right for your application if you need to provide:

➤ A workflow for working with data in multiple steps.

➤ An editable interface for an onscreen view.

➤ A secondary set of functionality that users can optionally engage while remaining in the context of the current view. For example, you can use a modal interface if you want to trigger the camera to take a photograph or choose a contact from your Address Book, and then provide the resulting data to the current view.

Figure 3-5 shows examples of modal interfaces.

Combination Interfaces

You should always keep in mind that radio, navigation, and modal interfaces don't have to be mutually exclusive. In fact, the various types of interfaces are often combined to provide users with an interface that presents multiple sets of hierarchical data for navigation. If you are familiar with any of the popular apps, you will see that the use of combination interfaces is very common. Navigation and modal interfaces are easily combined to create an application that can navigate through one of several hierarchical data sets. You can recognize the modal-navigation interface by a tab bar on the bottom of the screen that switches between table views at the top of the screen.

A combination interface might be right for your application if:

➤ You have complex data or functionality that would benefit from the use of different user interfaces.

➤ Your users will interact with your application using different modes for the same data set.

FIGURE 3-5

Figure 3-6 shows examples of combination interfaces.

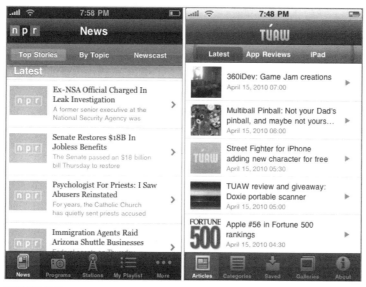

FIGURE 3-6

UILABEL

Now that you have an idea of the interaction patterns that iPhone applications commonly use, you are ready to get familiar with the controls available to you as Input & Value objects in Interface Builder. This chapter starts out with the most basic control in the library: the `UILabel`. The

`UILabel` represents a read-only text view. `UILabels` can contain varying amounts of text and may shrink, wrap, or truncate the text, depending on the size of the bounding rectangle and properties you set. Through its properties you can control the font, text color, alignment, highlighting, and shadowing of the text in the label. To do so, follow these steps:

1. Open Interface Builder.

2. Navigate to the Input & Value objects, and select a `UILabel`. Drag it onto your window/view and place it.

3. Create an outlet for this `UILabel` so that you can access this object from your code.

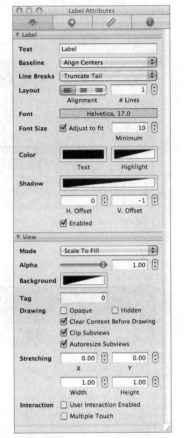

The members that you will most frequently work with in the `UILabel` are:

➤ `Text`: The actual text to be displayed by the label.

➤ `TextAlignment`: Use the `UITextAlignment` enum to choose `Left`, `Center`, or `Right`.

➤ `TextColor`: Assign a named color (such as `UIColor.Blue`) or a System color (such as `UIColor.DarkTextColor`), or a `From` method to use any other color.

➤ `Font`: Set the font typeface and size for the text.

➤ `Lines`: The maximum number of lines used to render the text.

Figure 3-7 shows the `UILabel` options in Interface Builder.

Not only can you set these from inside Interface Builder but you can also set these from inside your code. The `UILabel` is used to display read-only information and doesn't have any events to respond to clicks or any touch events. This will be a very static control and will mostly likely be used as a sub-view in other controls to display your data. Here is an example of using these basic properties in code:

FIGURE 3-7

```
// UILabel outlet is named Label
Label.Font = UIFont.FromName("Times New Roman", 17f);
Label.TextAlignment = UITextAlignment.Left;
Label.TextColor = UIColor.Red;
Label.Lines = 3;
Label.Text = "It's a UILabel from inside code with MonoTouch";
```

UIBUTTON

The `UIButton` is the control that you use to gather touch input from users. The use cases for the `UIButton` are much like buttons on web pages or in Windows Forms applications where you want the user to perform an action. The `UIButton` class can be customized through display attributes or with specialized drawing code. Before these are discussed, you should know some of the basic properties in Interface Builder:

➤ `Title`: The actual text displayed on the button.

➤ `Image`: An image displayed on the button.

➤ `Background`: An image used as the button's background.

➤ `TextColor`: Assign a named color (such as `UIColor.Blue`) or a System color (such as `UIColor.DarkTextColor`), or a `From` method to use any other color.

➤ `Shadow`: Assign a named color (such as `UIColor.Blue`) or a System color (such as `UIColor.DarkTextColor`), or a `From` method to use any other color.

Figure 3-8 shows the `UIButton` options in Interface Builder.

Each of the properties can be set for each of the different states of the `UIButton`; these are defined in the `UIControlState` enum to choose `Normal`, `Selected`, `Highlighted`, or `Disabled`. Within Interface Builder you can select these states and set properties accordingly; in code you will use the `SetXxx` method for the accompanying property.

You can create several types of buttons:

➤ `UIButtonTypeCustom`: No button style. Instead, a custom `drawRect:` method should be defined.

➤ `UIButtonTypeRoundedRect`: A rectangular button with rounded corners and a centered title. Used for all general-purpose buttons.

➤ `UIButtonTypeDetailDisclosure`: A circular button with a centered chevron (>). Used to display details of an associated object or record.

➤ `UIButtonTypeInfoLight`: A light-colored, circular button with an italicized lowercase "i" character. Used to flip a view over to display settings or additional information.

➤ `UIButtonTypeInfoDark`: A dark-colored, circular button with an italicized lowercase "i" character. Used to flip a view over to display settings or additional information.

➤ `UIButtonTypeContactAdd`: A rectangular button with rounded corners and a centered title. Used to display either a list of contacts or a form for adding a new contact.

FIGURE 3-8

The following is an example of setting some of the `UIButton` properties and responding to a click event, which for the `UIButton` is the `TouchUpInside` event:

```
// UIButton outlet is named button
UIImage bgImage = UIImage.FromFile("buttonBackground.png");
```

```
button.SetBackgroundImage(bgImage, UIControlState.Normal);
button.SetTitle("Click Me",UIControlState.Normal);
button.SetTitleColor(UIColor.White, UIControlState.Normal);
button.TouchUpInside += delegate(object sender, EventArgs e) {
    Label.Text = "Button Was Clicked!";
    Label.TextColor = UIColor.Brown;
};
```

UITEXTFIELD

The UITextField class provides you with single-line editing capabilities and has built-in support for editing secure data such as passwords or other sensitive items. When a user taps a text field, a keyboard appears; when a user taps Return in the keyboard, the keyboard disappears and the text field can handle the input in an application-specific way. UITextField supports overlay views to display additional information, such as a bookmarks icon. UITextField also provides a clear text control that a user taps to erase the contents of the text field. Via the properties of the UITextField you can control the font, style, color, and alignment of the text.

Here are some of the properties of the UITextField class:

➤ Text: The actual text displayed by the textbox.

➤ Placeholder: The text displayed when the user has not input actual text. You can use this as a visual cue to your user about what data you are expecting.

➤ TextAlignment: Use the UITextAlignment enum to choose Left, Center, or Right.

➤ TextColor: Assigns a named color (such as UIColor.Blue) or a System color (such as UIColor.DarkTextColor), or a From method to use any other color.

➤ SecureTextEntry: Determines if a mask is used to hide the displayed text.

➤ AutocapitalizationType: Determines when the Shift key is automatically used (for example, at the start of typing and new sentences). The default is None.

➤ AutocorrectionType: Shows whether auto-correction is enabled during typing. The default is correction enabled.

➤ ReturnKeyType: Note that UITextView does not support the same Done editing behavior as UITextField.

➤ KeyboardType: Allows the control to show a keyboard appropriate for the type of data you are expecting, for example, plain text, an e-mail address, or numeric data.

The code using these properties is shown here:

```
// UITextField outlet is named TextField
TextField.Font = UIFont.FromName("Times New Roman", 17f);
TextField.TextAlignment = UITextAlignment.Left;
TextField.TextColor = UIColor.Black;
TextField.SecureTextEntry = false;
```

Figure 3-9 shows the UITextField options in Interface Builder.

As noted earlier in this chapter, the UITextField responds when a user taps a text field, and a keyboard appears; when a user taps Return in the keyboard, the keyboard disappears. However, it should be noted that if the UITextField appears below where the modal keyboard view appears, the UITextField itself will be hidden unless you scroll the view to move the UITextField into the viewable area. That being said, it's generally the accepted practice that UITextFields are not to be used outside of UITableViews. When you use UITextField inside of a UITableView, the UITableView does all of the heavy lifting to ensure that the UITextField is in view for the user to see.

UISWITCH

The UISwitch is a rather simple control that displays an element and shows the user the Boolean state of a given value. Tapping the control toggles the state. Without subclassing and creating your own control based on the UISwitch, you can only display On or Off on the control. The UISwitch has very little in the way of properties as well; the one that you will most likely use is the State property, which tells you whether it represents On or Off.

Figure 3-10 shows the UISwitch options in Interface Builder.

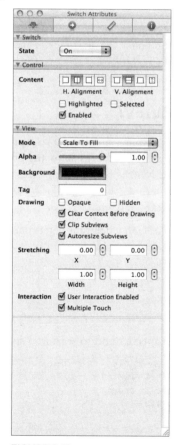

FIGURE 3-9   **FIGURE 3-10**

UISLIDER

The UISlider displays a horizontal bar, called a track, which represents a finite range of values. The current value is shown by the position of an indicator, or thumb. A user selects a value by sliding the thumb along the track. You can customize the appearance of both the track and the thumb:

➤ MinValue: The minimum value that the control will display.

➤ MaxValue: The maximum value that the control will display.

➤ MinValueImage: Contains the image that is drawn on the side of the slider representing the minimum value.

➤ MaxValueImage: Contains the image that is drawn on the side of the slider representing the maximum value.

Figure 3-11 shows the UISlider options in Interface Builder.

The following shows the code using these properties and creating a delegate for when the value is updated:

```
// UISlider outlet is named slider
slider.MinValue = 0.0f;
slider.MaxValue = 10.0f;
slider.SetValue(10.0f, false);
slider.ValueChanged += delegate(object sender, EventArgs e) {
    Console.WriteLine("New Value: " + slider.Value);
};
```

UIACTIVITYINDICATORVIEW

The UIActivityIndicatorView displays an element that provides user feedback on the progress of a task or process with an unknown duration (to show the progress of a task with known duration, use UIProgressView instead). As long as the task or process continues, the activity indicator spins. A user does not interact with an activity indicator. The following is a list of properties that are most frequently used with the UIActivityIndicatorView.

➤ HidesWhenStopped: A Boolean value that determines whether or not the control will display when it is not animated.

➤ ActivityIndicatorViewStyle: Use the UIActivityIndicatorViewStyle enum to choose Gray, White, or WhiteLarge.

Figure 3-12 shows the UIActivityIndicatorView options in Interface Builder.

The following code uses these properties and to start and stop the animation:

```
// UIActivityIndicatorView outlet is named activity
activity.ActivityIndicatorViewStyle = UIActivityIndicatorViewStyle.WhiteLarge;
activity.HidesWhenStopped = true;
activity.StartAnimating();
//Do Something
activity.StopAnimating();
```

UISEGMENTEDCONTROL

The `UISegmentedControl` provides a compact, persistent grouping of buttons that switch between views. According to the mobile HIG, segmented controls should provide feedback to users by swapping views or otherwise appropriately updating the UI. The feedback should be immediate, avoiding animation effects. That being said, it is, however, conceivable that you could use segmented controls for more complex view management. It displays an element that comprises multiple segments, each of which functions as a discrete button. Each segment can display either text or an image, but not both. `UISegmentedControl` ensures that the width of each segment is proportional, based on the total number of segments, unless you set a specific width.

➤ `NumberOfSegements`: This is a read-only property from inside code; but using Interface Builder you can use it to set the number of segments you want to display.

➤ `ControlStyle`: Use the `UISegmentedControlStyle` enum to choose `Plain`, `Bordered`, or `Bar`.

Figure 3-13 shows the `UISegmentedControl` options in Interface Builder.

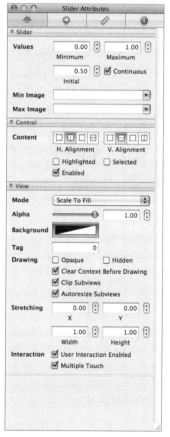

FIGURE 3-11

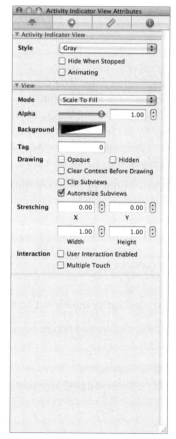

FIGURE 3-12

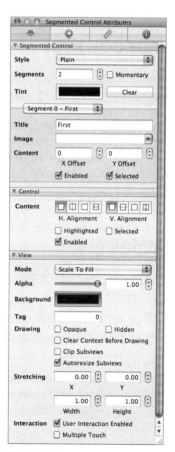

FIGURE 3-13

The following code uses these properties and to a delegate to respond to the value being changed:

```
// UISegmentedControl outlet is named segmentedControl
segmentedControl.InsertSegment("First", 0, false);
segmentedControl.InsertSegment("Second", 1, false);
segmentedControl.InsertSegment("Third", 2, false);
segmentedControl.SelectedSegment = 0;
segmentedControl.ControlStyle = UISegmentedControlStyle.Plain;

segmentedControl.ValueChanged += delegate {
   if (segmentedControl.SelectedSegment == 0)
      Console.WriteLine("First Selected");
   //Show Your View
   else if (segmentedControl.SelectedSegment == 1)
      Console.WriteLine("Second Selected");
   //Show Your View
   else if (segmentedControl.SelectedSegment == 2)
      Console.WriteLine("Third Selected");
   //Show Your View
};
```

UIPAGECONTROL

The `UIPageControl` indicates the number of open pages in an application by displaying a dot for each open page. The dot that corresponds to the currently viewed page is highlighted. `UIPageControl` supports navigation by sending the delegate an event when a user taps to the right or to the left of the currently highlighted dot. This control is generally used in conjunction with a `UIScrollView`. (`UIScrollView` is covered in Chapter 4.)

Figure 3-14 shows the `UIPageControl` options in Interface Builder.

SUMMARY

This chapter introduced the various types of interface patterns that are suggested by Apple:

➤ Command interfaces are best used for limited functionality.

➤ Radio interfaces use a `UITabBar` to provide access to related views.

➤ Navigation interfaces use a `UINavigationController` to provide hierarchical data or functionality that you'd like to allow users to traverse.

FIGURE 3-14

➤ Modal interfaces use a `UIViewController` to provide a secondary set of functionality that users can optionally engage while remaining in the context of the current view.

➤ Combination interfaces are good when you have complex data or functionality that would benefit from the use of different user interfaces.

You were also introduced to the Input & Value objects from the Interface Builder Objects Library, which gives you a great introduction to some of the controls that you'll use to create your user interfaces. This chapter combined with Chapter 4 should give you all the tools you need to build a great UI with MonoTouch.

Data Controls

WHAT'S IN THIS CHAPTER?

➤ Understanding windows, views, and controllers

➤ Displaying data and editing controls

➤ Using a toolbar

➤ Navigating with tabs

The Interface Builder Objects Library divides the Cocoa Touch controls into four groups: Controllers; Data Views; Inputs & Values; and Windows, Views & Bars. The Inputs & Values objects were introduced in Chapter 3, and a few other objects like Tables, Maps, and Image-related controls appear in Chapters 6, 7, and 10.

These are the remaining classes, which you are going to learn about in this chapter:

➤ Controllers

    ➤ `UIViewController`

    ➤ `UINavigationController`

    ➤ `UITabBarController`

    ➤ `UIToolBarController`

➤ Data Views

    ➤ `UIWebView`

    ➤ `UITextView`

    ➤ `UIScrollView`

    ➤ `UIPickerView`

    ➤ `UIDatePicker`

➤ Windows, Views & Bars

   ➤ `UIWindow`

   ➤ `UIView`

   ➤ `UINavigationBar`

   ➤ `UINavigationItem`

   ➤ `UIToolbar`

   ➤ `UIBarButtonItem`

   ➤ `UITabBar`

   ➤ `UITabBarItem`

Figure 4-1 shows how each of these classes appear in Interface Builder, so you know where to find them.

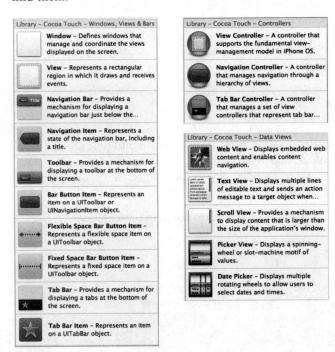

FIGURE 4-1

WINDOWS AND VIEWS

Windows and views form the underpinnings of all iPhone OS applications. They are the basis of the layout system and capture and handle user input. The `UIWindow` class in the iPhone OS is relatively simple and won't require a great deal of customization while `UIView` and its subclasses form the basis of every piece of your user interface.

UIWindow

An iPhone OS application generally has only one window — it provides the background upon which the rest of your user interface is displayed. Unlike windows in a desktop operating system, the UIWindow class has no "chrome" (no title bar; resize handles; borders; or minimize, maximize, or close buttons) and must always fill the entire screen. The only adornment is the status bar at the top of your window, which you can optionally show or hide.

When you create a new application solution in MonoDevelop it automatically adds MainWindow.xib to your project, which contains a UIWindow instance called window. It also adds the AppDelegate .FinishedLaunching method that includes the line window.MakeKeyAndVisible(), which shows the window.

It is possible to create a window directly in code. Listing 4-1 shows the simplest possible MonoTouch application requiring no Interface Builder files in order to display some text on the screen. Most examples in this book *do* use Interface Builder in the examples, but it's worthwhile remembering that you can always accomplish the same effect constructing your UIView objects in code.

LISTING 4-1: Creating UIWindow in code (Window01\AppController.cs)

Available for
download on
Wrox.com

```
using System;
using MonoTouch.Foundation;
using MonoTouch.UIKit;
namespace Window01
{
[Register("AppController")]
public class AppController : UIApplicationDelegate
{
    UIWindow window;
    public override void FinishedLaunching (UIApplication app)
    {
        window = new UIWindow (UIScreen.MainScreen.Bounds)
        {
            new UILabel(new System.Drawing.RectangleF (50,150,230,100))
            { Text = "Hello world" }
        };
        window.MakeKeyAndVisible();
    }
}
class HelloWorld
{
    static void Main (string[] args)
    { UIApplication.Main (args, null, "AppController"); }
}}
```

UIWindows should always fill the entire screen, hence the use of UIScreen.MainScreen.Bounds to size the window.

UIView

Although not an exact parallel, the `UIView` class has some similar characteristics to the User Control concept in ASP.NET, WinForms, and WPF.

`UIView` is the base class of every other control in the UIKit framework — it is responsible for both rendering content to the screen and responding to touch events within its bounds. A `UIView` can also contain other `UIView` instances — which are referred to as sub-views — in as deep a hierarchy as required. The parent (or superview) manages its sub-views' sizes and positions and may also respond to events that are not handled by a sub-view.

In *very simple* applications (such as many of the control-specific examples in this book) a `UIView` (or subclass) may be added directly to the `window` for display and user interaction. Most applications require more complex view handling, which is done by `UIViewControllers` such as the `UINavigationController` covered in this chapter and the `UITableViewController` covered in Chapter 6. `UIViewControllers` orchestrate all the different views in your application: showing and hiding them as appropriate and resizing them when the device's orientation changes.

As mentioned previously, an application should have only one `UIWindow`; the remainder of the views you add to your project will be a `UIView`, a `UIViewController`, or one of their subclasses. The key members to know on `UIView` are:

➤ `Bounds`: Location and size of the view in the view's coordinate system within its frame rectangle; that is, the default origin is (0, 0) at the top left of the screen.

➤ `Frame`: Position and size of the view in the coordinate system of its containing superview.

➤ `UIView(frame)`: Constructor for `UIView` that requires a `RectangleF` to set its size.

➤ `AddSubview`: Adds the supplied `UIView` instance as a sub-view to the current view. The new view is displayed on top of any existing sub-views and is positioned according to its `Frame` or `Bounds` property.

> *The* `Bounds` *and* `Frame` *properties are of type* `System.Drawing.RectangleF` *in MonoTouch, not* `CGRect` *from the* `CoreGraphics` *framework (which is what the underlying Objective-C methods accept). This is one of many examples where MonoTouch makes iPhone development more familiar to .NET developers by using familiar classes wherever possible.*

DATA VIEW CONTROLS

The Interface Builder Data Views library category contains a number of different types of views, including some important classes that deserve their own chapters: `UITableView` (Chapter 6), `UIMapView` (Chapter 8), and `UIImageView`, which is covered in Chapter 10. The rest are discussed in this section.

UIWebView

The `UIWebView` control allows you to embed web content in your application: Internet-based web sites, HTML files distributed in your application, or dynamically generated HTML strings. It is a very similar concept to the .NET WebBrowser control in Windows Forms and WPF, and for all intents and purposes is like having an instance of Safari inside your application.

Web-based Content

The most obvious use of the `UIWebView` is to display a web page in your application. There aren't many members on the control; the main ones are:

➤ `LoadRequest()`: This method passes a URL (in an `NSUrlRequest` object) to load that address from the Internet. In the following example this method is called from the Go button.

➤ `ScalesPageToFit`: This property controls whether the content is automatically scaled to fit (with zooming allowed) or whether it is forced to always be displayed "actual size." The default is `false`, which means web pages aren't scaled down for you. Users familiar with Mobile Safari will expect to be able to zoom in and out of web pages, so for web content you should usually set this to `true`, or check the Scales Page To Fit option in Interface Builder.

➤ `LoadStarted`: This event is triggered whenever new content is loaded by the web browser. The following example shows the Network Activity animation to give some visual feedback that something is happening.

➤ `LoadFinished`: This event is triggered when content has finished loading (the entire page and all its content, including images and scripts). Useful to hide the Network Activity animation.

➤ `LoadError`: This event is triggered when a page cannot be loaded. The following example stops the Network Activity animation and displays the error message to the user. In a real application you might filter out some of these errors or display a more user-friendly message.

To demonstrate loading a web page, one sample in this chapter's download — WebView01 — has three controls placed on a window in Interface Builder: `UIWebView`, `UITextField`, and a `UIButton`. This code added to `FinishedLaunching()` makes it work:

```
GoButton.TouchUpInside += delegate
{
    WebBrowser.LoadRequest(new NSUrlRequest(new NSUrl(UrlInput.Text)));
};
WebBrowser.LoadStarted += delegate
{
    UIApplication.SharedApplication.NetworkActivityIndicatorVisible = true;
};
WebBrowser.LoadFinished += delegate
{
    UIApplication.SharedApplication.NetworkActivityIndicatorVisible = false;
};
WebBrowser.LoadError += delegate(object sender, UIWebErrorArgs e)
{
    UIApplication.SharedApplication.NetworkActivityIndicatorVisible = false;
    using (var alert = new UIAlertView("WebView Error"
            ,e.Error.LocalizedDescription,null,"OK",null))
    { alert.Show(); }
};
```

WebView01\Main.cs

The result is shown in Figure 4-2. Try navigating to an invalid URL (for example, `http://wrox.co`) or testing it with no network connectivity to trigger the `LoadError` delegate.

> *If you read through Apple's documentation for `UIWebView` you will notice the events such as `LoadStarted`, `LoadFinished`, and `LoadError` are actually methods in another class — `UIWebViewDelegate`. This is an example of how MonoTouch makes the Objective-C APIs more familiar for .NET developers by exposing delegate methods as events on the object itself (in this case `UIWebView`).*
>
> *Although it is possible to subclass and use `Delegate` classes provided by the iPhone OS, throughout this book we use the MonoTouch events/delegates where they have been provided.*

To make this example work more like a real web browser you can use more `UIWebView` members to implement Back and Forward behavior and keep the address bar in-sync with the displayed web page. Using Interface Builder, add two `UIButtons` (labeled Back and Forward) that use these members:

➤ `CanGoBack`: Whether there is a previous address in the navigation history to show.

➤ `CanGoForward`: Whether there is a previously visited address to return to.

➤ `GoBack()`: Show the previous address in the navigation history.

➤ `GoForward()`: Return to an address that has previously been visited and "gone back" from.

Listing 4-2 shows the code required in `FinishedLaunching` and provided in the chapter download WebView02. The updated example with Back/Forward buttons is shown in Figure 4-3.

FIGURE 4-2

FIGURE 4-3

LISTING 4-2: Mini Web Browser (WebView02\Main.cs)

```
GoButton.TouchUpInside += delegate
{
    WebBrowser.LoadRequest(new NSUrlRequest(new NSUrl(UrlInput.Text)));
};
WebBrowser.LoadStarted += delegate
{
    UIApplication.SharedApplication.NetworkActivityIndicatorVisible = true;
    if (!String.IsNullOrEmpty(WebBrowser.Request.Url.AbsoluteString))
        UrlInput.Text = WebBrowser.Request.Url.AbsoluteString;
};
WebBrowser.LoadFinished += delegate
{
    UIApplication.SharedApplication.NetworkActivityIndicatorVisible = false;
    UrlInput.Text = WebBrowser.Request.Url.AbsoluteString;
    BackButton.Enabled = WebBrowser.CanGoBack;
    ForwardButton.Enabled = WebBrowser.CanGoForward;
};
WebBrowser.LoadError += delegate(object sender, UIWebErrorArgs e)
{
    UIApplication.SharedApplication.NetworkActivityIndicatorVisible = false;
    BackButton.Enabled = WebBrowser.CanGoBack;
    ForwardButton.Enabled = WebBrowser.CanGoForward;
    using (var alert = new UIAlertView("WebView Error"
            ,e.Error.LocalizedDescription,null,"OK",null))
    { alert.Show(); }
};
BackButton.TouchUpInside += delegate
{
    WebBrowser.GoBack();
    UrlInput.Text = WebBrowser.Request.Url.AbsoluteString;
};
ForwardButton.TouchUpInside += delegate
{
    WebBrowser.GoForward();
    UrlInput.Text = WebBrowser.Request.Url.AbsoluteString;
};
```

Local HTML Content

Another great use of the `UIWebView` control is to display HTML-formatted text and images. The simplest way to do this is add an HTML file to your project (don't forget to set the `Build Action: Content`) and load it into a `UIWebView` control. When you are writing HTML specifically for display on iPhone OS devices it is a good idea to target the exact width of the display and set `ScalesPagesToFit` to false.

```
NSUrl localFile = NSUrl.FromFilename("MyContent.html");
NSUrlRequest request = new NSUrlRequest(localFile);
WebBrowser.LoadRequest(request);
WebBrowser.ScalesPageToFit = false;
```

WebView03\Main.cs

A snippet of the HTML source from download WebView03 and the resulting output are shown in Figure 4-4.

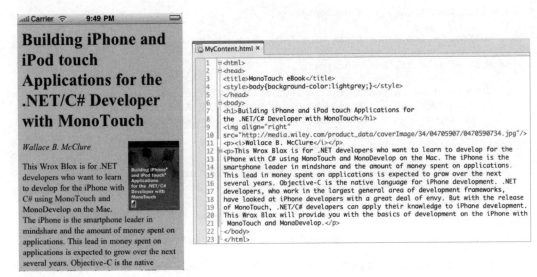

FIGURE 4-4

There are some things that you still can't do with an HTML file. You might want to generate the HTML dynamically in your code or reference local files such as images and style sheets. To allow the `UIWebView` to find local files you need to pass in the `basedirectory` that all the file references are relative to.

>
> *Any files (such as HTML and images) in your MonoTouch project that are marked as* `Build Action: Content` *will become part of your application bundle when deployed to the simulator or a device. You can discover the complete path (including the bundle name) using the static property* `NSBundle .MainBundle.BundlePath`.
>
> *That location is useful for displaying data files embedded in your application; however, you should not save files within the application bundle. If your code saves user data to a file, you should use a different path such as* `Environment .GetFolderPath (Environment.SpecialFolder.Personal)`, *which corresponds to the Documents folder — this data will be backed up by iTunes and won't be lost if the application is upgraded to a newer version.*

The next example in the download — WebView04 — shows how to display dynamically generated HTML and reference local files in the HTML. The code does the following:

➤ Determines the application bundle location.

➤ Generates an HTML string in code (the complete HTML string has been truncated in the printed example shown).

➤ Creates an NSUrl to the base directory set and passes that to the UIWebView along with the dynamically generated HTML string. Setting the base URL in this way tells the UIWebView to prepend that location to all relative addresses in the HTML, meaning it can then resolve image locations, style sheets, and even links to other HTML pages in your application bundle.

➤ Sets ScalesPageToFit = false because the dynamically generated HTML is intended to be viewed at normal zoom on the iPhone screen, and should not be resizable by the user.

Available for download on Wrox.com

```
basedir = NSBundle.MainBundle.BundlePath; // .app bundle
string name = "Reader";        // example of custom content
string html = @"<html><head>
<link rel='stylesheet' type='text/css'
      href='Styles/default.css' /></head>
<body>Dear "+ name +@",
<p>Styled text - <i>not possible</i> with
<b><code>UITextView</code></b>...
<img src='Images/Background.png' height='40'>..."; // truncated
WebBrowser.LoadHtmlString(html, new NSUrl(basedir, true));
WebBrowser.ScalesPageToFit = false;
```

WebView04\Main.cs

Figure 4-5 shows how this looks on the screen.

There is one more useful feature of the UIWebView control to learn about: the ability to intercept "navigation events" and perform some other behavior either before or instead of opening the link in the browser. ShouldStartLoad requires a delegate method with three parameters:

➤ UIWebView: The control that has triggered the navigation event.

➤ NSUrlRequest: The URL requested by the user.

➤ UIWebViewnavigationType: The type of navigation triggered by the user, listed in Table 4-1.

If ShouldStartLoad returns true, the requested navigation is allowed; if false, the navigation is cancelled. Your code could perform some alternate action such as showing another view or displaying an alert to the user.

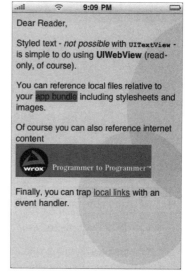
FIGURE 4-5

Available for download on Wrox.com

```
WebBrowser.ShouldStartLoad = delegate (UIWebView webView,
    NSUrlRequest request, UIWebViewNavigationType navigationType)
{
    if (navigationType == UIWebViewNavigationType.LinkClicked)
    { // open links in Safari rather than in the UIWebView
        UIApplication.SharedApplication.OpenUrl(request.Url);
        return false; // already handled
    }
    return true; // show everything else *in* the UIWebView
}
```

WebView04\Main.cs

Note that because the delegate must have a return value, it should be assigned to ShouldStartLoad *with an equals sign (=) and not attached using +=.*

The return type of the delegate must match the type it is being assigned to (WebBrowser.ShouldStartLoad *is a* boolean *in this example, which matches the return type of the delegate method).*

You can interrogate the target location from the request parameter and the type of navigation requested with the navigationType parameter in order to handle them differently (for example, open a link in Safari but allow a form post to continue in the UIWebView). The possible values for navigationType are shown in Table 4-1.

TABLE 4-1: UIWebViewNavigationType

VALUE	DESCRIPTION
LinkClicked	A link was tapped.
FormSubmitted	An HTML form was submitted.
BackForward	The GoBack() or GoForward() methods were triggered.
Reload	The currently displayed content is being reloaded.
FormResubmitted	A form was resubmitted.
Other	Another navigation action occurred.

Other Content

UIWebView can also be used to display other content too. Using the same C# that loads a local HTML file, you can display:

➤ PDF documents your application might contain or download from the Internet

➤ Images (which you can also display using UIImageView and UIScrollView, covered later)

UIScrollView

UIScrollView allows you to display and navigate content that is larger than the control itself (often sized to the entire device screen). It provides built-in support for swiping to move around the content and pinching to zoom (depending on the type of UIScrollView). It is also the base class for other controls that need to scroll content larger than their display Frame, like UITableView and UITextView.

Image Scrolling

The built-in Photos application is the most used example of a UIScrollView interface. Listing 4-3 shows the code required to load a large image into a UIScrollView and enable the user to pan and zoom around it.

➤ Bounces: If true, scrolling to the edges of the image will "bounce" beyond the edge of the image before stopping.

➤ BouncesZoom: If true, when you zoom to the minimum or maximum size the content temporarily exceeds the limits before animating to the correct size.

➤ ContentSize: The true size of the content being displayed. The UIScrollView needs to know this so that it can calculate the scroll indicators' size and position.

➤ IndicatorStyle: Use the UIScrollViewIndicatorStyle enum to select a Black or White scrollbar (or leave it as Default).

➤ MaximumZoomScale: The maximum scaling factor that can be applied to the content. The following example allows expanding the content to four times its original size.

➤ MinimumZoomScale: The minimum scaling factor that can be applied to the content. The following example allows shrinking to a quarter of its original size.

➤ ContentOffset: The current position of the content view's top-left corner in relation to the UIScrollView, represented as a System.Drawing.PointF.

➤ ZoomScale: The current scaling applied to the content (default is 1.0). Listing 4-3 initially displays the image at 80 percent of its actual size.

The default value for MaximumZoomScale and MinimumZoomScale is 1.0, which means that if neither is set, zooming is effectively disabled.

LISTING 4-3: Image Viewing with UIScrollView (ScrollView01\Main.cs)

```
UIImage image = UIImage.FromFile("GoldenGate.jpg");
UIImageView imageView = new UIImageView(image);
MyScrollView.AddSubview(imageView);
MyScrollView.ContentSize = imageView.Frame.Size;
MyScrollView.MaximumZoomScale = 4f;    // four times
MyScrollView.MinimumZoomScale = 0.25f; // one quarter size
MyScrollView.Bounces = false;
MyScrollView.BouncesZoom = false;
MyScrollView.IndicatorStyle = UIScrollViewIndicatorStyle.White;
MyScrollView.ViewForZoomingInScrollView = delegate (UIScrollView sender)
{ // could use a higher resolution copy here
   return imageView;
};
MyScrollView.ContentOffset = new System.Drawing.PointF(250,20);
MyScrollView.ZoomScale = 0.8f; // after assigning delegate
```

Figure 4-6 shows the relationship between the device's display and the UIScrollView's content being clipped to fit.

FIGURE 4-6

Paging

Paging with UIScrollView provides behavior like the iPhone OS Home screen and Weather application or third-party book-reading applications like Stanza and Kindle. Instead of allowing freeform scrolling around the image in the previous example, UIScrollView can skip to defined "pages" of the view (which are multiples of the view's Bounds).

The most important difference between this example and Listing 4-4 is setting PagingEnabled = true (which can be done in code or using the checkbox in Interface Builder). Figure 4-7 shows how the three Frames relate to the UIScrollView and the iPhone's screen.

LISTING 4-4: Paging with UIScrollView (ScrollView02\Main.cs)

```
RectangleF scrollFrame = MyScrollView.Frame;
scrollFrame.Width = scrollFrame.Width * 3;  // 3 pages
MyScrollView.PagingEnabled = true;
MyScrollView.ContentSize = scrollFrame.Size;
MyScrollView.ShowsHorizontalScrollIndicator = false;

RectangleF frame = MyScrollView.Frame;
frame.X = 0;                          // left-most 'page'
UITextView textView = new UITextView (frame);
```

```
textView.Editable = false;
textView.Text = "This is page one";
MyScrollView.AddSubview(textView);

frame.X = frame.Width + 1; ;      // middle-most 'page'
textView = new UITextView (frame);
textView.Editable = false;
textView.Text = "This is page two";
MyScrollView.AddSubview(textView);

frame.X = frame.Width * 2 + 1; ; // right-most 'page'
textView = new UITextView (frame);
textView.Editable = false;
textView.Text = "This is page three";
MyScrollView.AddSubview(textView);
```

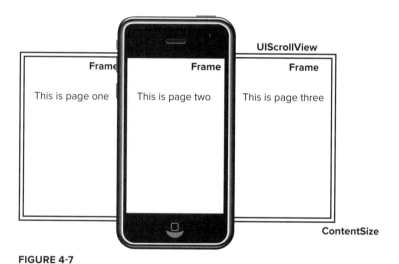

FIGURE 4-7

UITextView

The UITextView class is similar to the TextBox familiar to WPF programmers — it provides editable (or read-only) scrollable multiline text display. You can specify the font, style, color, and alignment for the all the text in the view; however you cannot style individual words or characters. To display styled text you need to use the UIWebView. Unfortunately there is no built-in control for *editing* styled text (that is, that mixes fonts, colors, or sizes).

Read-Only Text View

To display multiple lines of text you can simply drag a UITextView onto your window or view in Interface Builder and type the text into the Attributes window. You can also create the UITextView in code and use the Add or AddSubview methods to add it to a window or view, respectively. The following properties are demonstrated in the code download TextView01.

Some properties are easy to set in Interface Builder by simply checking a box, such as:

➤ **Detects Phone Numbers:** When checked, the UITextView automatically hyperlinks telephone numbers in the text, and if the view is *not* editable they initiate a call when touched. Recognized formats include 1-800-555-1234 and 555-1234.

➤ **Detects Links:** When checked, any URLs in the text are displayed as hyperlinks and open in Safari when touched. Recognized formats include http://wrox.com and www.wrox.com.

The following properties can be set via Interface Builder or in code:

➤ Editable: Defaults to true, which means the text is editable and shows a keyboard when touched. Set this to false to make the text read-only.

➤ TextAlignment: Use the UITextAlignment enum to choose Left, Center, or Right.

➤ TextColor: Assign a named color (such as UIColor.Blue) or a System color (such as UIColor.DarkTextColor), or a "From" method to use any other color (UIColor has a number of methods such as FromRGB and FromHSB to create specific colors from Red/Green/Blue or Hue/Saturation/Brightness values).

➤ ScrollsToTop: Enables the "shortcut," where touching the status bar (if shown) automatically scrolls a UITextView to the top of its content. This should be set to true if your text view is the main control on the screen.

➤ IndicatorStyle: Because UITextView inherits from UIScrollView you can set the color of the scrollbar using the UIScrollViewIndicatorStyle to Black or White so it is easy to see regardless of the background color you choose.

In code you can also modify:

➤ Font: Set the font typeface and size for the text.

The code using these properties is shown here:

```
// UITextView outlet is named TextBox
TextBox.Font = UIFont.FromName("Times New Roman", 24f);
TextBox.TextAlignment = UITextAlignment.Left;
TextBox.TextColor = UIColor.White;
TextBox.BackgroundColor = UIColor.DarkGray;
TextBox.ScrollsToTop = true;
TextBox.IndicatorStyle = UIScrollViewIndicatorStyle.White;
```

TextView01\Main.cs

Figure 4-8 shows the UITextView options in Interface Builder and an example showing Phone Numbers and Links. Refer back to Chapter 2 to review how to create outlets using Interface Builder.

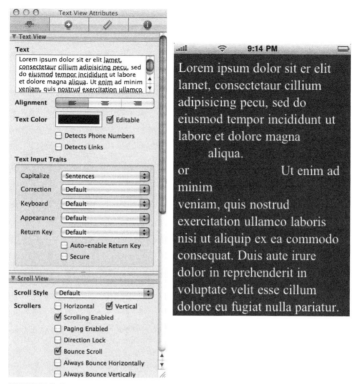

FIGURE 4-8

Editable Text View

To make a `UITextView` editable simply tick the Editable checkbox in Interface Builder or set `Editable = true`. When the view is first displayed it just displays scrollable content — it does not immediately accept input. Touching the view enables editing and the iPhone OS displays a keyboard (according to the `KeyboardType` chosen) ready to start typing. Listing 4-5 shows how to use notifications to respond to keyboard events and dynamically resize the input so that parts of it do not get obscured by the keyboard.

LISTING 4-5: TextView02\Main.cs

```
NSObject observer1, observer2; // for notifications
public override bool FinishedLaunching (UIApplication app, NSDictionary options)
{
    TextBox.Font = UIFont.FromName("Helvetica", 24f);
    TextBox.ScrollsToTop = true;
    DoneButton.Enabled = false; // set in notification
    DoneButton.TouchUpInside += delegate
    {
        TextBox.ResignFirstResponder(); // similar to 'losing focus' in .NET
    };
    // usually created in ViewWillAppear
    // on a ViewController, rather than AppDelegate
```

continues

LISTING 4-5 *(continued)*

```
      observer1 = NSNotificationCenter.DefaultCenter.AddObserver
          (UIKeyboard.WillShowNotification, delegate (NSNotification n)
      {
         var kbdRect = UIKeyboard.BoundsFromNotification (n);
         var frame = TextBox.Frame;
         frame.Height -= kbdRect.Height;
         TextBox.Frame = frame;
         DoneButton.Enabled = true;
      });
      observer2 = NSNotificationCenter.DefaultCenter.AddObserver
          (UIKeyboard.WillHideNotification, delegate (NSNotification n)
      {
         var kbdRect = UIKeyboard.BoundsFromNotification (n);
         var frame = TextBox.Frame;
         frame.Height += kbdRect.Height;
         TextBox.Frame = frame;
         DoneButton.Enabled = false;
      });
      window.MakeKeyAndVisible ();
      return true;
   }
   public override void WillTerminate (UIApplication application)
   {  // usually removed in ViewWillDisappear
      NSNotificationCenter.DefaultCenter.RemoveObserver (observer1);
      NSNotificationCenter.DefaultCenter.RemoveObserver (observer2);
   }
```

> *When a control has first responder status in the iPhone OS (that is,* `IsFirstResponder` = true), *it behaves similarly to a .NET control that "has focus": It is the first recipient of any user input.*
>
> *When a* `UITextView` *becomes editable, it becomes the* `FirstResponder` *and automatically causes the keyboard to appear. To make the keyboard disappear you must call* `ResignFirstResponder()`, *which is similar to a .NET control "losing focus".*

Figure 4-9 shows the `UITextView` in read and edit modes.

`UITextView` shares some features with `UITextField` from Chapter 3:

➤ `AutocapitalizationType`: Determines when the Shift key is automatically used (for example, at the start of typing and new sentences). The default is `None`.

➤ `AutocorrectionType`: Whether auto-correction is enabled during typing. The default is correction enabled.

➤ `ReturnKeyType`: Note that `UITextView` does not support the same Done editing behavior as `UITextField`.

➤ `KeyboardType`: Allows the control to show a keyboard appropriate for the type of data you are expecting, for example, plain text, an e-mail address, or numeric data.

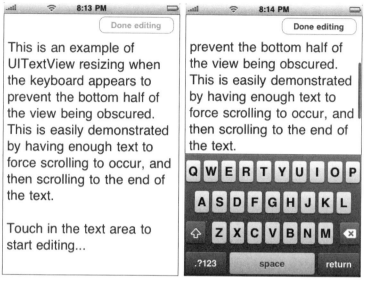

FIGURE 4-9

It also shares some properties with `UIWebView` that operate in the same way:

➤ Detects phone numbers

➤ Detects URLs

UIPickerView

The `UIPickerView` is analogous to a Drop Down List Box in Windows Forms or WPF or the `<asp:DropDownList>` element in ASP.NET; the iPhone OS just has a unique display style. It provides a fixed set of options for the user to scroll through and only supports a single selection from that list — the row currently displayed in the center of the picker. Figure 4-10 shows an example picker from Safari where the web page used a `<select>` element to capture user input.

FIGURE 4-10

Single Component Picker

`UIPickerView` instances should always sit on the edge of the window (normally the bottom) and take up the entire width of the screen. It has only two important members to discuss:

➤ `ShowsSelectionIndicator`: Whether the transparent blue guide is shown over the center row of the control.

➤ `Model`: Requires a delegate class that provides the picker with all the information it needs to display and react to user selection. The `Model` must contain or have a reference to the data you want to use for your picker.

The `Model` must be a subclass of `UIPickerViewModel` that implements the following methods:

➤ `GetComponentCount`: The number of wheels to display in the control. The following example shows a single wheel so it is hardcoded to `return 1`.

➤ `GetRowsInComponent`: The number of data items to display in the wheel.

➤ `GetTitle`: Returns the text to display in each row.

➤ `Selected`: Called when the user changes the row.

Listing 4-6 shows the code for the PickerView01 example in the code download for this chapter. It requires a `UIPickerView` and a `UITextBox` to be placed on the window using Interface Builder.

LISTING 4-6: PickerView01\Main.cs

```
public override bool FinishedLaunching (UIApplication app, NSDictionary options)
{
    ListBox.Model = new ListBoxModel(this);
    ListBox.ShowSelectionIndicator = true;
    window.MakeKeyAndVisible ();
    return true;
}
class ListBoxModel : UIPickerViewModel
{
    AppDelegate app;
    List<string> data;
    public ListBoxModel(AppDelegate appDelegate)
    {
        app = appDelegate;
        data = new List<string> {"Cirrus","Stratus","Cumulus","Fog"};
    }
    public override int GetComponentCount (UIPickerView picker)
    {
        return 1;
    }
    public override int GetRowsInComponent (UIPickerView picker, int component)
    {
        return data.Count;
    }
    public override string GetTitle (UIPickerView picker, int row, int component)
    {
        return data[row];
    }
    public override void Selected (UIPickerView picker, int row, int component)
    {
        app.DisplayText.Text = "You selected " + data[row];
    }
}
```

Figure 4-11 shows the preceding single component picker and an example of a multiple component picker (explained in the following section).

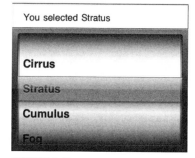 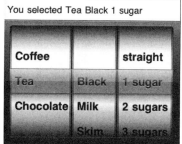

FIGURE 4-11

Multiple Component Picker

UIPickers can also show multiple components, which can be independent or related.

A multiple component picker uses the same methods as before, except the return values must change depending on which component is passed in. There is an additional method, GetComponentWidth, to set the width of each component.

Listing 4-7 shows the code required to enable the three-wheeled example from Figure 4-11.

LISTING 4-7: PickerView02\Main.cs

```
class ListBoxModel : UIPickerViewModel
{
    AppDelegate app;
    List<List<string>> data;
    public ListBoxModel(AppDelegate appDelegate)
    {
        app = appDelegate;
        data = new List<List<string>>();
        data.Add(new List<string> {"Coffee","Tea","Chocolate"});
        data.Add(new List<string> {"Black","Milk","Skim","Soy"});
        data.Add(new List<string> {"straight","1 sugar","2 sugars","3 sugars"});
    }
    public override int GetComponentCount (UIPickerView picker)
    {
        return data.Count;
    }
    public override int GetRowsInComponent (UIPickerView picker, int component)
    {
        return data[component].Count;
    }
    public override string GetTitle (UIPickerView picker, int row, int component)
    {
        return data[component][row];
    }
    public override float GetComponentWidth (UIPickerView picker, int component)
    {
        switch (component)
```

continues

LISTING 4-7 *(continued)*

```
        {
            case 0: return 110;
            case 1: return 80;
            default: return 100;   // 3rd wheel
        }
    }
    public override void Selected (UIPickerView picker, int row, int component)
    {
        app.DisplayText.Text = "You selected "
            + data[0][picker.SelectedRowInComponent(0)] + " "
            + data[1][picker.SelectedRowInComponent(1)] + " "
            + data[2][picker.SelectedRowInComponent(2)];
    }
}
```

If your components are dependent on each other, you might call the following two methods in your `Selected` method implementation:

➤ `ReloadComponent`: If the choice in one component affects what is displayed in the other/s, call this method for each one.

➤ `Select`: Forces selection of a specific row in a component. If you use `ReloadComponent`, you might also want to reset the selected row for that component to the first item, or you might keep track of previous selections and use that information.

Listing 4-8 shows how you would implement a two-level hierarchy in a `UIPickerView`, where different options in the second component depend on the choice in the first as shown in Figure 4-12.

Available for download on Wrox.com

LISTING 4-8: PickerView03\Main.cs

```
class ListBoxModel : UIPickerViewModel
{
    AppDelegate app;
    List<string> data1;
    List<List<string>> data2;
    public ListBoxModel (AppDelegate appDelegate)
    {
        app = appDelegate;
        // separate data for each component
        data1 = new List<string> {"Coffee", "Tea"};
        data2 = new List<List<string>> ();
        data2.Add (new List<string> {"Espresso", "Latte", "Cappuccino", "Macchiato"});
        data2.Add (new List<string> {"Black", "Green", "Peppermint", "Chai"});
    }
    public override int GetComponentCount (UIPickerView picker)
    {
        return 2;
    }
    public override int GetRowsInComponent (UIPickerView picker, int component)
    {
        if (component == 0)
            return data1.Count;
```

```
         else // which data to use depends on what's selected in component 0
            return data2[picker.SelectedRowInComponent(0)].Count;
      }
      public override string GetTitle (UIPickerView picker, int row, int component)
      {
         if (component == 0)
            return data1[row];
         else // which data to use depends on what's selected in component 0
            return data2[picker.SelectedRowInComponent(0)][row];
      }
      public override float GetComponentWidth (UIPickerView picker, int component)
      {
         switch (component)
         {
            case 0:
               return 110;
            case 1:
               return 200;
         }
         return 0;
      }
      public override void Selected (UIPickerView picker, int row, int component)
      {
         if (component == 0)
         { // whenever the first wheel is changed, reload the second
            picker.ReloadComponent (1);
            picker.Select (0, 1, true); // and select the top row
         }
         app.DisplayText.Text = "You selected " +
            data1[picker.SelectedRowInComponent (0)] + " " +
            data2[picker.SelectedRowInComponent(0)]
               [picker.SelectedRowInComponent (1)];
      }
   }
}
```

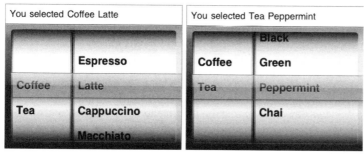

FIGURE 4-12

UIDatePicker

The UIDatePicker control is a specialized version of the UIPickerView, however it is much simpler to use because no Model class is required — the data source is just made up of dates and times. iPhone OS users see this view in the Calendar and Clock built-in applications.

Figure 4-13 shows the four different varieties of `UIDatePicker`: the countdown timer from Clock, the date view, the date & time view used in Calendar, and the time view also used in Clock.

FIGURE 4-13

The key members that you will use on the `UIDatePicker` control are:

➤ `Date`: This property defaults to the current date/time.

➤ `SetDate()`: Method to set the date/time for the control, optionally specifying that the transition should be animated (that is, the wheels "spin" to the new value) or instant (the wheels are simply set to the new value).

➤ `MinuteInterval`: The minimum value is 1, the maximum is 30, and the default is 5.

➤ `MinimumDate`: The earliest selectable date. If today's date is prior to this, the control still defaults to "today" but all values prior to this date in the list are greyed-out. Attempting to select a date prior to the minimum automatically selects the minimum date.

➤ `MaximumDate`: The latest selectable date. Any scrolling past this date resets the selection to this date and all values past this date are rendered in grey.

➤ `Mode`: One of the `UIDatePickerMode` values shown in Table 4-2.

TABLE 4-2: UIDatePickerMode Values

ENUM	DESCRIPTION
`CountDownTimer`	Select hours and minutes. Useful for selecting a `TimeSpan` that isn't directly related to the time of day.
`Date`	Shows month, date, and year (but not day of week). Used for selecting birthdays, holidays, or other dates where the year is significant.
`DateAndTime`	(default) Shows day of week with the month and date, hour, minute, and am/pm selection. Does not show the year. Useful for selecting appointments and reminders.
`Time`	Select hour, minute, and am/pm. Useful for setting alarms or the time.

The example DatePicker01 in the chapter download demonstrates a basic "appointment chooser" similar to the Calendar application where you choose the start and end time using the same

`UIDatePicker`. In Interface Builder you need two buttons, two labels, and a date picker on your window, with the following code in `FinishedLaunching`:

```
DateSelection.MinuteInterval = 6; // default 5
DateSelection.MinimumDate = new DateTime (2010,05,01);
DateSelection.MaximumDate = new DateTime (2011,01,01);
DateSelection.Mode = UIDatePickerMode.DateAndTime;
FromDate.Text = DateTime.Now.ToString("ddd dd MMM yyyy h:mm tt");
ToDate.Text = DateTime.Now.AddHours(1).ToString("ddd dd MMM yyyy h:mm tt");
FromButton.TouchUpInside += delegate
{   // edit the start time
    editingStart = true;
    DateSelection.Date = DateTime.Parse(FromDate.Text);
};
ToButton.TouchUpInside += delegate
{   // edit the finish time
    editingStart = false;
    DateSelection.SetDate(DateTime.Parse(ToDate.Text),false);
};
DateSelection.ValueChanged += delegate(object sender, EventArgs e)
{   // update the display
    var ctrl = (UIDatePicker)sender;
    var dateString = DateTime.Parse(ctrl.Date.ToString())
            .ToString("ddd dd MMM yyyy h:mm tt");
    if (editingStart) FromDate.Text = dateString;
    else ToDate.Text = dateString;
};
```

DatePicker01\Main.cs

The result is shown in Figure 4-14 — touch either of the two dates to edit them using the `UIDatePicker`.

CONTROLLERS AND BARS

Along with the `Window` and `View` classes mentioned at the start of the chapter, `UIViewController` and its subclasses form the basis of all iPhone OS applications. The `UIViewController` class itself is used to present a single full-screen view (and sub-views). Custom subclasses are a good way to re-use common view-related code in your applications.

Two of the other classes in this section — `UITabBarController` and `UINavigationController` — are used to orchestrate *multiple* different views in an application. The tab bar has the same purpose as a `TabControl` in WPF or Windows Forms: allowing the user to navigate back and forth between different views. The navigation controller is hierarchical in nature, allowing the user to "drill down" with support for a "back" button. Both use a number of supporting classes to provide their functionality, such as the `UITabBarItem` and the `UINavigationBar` and `UINavigationItem`, respectively.

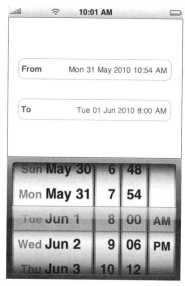

FIGURE 4-14

The `UIToolbar` is slightly different — it is designed to present options that are applicable *within a single view* using the `UIBarButtonItem` and the fixed and flexible spacing options.

UIViewController

The most common methods and properties of the `UIViewController` are:

➤ `ViewDidLoad`: Called after any associated views have been loaded. This method is where you typically put initialization code such as wiring up event delegates. It is called once in the object's lifetime.

➤ `ViewWillAppear`: Perform any additional tasks associated with presenting the view. This method is called straight after `ViewDidLoad` and then again whenever the view is re-displayed. Always call `base.ViewWillAppear()` in your implementation.

➤ `ViewWillDisappear`: Notification that the view is being hidden. You can use this method to commit editing changes, because you don't know whether the view will ever be re-displayed. Always call `base.ViewWillDisappear()` in your implementation. During the life cycle of the view controller `ViewWillDisappear` and `ViewWillAppear` can be called multiple times.

➤ `Title`: A property used to represent the view (see the `UINavigationController` example in Listing 4-13 later in the chapter).

If you override a method on a framework class and are unsure whether you need to call the base *method in your code, check the Apple or MonoTouch documentation.*

```
http://developer.apple.com/iphone/library/
http://go-mono.org/docs/
```

Apple's documentation for ViewWillAppear *and* ViewWillDisappear *explicitly states "If you override this method, you must call super at some point in your implementation".* super *is the Objective-C equivalent of* base *in C#.*

Other properties are only set (and used) when the view controller is associated with other classes discussed later in the chapter. They are briefly described here, but you should read the later sections to fully understand their purpose.

➤ `NavigationController`: `null` unless this controller is already in a navigation stack.

➤ `NavigationItem`: Read-only reference to the `UINavigationItem` that represents this controller, assuming it has been pushed onto a navigation stack.

➤ `TabBarController`: `null` unless this controller has been added to a tab bar.

➤ `TabBarItem`: If part of a tab bar, this references the `UITabBarItem` representing the controller (that is, the display text and image).

➤ `ToolbarItems`: If this controller is being used by a `UINavigationController`, contains an array of `UIToolbarItems`.

UIToolbar

A good example of the toolbar is the navigation buttons in Safari. To demonstrate the use of
`UIToolbar` you will add toolbar buttons to the `UIWebView` example from earlier in the chapter —
Toolbar01 in the code download. Figure 4-15 shows Safari on the left and our example on the right.

FIGURE 4-15

Starting with the WebView02 example code, delete the Back and Forward buttons and drag a
`UIToolbar` control onto the window. Then add four `UIBarButtonItems` and spacing items to
match Figure 4-16.

FIGURE 4-16

Update the items in Interface Builder as follows:

➤ The Back and Forward buttons can be connected to the existing outlets in the example code. These buttons use the `Bordered` style and have their Titles set as text.

➤ Create two additional outlets for the Reload and Stop buttons. They should be updated to use the `Plain` style and instead of display text choose one of the built-in Identifiers (`Refresh` and `Stop`, respectively). The other style options are listed in Table 4-3.

➤ Use the Fixed and Flexible spacing controls to arrange the icons in exactly the location you want.

TABLE 4-3: UIBarButtonItemStyle Options

VALUE	DESCRIPTION
Bordered	Button is displayed with a round-rectangle border.
Plain	Borderless button that glows when tapped.
Done	Similar to the `Bordered` style but with a blue background. Should be used only if the view will be dismissed when tapped.

Table 4-4 shows the available system values for toolbar buttons — if your application performs a similar function to what these options describe, you should use the system icon to adhere to Apple's consistent user interface. Conversely, you should *not* use a system icon for a feature that is not equivalent to the built-in functionality — this confuses the user and should instead be represented by a custom icon or text.

TABLE 4-4: UIBarButtonSystemItem Options

VALUE	IMAGE	DESCRIPTION
Add		Icon containing a plus sign (+)
Edit		Localized text
Done		Localized text
Cancel		Localized text
Save		Localized text
Undo		Text "Undo"
Redo		Text "Redo"
Compose		Icon of a notepad with a pencil (used in Mail app)

VALUE	IMAGE	DESCRIPTION
Reply		Icon of a left-pointing curved arrow (used in Mail app)
Action		Icon of a right-pointing curved arrow inside a square (used in Photos)
Organize		Icon of a folder with a down arrow (used in Mail app)
Trash		Trash can (used in Mail app)
Bookmarks		Icon of an open book (used in Safari)
Search		Magnifying glass icon
Refresh		Circular arrow icon (used in Safari)
Stop		Icon containing an X
Camera		Camera icon
Play		Icon of a right-facing triangle (used in iPod app)
Pause		Icon with two vertical bars (used in iPod app)
Rewind		Icon with two left-facing triangles (used in iPod app)
FastForward		Icon with two right-facing triangles (used in iPod app)

The following code must be added to FinishedLaunching to make the buttons work — note that UIBarButtonItems have a Clicked event rather than TouchUpInside. The methods are simple calls to the UIWebView's Reload and StopLoading functions, which are fairly self-explanatory.

```
BackButton.Clicked += delegate
{
    WebBrowser.GoBack();
    UrlInput.Text = WebBrowser.Request.Url.AbsoluteString;
};
BackButton.Clicked += delegate
{
    WebBrowser.GoForward();
    UrlInput.Text = WebBrowser.Request.Url.AbsoluteString;
};
RefreshButton.Clicked += delegate
{
```

```
    WebBrowser.Reload();
};
StopButton.Clicked += delegate
{
    WebBrowser.StopLoading();
};
```

Toolbar01\Main.cs

UITabBarController

The most obvious example of the tab bar is the iPod application (shown in Figure 4-17) with tabs for Artists, Albums, Videos, and more.

Recall the mention of the UIViewController's ViewWillAppear and ViewWillDisappear methods — each time the user touches a tab, the current tab's ViewWillDisappear method is called, and then the chosen tab's ViewWillAppear method is called. As the user navigates around the tab views, these two methods are called so that your views can respond to being hidden and shown.

Simple TabBar

The first UITabBarController example uses Interface Builder to construct the tabs and their contents. This is an easy way to build your user interface but requires some care because the XIB filenames for each tab are entered into the Attributes Inspector, so you must ensure they match the files themselves. The other problem is that Interface Builder currently doesn't show custom tab images on the design surface.

FIGURE 4-17

The MonoDevelop solution and the Interface Builder MainWindow.xib from TabBar01 in the code download are shown in Figure 4-18.

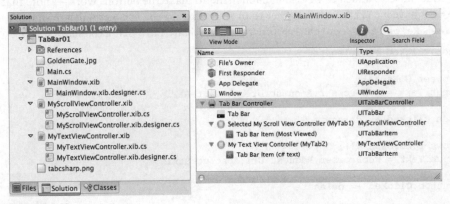

FIGURE 4-18

The following steps were required to create this project:

➤ `MainWindow.xib` was created as part of the MonoDevelop solution and opened in Interface Builder.

➤ A `UITabBarController` (the orange-circled icon in the Library window) was dragged onto the `MainWindow.xib` window (*not* onto the "window" design surface). This automatically creates the `Tab Bar` and two `Tab Bar Items` hierarchy that are shown in Figure 4-18.

➤ In MonoDevelop you add two View Interface Definition with Controller XIBs: `MyScrollViewController` and `MyTextViewController`.

➤ Back in Interface Builder you then hook up the tabs to the new XIB files. For each tab:

   ➤ Click *once* on the tab to set the XIB name and class name in the Attributes and Identity Inspectors, respectively, as shown in Figure 4-19.

FIGURE 4-19

   ➤ Click *twice* on the tab to choose its Title and Image in the Attributes Inspector. Figure 4-20 shows the two different tab settings. The first tab uses a built-in Identifier, which sets a specific Image and Title — the complete list is shown in Table 4-5. The second tab has a custom Title and Image — the image file must be added to the MonoDevelop solution with `Build Action: Content`. The image will not appear on the Interface Builder design surface but it will show when the application runs.

FIGURE 4-20

Making custom images for `UITabBarItem`s can be tricky. The images should be PNG format and 30x30 pixels in size. They cannot contain any color or gray-scale effect — you can only use black or varying degrees of transparency to create a shaded effect. The iPhone OS automatically renders them blue-on-black in the toolbar and black-on-white in the More list (if shown).

➤ Once the tabs have been "wired up" to specific `ViewControllers` you can implement whatever behavior you like. This example uses the `UIScrollView` and `UITextView` example code from earlier in the chapter for the tabs; Figure 4-21 shows the result.

FIGURE 4-21

TABLE 4-5: UITabBarSystemItem

VALUE	IMAGE	DESCRIPTION
More	•••	Ellipsis-like icon (three dots) normally used by the system to indicate that there are additional, hidden tabs.
Favorites	★	Star icon.
Featured	✹	Two spotlights, used in the App Store.
Top Rated	★	Star icon (same as Favorites but with different text).
Recents	🕘	Clock icon, used in the Phone app.
Contacts	👤	Head and shoulders icon, used in the Phone app.
History	🕘	Clock icon (same as Recents but with different text).
Bookmarks	📖	Open book icon.
Search	🔍	Magnifying glass icon, used in the App Store.

VALUE	IMAGE	DESCRIPTION
Downloads	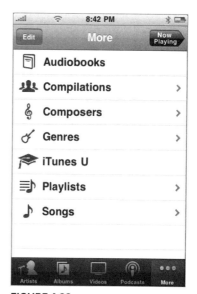	Down arrow inside a circle, used in iTunes.
Most Recent		Plus sign in a square.
Most Viewed		Three head and shoulders icons.

Editable TabBar

The iPhone screen is wide enough to support up to five tabs as the iPod application shows in Figure 4-22. When you add six or more tabs to your `UITabController` it automatically adds the More tab and presents the remaining options in a list. It can also (optionally) add an Edit button that allows the user to change the order of the tabs.

Demonstrating an editable tab bar requires a number of view controllers and associated code. To keep the example simple, and also to introduce another new concept, no Interface Builder files are used. Because of the lack of XIB files to define the user interface, a complete listing of the classes is shown in Listings 4-9 through 4-12.

Listing 4-9 shows the core of the application — it creates the `UIWindow`, `UITabBarController` and delegate, adds the tab view to the window, and shows it on the screen. The `UITabBarControllerDelegate` (Listing 4-11) is also created and assigned.

FIGURE 4-22

LISTING 4-9: TabBar02\Main.cs

```
public class Application
{
    static void Main (string[] args)
    {
        UIApplication.Main (args,"TabBar02", "AppDelegate");
    }
}
[Register ("TabBar02")]
public class TabBar02 : UIApplication {}

[Register ("AppDelegate")]
public partial class AppDelegate : UIApplicationDelegate
{
    UIWindow window;
    MyTabBarController tabBarController;
```

continues

LISTING 4-9 *(continued)*

```
public override bool FinishedLaunching (UIApplication app, NSDictionary options)
{
    window = new UIWindow (UIScreen.MainScreen.Bounds);
    tabBarController = new MyTabBarController();
    tabBarController.Delegate = new MyTabBarControllerDelegate();
    window.AddSubview (tabBarController.View);
    window.MakeKeyAndVisible ();
    return true;
}
// This method is required in iPhoneOS 3.0
public override void OnActivated (UIApplication application)
{}
}
```

Listing 4-10 shows the `UITabBarController` setting up the six views. In this example they are all image views showing a different photo (the initialization of all six has been hidden in the listing, for clarity). The second half of the method attempts to extract the custom tab order from `NSUserDefaults` (set in Listing 4-10) and re-order the tabs before they are displayed. Refer to Chapter 8 for more information on storing settings with `NSUserDefaults`.

LISTING 4-10: TabBar02\MyTabBarController.cs

```
public class MyTabBarController : UITabBarController
{

MyImageViewController imgController1,imgController2,imgController3,
                      imgController4,imgController5,imgController6;

public MyTabBarController () : base() {}

public override void ViewDidLoad ()
{
    imgController1 = new MyImageViewController("GoldenGate.jpg");
    imgController1.Title = "Golden Gate";
    imgController1.TabBarItem = new UITabBarItem(UITabBarSystemItem.Bookmarks, 0);
#region imgControllerX repeated 5 more times (repeated code not shown)

    // source array
    var tablist = new UIViewController[]
    {
        imgController1, imgController2, imgController3
      , imgController4, imgController5, imgController6
    };
    // this.ViewControllers = tablist; // if no customization req'd

    // sort the array according to edited preferences
    var tabOrder = new UIViewController[tablist.Length];
    var tabPrefs = NSUserDefaults.StandardUserDefaults.StringArrayForKey
        ("TabPreferences");
```

```
      if (tabPrefs == null)
      {
         tabOrder = tablist; // no sort saved
      }
      else
      {
         for (int i = 0; i < tabPrefs.Length; i++)
         {
            int index = Convert.ToInt32(tabPrefs[i]);
            tabOrder[i] = tablist[index];
         }
      }
      this.SelectedIndex = 0; // ensures the first icon is 'blue'
      this.ViewControllers = tabOrder;
   }
}
```

If you would prefer to disable editing of the tab order (and automatically hide the Edit button), pass an empty array like this:

```
this.CustomizableViewControllers = new UIViewController[]{};
```

Alternatively you can partially populate that array with only *some* of your UIViewControllers, and only those will be moveable when the tab controller is in edit mode.

Listing 4-11 shows the implementation of the delegate that keeps track of the edited tab order and saves it to NSUserDefaults. We have used the Tag values on the controllers as a reference to their array position, and stored that list as a comma-separated string. Your implementation may vary — this is just one way to persist the changes.

LISTING 4-11: TabBar02\MyTabBarControllerDelegate.cs

```
public class MyTabBarControllerDelegate : UITabBarControllerDelegate
{
   public MyTabBarControllerDelegate() : base() {}
   public override void FinishedCustomizingViewControllers
      (UITabBarController tabBarController,
       UIViewController[] viewControllers, bool changed)
   {
      if (changed)
      {
         var tabOrderList = new List<string>();
         foreach (var item in viewControllers)
         {
            tabOrderList .Add(item.TabBarItem.Tag.ToString());
         }
         NSArray array = NSArray.FromStrings(tabOrderList.ToArray())
         NSUserDefaults.StandardUserDefaults["TabPreferences"] = array;
      }
   }
}
```

Listing 4-12 shows the class being used for each of the tabs. It is very similar to the `UIScrollView` example, except that we have discarded the XIB and created the view entirely in C# code.

Available for download on Wrox.com

LISTING 4-12: TabBar02\MyImageViewController.cs

```
public class MyImageViewController : UIViewController
{
    UIScrollView ViewPort;
    string ImageName;
    public MyImageViewController (string imageName)
    {
        ImageName = imageName;
    }
    public override void ViewDidLoad ()
    {
        ViewPort = new UIScrollView(this.View.Bounds);

        UIImage image = UIImage.FromFile(ImageName);
        UIImageView imageView = new UIImageView(image);
        ViewPort.PagingEnabled = false; // freeform scrolling
        ViewPort.AddSubview(imageView);
        ViewPort.ContentSize = imageView.Frame.Size;
        ViewPort.ViewForZoomingInScrollView = delegate (UIScrollView sender)
        {   // could use a higher resolution copy here
            return imageView;
        };
        ViewPort.ZoomScale = 0.8f; // after assigning delegate

        this.View.AddSubview(ViewPort);
    }
}
```

UINavigationController

`UINavigationController` is used to manage multiple views that are related (such as drilling down into related information, which can be seen in the iPod application's Artist ➪ Album ➪ Song navigation). The controller keeps track of the views as though they are in a "stack" — when you make a selection that view is "pushed" onto the top of the stack, but you can always "pop" it off and return to the previous view.

The download example NavigationController01 is based on the MonoDevelop application template for Navigation-based applications. When you create the solution it is prepopulated with two XIB files:

➤ `MainWindow.xib` already contains an instance of `UINavigationController` and associated objects (`UINavigationBar` and `UINavigationItem`)

➤ `RootViewController.xib` initially contains a `UITableViewController`. However, they are covered in Chapter 6, so this example uses some `UIButtons` on a plain `UIViewController` instead.

It also contains three View Interface Definition with Controller classes (`View1Controller`, `View2Controller`, and `View3Controller`). On the views for these controllers we need some labels to identify the views and buttons to navigate between them, using the `UINavigationController` in `MainWindow.xib`. Figure 4-23 shows the final navigation sequence.

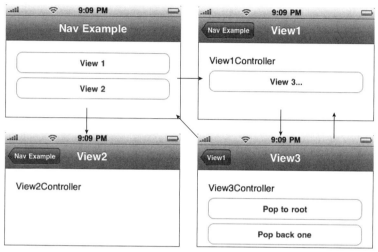

FIGURE 4-23

Figure 4-24 shows the `MainWindow.xib` view hierarchy that is automatically created. To make the navigation controller work you just need to add two buttons to the `RootController.xib` and wire them up. The code is shown in Listing 4-13: each button creates another view controller and pushes it onto the navigation stack.

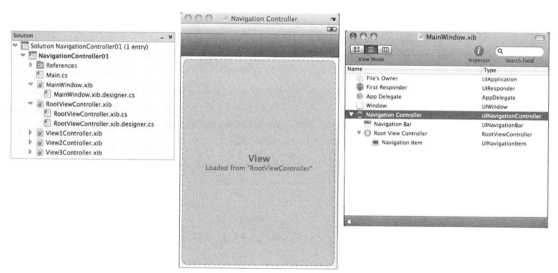

FIGURE 4-24

LISTING 4-13: NavigationController01\RootViewController.xib.cs

```
public override void ViewDidLoad ()
{
    this.Title = "Nav Example"; // shown top of screen, and 'back' button
    View1Button.TouchUpInside += delegate
    {
        var vc1 = new View1Controller ();
        vc1.Title = "View1"; // shown top of screen, and 'back' button
        this.NavigationController.PushViewController(vc1, true);
    };
    View2Button.TouchUpInside += delegate
    {
        var vc2 = new View2Controller ();
        vc2.Title = "View2"; // shown top of screen, and 'back' button
        this.NavigationController.PushViewController(vc2, true);
    };
}
```

Note that when a view is pushed onto the stack, the UINavigationBar across the top of the screen displays that view's Title, and the UINavigationBarItem acting as the Back button displays the Title of the previous view controller.

The following listings show two of the view controllers that also form part of this navigation stack. The code in Listing 4-14 creates another view controller and pushes it onto the navigation stack.

LISTING 4-14: NavigationController01\View1Controller.xib.cs

```
public override void ViewDidLoad ()
{
    View3Button.TouchUpInside += delegate
    {
        var vc3 = new View3Controller ();
        vc3.Title = "View3"; // shown top of screen, and 'back' button
        this.NavigationController.PushViewController(vc3, true);
    };
}
```

Listing 4-15 demonstrates the "back to start" method PopToRootViewController. If your navigation stack is particularly deep, you might want to provide the user with an option to start over, without having to touch the Back button in the navigation bar multiple times.

If you wish to mimic the behavior of the automatically provided "back" button in the navigation bar, the PopViewControllerAnimated method takes the user back to the previously displayed view.

LISTING 4-15: NavigationController01\View3Controller.xib.cs

```
public override void ViewDidLoad ()
{
    PopViewButton.TouchUpInside += delegate
    { // back to the 'base' view
```

```
      this.NavigationController.PopToRootViewController(true);
   };
   PopOneButton.TouchUpInside += delegate
   {  // pop one view - same behavior as 'back' button
      this.NavigationController.PopViewControllerAnimated(true);
   };


}
```

Navigation controllers are a particularly powerful class that lets you easily create user-friendly hierarchies of information. They are used throughout the built-in applications. `UINavigationController` is covered again in Chapter 6 because it is frequently coupled with `UITableView` where the table rows are used to present lists of navigation options.

SUMMARY

This chapter has introduced some of the fundamental building blocks of iPhone OS applications:

➤   `UIWindow`, `UIView`, and `UIViewController` are the underlying elements of the operating system's presentation of your code.

➤   `UITabBarController` and `UINavigationController` form the basis of most multi-view applications.

The remainder of the classes complement those in Chapter 3. Together these two chapters have introduced almost all the user interface elements you need to construct great iPhone OS applications.

5

Working with Data on the iPhone

WHAT'S IN THIS CHAPTER?

➤ Working with the SQLite database engine using ADO.NET

➤ Working with remote data using SOAP-based web services

➤ Working with REST-style web services using XML and JSON

➤ Storing data

Data is the lifeblood of applications. The application might be an app to interact with Twitter, an instant message application, or your own personal address book. This chapter looks at the SQLite database engine as well as strategies to store data off the device on a central server through SOAP and REST without tying up the user interface.

 This chapter is not an overview of ADO.NET, SOAP, or REST. The goal of this chapter is to show that the basic features work and help in areas that are specific to the iPhone.

WORKING WITH SQLITE

SQLite is an embedded data engine running in the iPhone and is the native database on the iPhone. It is different from client-server style databases, such as SQL Server, Oracle, and DB/2. With a client-server style database, a query, or operation, is sent to the database engine, the operation is performed, and the result is sent back to the client. With this type of database engine, the database runs in a separate process and typically on a separate machine. SQLite does not run on a separate machine; it runs on the same machine, the iPhone, and runs in the same process as the application. SQLite is embedded in the application and linked to the app during the compilation process. Calls made to SQLite are not made over a network, but stay on the physical device. SQLite uses SQL (Structured Query Language) to interact with it. Another good feature of SQLite is that it is 100 percent free.

This chapter is not meant to be an introduction to the SQL language, databases, tables, columns, data types, foreign keys, rows, or any other type database feature. The reader is expected to understand these concepts.

Using Mono.Data.Sqlite

The data provider for SQLite is contained within the Mono.Data.Sqlite assembly. This assembly provides support for SQLite version 3. The assembly is intended for ADO.NET 2.0, which isn't a problem for writing an application in MonoTouch. For the purposes of this chapter, we use a connection string of Data Source=filename.db3.

> *The code for the SQLite database example is taken from the Sqlite MonoDevelop project, which is available as part of this chapter's download from* www.wrox.com.
>
> *This example does authentication against Twitter. As a result, you need to change the private variables* TwitterUserId *and* TwitterPassWord *that are in the Main.cs file*

Setting Up a Database

The first step in getting an app to work with SQLite is to set up the database. With server-based databases, this is done a single time by a DBA. With SQLite, the creation of a database must be done on the initial run of an application on a device and it must be done on each device that the application runs on. Because the application must run on the end user's device, the database setup process must work without user intervention and it must run within the time constraints of the device. Take a look at some code that creates a database:

Available for download on Wrox.com

```
string DatabaseName = "TwitterData.db3";
string documents = Environment.GetFolderPath(Environment.SpecialFolder.Personal);
string db = Path.Combine(documents, DatabaseName);
bool exists = File.Exists(db);
if (!exists)
{
    SqliteConnection.CreateFile(db);
}
```

Found in the Sqlite/Main.cs file of the download

This code creates a database through the following steps:

1. A string with the folder name of the personal folder on the iPhone is determined.

2. A string with the full path plus filename to the database is created.

3. If the file does not exist, the database is created by calling the CreateFile() static method of the SqliteConnection object.

Setting Up Tables

Now that your database has been created, the next step is to set up tables, indexes, triggers, and any other particular database objects that are needed. Listing 5-1 shows some code that creates tables, triggers, and indexes:

LISTING 5-1: Creating tables and other objects

```
string DatabaseName = "TwitterData.db3";
string documents = Environment.GetFolderPath (Environment.SpecialFolder.Personal);
string db = Path.Combine (documents, DatabaseName);
var conn = new SqliteConnection("Data Source=" + db);
var commands = new[] {
    "DROP TABLE IF EXISTS TWITTERDATA",
    "DROP TRIGGER IF EXISTS TWITTERDATA_INSERT",
    "CREATE TABLE TWITTERDATA (STATUSID BIGINT PRIMARY KEY, " +
        "TWITTERID VARCHAR(20), STATUS VARCHAR(140), TWEETDATE DATETIME, " +
        "DATEENTERED DATETIME)",
    "CREATE TRIGGER TWITTERDATA_INSERT INSERT ON TWITTERDATA " +
    "BEGIN UPDATE TWITTERDATA SET DATEENTERED=DATE('now') " +
        "WHERE STATUSID=NEW.STATUSID; END;",
    "CREATE INDEX IDX_TWITTERID ON TWITTERDATA (TWITTERID)",
    "CREATE INDEX IDX_DATEENTERED ON TWITTERDATA (DATEENTERED)",
    "CREATE INDEX IDX_TWEETDATE ON TWITTERDATA (TWEETDATE)"
};
foreach (var cmd in commands)
    using (var sqlitecmd = conn.CreateCommand()) {
        sqlitecmd.CommandText = cmd;
        sqlitecmd.CommandType = CommandType.Text;
        conn.Open ();
        sqlitecmd.ExecuteNonQuery ();
        conn.Close ();
    }
```

Found in the Sqlite/Main.cs file of the download

This code creates a set of database objects. Here are the specifics:

➤ A SqliteConnection object is created.

➤ A series of SQL commands are placed within a string array. Each string within the array is a database command.

➤ The commands will drop a table if it exists, create a table, create a trigger, and then create a set of indexes.

➤ A `foreach` iteration is used to iterate through the commands and execute each command in the string array.

One thing that you will notice is that there is no GUI tool for creating the files in SQLite. Also, developers should not expect a user to be able to follow a sequence of commands to create a database, tables, and the other objects necessary for an application.

Using SQL Statements

Creating, altering, and dropping database objects is interesting. However, CRUD (create, read, update, delete) is the lifeblood of database applications. The ability to select, insert, update, and delete data through SQL is at the core of an application.

Using Read/Select to Read Data

Reading data is a very important operation for an application. Reading data out of a database table is the operation that is done 95+ percent of the time in an application. The .NET Framework provides us with datareaders, connections, and a series of objects that allow us to access database tables. MonoTouch provides an implementation of these .NET methods for the iPhone. Listing 5-2 shows some code that shows how to read data out of a table:

LISTING 5-2: Reading data from a table

```
string documents = Environment.GetFolderPath (Environment.SpecialFolder.Personal);
string db = Path.Combine (documents, DatabaseName);
string strSql = "select Max(TweetDate) as MaxTweetDate, Count(Status) " +
        "as StatusCount from TwitterData";
string output = String.Empty;
var conn = new SqliteConnection("Data Source=" + db);
SqliteDataReader dr;
var cmd = new SqliteCommand(strSql, conn);
conn.Open();
dr = cmd.ExecuteReader();
if ( dr.HasRows == true ) {
    while(dr.Read())
    {
        output = "Number of records: " + Convert.ToString(dr["StatusCount"]) +
            " Most recent post date: " + Convert.ToString(dr["MaxTweetDate"]);
    }
}
else{
    output = "No records found.";
}
conn.Close();
Status.Text = output;
```

Found in the Sqlite/Main.cs file of the download

As you can see, it's possible to use objects that you know and understand. You can create a connection object, `SqliteConnection`, and then create a datareader. With the datareader, you can iterate through the records returned and use the records just like in a .NET application.

At the time of this writing, there is a bug in the `SqliteDataAdapter` when call-ing `.Fill()` and `DataTable`. This bug has been documented and submitted to the MonoTouch bugzilla system, but no ETA has been determined for this bug to be fixed.

Using SQL Statements to Get Data

Now that you know how to read data out of a database table, the next obvious question is "How do I put data into a table?" Your first step is to go get some data. Follow these steps and take a look at Listing 5-3:

1. Make a call to the Twitter.com API to get data through XML.

2. Use LINQ to XML to convert the data into a set of objects. With these objects, the code can then process the data fairly easily.

3. Once the query is created, your next step is loop through the result. Remember, with LINQ, the query is not executed until the data is needed.

4. The next step is to save the data. This is done in the custom written SaveData method.

Available for
download on
Wrox.com

LISTING 5-3: Getting data from Twitter and saving it to SQLite

```
string url = "http://twitter.com/statuses/friends_timeline.xml";
HttpWebRequest request = (HttpWebRequest)HttpWebRequest.Create(url);
request.Method = "GET";
request.Credentials = new NetworkCredential(TwitterUserId, TwitterPassWord);
WebResponse response = request.GetResponse();
StreamReader reader = new StreamReader(response.GetResponseStream());
string responseString = reader.ReadToEnd();
reader.Close();
XDocument document = XDocument.Parse(responseString);
var query = from e in document.Root.Descendants()
        where e.Element("user") != null
        select new UserStatusSvc
        {
            StatusId = Convert.ToInt64(e.Element("id").Value),
            UserName = e.Element("user").Element("screen_name").Value,
            ProfileImage = e.Element("user").Element("profile_image_url").Value,
            Status = e.Element("text").Value,
            StatusDate = e.Value.ParseDateTime().ToString()
        };
foreach(UserStatusSvc uss in query)
{
        SaveData(uss);
}
```

Found in the Sqlite/Main.cs file of the download

The SaveData method does a simple check to verify whether a record already exists. If the record does not already exist, that record is then inserted into the table. The insert is performed using a prepared statement and a set of parameters. See Listing 5-4. If the record already exists locally, no action is taken.

LISTING 5-4: Inserting data into SQLite

```
private void SaveData(UserStatusSvc uss)
{
var documents = Environment.GetFolderPath (Environment.SpecialFolder.Personal);
string db = Path.Combine (documents, DatabaseName);
var conn = new SqliteConnection("Data Source=" + db);
var sql = "SELECT COUNT(*) FROM TWITTERDATA WHERE STATUSID=" + uss.StatusId;
var cmd = new SqliteCommand(sql, conn);
try{
        conn.Open();
        var Count = Convert.ToInt32(cmd.ExecuteScalar());
        if ( Count == 0 ) {
            var sqlStatusId = new SqliteParameter("@StatusId", uss.StatusId);
            cmd.Parameters.Add(sqlStatusId);
            var sqlTwitterId = new SqliteParameter("@TwitterId", uss.UserName);
            cmd.Parameters.Add(sqlTwitterId);
            var sqlStatus = new SqliteParameter("@Status", uss.Status);
            cmd.Parameters.Add(sqlStatus);
            var sqlTweetDate = new SqliteParameter("@TweetDate", uss.StatusDate);
            cmd.Parameters.Add(sqlTweetDate);
            sql = "insert into twitterdata (STATUSID, TWITTERID, STATUS, TWEETDATE) VALUES
                (" + "@StatusId, @TwitterId, @Status, @TweetDate)";
            cmd.CommandText = sql;
            cmd.ExecuteNonQuery();
        }
}
finally{
        if ( conn.State != ConnectionState.Closed ) {
            conn.Close();
        }
        conn.Dispose();
        cmd.Dispose();
}
}
```

Found in the Sqlite/Main.cs file of the download

Now that you are able to insert data into the table, handling other operations is similar. Update and Delete operations can easily be handled through SQLite's command object. The command can be a direct SQL statement or a prepared statement. Either will work. One word of warning: If you choose to use a simple SQL statement, don't open code up to a SQL injection attack.

Figure 5-1 shows the app reporting that data exists in your SQLite database.

Upgrading Strategies

With a web application, there is typically only one database instance that has to be managed. With an application installed on an iPhone and using SQLite, there are as many database instances as installations of the application. With a new version of your application, there is most likely a new version of the database schema to support the new features in that upgraded application. What are the strategies that can be inserted into an application to handle upgrading a database that is out in the wild?

Upgrading in Place

With an existing application's database, one strategy is to track the version of an application within a table. By tracking the database schema version, the application can check the version on startup. If the version is not the current version, an upgrade of the schema can be done by executing a series of SQLite commands against the database. This strategy requires a check on each startup of the application. This strategy would be good for a complicated database schema.

Copying Data

The upgrade in place solution requests a check each time the application starts. Another option is to check on startup and if the schema is not the correct version to create a new instance of the database and copy the necessary data over. Then you can assume that the schema is correct. This strategy requires a significant number of commands to be executed and potentially a lot of data to be moved. The more com-

FIGURE 5-1

mands that must be executed and the more data that is moved, the more opportunity there is for a mistake to be made. This option would be a good idea for an application that must make an extensive number of changes.

Storing Data Remotely

The two options mentioned — and there are most likely others — both result in data being stored in the application. Neither takes into account what happens if the device is lost or damaged. Another option to the problem of storing data is storing that data remotely. The next section focuses on the web services support necessary to store data remotely.

WORKING WITH REMOTE DATA

Applications no longer live as little islands of data. Everything is interconnected, or will be. The ability to connect with remote data is not only nice to have, but a requirement with today's applications. When I got my first cell phone, I had all kinds of places where I lost connection or didn't have any signal. Those days are over. Signal connections are available in all of the places that I frequent, though I do have problems when I am surrounded by metal, such as in a gym locker room. Typically, the remote data problem is seen as a problem that has been solved. This section looks at two primary ways to connect to data services over the Internet: SOAP and REST. Each operates over HTTP and port 80. Other mechanisms exist to interchange data, but this section just looks at these two.

One of the problems that I ran into when working on this section was in creating examples with code that I was familiar with. My first thought was to create a series of examples using the Twitter.com API. Unfortunately, the Twitter.com API is based on REST and there is no SOAP-based API. Therefore, there is no ASMX or WCF native solution to Twitter. I decided to use some simple web services to illustrate the issues. The ASMX web service example was found through the MonoTouch site and its examples. The WCF web service example was built on a sample found through the MonoTouch site as well; however, the WCF service was running on another computer within the network.

After speaking with many other developers, I found a lot of new development being done with WCF; however, a large number of ASMX-based web services out there are currently used in production, so I decided that it was important to add a short section on ASMX-based web services.

Using SOAP

SOAP refers to the Simple Object Access Protocol, which is a mechanism to exchange information in the form of web services over computer networks. SOAP is highly reliant on XML. Due to this reliance on web standards and XML, SOAP is a natural tool to easily allow different systems to communicate. For example, a Windows-based system can easily communicate with a UNIX or mainframe system over HTTP without requiring the heavy layer of access software that is normally associated with such communication. One of the big advantages that SOAP has is that developers are familiar with creating and using SOAP-based web services in Visual Studio. With .NET, there are ASMX- as well as WCF-based web services that support SOAP.

Working with ASMX Web Services

ASMX web services are the first mechanism in ASP.NET for building web services. ASMX web services operate with the Web Services Description Language (WSDL) and SOAP. Consuming an ASMX web service to operate with MonoTouch is similar in concept to consuming a WCF web service to run in MonoTouch.

I do not have an ASMX web service handy to work with. Instead of creating one and potentially causing my own DDOS attack on one of my services with an example application, I decided to use a simple web service that allows for converting Celsius to Fahrenheit and back.

The next example takes a look at how to call an ASMX-based web service using MonoTouch. The steps are:

1. Add the `System.Web.Services.dll` assembly to your project.

2. Add a reference to the web service's wsdl within a project. You do this by right-clicking the project and adding the location of the URL. The URL is `http://www.w3schools.com/WebServices/TempConvert.asmx`. The Add Web Reference dialog box is shown in Figure 5-2.

3. Now that the reference has been created for the code, it is possible to program against that API. Figure 5-3 shows programming against the API exposed by the web service.

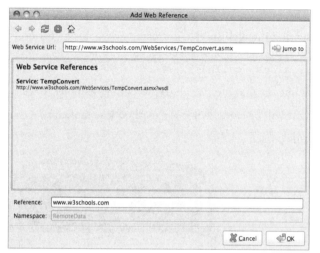

FIGURE 5-2

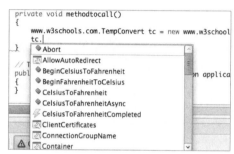

FIGURE 5-3

Now that this is set up, take a look at Listing 5-5.

LISTING 5-5: Calling an ASMX service

```
public override bool FinishedLaunching (UIApplication app, NSDictionary options)
{
    Calculate.TouchUpInside += delegate(object sender, EventArgs e) {
    string TempC = TempInC.Text;
    www.w3schools.com.TempConvert tc = new www.w3schools.com.TempConvert();
    AsyncCallback ac = new AsyncCallback( FarenheitCallback );
    tc.BeginCelsiusToFahrenheit( TempC, ac, tc );
    };
    TempInC.EditingDidEndOnExit += delegate(object sender, EventArgs e) {
        TempInC.ResignFirstResponder();
    };
    window.MakeKeyAndVisible ();
    return true;
}
private void FarenheitCallback(IAsyncResult iar)
{
    www.w3schools.com.TempConvert tc = (www.w3schools.com.TempConvert)iar.AsyncState;
     string faren = tc.EndCelsiusToFahrenheit( iar );
    InvokeOnMainThread (delegate {
        TempInF.Text = faren;
    });
    Console.WriteLine("Temp: " + faren);
}
```

Found in the ConsumeASMXWebService/Main.cs file of the download

Take notice of the following points in Listing 5-5:

➤ In the `FinishedLaunching` method, a delegate is created to handle the touching of the Calculate button.

➤ Within the delegate, a class representing the web service is created and an asynchronous call is made. The calling sequence for an asynchronous web service call is `Method( param1, param2, ..., paramN, callback, state)`.

➤ The first set of parameters is the parameters that are passed to the calling methods.

➤ The next parameter is the method that will be called when the method is completed.

➤ The final parameter is an object that is passed into the callback.

➤ Setting up the event `EditingDidEndOnExit` and calling `ResignFirstResponder()` results in the keyboard being hidden after input is finished.

➤ The callback method, `FarenheitCallback`, accepts an `IAsyncResult` parameter. This parameter is used to get the asynchronous state that was passed in.

➤ Calling the `EndCelsiusToFarenheit` method allows the program to retrieve the result of the web service call.

➤ The final issue is how to return the value to the user interface so that the data can be available to the user. This is done through the `InvokeOnMainThread` method. The reason that `InvokeOnMainThread` must be used is that the response from the web service is handled in a different thread from the main thread. To write to the user interface, the command must be written on the main thread.

➤ The final line results in debugging information being sent to the connected computer.

Figure 5-4 shows the output of the asynchronous call to a web service.

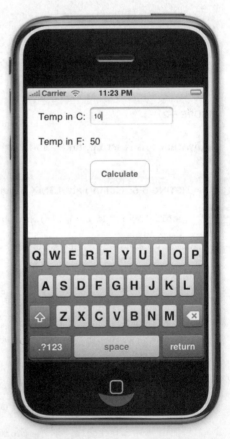

FIGURE 5-4

Working with Windows Communication Foundation (WCF)

This section explores WCF-based web services. *WCF* was released with .NET 3.5, and is an API designed to build service-oriented applications.

Visual Studio hides a number of the complexities of SOAP-based web services from developers. One of the complexities is the creation and generation of web service proxies. These proxies allow developers to generate and use these web services as if they are local libraries on a computer. Unfortunately, the iPhone does not allow for code to be generated dynamically at runtime. This creates a problem for an application because, typically, we now have to generate the proxies manually. The steps to generate the proxies and get things running are:

1. Manually generate the runtime proxy. Silverlight version 3 ships with a utility to generate a proxy. This utility is available on a Windows system with Silverlight Version 3 installed and is called by `C:\Program Files\Microsoft SDKs\Silverlight\v3.0\Tools\SlSvcUtil.exe/noConfig http://example.com/service.svc?wsdl`. The result is a proxy that can be used in a MonoTouch application. The resulting file can be imported into a MonoDevelop project.

2. Add the generated proxy to your project.

3. Add references to `System.Runtime.Serialization`, `System.ServiceModel`, and `System.ServiceModel.Web` to your project.

4. Make requests against the service. The constructor for the method should use the `BasicHttpBinding` type and the endpoint address.

5. Add the `System.ServiceModel` namespace n the Main.cs file (or any file that calls code in the proxy class).

Listing 5-6 shows the MonoTouch code for calling a remote method hosted in WCF.

Available for download on Wrox.com

LISTING 5-6: Calling a WCF web service

```
btnDoIt.TouchUpInside += delegate(object sender, EventArgs e) {
    AddNumberServiceClient asc = new AddNumberServiceClient(
        new BasicHttpBinding (),
        new EndpointAddress ("http://10.1.10.92/webservices/AddNumberService.svc") );
    asc.AddNumbersCompleted += HandleAscAddNumbersCompleted;
    asc.AddNumbersAsync(3, 4);
};
void HandleAscAddNumbersCompleted (object sender, AddNumbersCompletedEventArgs e)
{
    InvokeOnMainThread( delegate{
        lblOutput.Text = "Result: " + e.Result.TotalNum.ToString();
    });
}
```

Found in the WCFTestService/Main.cs file of the download. The WebServices directory in the download contains the WCF web service that is called.

Take note of the following in Listing 5-6:

➤ On a simple button touch-up event, code is called.

➤ The `AddNumberServiceClient` class is created. When the class is instantiated, the `BasicHttpBinding` is passed as the binding, and the `EndPointAddress` is created and passed with the URI to the WCF service.

➤ Because the WCF service is asynchronous, the completed event is set up. In this case, it is calling a defined method; however, it could just as easily be calling a delegate.

➤   In the callback, the result is received through the event arguments that are passed in.

➤   The final step is to do something with the result. In this case, the code will just display data to the user. The result is that `InvokeOnMainThread` is called to put data back in the UI.

Figure 5-5 shows the output of a call to the test WCF service.

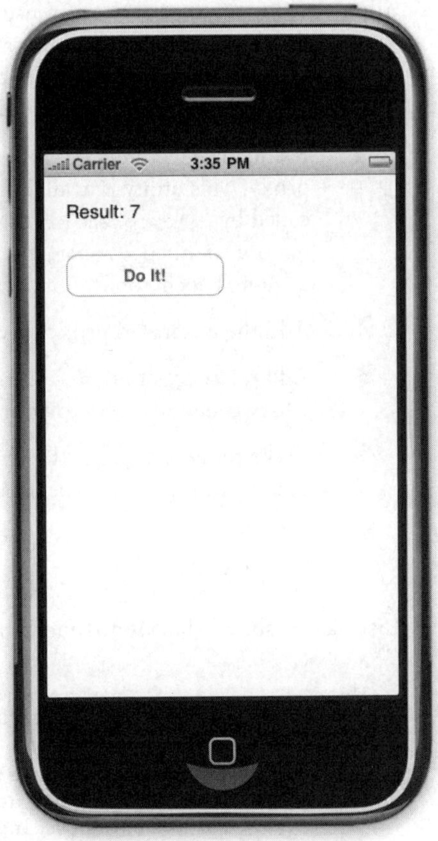

Using REST-Based Web Services

REST stands for *REpresenational State Transfer*, and it is a general architecture for distributed systems, such as the World Wide Web. REST architectures are made up of clients and servers. Servers process requests that come from clients.

REST-based web services are web services that run over HTTP and implement a more readable (and simpler) interface than SOAP. With REST, there is no need for proxies or some of the other things that make SOAP somewhat complicated.

REST-based web services typically have these three features:

1.   Addressability of the resources. Some portion of the data is available over a URL.

FIGURE 5-5

2.   Data is sent over various HTTP verbs, such as POST, GET, PUT, and DELETE. The verbs are typically used as:

➤   GET: A GET operation will have input data sent over the URL. This is thought of as a request for data.

➤   POST: A POST operation will have input data sent in the body of the request. A POST is used to add/insert data.

➤   PUT: A PUT operation will have input data sent in the body of the request. A PUT is used to update data.

➤   DELETE: A DELETE operation will have all data sent in the body of the request. A DELETE is used to delete data.

While some purists will argue the point, there may be valid reasons to perform REST-style operations by using different HTTP verbs. In addition, some operating systems and devices do not support all of the HTTP verbs. The examples here use the GET and POST verbs for operations.

3. Data may be sent encoded in various formats, such as text, XML, and any other valid data type. Officially, this is referred to as the MIME type.

Using JavaScript Object Notation (JSON)

Most developers are familiar with the eXtensible Markup Language (XML), which is used for data interchange. *JSON* is a similar technology; it is a data-interchange format based on the JavaScript scripting language. The JSON format uses a series of conventions that are familiar to most programmers that use the C-family of languages. JSON is built on two concepts:

➤ Data is transmitted as a series of name-value pairs. The values may be a single value or a series of values, such as an array.

➤ Data is stored in a structure that can be thought of as a sequence.

Because these concepts are commonly accepted, the concepts are available across nearly all modern programming languages. As a result, nearly all programming languages have some support for JSON. In .NET, Microsoft introduced support for JSON with the ASP.NET 2 AJAX library that shipped in 2007. Now programmers have various options for JSON in .NET thanks to WCF, the popular JSON.NET library, and various other libraries.

Following is an example of a JSON data packet:

```
{
    "ld":{
        "UserName":"tiger",
        "PassWord":"scott",
        "AppKey":"blah"
    },
    "TwitterId":"wbm",
    "PageIndex":"1"
}
```

In this example, three parameters are shown:

➤ ld: This object has three properties within it:

  ➤ UserName: The UserName property has a value of tiger.

  ➤ PassWord: The PassWord property has a value of scott.

  ➤ AppKey: The AppKey property has a value of blah.

➤ TwitterId: The TwitterId property has a value of wbm.

➤ PageIndex: The PageIndex property has a value of 1.

Retrieving Data

This section is an introduction to getting data from Twitter using the Twitter Search API.

Using LINQ to XML

Language Integrated Query (LINQ) is a set of methods, operations, rules, and types that allow for data to be queried within a .NET language such as Visual Basic or C#. LINQ shipped within the .NET 3.5 Framework, and LINQ support for several data providers exists within the Mono project.

LINQ to XML is a technology that allows for XML documents to be converted into XElement objects, queried based on some criteria, and to be converted into a collection of objects. The queries are performed within the local execution engine.

Listing 5-7 shows a simple example of querying data from Twitter:

Available for
download on
Wrox.com

LISTING 5-7: Retrieving data from Twitter

```
private Dictionary<int, TCController> controllers;
private String[] str;
public void SearchByTerm(string SearchTerm)
{
        string strUrl = "http://search.twitter.com/search.atom?q=";
        SearchTwitterResult sr = new SearchTwitterResult();
        if ( controllers == null )
        {
           controllers = new Dictionary<int, TCController>();
        }
        List<SearchTwitterResult> strl = new List<SearchTwitterResult>();
        if ((!String.IsNullOrEmpty(SearchTerm)))
        {
           strUrl += SearchTerm;
           XDocument xdoc = XDocument.Load(strUrl);
           Console.WriteLine("Document Loaded.");
           XNamespace atomNS = "http://www.w3.org/2005/Atom";
           XNamespace google = "http://base.google.com/ns/1.0";
           var query = (from tweet in xdoc.Descendants(atomNS + "entry")
                   where tweet != null
                   select new SearchTwitterResult
                   {
                       TwitterUri = tweet.Element(atomNS + "author").Element(atomNS +
                                       "uri").Value,
                       TwitterName = tweet.Element(atomNS + "author").Element(atomNS +
                                       "name").Value,
                       StatusDate = Convert.ToDateTime(tweet.Element(atomNS +
                                       "updated").Value),
                       Status = tweet.Element(atomNS + "title").Value,
                   });
           Console.WriteLine("Query formed.");
           strl = query.ToList();
           Console.WriteLine("Query Completed.");
           Console.WriteLine("Records stored: " + strl.Count);
        }
        str = strl.ToArray();
}

public class SearchTwitterResult
```

```
{
    public string TwitterName { get; set; }
    public string TwitterUri { get; set; }
    public string Location { get; set; }
    public string Status { get; set; }
    public DateTime StatusDate { get; set; }
    public int StatusID { get; set; }
    public double? Latitude { get; set; }
    public double? Longitude { get; set; }
}
```

Found in the RemoteData/Main.cs and the RemoteData/UserStatusSvc.cs files of the download

In this example, a query is made against the Twitter Search API based on a specific term. The term is entered through the user interface, and data is passed through to the Twitter Search API. The programmatic steps are:

1. Data is loaded by a call to `XDocument.Load(...)`. The `XDocument.Load()` method is a synchronous method.

2. A query is formed against the `XDocument`. When the query is executed, the data is converted from an XML format into a collection of objects.

3. LINQ queries are executed when the results are enumerated. The `.ToList()` method is called to cause the data to be retrieved.

Several pieces of code might seem strange or out of place to you in this listing, but they are there for a reason. These objects and lines of code are as follows:

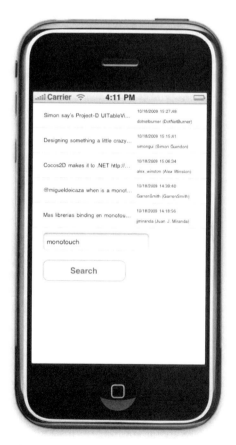

➤ The `if(controllers == null)` section: With the `UITableView`, the controllers for the `UITableCells` should be cached. The `controllers` object is a `Dictionary` that contains the `UITableCells`' controllers.

➤ A check is performed to verify that a string is passed in. This is not really necessary in example code.

➤ The result is shown in Figure 5-6.

FIGURE 5-6

You may have noticed that the above code makes a request synchronously. There is one negative to performing synchronous operations. Performing a synchronous operation over a wireless network may not be a reliable mechanism. If the connection is unreliable, the application may freeze for more than the iPhone's self-imposed 20-second limit. The result would be that the iPhone would detect the timeout and close the application. The easiest way around this issue is to perform the operation asynchronously. Some examples of asynchronous operations in MonoTouch follow.

Using Asynchronous Data Retrieval

Performing an asynchronous call to a REST-based web service is possible. Though the iPhone is limited in its ability to multitask third-party applications, it is possible to make asynchronous calls through MonoTouch. Calling a REST-based web service asynchronously is an easy way to get around the iPhone's 20-second time spent in an application executing code. Another positive is that this is done through the exact same API as in .NET. Chances are that a developer is familiar with the .NET asynchronous programming methodologies of calling BeginXXX/EndXXX.

In Listing 5-8, the code makes asynchronous requests against a set of third-party web services hosted on the twtmstr.com domain. TwtMstr is an application that interfaces to Twitter and allows for the scheduling of Twitter entries.

LISTING 5-8: Calling a REST web service asynchronously

```
void HandleGetDataTouchUpInside (object sender, EventArgs e)
{
        string Url = "http://www.twtmstr.com/WebServices/RemoteAPI.svc/GetUserTimeLine";
        string Body = "{\"ld\":{\"UserName\":\"userid1\",\"PassWord\":\"pwd1\",
            \"AppKey\":\"blah\"}, \"TwitterId\":\"wbm\", \"PageIndex\":\"1\"}";
        byte[] byteData = UTF8Encoding.UTF8.GetBytes(Body);
        try
        {
           // Create the web request
           HttpWebRequest request = WebRequest.Create(Url) as HttpWebRequest;
           request.ContentLength = Body.Length;
           // Set type to POST
           request.Method = "POST";
           request.ContentType = "text/json";
           // Write the parameters
           StreamWriter stOut = new StreamWriter(request.GetRequestStream(),
               System.Text.Encoding.ASCII);
           stOut.Write(Body);
           stOut.Close();
           request.BeginGetResponse(new AsyncCallback(ProcessHttpResponse), request);
        }
        catch (WebException we)
        {
            Console.Error.WriteLine("Exception: " + we.Message);
        }
    }
}
```

Found in the RemoteData/Main.cs file of the download

Here are the specifics of this code:

1. A URL to call is set up. This URL is to a REST-based WCF service. This method will return a set of user statuses and has the following signature:

    ```
    [OperationContract]
    UserStatusSvc[] GetUserTimeLine(LoginData ld, string TwitterId, int PageIndex);
    ```

2. Due to the necessity of providing userid/password information to the application, it was determined that this was a security vulnerability. As a result, a POST is required.

3. A body is set up to pass information through. This body contains the content that is passed to the method.

4. The body is set up manually. Another way to handle this is to use a library that will serialize/deserialize JSON.

5. The HTTP request is set up as the JSON MIME type.

6. The HTTP request is made asynchronously. A callback is set up so that when data returns from the web service, a method is called to handle the returned data.

7. The ProcessHttpResponse method takes the result that is returned from the web service.

8. Within the ProcessHttpResponse callback method (Listing 5-9) are two things to note:

➤ JSON serialization is performed through the Mono JavaScript serializer that is compatible with ASP.NET 2 AJAX. With this serializer, the properties must match up in their names for the properties to flow across. Other JSON serializers could be used as well.

➤ It is important to close the HttpWebResponse after data has been retrieved.

LISTING 5-9: Processing the callback from a web service called asynchronously

```
private void ProcessHttpResponse(IAsyncResult iar)
{
        HttpWebRequest request = (HttpWebRequest)iar.AsyncState;
        HttpWebResponse response;
        response = (HttpWebResponse)request.EndGetResponse(iar);
        Console.Error.WriteLine("get response.");
        System.IO.StreamReader strm = new System.IO.StreamReader(
        response.GetResponseStream());
        string responseString = strm.ReadToEnd();
        responseString = responseString.Replace("{\"GetUserTimeLineResult\":",
            String.Empty);
        responseString = responseString.Substring(0, responseString.Length - 1);
        response.Close();
        Console.Error.WriteLine("response: " + responseString);
        JavaScriptSerializer ser = new JavaScriptSerializer();
        List<UserStatusSvc> uss = ser.Deserialize<List<UserStatusSvc>>(responseString);
        Console.Error.WriteLine("Count: " + uss.Count.ToString());
}
```

Found in the RemoteData/Main.cs file of the download

Now that the callback has processed, you have a set of objects that you can work with. Though this code will just output to the Mono debugger that a set of objects has been returned, it is possible to save the data in another format, such as SQLite, presented to the user in the UITableView, or processed in any set of ways.

Posting Data with POST

Now that you have learned how to get data from a service, you need to take a closer look at how to post data to a service. In this example, you look at posting data to a service with JSON.

First some background on the service: TwtMstr is a service that provides a number of enhancements to businesses that are using Twitter as part of their social media efforts. TwtMstr exposes a set of REST-based JSON web services that allow third-party applications to integrate with it. One of the features that TwtMstr provides is the ability to schedule Tweets to go out on Twitter in the future.

Listing 5-10 shows some example code that would schedule a post to be done in the future. The code will schedule a post one hour in the future.

LISTING 5-10: Posting data asynchronously

Available for
download on
Wrox.com

```
void HandleTweetTouchUpInside (object sender, EventArgs e)
{
    string Url = "http://www.twtmstr.com/WebServices/RemoteAPI.svc/ScheduleMessage";
    string DateToPost = DateTime.Now.AddHours(1).ToString("MM/dd/yyyy");
    string TimeToPost = DateTime.Now.AddHours(1).ToString("HH:mm");
    string Body = "{\"ld\":{\"UserName\":\"xxxx\",\"PassWord\":\"yyyyy\",
        \"AppKey\":\"blah\"}, " +
        \"TwitterId\":\"zzzzz\",
        \"ReplyStatusId\":\"\", \"DateToPost\":\"" + DateToPost + "\",
        \"TimeToPost\":\"" + TimeToPost + "\", \"Tweet\":\"" + TweetText.Text + "\" }";
    byte[] byteData = UTF8Encoding.UTF8.GetBytes(Body);
    // Create the web request
    HttpWebRequest request = WebRequest.Create(Url) as HttpWebRequest;
    request.ContentLength = Body.Length;
    // Set type to POST
    request.Method = "POST";
    request.ContentType = "text/json";
    // Write the parameters
    StreamWriter stOut = new StreamWriter(request.GetRequestStream(),
        System.Text.Encoding.ASCII);
    stOut.Write(Body);
    stOut.Close();
    request.BeginGetResponse(new AsyncCallback(ProcessHttpResponseAndForget), request);
}
```

Found in the RemoteData/Main.cs of the download

Note the following in the code:

➤ You create the URL for calling this method. This is stored in the `Url` variable.

➤ The code creates a date and a time to post. In this simple example, the date and time are separate controls and are passed separately to the method.

➤ The body of the method is created. Ideally, this would be done with a custom object that is serialized. The reason for showing it here is merely to display the content. The body is put into a byte array.

➤ An `HttpWebRequest` is created with several properties set. The key is the `Method` and the `ContentType`. The `Method` is set to `POST` and the `ContentType` is set as a JSON data packet.

➤ Finally, `BeginGetResponse()` is called. This results in the web request being made asynchronously.

➤ When the response returns, a call is made into the method `ProcessHttpResponseAndForget()`. This method handles the callback event.

➤ The `ProcessHttpResponseAndForget()` method, shown in the following code block, does nothing more than close the web request when it is finished.

```
private void ProcessHttpResponseAndForget(IAsyncResult iar)
{
    HttpWebRequest request = (HttpWebRequest)iar.AsyncState;
    HttpWebResponse response;
    response = (HttpWebResponse)request.EndGetResponse(iar);
    Console.Error.WriteLine("get response.");
    System.IO.StreamReader strm = new System.IO.StreamReader(
        response.GetResponseStream());
    string responseString = strm.ReadToEnd();
    response.Close();
}
```

Figure 5-7 shows that a record has been successfully entered into TwtMstr for the supplied user id.

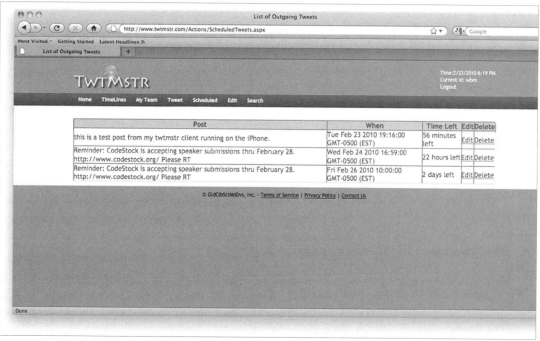

FIGURE 5-7

Using Web Services Responsibly

Now that you have learned how to use web services in various forms in MonoTouch, let's look at some issues. Web services are great tools for:

➤ Building apps that run over the Internet. Because they run over port 80, there is a very small chance that the communication will be blocked.

➤ Keeping information centralized.

➤ Easily allowing for disparate systems to communicate.

At the same time, web services have their drawbacks. Some of the cons of web services over wireless are:

➤ Web services tend to be slow. Sending information over a textual format, such as JSON or XML, can be slower than sending the same information over a binary/compressed protocol.

➤ Wireless communications tend to be unreliable.

➤ Sending data over numerous networks, which the Internet is, tends to be unreliable.

As a result, it is important to remember to use web services in a responsible manner:

➤ Be efficient in the amount of data that is sent to the web service and sent back to the iPhone. There is no reason to overburden the iPhone or the connection to the web service.

➤ The iPhone has a limit of 20 seconds to wait on user code to finish executing. After 20 seconds, the code that is being executed will terminate. As a result, for calling web services, it makes sense to call web services asynchronously or in another thread.

SUMMARY

This chapter looked at data strategies on the iPhone. By using these technologies, developers can build native applications that run when a network connection is not available. You've learned how to:

➤ Set up a local database in SQLite on the iPhone

➤ Run commands against the SQLite database on the iPhone

➤ Work with SOAP-based web services on the iPhone

➤ Work with REST-based web services on the iPhone

When they add in the ability to call web services, iPhone developers and their applications can integrate with central datastores. This allows an application's users to interact with other users. For example, Twitter users on their iPhone can interact with other Twitter users without ever having to go to the Twitter.com web site. By taking advantage of the features in the iPhone, developers can create applications that provide more features for users and are more resistant to problems when connecting to the Internet and its datasources.

Displaying Data Using Tables

WHAT'S IN THIS CHAPTER?

➤   Displaying information in a table

➤   Using tables for navigation

➤   Taking advantage of UITableView's built-in editing features

➤   Adding a search bar to a table

Most programmers visualize a "table" as a grid: a set of rows and columns used to display structured information similar to a spreadsheet. C#/.NET developers probably think of the DataGrid or GridView control in their area of expertise (WinForms, ASP.NET, or WPF).

Tables on the iPhone are a more like a Repeater control in ASP.NET, with an almost infinitely flexible ItemTemplate. The two key classes are UITableView and the UITableViewCell. Both are provided with useful default functionality and can be highly customized via either Interface Builder or in code to produce almost any structured content display you can imagine. Coupled with the UINavigationController to help manage multiple levels of navigation, the UITableView forms the basis for much of the iPhone OS UI that you are familiar with. Tables and how you use and manage them in the iPhone OS are what this chapter is all about.

Tables are used throughout the iPhone OS, from obvious places like the iPod Album/Artist/ Track and Contact lists to the Messages application and the display/editing of values in Settings. Figure 6-1 shows a variety of different examples, highlighting how flexible and customizable the UITableView control can be.

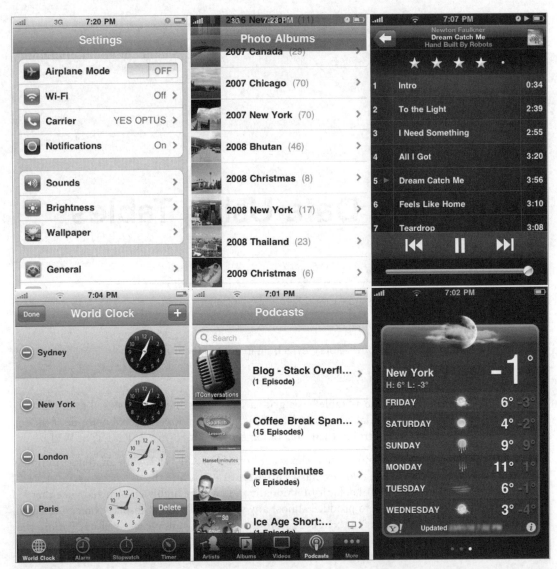

FIGURE 6-1

The main classes required to create these user interfaces are UITableView and its associated UITableViewSource delegate. UITableViewCell is also used when customizing the display beyond the built-in options, and the UISearchBar and Search Display Controller provides an easy way to set up a search function with the results in a table. UITableView can also be combined with a NavigationController to facilitate navigating through a hierarchy of options with built-in "back" functionality.

DISPLAYING DATA IN A TABLE

The simplest form of table renders a list of data on the screen using a built-in cell style. Create a new solution Tables01 in MonoDevelop, drag a UITableView onto the main window using Interface Builder, and create an outlet called Table for it. Add the code in Listing 6-1 to Main.cs to create a basic table. The key aspects of the code are:

➤ Creating some data to display, in this case a simple array of strings called colors. Data for your table could come from anywhere — a hardcoded list, a database query, or web service call.

➤ Assigning the UITableView.Source property an instance of a custom UITableViewSource subclass, passing a reference to the data being displayed. This is the key to the delegate pattern — the UITableView instance "asks" the UITableViewSource for the information it needs to render, including the number of rows and what view object to display in each cell.

➤ Implementing the two required methods in the UITableViewSource subclass:

➤ RowsInSection: Tells the table how many rows will be required to display the entire data set.

➤ GetCell: Called by the table when it is rendering the user interface. Here you simply create a new UITableViewCell each time and assign your data to the TextLabel. Notice that you pass a reuseidentifier "mycell" to the constructor — it isn't used elsewhere in this code but it becomes very important for larger tables later in the chapter.

LISTING 6-1: Basic table display (Tables01\Main.cs)

```
using System;
using System.Collections.Generic;
using System.Linq;
using MonoTouch.Foundation;
using MonoTouch.UIKit;
namespace Tables01
{
public class Application
{
    static void Main (string[] args)
    { UIApplication.Main (args);}
}
public partial class AppDelegate : UIApplicationDelegate
{
    // This method is required in iPhoneOS 3.0
    public override void OnActivated (UIApplication application) {}
    private List<string> colors;
    public override bool FinishedLaunching
                        (UIApplication app, NSDictionary options)
```

continues

LISTING 6-1 *(continued)*

```
        {
            colors = new List<string>
                {"Red","Orange","Yellow","Green","Blue","Indigo","Violet"};
            Table.Source = new MyTableViewSource (colors);
            window.MakeKeyAndVisible ();
            return true;
        }
        // Replaces/combines UITableViewDataSource and UITableViewDelegate
        private class MyTableViewSource : UITableViewSource
        {
            private List<string> rows;
            public MyTableViewSource (List<string> list)
            { // store the data in this class
                rows = list;
            }
            public override int RowsInSection (UITableView tableview, int section)
            {  // tell the table how many rows will be needed
                return rows.Count;
            }
            public override UITableViewCell GetCell
                        (UITableView tableView, NSIndexPath indexPath)
            {   // we will learn what "mycell" is for later...
                UITableViewCell cell = new
                        UITableViewCell(UITableViewCellStyle.Default,"mycell");
                cell.TextLabel.Text = rows[indexPath.Row];
                return cell;
            }
        }
    }}
```

The "format" of your data (for example, the underlying class or type of collection you use) isn't important because you are responsible for determining the number of rows and for instructing the table how to display each row via the GetCell method. The result of this very simple code is shown in Figure 6-2.

FIGURE 6-2

If you are converting an Objective-C example or reading Apple's documentation you will find references to UITableView's Delegate *and* DataSource *properties. In Objective-C* UITableViewDelegate *and* UITableViewDataSource *are protocols that can both be implemented by the same class, but in C# they are exposed as abstract classes, which means you must implement two subclasses for every table you create.*

In MonoTouch the properties and methods of those two classes have been "merged" into UITableViewSource *as a convenience for C# developers. MonoTouch allows you to use either approach: Implement* UITableViewSource *only OR implement both* UITableViewDelegate *and* UITableViewDataSource. *There is no difference in functionality — in this chapter only the* UITableViewSource *approach has been used because it involves less typing.*

Selecting a Cell

UITableView provides a lot of default functionality with little or no additional coding — already the example behaves like an iPhone OS application by inheriting the default font and text settings and supporting smooth scrolling. Responding to the user touching a cell takes only a few lines of code — first create this helper method in the UITableViewSource subclass to pop up a message:

```
public void ShowAlert (string title, string message)
{
    using(var alert=new UIAlertView(title,message,null,"OK",null))
    {
        alert.Show();
    }
}
```

Then implement the RowSelected method on the UITableViewSource subclass. The NSIndexPath object contains information on which row was selected — the Row property tells you the index that is used to retrieve the value in the rows array:

```
public override void RowSelected
                (UITableView tableView, NSIndexPath indexPath)
{
    ShowAlert("RowSelected","You selected "+rows[indexPath.Row]);
}
```

An instance of NSIndexPath *contains enough information to identify a specific row in a* UITableView. *In these simple examples only the* Row *property is used, but when grouping is used (later in the chapter) the* Section *property is also required.*

You can take many actions when a table cell is touched: Add a checkmark to the cell, open a new view, navigate elsewhere in your application, or whatever else you can think of. Some of these other actions are covered later in the chapter.

There is another type of "row selection" provided by the UITableView — the DetailDisclosureButton — most commonly seen in the Phone application. This user interface element has a special meaning: It indicates that touching the main part of the cell can perform one action (for example, initiating a telephone call) whereas touching the blue-circle-arrow performs a *different* action (such as opening the contact details). To use this feature, set the Accessory property of cell in the GetCell method.

```
cell.Accessory = UITableViewCellAccessory.DetailDisclosureButton;
```

and implement this method in the UITableViewSource subclass:

```
public override void AccessoryButtonTapped
                (UITableView tableView, NSIndexPath indexPath)
{
    app.ShowAlert ("AccessoryButton", "You tapped "+text[indexPath.Row]);
}
```

Figure 6-3 shows the RowSelected and AccessoryButtonTapped methods in action — touching the row calls RowSelected and touching the DetailDisclosureButton calls AccessoryButtonTapped so you can respond to two different actions from the row.

FIGURE 6-3

In addition to the special DetailDisclosureButton, as you can see in Table 6-1, there are two other possible values for cell.Accessory, each with a specific purpose in the *iPhone Human Interface Guidelines*.

TABLE 6-1: UITableViewCellAccessory Options

TYPE	DESCRIPTION
None	The default value — no accessory is displayed. Either this cell is a read-only piece of data or it responds to a touch.
Checkmark	Use this to indicate single- or multi-selection in a table. Do *not* use the blue selection state — that is only intended as a visual indicator that the cell has been touched.

TYPE	DESCRIPTION
Disclosure	Simple grey > arrow usually used to indicate that touching this cell results in some sort of navigation.
DetailDisclosure	Blue circle with small white > arrow, which indicates that touching this accessory has a *different behavior* than touching the rest of the cell.

Changing the Cell Layout

The table would be fairly uninspiring if you could not include some additional text or images in each cell. Four predefined layouts are available (see Table 6-2) that are used by the built-in applications.

TABLE 6-2: UITableViewCellStyle Options

STYLE	DESCRIPTION
Default	Shows a single black TextLabel and an optional image on the left of the text. Does *not* support DetailTextLabel. This style is used in the iPod application.
Subtitle	Displays two left-aligned fields: TextLabel uses larger black text; DetailTextLabel uses smaller grey text. An image can optionally be added to the left of both labels. This style is used in the iPod application.
Value1	TextLabel is smaller than the Default, right-aligned and blue. DetailTextLabel is left-aligned and black. It doesn't support an image. This style is used in the Contacts list.
Value2	TextLabel is left-aligned black text. DetailTextLabel is right-aligned blue text. It doesn't support an image. This style is used in the Settings application.

 When using these styles do not attempt to set unsupported properties (for example, the DetailTextLabel isn't supported by Default; and the ImageView isn't supported by Value1) because a null reference exception will result.

The code download folder Tables02 in the code download for this chapter contains seven PNG images (one for each color), and an additional Hex property has been added to the Color class to demonstrate the different styles. Change the instantiation of each UITableViewCell in the GetCell method to use a different style like this:

```
var cell = new UITableViewCell (UITableViewCellStyle.Subtitle,
                                "mycell");
MyColor display = sectionColors[indexPath.Section][indexPath.Row];
cell.TextLabel.Text = display.Name;
cell.DetailTextLabel.Text = display.Hex;
cell.ImageView.Image = UIImage.FromFile(display.Name + ".png");
```

Figure 6-4 shows the four different cell style options using the preceding code as well as an example of each style from the built-in applications.

FIGURE 6-4

The visual styles such as the text font size and color of the built-in views can also be changed in `GetCell` like this:

```
cell.DetailTextLabel.Font = UIFont.SystemFontOfSize(20); //bigger
cell.DetailTextLabel.TextColor = new UIColor(0,0,255,255); //blue
```

Presenting Grouped Data

Short lists such as the seven colors used in previous examples are easy to navigate and unlikely to cause performance problems. However, when you need to display dozens, hundreds, or *thousands* of rows (for example, the Songs list in the iPod application), a little more code is required to ensure your application is responsive and follows the *iPhone Human Interface Guidelines*. To address these concerns you need to:

➤ Implement reusable cell objects in your table

➤ Use grouping and possibly an index to make your table easier to navigate

The `GetCell` method is called whenever a new row is scrolled into view, so the code shown in Listing 6-1 would return a new `UITableViewCell` object for every row that comes into view. A table with the default layout and cell size shows only about 10 rows on an iPhone-sized screen, but without reusing cell objects there would potentially be hundreds (or thousands) created if you scrolled through a very long list — your application would slow down and possibly run out of memory.

The iPhone OS provides a neat solution to this problem that resembles the VirtualizingStackPanel familiar to .NET/WPF developers. When a row moves *offscreen*, the view object for that row is placed in a queue for reuse, and a method is provided by UITableView to look for objects in this queue before creating new ones. An improved GetCell method that uses this approach is shown in the following code:

```
public override UITableViewCell GetCell
              (UITableView tableView, NSIndexPath indexPath)
{
    UITableViewCell cell = tableView.DequeueReusableCell("mycell");
    if (cell == null)
    { // none to re-use, create a new object
        cell = new UITableViewCell (UITableViewCellStyle.Value1,"mycell");
    }
    Element display = sectionElements[indexPath.Section][indexPath.Row];
    cell.TextLabel.Text = display.Symbol;
    return cell;
}
```

The DequeueReusableCell method asks the table if there are any spare UITableViewCell objects that can be reused, and returns null if none are available. In that case your code creates a new UITableViewCell object and returns it at the end of the method (and ultimately back into the queue if it is scrolled off-screen).

The "mycell" parameter is used to distinguish between cell layouts that can be re-used interchangeably. Because this example only has one cell layout, you pass the same string into the UITableViewCell constructor and DequeueReusableCell. The Messages application uses a table to display each conversation with grey and green "speech bubble" cells that would need different identifiers because you obviously can't re-use a green cell when you need a grey one. In that case you would probably check the contents of indexPath *first* to determine what type of cell is required and potentially dequeue or instantiate different UITableViewCell implementations with "greycell" or "greencell" identifiers. The actual strings you choose are not important; all that matters is different cell layouts have different identifiers.

To demonstrate DequeueReusableCell and grouping/indexing the next few examples use a collection of Elements (too long to reprint here) that is included in the code download for this chapter (folder Tables03). The initialization of the collection starts like this:

```
elements = new List<Element>{
  new Element{Name="hydrogen",Number="1",Symbol="H", Family="Hydrogen"},
  new Element{Name="helium",  Number="2",Symbol="He",Family="Noble gas"},
  // etc...
```

In most cases the data you present in a table will be a single flat structure like this list of Elements. Using the grouping functionality of the UITableView requires you to restructure your data so that your UITableViewSource delegate can tell the table how many groups to display and how many items are in each group.

Figure 6-5 shows the difference between a data structure used for the plain and grouped tables. For the previous examples a simple array is sufficient to display a table because there is an "implicit" single section and the row index is enough to identify each cell. When grouping is used UITableView uses Section and Row to identify each cell (the two properties of NSIndexPath) so a two-dimensional-array–type structure works better.

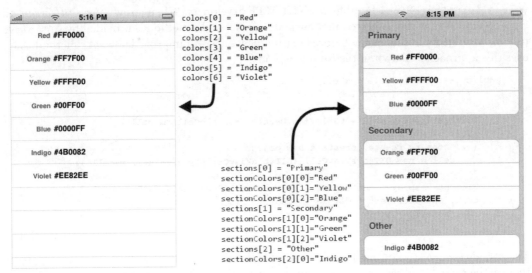

FIGURE 6-5

Listing 6-2 contains an example UITableViewSource implementation using LINQ to create a SortedDictionary that conforms to the Section-Row hierarchy and makes displaying the groups easy:

➤ In the constructor for MyTableViewSource the list of Element objects is turned into a two-level hierarchy:

> ➤ First it extracts the criteria for each group using a Distinct LINQ query and the Sort() method to create an array of the first letters of each Element. This creates the sectionTitles list, which is used to populate the index bar and to help divide the Elements into groups in the next step.

> ➤ Then it loops through the Elements to create a SortedDictionary where the key is the integer position of the starting letter and the element is a collection of Element objects to display in that group.

The result is two collections that are easily referenced with integer parameters for the section and row number.

➤ NumberOfSections: The number of groups to be displayed.

➤ TitleForHeader: The display name of the group, in this case a letter of the alphabet.

➤ RowsInSection: Returns the count of items in the specified group.

➤ RowSelected: The previous simple example only checked indexPath.Row to determine which cell was touched. Now that your cells are grouped you need to check the indexPath.Section value as well.

➤ GetCell: Similar to the RowSelected method, you now need to check both Row and Section properties of IndexPath.

LISTING 6-2: Grouped data table (Tables03\Main.cs)

```csharp
private class MyTableViewSource : UITableViewSource
{
   private AppDelegate app;
   private List<string> sectionTitles;
   private SortedDictionary<int,List<Element>> sectionElements
                       = new SortedDictionary<int, List<Element>>();
   public MyTableViewSource (AppDelegate appDelegate, List<Element> list)
   {
      sectionTitles = (from c in list
                  select c.StartsWith).Distinct().ToList();
      sectionTitles.Sort();
      foreach (var c in list)
      { // 'group' elements together into alphabet
         int sectionNum = sectionTitles.IndexOf(c.StartsWith);
         if (sectionElements.ContainsKey(sectionNum))
            sectionElements[sectionNum].Add(c);
         else
            sectionElements.Add(sectionNum, new List<Element> {c});
      }
      app = appDelegate;
   }
   public override int NumberOfSections (UITableView tableView)
   { // ie. 26 if you were using the English alphabet
      return sectionTitles.Count;
   }
   public override string TitleForHeader (UITableView tableView, int section)
   { // ie. "A", "B", "C", etc if you were using the alphabet,
      // but could also be a word/heading
      return sectionTitles[section];
   }
   public override int RowsInSection (UITableView tableview, int section)
   {
      return sectionElements[section].Count;
   }
   public override void RowSelected (UITableView tableView, NSIndexPath indexPath)
   {
      Element display = sectionElements[indexPath.Section][indexPath.Row];
      app.ShowAlert ("RowSelected", "You selected " + display.Name);
   }
   public override UITableViewCell GetCell (UITableView tableView, NSIndexPath indexPath)
   {
      UITableViewCell cell = tableView.DequeueReusableCell ("mycell");
      if (cell == null)
      {
         cell = new UITableViewCell (UITableViewCellStyle.Value2, "mycell");
      }
      Element display = sectionElements[indexPath.Section][indexPath.Row];
      cell.TextLabel.Text = display.Symbol;
      cell.DetailTextLabel.Text = display.Name;
      return cell;
   }
}
```

Adding an Index

Adding an index (the alphabetic list down the right side of the table that lets you jump directly to any part of the table) is as easy as implementing a method to describe what values should be displayed for each section: `SectionIndexTitles`. It is your responsibility to ensure the number of elements in this array is the same as the number of groups in your data.

```
public override string[] SectionIndexTitles (UITableView tableView)
{   // for the right-vertical index: preferably only one character
    // ie. "A", "B", "C", etc if you were using the alphabet
    return sectionTitles.ToArray();
}
```

There is limited vertical space for the index on iPhone-sized devices so choose your indexing strategy carefully — an index is most commonly used to display the alphabet (such as in the Contacts and iPod applications). Use too few items and it looks sparse and unfamiliar to users; with too many items it will be crowded and unusable. Figure 6-6 shows a table with and without an index — it's much easier to scroll quickly to "Z" with the index.

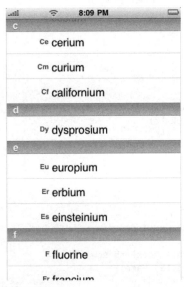
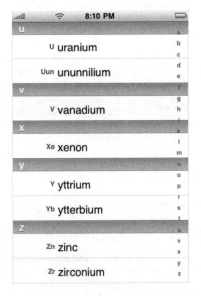

FIGURE 6-6

 To show the search magnifying glass that the built-in applications use in their indexes, return `"{search}"` *as an element of the* `SectionIndexTitles` *array. This is equivalent to using the constant* `UITableViewIndexSearch` *in Objective-C.*

Grouped Table Style

When you are placing a `UITableView` in Interface Builder it defaults to the `Plain` style shown in the previous examples. There is another style — `Grouped` — which provides a more visual connection between grouped elements. The `Grouped` style can be used for long lists but is also commonly used to display tables containing short lists of perhaps unrelated information (such as in the Settings application).

Because the style of a table is set during its initialization, the `Style` property is read-only and cannot be changed in `FinishedLaunching`. Unless you are creating your `UITableView` in code (beyond the scope of this chapter), you should choose the style in Interface Builder when you are designing the window (as shown in Figure 6-7).

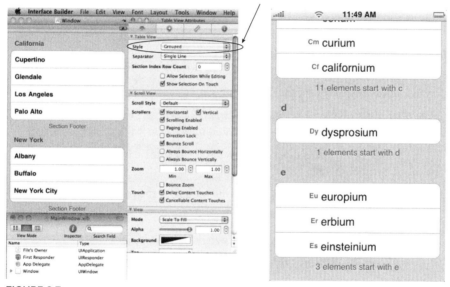

FIGURE 6-7

`UITableView` also allows a footer to be shown at the end of each section. It can be added in both `Plain` and `Grouped` styles, although it looks better with `Grouped` tables. You can easily add footers to the table with another method in the delegate class: `TitleForFooter`.

```
public override string TitleForFooter (UITableView tableView, int section)
{
    int count = sectionElements[section].Count;
    return String.Format("{0} elements start with {1}",
                         count, sectionTitles[section]);
}
```

`Grouped` tables aren't *usually* used for alphabetic grouping but more often for when you want to show smaller sets of data or for when the table is being used to display a form. The *iPhone Human Interface Guidelines* state that you should *not* use an index (that is, implement `SectionIndexTitles`) with the `Grouped` table style.

Customizing the Cell Layout

In addition to the four built-in cell layouts shown in Figure 6-4 there are many other examples (both built-in and third party) of tables with much more sophisticated cell layouts. These layouts can be designed in Interface Builder by creating a custom `UITableViewCell` and then loading it dynamically in the `UITableViewSource.GetCell` method. This requires some careful use of Interface Builder to ensure your XIB is set up correctly for access via MonoTouch.

To build a table with custom cells, use MonoDevelop to create a new iPhone Window-based Project called Tables04 and add a fullscreen `UITableView` to `MainWindow.xib` (or look for it in the code download for this chapter). From within MonoDevelop right-click on the project, choose Add ➪ New File, choose View Interface Definition, and name it `MyTableViewCell.xib`.

In Interface Builder perform the following steps, partly depicted in Figure 6-8:

1. Delete the default `UIView` from the XIB — a more specific view class is required.

2. Drag a `UITableViewCell` from the Objects Library into `MyTableViewCell.xib`. Open it and drag four `UILabels` from the Objects Library; position and format them as required.

   ➤ In the Identity Inspector set the Class to `MyTableViewCell` (matching the filename).

   ➤ In the Attributes Inspector set the Identifier to `MyCellIdentifier`. This is the re-use identifier that is referenced in `DequeueReusableCell()` calls.

   ➤ In the Classes Library select `MyTableViewCell` and create outlets for each label (Number, Symbol, Name, Family).

   ➤ In the Connections Inspector "wire up" the outlets to the four labels.

3. Make the following changes to `File's Owner`:

   ➤ In the Identity Inspector set the Class to `MyTableViewController`.

   ➤ In the Library select `MyTableViewController` from the Classes list and add an outlet named `Cell`.

   ➤ In the Connections Inspector "wire up" the `Cell` outlet to `MyTableViewCell`.

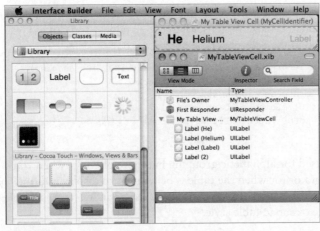

FIGURE 6-8

After you save the XIB in Interface Builder and return to MonoDevelop, the `designer.cs` file contains two partial class definitions: `MyTableViewController` should have a `Cell` property, and `MyTableCellView` has the four labels. The `designer.cs` should never be edited; however, notice that MonoTouch adds the following helpful comments on each class:

```
// Base type probably should be MonoTouch.UIKit.UIViewController or subclass
[MonoTouch.Foundation.Register("MyTableViewController")]
public partial class MyTableViewController {
```

and

```
// Base type probably should be MonoTouch.UIKit.UITableViewCell or subclass
[MonoTouch.Foundation.Register("MyTableViewCell")]
public partial class MyTableViewCell {
```

These generated comments provide guidance for how to complete the class definitions. Listing 6-3 shows the code you need to complete the partial classes, by inheriting from `UITableViewController` and `UITableViewCell`, respectively. You also need to add four public properties for the privately defined outlets and two constructors required to load the `MyTableViewCell` from an XIB (most importantly they call the `base` constructor).

LISTING 6-3: Tables04\MyTableViewCell.xib.cs

```
public partial class MyTableViewCell : UITableViewCell
{
// The IntPtr and NSCoder constructors are required for controllers that need
// to be able to be created from a xib rather than from managed code
    public MyTableViewCell (IntPtr handle) : base(handle)
    { Initialize (); }
    [Export("initWithCoder:")]
    public MyTableViewCell (NSCoder coder) : base(coder)
    {
        Initialize ();
    }
    void Initialize () {}
    public string ElementName
    {
        get {return Name.Text;}
        set {Name.Text = value;}
    }
    #region Other properties: ElementSymbol, ElementNumber, ElementFamily
}
```

Only a few minor changes are required in `Main.cs` to complete the implementation. The `AppDelegate` requires a field for the `UITableViewController` that has been "created" through Interface Builder

```
MyTableViewController myTVC = new MyTableViewController();
```

and the `GetCell` method uses that field to load the XIB with `LoadNib()`. The controller is not actually connected to the table in this case and exists solely to load its `MyCell` property from the XIB.

```
public override UITableViewCell GetCell
                        (UITableView tableView, NSIndexPath indexPath)
{
    UITableViewCell cell = tableView.DequeueReusableCell
                            ("MyCellIdentifier"); // set in XIB
    MyTableViewCell mycell = null;
    if (cell == null)
    { // no re-usable cell found, load new object (from XIB file)
        NSBundle.MainBundle.LoadNib("MyTableViewCell", app.myTVC, null);
        mycell = app.myTVC.MyCell;
        app.myTVC.MyCell = null;
    }
    else
    {
        mycell = (MyTableViewCell)cell;
    }
    // now we have a cell, set the display properties
    Element display = sectionElements[indexPath.Section][indexPath.Row];
    mycell.ElementName   = display.Name;
    mycell.ElementSymbol = display.Symbol;
    mycell.ElementNumber = display.Number;
    mycell.ElementFamily = display.Family;
    return mycell;
}
```

The finished table with custom cells is shown in Figure 6-9.

FIGURE 6-9

NAVIGATING WITH TABLES

Many iPhone OS applications use tables to navigate through hierarchical data structures, such as the iPod Artists list, which takes you to a list of Albums and then a list of Songs. The previous examples in this chapter have the `UITableView` as the window's only view. To use tables for navigation you need to introduce a new class — `UINavigationController` — which manages a collection of `UITableViews` as sub-views, showing and hiding them as required. Figure 6-10 shows two levels of table navigation leading to a static table being used as a "detail view."

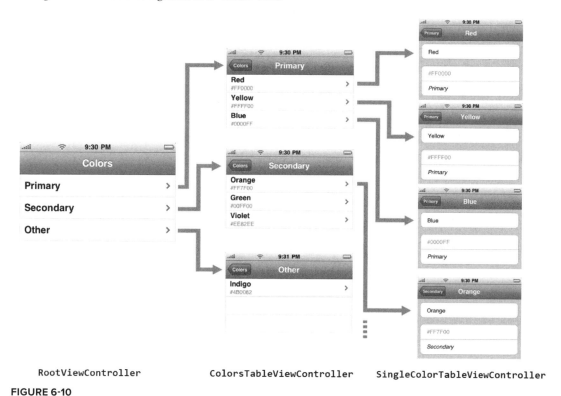

RootViewController   ColorsTableViewController   SingleColorTableViewController

FIGURE 6-10

Using UINavigationController

This example uses a small list to keep it simple — the seven colors from the earlier example in the chapter. You start with the list of three color groups, drill down into a subset of colors, and then show a "color detail" view.

To create an example table navigation create a new MonoDevelop "iPhone Navigation Application" called Tables05 (you can find it in the download for this chapter).

The new solution will already have some of the required classes included as shown in Figure 6-11.

`MainWindow.xib` already contains a `UINavigationController`, `UINavigationBar`, a class called `RootViewController`, and a `UINavigationItem`, as shown in Figure 6-12. None of these classes requires any change in Interface Builder — if you click the Navigation Controller, the designer shows the navigation bar along the top of the window and the content area with a message Loaded from "RootViewController" (as in Figure 6-12).

FIGURE 6-11

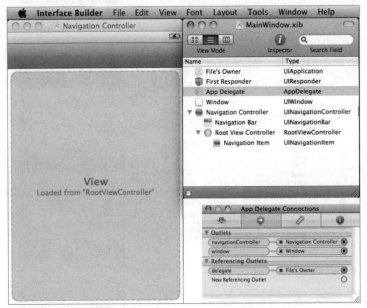

FIGURE 6-12

Figure 6-12 also shows if you click the App Delegate two outlets are already defined in the Connections Inspector: `window` and `navigationController`. These two objects are already referenced in `FinishedLaunching` and allow the window to reference the navigation controller and — if you start/debug the application now — display an empty table.

```
public override bool FinishedLaunching
            (UIApplication app, NSDictionary options)
{
    window.AddSubview (navigationController.View);
    window.MakeKeyAndVisible ();
    return true;
}
```

To get the first table view working you need to "finish" the `RootViewController` provided by the template. Nothing needs to be edited in Interface Builder — `RootViewController.xib` already contains a `UITableView` — but you need to provide the `UITableViewSource` implementation so it has some data to display. The code is shown in Listing 6-4, and should look very familiar. The only new code is `Title = "Colors";`, which appears in the navigation bar at the top of the screen.

LISTING 6-4: Tables05\RootViewController.xib.cs

```
partial class RootViewController : UITableViewController
{  // constructor required to create class
    public RootViewController (IntPtr handle) : base(handle) {}
    public override void ViewDidLoad ()
    {
        Title = "Colors";  // appears at top of screen
        colors = new List<MyColor>
        {
        new MyColor{Name="Red",Hex="#FF0000",Group="Primary"},
// etc...
        };
        groups = (from c in colors
            select c.Group).Distinct().ToList();
        this.TableView.Source = new DataSource (this, groups);
    }
    private List<MyColor> colors;
    private List<string> groups;
    class DataSource : UITableViewSource
    {
        RootViewController controller;
        List<string> rows;
        public DataSource (RootViewController controller, List<string> data)
        {
            this.controller = controller;
            rows = data;
        }
        public override int RowsInSection (UITableView tableview, int section)
        {
            return rows.Count;
        }
        public override UITableViewCell GetCell
            (UITableView tableView, MonoTouch.Foundation.NSIndexPath indexPath)
        {
            string cellIdentifier = "Cell";
            var cell = tableView.DequeueReusableCell (cellIdentifier);
            if (cell == null)
            {
              cell = new UITableViewCell
                        (UITableViewCellStyle.Default, cellIdentifier);
            }
            cell.TextLabel.Text = rows[indexPath.Row];
            return cell;
        }
        // TODO: Add RowSelected method after creating 2nd level
    }
}
```

The application will now show a list of color groups in a table, but notice there is a //TODO: place-holder where the RowSelected method should be. First you need to create the next level of the navigation hierarchy.

Implementing a Second Level of Navigation

In MonoDevelop choose to add a New File and select View Interface Definition with Controller to add `ColorsTableViewController`. Then double-click to open it in Interface Builder.

➤ Delete the `UIView` from the XIB.

➤ Drag a `UITableView` from the Objects Library into the XIB.

➤ Connect the `File's Owner` view outlet to the `UITableView`. Notice the `File's Owner` is already of type `ColorsTableViewController`.

Close Interface Builder and open `ColorsTableViewController.xib.cs` in MonoDevelop so you can complete the partial class that was created by parsing your Interface Builder XIB file. The complete class should look *very* similar to Listing 6-4, replacing the constructors and `ViewDidLoad` method with the constructors shown in Listing 6-5.

LISTING 6-5: Tables05\ColorsTableViewController.xib.cs

```
public partial class ColorsTableViewController : UITableViewController
{   // constructors:base reference XIB filename to load from
    public ColorsTableViewController () :
                    base ("ColorsTableViewController", null) {}
    public ColorsTableViewController (List<MyColor> data, string key) :
                    base ("ColorsTableViewController", null)
    {   // find the colors that match the group key
        colors = (from c in data
                  where c.Group == key
                  select c).ToList();
        this.TableView.Source = new DataSource (this, colors);
    }
    private List<MyColor> colors;
    // TODO: insert DataSource from Listing 6-4 (without RowSelected)
}
```

Now that you have a table to show, implement this `RowSelected` method in the `RootViewController` `.xib.cs` from Listing 6-4. When a row is selected you create an instance of the new `ColorsTableViewController` and pass it a reference to the data (`controller.colors`) and the value of the selected row (`rows[indexPath]`) so that it can display the correct subset of the data. It also sets the `Title` property, which is displayed in the navigation area of the table, and then calls `PushViewController`, which tells the `UINavigationController` to put that view on the "top of the stack" and display it.

```
// for Listing 6-4 RootViewController.xib.cs
public override void RowSelected
    (UITableView tableView, MonoTouch.Foundation.NSIndexPath indexPath)
{
    var colorsViewController = new ColorsTableViewController
                        (controller.colors, rows[indexPath.Row]);
    colorsViewController.Title = rows[indexPath.Row];
    controller.NavigationController.PushViewController
```

```
                                          (colorsViewController, true);
        tableView.DeselectRow(indexPath, true);
    }
```

 `DeselectRow()` *is called to remove the blue selection indicator from this table. If* `DeselectRow` *isn't called and the user returns to this table (using the Back functionality of the navigation controller), the row will still appear selected — not the expected behavior for iPhone OS applications.*

Running the application now will display a two-level hierarchy that you can easily navigate by touching the rows and the Back button provided by the navigation controller.

Creating Static Row Content

The final step in this example is a different kind of table — a "detail view" using table cells — for the third level of the hierarchy. Create another New File in MonoDevelop and select the View Interface Definition with Controller to add `ColorsTableViewController`. Then double-click to open it in Interface Builder. These will be the most involved Interface Builder steps in this chapter — a snapshot is shown in Figure 6-13 and the detailed instructions follow. The goal is to create a table and the cells it will use in a single XIB file to be wired up in a `GetCell` method using hardcoded references to the outlets you create.

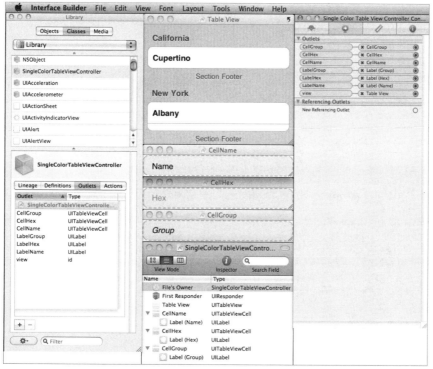

FIGURE 6-13

To create this table and its cells:

1. Delete the `UIView` from the XIB.

2. Drag a `UITableView` from the Objects Library into the XIB.

3. Click the table view and change its style to `Grouped` in the Attributes Inspector.

4. Drag three `UITableViewCell`s from the Objects Library into the XIB. Click each and give them a name (`CellGroup`, `CellHex`, and `Cellname`).

5. Open all three cells and drag a `UILabel` into each one. Apply some formatting (for example, italics or grey color) to each one to distinguish them.

6. Select the `SingleColorTableViewController` in the Classes Library and add the following outlets: `CellGroup`, `CellHex`, `Cellname`, `LabelGroup`, `LabelHex`, `LabelName`.

7. Select `File's Owner` in the XIB and in the Connections Inspector connect the cell and label outlets.

The code for this table is shown in Listing 6-6. It has the same structure as the previous `UITableViewControllers`; however, there is an important difference: Most of the `UITableViewSource` methods are hardcoded to reflect a specific layout of cells and data. The `NumberOfSections` and `RowsInSection` both return numbers to show a very specific design. `GetCell` is even more unusual — there is no object instantiation, and there are no `DequeueReusableCell` calls. Instead you reference the labels and cells directly from the XIB via the outlets. In previous examples you used `UITableView` to present a list of data where each cell uses the same layout to display a row of data. This code does the opposite: Each cell can have a totally different layout — they can be designed independently in Interface Builder and can display different pieces of data.

LISTING 6-6: Tables05\SingleColorTableViewController.xib.cs

```
public partial class SingleColorTableViewController : UITableViewController
{
    public SingleColorTableViewController() : base() {}
    public SingleColorTableViewController(MyColor data)
                        : base("SingleColorTableViewController", null)
    {  // loads from XIB via base, then sets DataSource
        this.TableView.Source = new DataSource(this, data);
        this.TableView.AllowsSelection = false;
    }
    class DataSource : UITableViewSource
    {
        public DataSource
                (SingleColorTableViewController controller, MyColor data)
        {
            this.controller = controller;
            row = data;
        }
        SingleColorTableViewController controller;
        MyColor row;
        public override int NumberOfSections (UITableView tableView)
        {
```

```
         return 2; // yes, hardcoding to reflect the layout we want
      }
      public override int RowsInSection (UITableView tableview, int section)
      { // more hardcoding to break the cells into sections
         if (section == 0)
            return 1;
         else
            return 2;
      }
      public override UITableViewCell GetCell
                        (UITableView tableView, NSIndexPath indexPath)
      { // even more hardcoding to layout correctly
         if (indexPath.Section == 0)
         {
            controller.LabelName.Text = row.Name;
            return controller.CellName;
         }
         else // Section == 1
            if (indexPath.Row == 0)
            {
               controller.LabelHex.Text = row.Hex;
               return controller.CellHex;
            }
            else
            {
               controller.LabelGroup.Text = row.Group;
               return controller.CellGroup;
            }
      }
   }
}
```

Now you can implement the final RowSelected method in the ColorsTableViewController.xib
.cs from Listing 6-5. When a row is selected, you create an instance of the "single color view,"
passing in the object to display (rows[indexPath.Row]) — all the work wiring up the objects properties to the UILabels is done in GetCell. The next line sets the Title, and then you push the view
(which displays it) and deselect the row.

```
// for Listing 6-5 ColorsViewController.xib.cs
public override void RowSelected
                  (UITableView tableView, NSIndexPath indexPath)
{
   var single = new SingleColorTableViewController (rows[indexPath.Row]);
   single.Title = rows[indexPath.Row].Name;
   controller.NavigationController.PushViewController (single, true);
   tableView.DeselectRow(indexPath, true);
}
```

Now you have a complete three-level navigation hierarchy (refer back to Figure 6-10) managed by a
UINagivationController. Using the built-in navigation controller provides a simple way to navigate back and forth between views, operating like a stack where new windows are *pushed* to the
top and when going back they are *popped* off. This example uses tables and RowSelected for every
navigation action. However, NavigationController.PushViewController could also be called
from within a UIButton.TouchDown event or other control depending on your requirements.

EDITING TABLE ROWS

Another of the `UITableView`'s features is the built-in editing: deleting cells, re-ordering cells, and providing a consistent user interface to add new rows. Each of these elements can be individually enabled with the implementation of methods on the `UITableViewSource` delegate class.

Once again you will start with the Colors list for this example. The code for Tables06 is in the download for this chapter.

Adding Swipe to Delete

The simplest editing function to implement is *swipe and delete*. There is no visual indicator on the table that any editing functionality is enabled, but if the user swipes across the row a Delete button appears. Touching the button immediately deletes the row. The following three methods are used by the `UITableViewSource` subclass to enable this functionality:

➤ `CanEditRow`: This method is called when the table is being rendered so that it can respond to "editing input" (such as a swipe). `indexPath` is a parameter, so the response can be changed for each row. However, for this example it is hardcoded `true`. Every row in the table will respond to the swipe gesture and display a Delete button.

➤ `CommitEditingStyle`: Called when "editing" takes place. Because only Delete is functional in this simple example, the code shows only how Delete works. First delete the data from the underlying data structure (`rows.RemoveAt` is called in this case) and then call `DeleteRows` on the table to remove the corresponding cell from the table.

➤ `TitleForDeleteConfirmation`: Optional customization of the text in the button.

```
public override int RowsInSection (UITableView tableview, int section)
{
    return rows.Count;
}
public override bool CanEditRow (UITableView tableView,
                      MonoTouch.Foundation.NSIndexPath indexPath)
{
    return true;
}
// Override to support editing the table view.
public override void CommitEditingStyle (UITableView tableView,
    UITableViewCellEditingStyle editingStyle, NSIndexPath indexPath)
{
    rows.RemoveAt(indexPath.Row);
    tableView.DeleteRows (
      new NSIndexPath[] { indexPath }, UITableViewRowAnimation.Fade);
}
public override string TitleForDeleteConfirmation
                  (UITableView tableView, NSIndexPath indexPath)
{ // OPTIONAL: Defaults to Delete
    return "Trash this";
}
```

`DeleteRows` takes an array of `indexPaths` so it knows which visual representations (cells) to animate out of the table; it also accepts a parameter to choose how to animate the deletion. The animation options are listed in Table 6-3 and apply to row insertion, which is covered later in the chapter.

TABLE 6-3: UITableViewRowAnimation

ANIMATION	BEHAVIOR (FOR INSERTION AND DELETION)
None	No animation
Fade	Cell fades in or out
Right	Slides in from or out to the right
Left	Slides in from or out to the left
Top	Slides down from or up toward the top
Bottom	Slides up from or down to the bottom

Enabling Edit "Mode"

The UITableView also provides a more obvious editing UI, which is enabled with the SetEditing method. This mode uses a red stop-sign switch in each row, which causes the Delete button to appear. Most applications provide an Edit button to show these switches, and UINavigationController makes it easy to add a button as shown in the following code. ViewDidLoad creates two buttons with slightly different appearances, and Clicked toggles the Editing mode and displays the appropriate button.

```
public override void ViewDidLoad ()
{
   // ... initialization code here ...
   editButton = new UIBarButtonItem
               ("Edit", UIBarButtonItemStyle.Bordered, Clicked);
   doneButton = new UIBarButtonItem
               ("Done", UIBarButtonItemStyle.Done, Clicked);
   NavigationItem.RightBarButtonItem = editButton;
   TableView.Source = new DataSource (this, colors);
}
void Clicked (object sender, EventArgs ea)
{
   if (TableView.Editing)
   { // toggle off, show edit
     TableView.SetEditing (false, true);
     NavigationItem.RightBarButtonItem = editButton;
   }
   else
   { // toggle on, show done
     TableView.SetEditing (true, true);
     NavigationItem.RightBarButtonItem = doneButton;
    }
 }
```

After SetEditing is called the table will normally display *both* delete and move visual cues. CanMoveRow is called for each row to determine whether it can be moved — if you *don't* want to support re-ordering (as shown in Figure 6-14), return false.

```
class DataSource : UITableViewSource
   // ... other methods here ...
```

```
public override bool CanMoveRow
            (UITableView tableView, NSIndexPath indexPath)
{
    return false; // can't move (yet)
}
```

FIGURE 6-14

Re-Ordering Cells

Some tables do need re-ordering (such as the Stocks app), which requires the following two methods:

➤   CanMoveRow: Returns true for each row, causing the move indicator to display and the row to be moveable.

➤   MoveRow: Gets passed two parameters for the old and new location of the row, making it easy to update the underlying data. The UITableView isn't updated because it already knows about the movement and has reflected it in the user interface (in contrast to the DeleteRows method, which is called on the table from CommitEditingStyle).

```
public override bool CanMoveRow
            (UITableView tableView, NSIndexPath indexPath)
{   // all rows are moveable, always return true
    return true;
}
public override void MoveRow (UITableView tableView,
    NSIndexPath sourceIndexPath, NSIndexPath destinationIndexPath)
{
    var tempRow = rows[sourceIndexPath.Row];
    rows.Remove(tempRow);              // remove it from here
    int targetRowIndex = destinationIndexPath.Row;
    rows.Insert(targetRowIndex, tempRow); // and put it here
}
```

Figure 6-15 shows a row in the process of being moved.

FIGURE 6-15

Moving rows in the simulator can be a bit tricky — the Move indicator (three horizontal bars) is designed to be activated by a finger and the tiny single-pixel mouse pointer sometimes has trouble "grabbing" it. It is much easier to test on a device.

Creating an Insert Icon

The final editing feature supported by `UITableView` is adding a new row. The Contacts application uses the green plus (+) icon to add new items, so you'll put a similar option at the end of your table. Implementing the (+) row requires changes to almost every method in the `UITableViewSource` because in addition to displaying your data you must also keep track of the new non-data-related cell. Each method now contains an `if-else` clause that checks whether it is being called for a data display row or for the (+) row. The changes are described here and shown in Listing 6-7:

➤   `GetCell`: Creates two different cell styles — `Subtitle` for the data and `Value2` for the "add new" row.

➤   `EditingStyleForRow`: Sets the `Delete` style on all the data rows and the `Insert` style on the last row.

➤   `RowSelected`: If the data rows are touched, an alert is shown. However, if the (+) row is touched, `AddNewRows` is called. In a real application this might instead open a new view for data entry, but for this example you will just insert some hardcoded data.

➤   `CommitEditingStyle`: Called when an editing action is triggered — either touching the Delete button or the (+) icon. The method parameters contain which action has been requested on a specific row.

LISTING 6-7: Tables06\RootViewController.xib.cs

```
public override UITableViewCell GetCell
              (UITableView tableVicw, NSIndexPath indexPath)
{
   UITableViewCell cell = null;
   if (indexPath.Row < rows.Count)
   {  // normal data
      cell = tableView.DequeueReusableCell ("Cell");
      if (cell == null)
      {
         cell = new UITableViewCell
                (UITableViewCellStyle.Subtitle, "Cell");
      }
      cell.TextLabel.Text = rows[indexPath.Row].Name;
      cell.DetailTextLabel.Text = rows[indexPath.Row].Hex;
   }
   else
   {  // the '(+) add new cell
      cell = tableView.DequeueReusableCell ("Cell2");
      if (cell == null)
```

continues

LISTING 6-7 *(continued)*

```
        {
          cell = new UITableViewCell
                  (UITableViewCellStyle.Value2, "Cell2");
        }
        cell.TextLabel.Text = "add new color";
      }
      return cell;
  }
  public override UITableViewCellEditingStyle EditingStyleForRow
      (UITableView tableView, NSIndexPath indexPath)
  {
    if (indexPath.Row < rows.Count)          // data row
      return UITableViewCellEditingStyle.Delete;
    else                                     // (+) 'add new' row
      return UITableViewCellEditingStyle.Insert;
  }
  public override void RowSelected
                       (UITableView tableView, NSIndexPath indexPath)
  {
    if (indexPath.Row < rows.Count)
    {   // a data row was touched
      displayText = rows[indexPath.Row].Name;
      ShowAlert ("RowSelected","You selected "+displayText);
    }
    else
    { // the (+) 'add new' row was touched
      AddNewRows(tableView, indexPath); // or show data-entry view
    }
    tableView.DeselectRow(indexPath,true);
  }
  public override void CommitEditingStyle (UITableView tableView,
      UITableViewCellEditingStyle editingStyle, NSIndexPath indexPath)
  {
    if (editingStyle == UITableViewCellEditingStyle.Delete)
    { // the delete button was touched on this row
      rows.RemoveAt(indexPath.Row);
      tableView.DeleteRows
          (new NSIndexPath[] {indexPath}, UITableViewRowAnimation.Fade);
    }
    else if (editingStyle == UITableViewCellEditingStyle.Insert)
    { // the insert icon (+) was touched on this row
      AddNewRows (tableView, indexPath);
    }
  }
```

Figure 6-16 shows a table with the final cell rendered with an insert (+) icon. In your code the `RowSelected` method might display a new data-entry view rather than directly insert data as the example does.

Adding New Rows

The `InsertRows` method allows you to add multiple rows to a table and take advantage of the built-in animation to update the table's appearance. You might need to add multiple rows if you are creating an editable table such as the Contacts application's user interface (the animation occurs between View and Edit Contact as shown in Figure 6-17) or if your underlying datasource is being updated externally (such as new e-mails or tweets appearing at the top of the Inbox or a Twitter client).

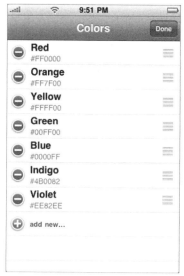

FIGURE 6-16   **FIGURE 6-17**

The `AddNewRows` method shown below demonstrates how to use `InsertRows`. The most important aspects of this method are:

➤ Calling `BeginUpdates` and `EndUpdates` around your modifications to the table and the data.

➤ Creating and passing `NSIndexPath` instances that inform the table which rows are to be inserted. Here you are adding three rows to table starting at the index of the row that was touched, hence the array containing the passed-in `indexPath` and two additional `NSIndexPaths` offset by 1 and 2.

➤ Ensuring that you add the same number of rows to the data as you pass to `InsertRows`, so that when the table animates the appearance of these rows they are already present in the collection and available for `GetCell` to access. In this case you add the objects to the end of the collection using `rows.Add()`, but if you had specified a different location using the `NSIndexPath` array, you should ensure the data is inserted into exactly those positions as well.

➤ Choosing the type of animation to use.

```
void AddNewRows (UITableView tableView, NSIndexPath indexPath)
{
    tableView.BeginUpdates();            // data for rows being inserted
    rows.Add(new MyColor{Name="Puce",    Group="Other", Hex="#CC8899"});
    rows.Add(new MyColor{Name="Avocado", Group="Other", Hex="#98A148"});
    rows.Add(new MyColor{Name="Azure",   Group="Other", Hex="#F0FFFF"});
    NSIndexPath indexPath1, i2indexPath2;// location of rows being inserted
    indexPath1 = NSIndexPath.FromRowSection(indexPath.Row + 1, 0);
    indexPath2 = NSIndexPath.FromRowSection(indexPath.Row + 2, 0);
```

```
    controller.TableView.InsertRows(
            new NSIndexPath[] {indexPath, indexPath1, indexPath2},
            UITableViewRowAnimation.Fade);
    tableView.EndUpdates();
}
```

This example showing the insertion of three hardcoded objects is not very realistic. Most applications would use the insert icon to show a *new view* for data entry, update the table's data, and call `ReloadData`when navigating back to this view. You should also use `ReloadData` instead of `InsertRows` when a large proportion of the table's data is changing or if you do not want to show the animation.

The editing commands you've implemented in this chapter ensure the underlying data structure (for example, the `rows List<>` in this case) is modified as the user interacts with the application. However, you must remember to provide a mechanism to save/persist the changes as well. You might choose to persist changes in the `MoveRow` and `CommitEditingStyle` methods or else keep them in memory and save at a later point in the application's life cycle (such as `WillTerminate`).

ADDING A SEARCH BAR TO A TABLE

Many tables in the built-in applications include a search bar to make navigating long lists easier, including the Mail Inbox and all of the tabs in the iPod application. Touching in the search input of these tables "greys out" the underlying rows and shows the keyboard. Typing in the search box produces only matching rows in a new `UITableView` displayed on top of the original data.

The search bar example is based on the Elements data used in the Tables03 example from earlier in the chapter. You can add the search functionality with the Search Bar and Search Display Controller from the Interface Builder Library, which is included as example Tables07 in the code download. Figure 6-18 shows how to drag the controller onto your table. Be sure to choose the Search Bar and Search Display Controller class (and not the regular Search Bar).

FIGURE 6-18

Notice that the object should be dragged onto the `UITableView` itself (and not elsewhere in the view); doing so causes Interface Builder to wire up a number of outlets automatically, including the

`UISearchDisplayController`. Figure 6-19 shows all the automatically generated outlets for the App Delegate, Table View Controller, and Search Display Controller. The only two outlets that need to be defined by you are circled: `MyTableView` and `MySearchDisplayController`.

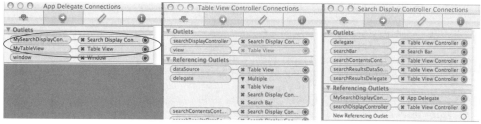

FIGURE 6-19

Enabling the Search Bar

After you have dragged the control onto the table view, you must add the following three things to enable the search bar:

➤ A collection to hold the results matching the search criteria. This collection will be updated every time the search criteria change.

➤ A `UITableViewSource` subclass to be used by the `UITableView` created by the search controller. This class will be responsible for displaying the results rows.

➤ A `UISearchDisplayDelegate` subclass that can respond to events from the `UISearchBarController`. You must use the methods on this class to respond to search events, such as updating the results collection so that the `UITableView` can display them.

First, add a `FilteredElements` property to the `AppDelegate` that will be used to store the search results. This will be populated by the search controller and then displayed by the search controller's table view.

```
List<Element> FilteredElements { get; set; }
```

You must then implement a `UITableViewSource` that will use the `FilteredElements` collection as its data, as shown in Listing 6-8. To access the collection you can pass the `AppDelegate` into the class and reference the `FilteredElements` property.

LISTING 6-8: UITableViewSource to support searching (Tables07\Main.cs)

```
class MySearchResultsSource : UITableViewSource
{
    AppDelegate _appd;
    public MySearchResultsSource (AppDelegate appd)
    {
```

continues

LISTING 6-8 *(continued)*

```
    _appd = appd; // to access FilteredElements for display
}
public override int RowsInSection(UITableView tableview, int section)
{
    return _appd.FilteredElements.Count;
}
public override UITableViewCell GetCell
    (UITableView tableView, NSIndexPath indexPath)
{
    string kCellIdentifier = "mycell";
    UITableViewCell cell = tableView.DequeueReusableCell(kCellIdentifier);
    if (cell == null)
    {  // No re-usable cell found, create a new one
        cell = new UITableViewCell
            (UITableViewCellStyle.Default, kCellIdentifier);
    }
    Element display = _appd.FilteredElements[indexPath.Row];
    cell.TextLabel.Text = display.Name;
    return cell;
}
public override void RowSelected
    (UITableView tableView, NSIndexPath indexPath)
{
    Element display = _appd.FilteredElements[indexPath.Row];
    ShowAlert ("RowSelected", "You selected " + display.Name);
    tableView.DeselectRow(indexPath,true);
}
public void ShowAlert (string title, string message)
{
    using (var alert = new UIAlertView(title,message,null,"OK",null))
    { alert.Show(); }
}
}
```

The next step is to create the UISearchDisplayDelegate that responds to input in the search bar and sets the FilteredElements property, as shown in Listing 6-9. You must override the ShouldReloadForSearchString() method to perform the actual search against the source data (Elements collection) and populate the FilteredElements search results. The method must then return true, which instructs the search controller to call ReloadData() on the UITableView for you, picking up the updated FilteredElements collection and displaying the search results.

LISTING 6-9: Custom UISearchDisplayDelegate class (Tables07\Main.cs)

```
class MySearchDisplayDelegate : UISearchDisplayDelegate
{
    AppDelegate _appd;
    public MySearchDisplayDelegate(AppDelegate appd)
    {
```

```
        _appd = appd;
    }
    public override bool ShouldReloadForSearchString
      (UISearchDisplayController controller, string forSearchString)
    {
    // updated the filtered list on the AppDelegate
    _appd.FilteredElements = _appd.Elements.Where(
        r => r.Name.ToLower().StartsWith(forSearchString.ToLower())
    ).ToList();
    // sort the filtered list
    _appd.FilteredElements.Sort(delegate(Element e1, Element e2)
        {
            return e1.Name.CompareTo(e2.Name);
        });
    return true; // tells the controller to call ReloadData()
    }
```

Finally, add the following lines to `FinishedLaunching` to wire up these new classes (and the existing `MyTableViewSource` from the Tables03 example).

```
MyTableView.Source  = new MyTableViewSource(Elements); // existing class
MySearchDisplayController.Delegate
      = new MySearchDisplayDelegate(this); // pass reference to AppDelegate
MySearchDisplayController.SearchResultsSource
      = new MySearchResultsSource(this);   // pass reference to AppDelegate
```

Figure 6-20 shows the example with the original table, an empty search, and with some filtering applied.

FIGURE 6-20

Customizing Search Appearance

There are a number of properties on the `UISearchBar` that you can use to customize the appearance and behavior of the search. These properties include:

➤ `Placeholder`: The "watermark" grey text that appears when the search box is empty.

➤ `Prompt`: Instructional text that appears above the search box when it is in use.

➤ `Text`: Allows you to pre-set the search text to a specific value.

➤ `KeyboardType`: Used to specify which keyboard appears to type the search text (for example, `EmailAddress`, `NumberPad`, or `PhonePad` if you are searching for specific data types).

➤ `AutocorrectionType`: Whether or not the search input text should be autocorrected.

➤ `AutocapitalizationType`: Whether or not the search input text should be autocapitalized. Regardless of this setting you should consider making your search code case-insensitive, as most users will not expect searches to fail because of different capitalization.

➤ `BarStyle`: The color of the search bar (`Default` or `Black`).

The following is an example of how to set these properties in `FinishedLaunching`; in this case the code sets the watermark text when the search input is empty:

```
MySearchDisplayController.SearchBar.Placeholder = "Begin typing element...";
```

You can set the other properties as required to reflect the type of data your code is searching.

SUMMARY

This chapter has covered one of the key user interface elements in the iPhone OS: the table. Tables are used throughout the operating system and built-in applications. This chapter covered the essentials of using a `UITableView` and related classes to:

➤ Display a simple list of data in a table

➤ Change the appearance of table cells using built-in designs or creating a custom layout in Interface Builder

➤ Use grouping and indexing to make a table easier to read and use

➤ Implement `DequeueReusableCell` to improve performance

➤ Add the ability to edit a table's contents

➤ Implement search functionality in a table

Along the way you used MonoTouch's special `UITableViewSource` class instead of Apple's `UITableViewDataSource` and `UITableViewDelegate` and used the `UINavigationController` to create a hierarchical menu user interface.

7

Mapping

WHAT'S IN THIS CHAPTER?

➤   Understanding CoreLocation and MapKit

➤   Using Location Services

➤   Adding maps and geocoding to your application

The display of location-specific information including maps, addresses, and points of interest is a natural feature for mobile devices such as the iPhone and iPod Touch. Outside of some niche markets it has never had great success on the desktop, primarily because the desktop PC is often stuck in a single location. Mobile devices, on the other hand, are naturally going to be carried around wherever the user goes; and as GPS technology has become smaller and cheaper it has found its way into the cell phone market.

When the iPhone first appeared its Maps application (shown in Figure 7-1) was one of the key selling features — a perfect example of the iPhone's multitouch user interface. No other mobile device had previously made navigating maps as elegant as the pinch-to-zoom, swipe-to-pan operation of Maps on the iPhone's large screen. This chapter shows you how to incorporate that same user experience into your own MonoTouch applications.

FIGURE 7-1

MAP BASICS

Before you start looking at the mapping capabilities of iPhone OS and MonoTouch, here are some mapping terms that are used throughout this chapter:

➤ **Latitude:** The Y value of a location (90 to –90 degrees north to south).

➤ **Longitude:** The X value of a location (180 to –180 degrees east to west).

➤ **Heading:** Compass direction expressed in degrees (0–360).

➤ **GPS:** Global Positioning System. A collection of satellites using radio signals to enable earth-based receivers to determine their location with a high degree of accuracy.

➤ **Geocode:** Resolving a search string (for example, an address, business, or landmark name) to a geographic location (latitude/longitude).

➤ **Reverse geocode:** Finding the "human readable" address for a specific latitude/longitude location.

The iPhone SDK provides two frameworks to enable mapping-related functionality within your application:

➤ **MapKit:** Provides a control to display map imagery, allows you to add markers (pins) and reverse geocode a location.

➤ **CoreLocation:** Uses whatever capabilities the device supports to determine the user's location and heading (if possible).

Used together these enable you to add mapping and location-based services to iPhone applications, and MonoTouch provides easy access to all the features they provide.

Introducing MapKit

The `MapKit` framework provides a visual representation of geographic information using Google Maps images and data. Users can access the same road, satellite, and hybrid maps that they are familiar with from web-based mapping applications; and you can look up the closest "real" address for a given latitude/longitude location. The map is navigated with the same drag and pinch gestures used across the iPhone OS without any additional coding.

The `MapKit` framework is exposed in MonoTouch via the `MonoTouch.MapKit` namespace.

Introducing CoreLocation

`CoreLocation` works on a number of iPhone OS devices using a variety of technologies to determine position, and using the built-in compass of newer devices provides the heading the device is pointing to. Using this information you can determine where users are and what direction their device is facing, and by monitoring changes to that data how fast they are moving and how far they have traveled.

The `CoreLocation` framework is exposed in MonoTouch via the `MonoTouch.CoreLocation` namespace and deals with two types of information:

➤ Location

➤ Heading

Location

The location of a device is expressed in latitude and longitude, and is typically determined by a GPS device. Consumer GPS devices were previously limited to bulky car navigation systems but are now small enough to fit inside a cell phone!

Devices without GPS capability (for example, the original iPhone and the iPod Touch range) can still calculate location information using a combination of cell tower triangulation and Wi-Fi network lookups. This means a large proportion of iPhone OS devices have *some* sort of Location Services capability that you can program against.

Because `CoreLocation` uses these different technologies to determine the device's position, the availability and accuracy of the data can vary widely. Devices with GPS capability can determine a very accurate latitude/longitude position under the right conditions (usually outdoors with a clear view of the sky). When no GPS is available and cell-tower or wireless network information is used, the data is much less accurate. Each different data source offers differing levels of accuracy: from a few feet to a few kilometers. Location-enabled applications should consider the accuracy of the data they receive to ensure they don't present misleading information. `CoreLocation` provides an accuracy estimate with each reading — the "margin of error" of the location information in meters — which should be taken into account in your code.

Sometimes `CoreLocation` will be unable to provide data — this could be due to a number of reasons:

➤ GPS reading could not be taken (user is inside or otherwise out of range of GPS signals).

➤ Other location providers cannot be accessed (for example, cell towers or Wi-Fi network info).

➤ The user has prevented `CoreLocation` from supplying data to your application. To prevent applications from accessing a user's location without their knowledge, the operating system will ask for their permission before sending the data to your application. The warning in Figure 7-2 will be displayed the first few times your application is used; after that the operating system remembers the user's preference.

FIGURE 7-2

➤ The user has disabled Location Services. For privacy or battery-saving reasons Location Services can be turned off in Settings. You should always check whether Location Services are available and for any error condition (including the user denying access) before using location data in your code. Use the boolean `LocationServicesEnabled` property of the

`CLLocationManager` class to determine if Location Services are available. If they have been turned off and your application attempts to access location data, the message in Figure 7-3 will be displayed to prompt the user to turn Location Services back on.

FIGURE 7-3

Application code should gracefully handle situations where no location information is available. If your application *cannot operate* without Location Services you can add an entry in your `Info.plist` to prevent it from installing or running unless the correct capabilities are present on the device. Table 7-1 describes the entries you can include to control this behavior. Refer to Chapter 8 for details on how to configure `Info.plist`.

TABLE 7-1: UIRequiredDeviceCapabilities Key in Info.plist

KEY	DESCRIPTION
location-services	The device must support Location Services and they must be enabled in Settings before the application will run.
gps	The device must specifically support GPS hardware before the application will install or run.
magnometer	The device must specifically support compass hardware before the application will install or run.

iPhone Application Programming Guide

Heading

Only newer iPhone OS devices (for example, the 3GS) have a built-in compass to provide heading information. You should use the `HeadingAvailable` property of the `CLLocationManager` class to determine whether you can access heading data to ensure your application displays relevant information on devices without a compass.

 The simulator has a number of limitations compared to testing with a real device. When testing Location Services in the simulator the location will always be 37.331689, –122.030731, which is Apple's headquarters in Cupertino, California. The heading will always return 103.27 degrees.

This means some mapping and location features (such as tracking a user's movement to measure speed or distance) can only be tested on a device.

USING CORELOCATION

The main `CoreLocation` classes are shown in Figure 7-4.

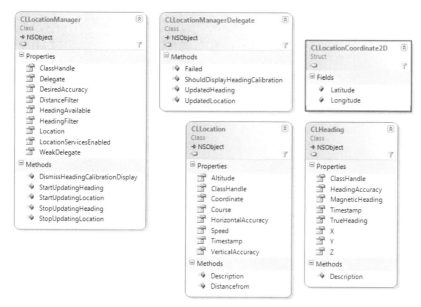

FIGURE 7-4

`CLLocationManager` is the class responsible for interfacing with the hardware and a subclass of `CLLocationManagerDelegate` is required to receive "events" from it.

Delegate classes and methods in the iPhone SDK perform a similar function to event handlers in .NET. The delegate subclass implements certain methods and then gets assigned to a framework class that is responsible for interfacing with the hardware. As data becomes available from the hardware the delegate methods are called on your subclass and your application can respond.

It takes some time (possibly many seconds) to retrieve location information so using a delegate class allows your `FinishedLaunching` "startup code" to call `StartUpdatingLocation()` and then continue to run, knowing that when the data becomes available your delegate method will be called for you to process it.

Determining Device Location

The first example in this chapter uses `CLLocationManager` with custom delegate classes to build an application that displays latitude, longitude, heading, and the nearest address on the screen. `CoreLocation` does not have any visual classes so to start using it you need to create some regular buttons and labels using Interface Builder. Create a new MonoTouch iPhone application called

Mapping01 in MonoDevelop and drag the controls onto your window, as shown in Figure 7-5 (make sure you link the outlets to the correct controls).

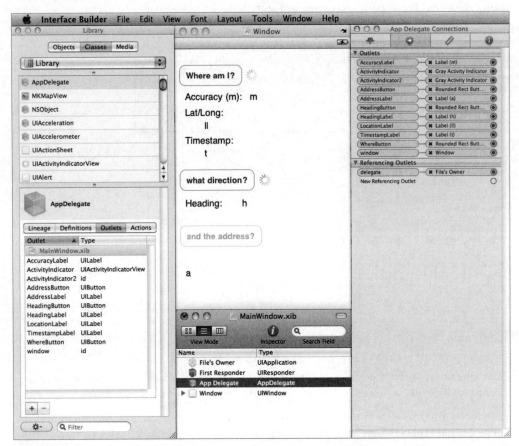

FIGURE 7-5

Once the `MainWindow.xib` has been constructed in Interface Builder you need to add the code in Listing 7-1 to `Main.cs`.

The custom subclass `MyLocationManagerDelegate` is shown first. It receives notifications of updated data through the overridden `UpdatedLocation` and `UpdatedHeading` methods and displays the data using `UILabel` controls. Each method then tells the `CLLocationManager` not to send any more notifications using the `StopUpdatingLocation()` and `StopUpdatingHeading()` methods.

The `Failed` method checks the `NSError.Code` against the `CLError` enumeration to decide what action to take. If the value is `Denied` then you should always stop the location manager from attempting further updates, however other errors can be ignored as the operating system will keep trying to obtain a reading.

LISTING 7-1: CLLocationManagerDelegate subclass (Mapping01\Main.cs)

```
private class MyLocationManagerDelegate: CLLocationManagerDelegate
{
    private AppDelegate app;
    public MyLocationManagerDelegate (AppDelegate appd):base()
    {
        app = appd;
    }
    public override void UpdatedLocation (CLLocationManager locationMgr,
                    CLLocation newLocation, CLLocation oldLocation)
    {
        app.LocationLabel.Text = newLocation.Coordinate.Latitude
                + "," + newLocation.Coordinate.Longitude;
        app.AccuracyLabel.Text = newLocation.HorizontalAccuracy.ToString();
        app.TimestampLabel.Text = newLocation.Timestamp.ToString();
        locationMgr.StopUpdatingLocation(); // stop updating after the first time
        app.ActivityIndicator.StopAnimating();
        app.AddressButton.Hidden = false;
    }
    public override void UpdatedHeading (CLLocationManager locationMgr, CLHeading h)
    {
        app.HeadingLabel.Text = h.TrueHeading.ToString();
        locationMgr.StopUpdatingHeading();
        app.ActivityIndicator2.StopAnimating();
    }
    public override void Failed (CLLocationManager locationMgr, NSError e)
    {

            switch (e.Code)
            {
            case (int)CLError.LocationUnknown:
            app.LocationLabel.Text = "Failed to get location, still trying";
            break;
            case (int)CLError.Denied:
            locationMgr.StopUpdatingHeading ();
            app.ActivityIndicator.StopAnimating ();
            app.LocationLabel.Text = "Access to location denied. Stop trying.";
            break;
            case (int)CLError.Network:
            app.LocationLabel.Text = "Failed to get location, still trying";
            break;
            case (int)CLError.HeadingFailure:
            app.LocationLabel.Text =
                    "Heading could not be determined (magnetic interference)";
            break;
            }
    }
}
```

This delegate class doesn't work without being assigned to a CLLocationManager and calling the StartUpdatingLocation() and StartUpdatingHeading() methods. Listing 7-2 shows how to do that — add the delegate code above where the //TODO: comment indicates.

LISTING 7-2: Showing device location (Mapping01\Main.cs)

```
public partial class AppDelegate : UIApplicationDelegate
{    public override void OnActivated (UIApplication application) {}
    CLLocationManager locationMgr;
    public override bool FinishedLaunching (UIApplication a, NSDictionary o)
    {
        locationMgr= new CLLocationManager();
        locationMgr.Delegate = new MyLocationManagerDelegate(this);

        WhereButton.TouchUpInside += delegate
        { // latitude,longitude
            if (locationMgr.LocationServicesEnabled)
            {
                ActivityIndicator.Hidden = false;
                ActivityIndicator.StartAnimating();
                locationMgr.StartUpdatingLocation();
            }
            else ShowAlert ("Not Supported","LocationServicesEnabled==false");
        };
        HeadingButton.TouchUpInside += delegate
        { // compass direction
            if (locationMgr.HeadingAvailable)
            {
                ActivityIndicator2.Hidden = false;
                ActivityIndicator2.StartAnimating();
                locationMgr.StartUpdatingHeading();
            }
            else ShowAlert ("Not Supported","HeadingAvailable==false");
        };
        window.MakeKeyAndVisible ();
        return true;
    }
    private void ShowAlert (string title, string message)
    {
        using (var alert = new UIAlertView(title,
                message, null, "OK", null))
        { alert.Show(); }
    }
    //TODO: Delegate implementation go here
}
```

The `WhereButton.TouchUpInside` delegate first checks whether Location Services are turned on
and then calls `StartUpdatingLocation`. `HeadingButton.TouchUpInside` does a similar job for the
compass. They both require that the `CLLocationManager` variable is declared at the `AppDelegate`
level. When the device has calculated that information the `Updated` methods are called on the delegate class, which then displays it on the screen.

Running the application should display the location and heading after a few seconds (the simulator
will say it is in Cupertino!).

Reverse Geocoding

Having determined the latitude and longitude using `CoreLocation`, the "real" address can be determined using `MapKit`'s reverse geocoding functionality. The required classes are shown in Figure 7-6.

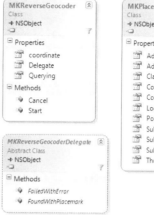
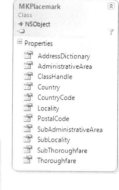

The following changes to `Main.cs` are required (as well as ensuring there is an `AddressLabel` in Interface Builder). First, the `MapKit` namespace must be added:

```
using MonoTouch.MapKit;
```

Then an instance variable declared in the `AppDelegate` class:

```
MKReverseGeocoder geocoder;
```

FIGURE 7-6

Add the following code in the `FinishedLaunching` method:

```
AddressButton.TouchUpInside += delegate
{ // reverse geocode
  geocoder = new MKReverseGeocoder (locMgr.Location.Coordinate);
  geocoder.Delegate = new MyGeocoderDelegate (this);
  geocoder.Start();
};
```

And declare this delegate subclass within `AppDelegate`:

```
private class MyGeocoderDelegate : MKReverseGeocoderDelegate
{
  AppDelegate app;
  public MyGeocoderDelegate (AppDelegate appd)
  {
    app = appd;
  }
  public override void FoundWithPlacemark
                  (MKReverseGeocoder geocoder, MKPlacemark place)
  {
    app.AddressLabel.Text = place.SubThoroughfare + " "
        + place.Thoroughfare+ " " + place.Locality + " "
        + place.AdministrativeArea + " " + place.Country;
  }
  public override void FailedWithError (MKReverseGeocoder geocoder, NSError e)
  {
    app.AddressLabel.Text = "Geocode error: " + e.LocalizedDescription;
  }
}
```

Mapping01\Main.cs

When the `AddressButton` is touched it calls the `MKReverseGeocoder`'s `Start()` method, which starts a web service request to reverse geocode the latitude/longitude. The web service is managed by the framework and uses Google Maps data to determine the address. When the web service returns it calls the `FoundWithPlacemark` delegate method, which displays the information on-screen.

The completed application is shown in Figure 7-7, displaying the hardcoded location information that the simulator always returns.

Tracking Device Movement

`CoreLocation` doesn't just provide a single location reading — it can be configured to continuously provide your application with a stream of location updates as the device moves around. You can affect the frequency of these updates by setting the following properties on `CLLocationManager`:

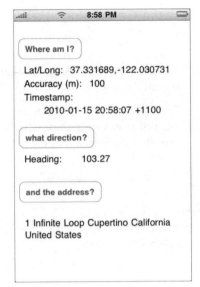

FIGURE 7-7

➤ `DistanceFilter`: Number of meters that the device must move before an updated location event is generated. The default value is to be notified of all events.

➤ `HeadingFilter`: Number of degrees the device needs to turn before an updated compass reading is generated. The default value is to be notified of all events.

➤ `DesiredAccuracy`: The level of accuracy of location data that your application requires. If you are simply trying to determine the user's city or country, then `ThreeKilometers` should be sufficient; if you are trying to determine a street address you need the `Best` available. The default value is to require the best available accuracy, otherwise use the following `enum` to choose a value:

```
enum CLLocationAccuracy
{
    Best = -1
,   NearestTenMeters = 10
,   HundredMeters  = 100
,   Kilometer = 1000
,   ThreeKilometers = 3000
}
```

 `MyLocationManagerDelegate` and `MyGeocoderDelegate` are implemented as "nested types" within the `AppDelegate` class for good reason. Because the buttons and labels created in Interface Builder have references automatically generated by MonoTouch in `MainWindow.xib.designer.cs` as private *properties, classes defined outside the `AppDelegate` cannot access them. Nested classes can access the private properties of their containing class (for example, `app.LocationLabel` and `app.Addresslabel`), which is why delegate subclasses in MonoTouch are usually declared inside the class that uses them.*

To see how this works create a new MonoTouch iPhone application Mapping02 and create a window like the one shown in Figure 7-8 in Interface Builder.

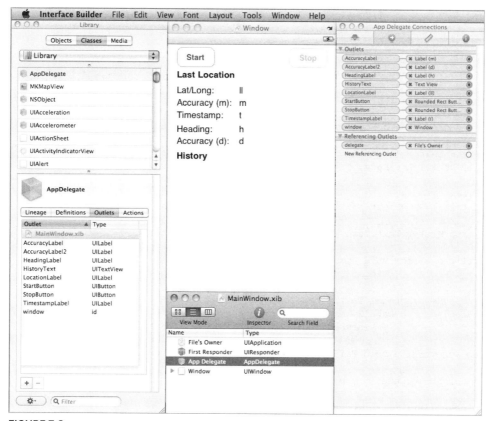

FIGURE 7-8

Like the previous example, a delegate subclass is required to handle the location data as it is recorded. In this case we have changed the `UpdatedLocation` method to *append* each reading to a `UITextView` so it will continually update on the screen as the device is moved. Rounding has been applied for easy reading on the limited screen space of iPhone devices. The new delegate class is shown in Listing 7-3.

LISTING 7-3: Tracking position with CLLocationManagerDelegate (Mapping02\Main.cs)

```
private class MyLocationManagerDelegate: CLLocationManagerDelegate
{
    private AppDelegate app;
    int updateCount = 0;
    public LocationManagerDelegate(AppDelegate appd):base() {
        app = appd;
    }
    public override void UpdatedLocation (CLLocationManager locManager,
                    CLLocation newLocation, CLLocation oldLocation)
```

continues

LISTING 7-3 *(continued)*

```
{
    var latLong = Math.Round(newLocation.Coordinate.Latitude,4)
        + "," + Math.Round(newLocation.Coordinate.Longitude,4);
    app.LocationLabel.Text = latLong;
    app.AccuracyLabel.Text = newLocation.HorizontalAccuracy.ToString();
    app.TimestampLabel.Text = newLocation.Timestamp.ToString();
    var dist = 0.0;
    if (oldLocation != null)
    {
        dist = Math.Round(newLocation.Distancefrom(oldLocation),1);
    }
    var text = "Location: " + latLong + Environment.NewLine;
    text += "Accuracy: " + newLocation.HorizontalAccuracy
                             + Environment.NewLine;
    text += dist + "m from last reading" + Environment.NewLine;
    text += newLocation.Timestamp + Environment.NewLine;
    text += "_____"+ Environment.NewLine;
    app.HistoryText.Text += text;
}
public override void UpdatedHeading
            (CLLocationManager locManager, CLHeading newHeading)
{
    app.HeadingLabel.Text = newHeading.TrueHeading.ToString();
    app.AccuracyLabel2.Text = Math.Round
                    (newHeading.HeadingAccuracy,2).ToString();
}
public override void Failed (CLLocationManager locManager, NSError e)
{
    switch (e.Code)
    {
    case (int)CLError.LocationUnknown:
        app.LocationLabel.Text = "Failed to get location, still trying";
        break;
    case (int)CLError.Denied:
        locationMgr.StopUpdatingHeading ();
        app.ActivityIndicator.StopAnimating ();
        app.LocationLabel.Text = "Access to location denied. Stop trying.";
        break;
    case (int)CLError.Network:
        app.LocationLabel.Text = "Failed to get location, still trying";
        break;
    case (int)CLError.HeadingFailure:
        app.LocationLabel.Text =
            "Heading could not be determined (magnetic interference)";
        break;
    }
}
}
```

The code for the `AppDelegate` class is shown in Listing 7-4; in addition to the button `TouchUpInside` handlers that can be used to start and stop location updates there are additional lines setting the `DesiredAccuracy`, `DistanceFilter`, and `HeadingFilter` properties.

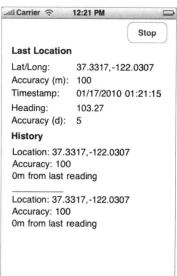

LISTING 7-4: Start and stop location updates (Mapping02\Main.cs)

```
public partial class AppDelegate : UIApplicationDelegate
{   public override void OnActivated (UIApplication application) {}
    CLLocationManager locationMgr;
    public override bool FinishedLaunching (UIApplication a, NSDictionary o)
    {
        StartButton.TouchUpInside += delegate
        {
            locationMgr.StartUpdatingLocation();
            if (locationMgr.HeadingAvailable)
            {
                locationMgr.StartUpdatingHeading();
            }
            StopButton.Hidden = false; StartButton.Hidden = true;
        };
        StopButton.TouchUpInside += delegate
        {
            locationMgr.StopUpdatingLocation();
            if (locMgr.HeadingAvailable)
            {
                locationMgr.StopUpdatingHeading();
            }
            StopButton.Hidden = true; StartButton.Hidden = false;
        };
        locationMgr = new CLLocationManager();
        locationMgr.DesiredAccuracy = 10;
        locationMgr.DistanceFilter = 10;
        locationMgr.HeadingFilter = 1;
        locationMgr.Delegate = new MyLocationManagerDelegate(this);
        window.MakeKeyAndVisible ();
        return true;
    }
    // Delegate goes here
}
```

The output in the simulator is shown in Figure 7-9. Because the simulator only returns the same location data, this example works much better on a real device. Try changing the DesiredAccuracy and DistanceFilter values to see how the frequency and accuracy of the data is affected.

This example highlights one of the problems with using location data — the varying accuracy of readings and how your application should interpret them. Notice the code that reports distance using newLocation.Distancefrom(oldLocation), which calculates and displays the distance in meters between this location and the last recorded location. Intuitively that might sound like an easy way to track the distance that a user has traveled (for example, how far they have walked or driven while your application is running).

FIGURE 7-9

However it is not quite that easy! When this example is tested on a GPS-enabled device the first few readings might look like those shown in Table 7-2 even though the *device is perfectly stationary.*

TABLE 7-2: Mapping02 Example Output

LOCATION (ROUNDED)	ACCURACY	DISTANCE FROM LAST READING (ROUNDED)
−33.8898,151.249	2917	0
−33.8909,151.251	2283	227.2
−33.8907,151.2486	162	223.9
−33.8911,151.2488	76	43.9
−33.8911,151.2497	17	7.4

What's happening? The code is receiving multiple notifications with varying levels of accuracy, which affects the reported location. As the accuracy improves, the location is (likely to be) closer to the actual location of the device. Even though the device hasn't moved, the reported location *is* moving. Unless your code has some intelligence to deal with varying accuracy, it might try to tell the user in this situation that he has traveled 502.4 meters when he hasn't actually moved an inch!

Strategies to address this issue include:

➤ Setting the distance and accuracy filter to the level of detail that you need.

➤ Evaluating the accuracy of location data to see whether it meets your requirements: If you need high levels of accuracy you might ignore inaccurate readings.

➤ Comparing location data to recent historical reports to determine whether they fall within a reasonable range (in particular for the elapsed time period).

➤ Communicating the margin of error to the user (such as the blue "halo" of uncertainty displayed around the Current Location marker in the built-in Maps application).

➤ Checking the `Timestamp` on location reports: Often the first location returned will be cached from a previous `CoreLocation` request. This might cause an obvious "bug" if the user has just turned on his phone after stepping off a plane, and the cached location data is from another city or country!

USING MAPKIT

The `MapKit` framework consists of the `MKMapView` visual control and a number of supporting classes to manipulate and annotate the map's display. Figure 7-10 shows the most commonly used `MapKit` classes.

FIGURE 7-10

Because the data used by MapKit *(both the imagery and the reverse geocoding service) is provided by Google, the use of that data in your application must adhere to certain terms. Apple's developer web site contains the following message:*

Important: *The* MapKit *framework uses Google services to provide map data. Use of this class and the associated interfaces binds you to the Google Maps/ Google Earth API terms of service. You can find these terms of service at* http://code.google.com/apis/maps/iphone/terms.html.

Showing a Map

The `MKMapView` control provides a sophisticated user interface to present mapping data on the device with no additional coding. Once the `MKMapView` control has been placed on a window in Interface Builder your application immediately has the ability to display, pan, and zoom Google Maps imagery and show the current location of the device (using `CoreLocation` of course).

The only caveat is that because the map images are downloaded from the Internet, using `MKMapView` requires a network connection (either cellular data or a wireless network). The control itself does cache images so when the device is offline it will show map data for the most recently viewed location, however new map data can't be downloaded. This is of particular interest to applications on the iPod Touch, which are less likely to be constantly networked.

`MKMapView` has a number of properties that control how the user can interact with it.

➤ `UserInteractionEnabled`: When set to `false` the map does not respond to any user input; it cannot be scrolled or zoomed and pins (including the current user location) will not show their callout when touched. This property overrides `ZoomEnabled` and `ScrollEnabled`.

➤ `ZoomEnabled`: When `false` the user cannot pinch to zoom in or out of the map, although scrolling and pin callouts will still work.

➤ `ScrollEnabled`: When `false` the user cannot scroll around the map (that is, cannot change the center point from whatever is set in code). Zooming and pin callouts will still work.

➤ `ShowUserLocation`: This is a simple property that causes the map to display a blue dot (and "accuracy halo") if the device location can be determined. The map will also be centered and zoomed to that location. It can be set via a checkbox in Interface Builder or programmatically set on the `MKMapView` instance.

➤ `MapType`: This is an enumeration that defines the types of map imagery available for display; the same three options that Internet users have become familiar with using Google Maps:

  ➤ `Standard`: Road map

  ➤ `Satellite`: Aerial photographic images

  ➤ `Hybrid`: Aerial images overlaid with roads and place names

The following `MapKit` example demonstrates these properties. Create a new MonoTouch application Mapping03 and use Interface Builder to drag an `MKMapView` and `UISegmentedControl` onto the window as shown in Figure 7-11.

Then add the code from Listing 7-5 to `Main.cs` to wire up the map type selection and set the properties just described.

LISTING 7-5: Simple map display (Mapping03\Main.cs)

```
public partial class AppDelegate : UIApplicationDelegate
{  public override void OnActivated (UIApplication application) {}
   public override bool FinishedLaunching (UIApplication a, NSDictionary o)
   {
```

```
        MapType.ValueChanged += delegate
        {
            if (MapType.SelectedSegment == 0)
                Map.MapType = MKMapType.Standard;
            else if (MapType.SelectedSegment == 1)
                Map.MapType = MKMapType.Satellite;
            else if (MapType.SelectedSegment == 2)
                Map.MapType = MKMapType.Hybrid;
        };
        Map.ShowsUserLocation = true;
        Map.MapType = MonoTouch.MapKit.MKMapType.Standard; // Hybrid | Satellite
        Map.Region = new MKCoordinateRegion (
                        new CLLocationCoordinate2D(37.331689, -122.030731)
                        , new MKCoordinateSpan(0.5,0.5));
        Map.ZoomEnabled = true;            // false=cannot zoom
        Map.ScrollEnabled = true;          // false=cannot scroll
        Map.UserInteractionEnabled = true; // false=cannot even click on pin
        window.MakeKeyAndVisible ();
        return true;
    }
}
```

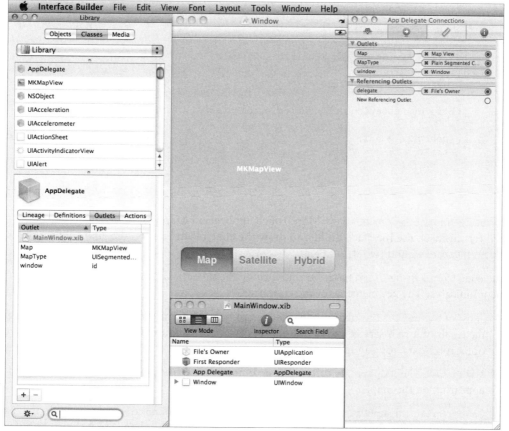

FIGURE 7-11

Annotating the Map

Adding pin markers to the map requires creating and adding `MKAnnotations` to the `MKMapView`. When using the `MapKit` framework from Objective-C, `MKAnnotation` is a *protocol* — a similar concept to interfaces in C# except that protocols can have optional members. In MonoTouch, protocols like `MKAnnotation` are modeled as abstract classes to be implemented in your application. In the case of `MKAnnotation` three properties are required: `Coordinate`, `Title`, and `Subtitle`. The subclass in Listing 7-6 adds private backing variables and a constructor to set them; however, other implementations could vary.

LISTING 7-6: MKAnnotation subclass (Mapping04\Main.cs)

```
public class MyAnnotation : MKAnnotation
{
    private CLLocationCoordinate2D coordinate;
    private string title, subtitle;
    public override CLLocationCoordinate2D Coordinate
    {
        get { return coordinate; }
    }
    public override string Title
    {
        get { return title; }
    }
    public override string Subtitle
    {
        get { return subtitle; }
    }
    public MyAnnotation (CLLocationCoordinate2D l, string t, string s)
    {
        coordinate = l;
        title = t;
        subtitle = s;
    }
}
```

To try out `MyAnnotation` create a new MonoTouch application Mapping04 (which has been updated for this use), use Interface Builder to draw the controls in Figure 7-12, and connect the outlets for the `MKMapView` and two `UIButtons`.

Add the code from Listing 7-7 to `Main.cs` and include the `MyAnnotation` class where the `//TODO:` comment indicates. The key elements of the code are:

➤ A list of `MyAnnotation` objects is hardcoded to be used in the application. This list could be the result of a web-service call, a custom set of data in your application, or any other source of location data you can find.

➤ `AddButton.TouchUpInside` calls `Map.AddAnnotationObject()`, which results in the pin appearing on the map.

➤ `CenterButton.TouchUpInside` calls `Map.SetCenterCoordinate()`, which moves the map to show the pin in the center. The second parameter causes the change to be animated; if set to `false` the map just re-draws at the new location.

➤ `Map.GetViewForAnnotation` allows the pin and associated callout to be customized before appearing on the map. Notice how this delegate is *assigned* with an equals sign rather than *attached* with plus-equals like the button delegates. This is an important distinction: `GetViewForAnnotation` is a property of the `MKMapView` class and *not* an event.

➤ Two `UserLocation` properties are customized, changing the text that appears when you touch the blue Current Location marker.

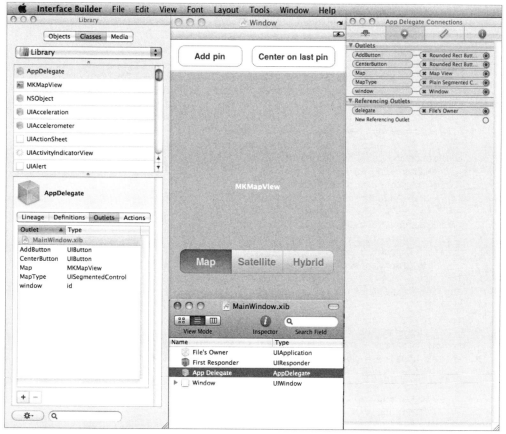

FIGURE 7-12

LISTING 7-7: Annotating the map (Mapping04\Main.cs)

```
public partial class AppDelegate : UIApplicationDelegate
{
    // This method is required in iPhoneOS 3.0
    public override void OnActivated (UIApplication application) {}
    List<MyAnnotation> pins = new List<MyAnnotation>();
    public override bool FinishedLaunching (UIApplication a, NSDictionary o)
    {
```

continues

LISTING 7-7 *(continued)*

```
        MapType.ValueChanged += delegate
        {
            if (MapType.SelectedSegment == 0)
                Map.MapType = MKMapType.Standard;
            else if (MapType.SelectedSegment == 1)
                Map.MapType = MKMapType.Satellite;
            else if (MapType.SelectedSegment == 2)
                Map.MapType = MKMapType.Hybrid;
        };
        int pinCount=0;
        // initialize Pins collection
        pins.Add(new MyAnnotation(new CLLocationCoordinate2D(37.2, -122.4)
                             , "Annotation #1", "Red pin"));
        pins.Add(new MyAnnotation(new CLLocationCoordinate2D(37.6, -122.2)
                             , "Annotation #2", "Red pin"));
        pins.Add(new MyAnnotation(new CLLocationCoordinate2D(37.4, -122.0)
                             , "Annotation #3", "Red pin"));
        AddButton.TouchUpInside += delegate
        { // Add a pin
          if (pinCount < pins.Count)
              Map.AddAnnotationObject(pins[pinCount++]);
        };
        CenterButton.TouchUpInside += delegate
        { // navigate to pin location
            if (pinCount > 0)
                Map.SetCenterCoordinate(pins[pinCount-1].Coordinate, true);
        };
        Map.GetViewForAnnotation = delegate
                            (MKMapView mapView, NSObject annotation)
        {
            if (annotation is MKUserLocation) return null;      // line 1
            var mapAnnotation = (MyAnnotation)annotation;        // line 2
            var pinView = new MKPinAnnotationView(mapAnnotation,"mypin");  // line 3
            pinView.AnimatesDrop = true;                         // line 4
            pinView.CanShowCallout = true;
            //TODO: add callouts here later
            //TODO: add pin color customisation here later
            return pinView;                                      // line 8
        };
        Map.Region = new KMCoordinateRegion (
                new CLLocationCoordinate2D (37.331689, -122.0307311)
               , new MKCoordinateSpan (0.5, .05));
        Map.UserLocation.Title = "You are here";
        Map.UserLocation.Subtitle = "Location of your device";
        window.MakeKeyAndVisible ();
        return true;
    }
    //TODO: MyAnnotation class goes here (Listing 7-6)
}
```

The annotation (or callout) is added by the call to `Map.AddAnnotationObject()`. `Map .GetViewForAnnotation` usually gets called soon after — it is executed every time an annotation *becomes visible* on the map in order for the relevant `View` object to be fetched so that the annotation can be placed within it. Here are some important features of the `GetViewForAnnotation` method to review:

➤ Line 1 `returns` immediately if the `annotation` parameter is of type `MKUserLocation`. This is because the method is called for *every* annotation added to the map, including the Current Location marker, which you do not want to customize.

➤ Line 2 casts the `annotation` parameter to a subclass of `MKAnnotation`. This is important because the type of the parameter is `NSObject`, which does not allow you to access any of the `MKAnnotation` properties required to customize the pin.

➤ Line 3 creates a new instance of `MKPinAnnotationView` passing the `MyAnnotation` class to provide the callout text and location information. The second parameter `"mypin"` is for re-using objects to save memory, which is discussed in more detail later in the chapter.

➤ `AnimatesDrop` determines whether the pin "drops" from the top of the screen onto the map, or just appears in place.

➤ `CanShowCallout` determines whether a callout appears when the pin is touched. If this is `false` the callout won't appear, even if it has been created.

➤ Line 8 returns `MKPinAnnotationView` to be added to the `MKMapView`.

The finished application in Figure 7-13 shows an annotation with its callout displayed.

FIGURE 7-13

Objective-C doesn't have the same event *concept that .NET does, which is why the iPhone SDK uses the delegate class pattern to provide a mechanism to "call back" into your code. The delegate pattern has been used a number of times in this chapter for* `CoreLocation` *functionality.*

Early versions of MonoTouch also required `MKMapKit` *to use a subclass of* `MKMapViewDelegate` *to handle methods like* `GetViewForAnnotation` *and* `RegionDidChange`; *however, this pattern is unfamiliar to C# programmers. The MonoTouch team is gradually making the Objective-C APIs more .NET-like by exposing .NET events and properties in place of the delegate classes.*

The result is the `GetViewForAnnotation` *delegate in this example — much easier to use because no additional classes are required. The* `MKMapView .Delegate = MKMapViewDelegate` *subclass approach still works, but offers no advantage over the neater C# syntax.*

Over time it is likely that other areas of the iPhone SDK that use delegates will be similarly "improved" in MonoTouch by the addition of C# events.

Zoom Level

Setting the `Region` in the previous code uses the `MKCoordinateSpan` struct and is equivalent to setting the "zoom level." The units passed to `MKCoordinateSpan` are *degrees of latitude and longitude* — around the equator a degree of latitude or longitude is approximately 111 kilometers/70 miles. As you approach the poles, degrees of longitude converge and the distance between them diminishes while degrees of latitude remain about the same distance apart. You needn't calculate exactly the correct aspect ratio for the screen because the map control will automatically attempt to accommodate the span you requested and match it to the closest available "actual" zoom level. As an example, the code in Listing 7-5 uses `MKCoordinateSpan(0.5,0.5)`; however, querying `Map.Region.Span.LatitudeDelta` and `LongitudeDelta` after the map is drawn shows the actual values were `0.88447,0.87890`. That's approximately 95 km/61 miles of visible terrain, which is pretty close to what you see on the screen.

Looking at it another way, the popular web-based mapping tools typically treat their "most zoomed out" display as level 1 and *halve* the size of the viewport for each level of zoom. Table 7-3 shows a rough comparison of those levels to degrees that you can pass to `MKCoordinateSpan` — notice how level 13 is very close to the map's resolution of (0.5, 0.5) as described earlier.

TABLE 7-3: Rough Comparison to Web-based Mapping Zoom Levels

ZOOM LEVEL	DEGREES	ZOOM LEVEL	DEGREES
1	360 (world)	10	0.70313
2	180	11	0.35156 (city)
3	90	12	0.17578
4	45 (country)	13	0.08789
5	22.5	14	0.04395
6	11.25	15	0.02197 (suburb)
7	5.625 (state)	16	0.01099
8	2.8125	17	0.00549
9	1.40625	18	0.00275 (street)

Figure 7-14 shows the map using these parameters (180, 180), (10, 10), (0.5, 0.5), (0.02, 0.02), and (0.00275, 0.00275).

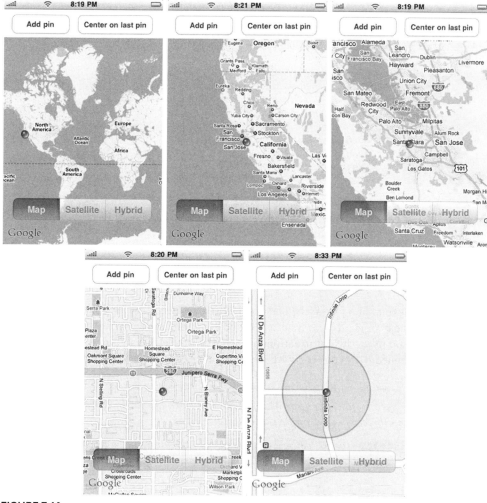

FIGURE 7-14

You can use the preceding table to select an appropriate zoom level to display a single point, or if you have a group of locations you can calculate an appropriate Span. Replace the CenterButton .TouchUpInside delegate with the following to calculate an appropriate Span that includes all current Annotations placed on the map:

```
// Centering on a group of locations
CenterButton.TouchUpInside += delegate
{  // expects at least one Annotation
   var userWasVisible = Map.ShowsUserLocation;
   Map.ShowsUserLocation = false; // ignoring the blue blip
   // start with the widest possible viewport
   var tl = new CLLocationCoordinate2D (-90,180); // top left
   var br = new CLLocationCoordinate2D (90,-180); // bottom right
   foreach (var an in Map.Annotations)
   {  // narrow the viewport bit-by-bit
```

```
        tl.Longitude = Math.Min(tl.Longitude, an.Coordinate.Longitude);
        tl.Latitude = Math.Max(tl.Latitude, an.Coordinate.Latitude);
        br.Longitude = Math.Max(br.Longitude, an.Coordinate.Longitude);
        br.Latitude = Math.Min(br.Latitude, an.Coordinate.Latitude);
    }
    var center = new CLLocationCoordinate2D
    { // divide the range by two to get the center
        Latitude = tl.Latitude - (tl.Latitude - br.Latitude) * 0.5
      , Longitude = tl.Longitude + (br.Longitude - tl.Longitude) * 0.5
    };
    var span = new MKCoordinateSpan
    { // calculate the span, with 20% margin so pins aren't on the edge
        LatitudeDelta = Math.Abs(tl.Latitude - br.Latitude) * 1.2
      , LongitudeDelta = Math.Abs(br.Longitude - tl.Longitude) * 1.2
    };
    var region = new MKCoordinateRegion { Center = center, Span = span};
    region = Map.RegionThatFits (region); // adjusts zoom level too
    Map.SetRegion (region, true);        // animated transition
    Map.ShowsUserLocation = userWasVisible;
};
```

Mapping04a\Main.cs

The math is fairly self-explanatory — at the end you have calculated a center-point and rectangle bounded by the outermost `Annotations` (plus a 20% buffer so the pins aren't obscured). The `RegionThatFits` method takes this information and adjusts it to return a `Region` that fits the maps view, which is then supplied to `SetRegion` with the parameter to animate the changed view.

The algorithm used to find the appropriate zoom level and bounding box was inspired by the Objective-C example on this site:

`http://codisllc.com/blog/zoom-mkmapview-to-fit-annotations`

Functional Annotations

The default pin callout is not very functional — in the Maps application there is an icon and a disclosure button on either side of the callout text. Add the code in Listing 7-8 where the Listing 7-7 says `//TODO:` (don't forget to also include a `wrox.png` image in your MonoTouch solution and set its `Build Action` to `Content`) to improve the callout's appearance and functionality. The image file and completed code is in the chapter download folder Mapping05.

Available for download on Wrox.com

LISTING 7-8: Setting accessory views (Mapping05\Main.cs)

```
// Left callout image
UIImage img = UIImage.FromFile("wrox.png");
UIImageView imgView = new UIImageView();
imgView.Image = img;
pinView.LeftCalloutAccessoryView = imgView;
// Right callout button
```

```
UIButton rightCallout = UIButton.FromType(UIButtonType.DetailDisclosure);
rightCallout.Frame = new System.Drawing.RectangleF(250,8f,25f,25f);
rightCallout.TouchUpInside += delegate
{
   NSUrl url = new NSUrl("http://wrox.com/");
   UIApplication.SharedApplication.OpenUrl(url);
};
pinView.RightCalloutAccessoryView = rightCallout;
```

The new callout is shown in Figure 7-15. Clicking the disclosure button opens Safari and navigates to the Wrox web site!

FIGURE 7-15

In the `rightCallout` declaration from Listing 7-8 a delegate was explicitly created and attached to the `TouchUpInside` method to make it functional. There is also an event `CalloutAccessoryControlTapped` on `MKMapView` that can provide similar functionality with a single event that is called when any annotation on the map is touched.

To test the `CalloutAccessoryControlTapped` event, change the `LeftCalloutAccessoryView` in Listing 7-8 to a `UIButton` instead of a `UIImageView`:

Available for
download on
Wrox.com

```
// Left callout image
UIButton leftCallout = UIButton.FromType(UIButton.InfoLight);
pinView.LeftCalloutAccessoryView = leftCallout;
```

and add this event handler to the `MKMapView` instance:

```
Map.AccessoryControlTapped += delegate
        (object sender, MKMapViewAccessoryTappedEventArgs e)
{
   var tapped = e.View.Annotation as MyAnnotation;
   using (var alert = new UIAlertView (tapped.Title,
            tapped.Subtitle + " clicked", null, "OK", null))
   {
      alert.Show();
   }
}
```

Mapping05\Main.cs

The results are shown in Figure 7-16 — rather than adding a `TouchUpInside` handler to every pin you can centralize behavior in this single method. The only restriction on the use of `CalloutAccessoryControlTapped` is that the view you specify must be a subclass of `UIControl` — which does *not* include `UIImage`.

FIGURE 7-16

Colorful Annotations

The color of the pin associated with the MKPinViewAnnotation can also be customized with three small updates to the code. First, add a Color property to your MKAnnotation subclass with the following code:

```
public class MyAnnotation : MKAnnotation
{
    private CLLocationCoordinate2D color;
    public override MKPinAnnotationColor Color
    {
        get { return color; }
    }
    public MyAnnotation (CLLocationCoordinate2D l, string t, string s,
                         MKPinAnnotationColor c)
    {
        coordinate = l;
        title = t;
        subtitle = s;
        color = c;
    }
}
```

Then initialize the example pins with a color value — currently only three colors are supported in the MKPinAnnotationColor enumeration: Purple, Green and Red.

```
pins.Add(new MyAnnotation(new CLLocationCoordinate2D(37.2, -122.4)
        , "Annotation #1", "Purple pin", MKPinAnnotationColor.Purple));
pins.Add(new MyAnnotation(new CLLocationCoordinate2D(37.6, -122.2)
        , "Annotation #2", "Green pin", MKPinAnnotationColor.Green));
pins.Add(new MyAnnotation(new CLLocationCoordinate2D(37.4, -122.0)
        , "Annotation #3", "Red pin", MKPinAnnotationColor.Red));
```

Finally, set the color in the GetViewForAnnotation delegate and the code should now display three different colored pins on the map.

```
pinView.PinColor = mapAnnotation.Color;
```

Mapping05\Main.cs

Better Performing Annotations

The preceding example adds only three annotations to the map so it is unlikely to cause memory pressure or performance issues. However, some applications will use dozens or hundreds of annotations and in those cases you don't want to create that many views if only a small portion appear on-screen at any one time.

MapKit provides for this by calling Map.GetViewForAnnotation only when an annotation is required to appear on-screen. If your data contains a large number of annotations you can safely add them all to the MKMapView — it only attempts to render them as required (that is, their Coordinate falls within the current MKMapRegion). As the map is panned and zoomed some annotations will go out of view as others come into view — MapKit also provides a facility to re-use MKPinAnnotationViews (in much the same way as table cells are re-used by UITableView in Chapter 6; and similar to virtualized list controls in Windows Presentation Foundation).

The updated GetViewForAnnotation code in Listing 7-9 shows how this works.

LISTING 7-9: Reusable annotations in GetViewForAnnotation (Mapping05\Main.cs)

```
Map.GetViewForAnnotation = delegate
                        (MKMapView mapView, NSObject annotation)
{
    if (annotation is MKUserLocation) return null;      // line 1
    MyAnnotation ma - annotation as MyAnnotation;       // line 2
    var pinView=mapView.DequeueReusableAnnotation("mypin");// line 3
    if (pinView == null)                                // line 4
    { // new object with same identifier, passing in the annotation
        pinView = new MKPinAnnotationView(ma, "mypin"); // line 5
    }
    else
    { // re-use MKPinAnnotationView with 'mypin' identifier
        pinView.Annotation = annotation;                // line 7
    }
    pinView.AnimatesDrop = true;                        // line 8
    pinView.CanShowCallout = true;
    pinView.PinColor = ma.Color;
    return pinView;
};
```

Changes from the previous implementation of GetViewForAnnotation are:

➤ Line 3 shows DequeueReusableAnnotation requesting an existing MKPinAnnotationView from the MKMapViews unused object queue, using the identifier "mypin".

➤ Line 5 shows the creation of a new object if null was returned (meaning there was no object to reuse). The reuseidentifier "mypin" is passed to the new object: This is how the MKMapView distinguishes different types of views in the unused object queue.

➤ Line 7 shows the annotation to be displayed being assigned to a re-used View object.

➤ Lines 8, 9, and 10 set properties on the View before it is returned to the map for display.

To conform to Apple's Human Interface Guidelines most mapping applications use the standard MKPinAnnotationView to place markers, which means you can use a single re-use identifier to retrieve those objects from the queue. If you create your own subclasses of MKAnnotationView, you should use different reuseidentifier strings for each different type of view, otherwise you might get unexpected results. The code would check some property of the annotation to see what view is required and then call DequeueReusableAnnotation with the correct reuseidentifier before trying to create the object.

Using the Geocoding Feature

Geocoding functionality is not directly provided by any of the built-in frameworks but is a very useful feature of location-aware applications. One of the great advantages of MonoTouch is the vast array of existing .NET code and samples that you can bring to the iPhone OS. The simple `Geocoder` class in Listing 7-9 uses a number of familiar .NET libraries such as `System.Xml`, `System.IO`, and `System.Net`.

To implement the geocoding sample, create a new MonoTouch iPhone application Mapping06 and add the code from Listing 7-10 to a new C# file `Geocoder.cs`.

LISTING 7-10: Geocoding an address with the Google Maps API (Mapping06\Geocoder.cs)

```
/// <summary>
/// Documentation for the service
/// http://code.google.com/apis/maps/documentation/geocoding/
/// </summary>
public class Geocoder
{
    /// <summary>
    /// Sign up for a Google Maps key to pass in
    /// http://code.google.com/apis/maps/signup.html
    /// </summary>
    public Geocoder (string key)
    {
        _GoogleMapsKey = key;
    }
    private string _GoogleMapsKey = "";
    private string xmlString = "";
    public bool LocateGoogle(string query, out CLLocationCoordinate2D result)
    {
        string url = "http://maps.google.com/maps/geo?q={0}&output=xml&key="
                    + _GoogleMapsKey;
        url = String.Format(url, query);
        XmlNode coords = null;
        result = new CLLocationCoordinate2D (0,0);
        try
        {
            xmlString = GetUrl(url);
            XmlDocument xd = new XmlDocument();
            xd.LoadXml(xmlString);
            XmlNamespaceManager xnm = new XmlNamespaceManager(xd.NameTable);
            coords = xd.GetElementsByTagName("coordinates")[0];
        }
        catch { }
        string gl = "";
        if (coords != null)
        {
            string[] coordinateArray = coords.InnerText.Split(',');
            if (coordinateArray.Length >= 2)
            {
                result = new CLLocationCoordinate2D
                        (Convert.ToDouble(coordinateArray[1].ToString())
                        , Convert.ToDouble(coordinateArray[0].ToString()));
                return true;
            }
```

```
            return false;
        }
        private static string GetUrl(string url)
        {
            string result = string.Empty;
            System.Net.WebClient Client = new WebClient();
            using (Stream strm = Client.OpenRead(url))
            {
                StreamReader sr = new StreamReader(strm);
                result = sr.ReadToEnd();
            }
            return result;
        }
    }
```

To build the user interface add a `UISearchBar` and `MKMapView` to `MainWindow.xib` using Interface Builder (see Figure 7-17) and create the necessary outlets.

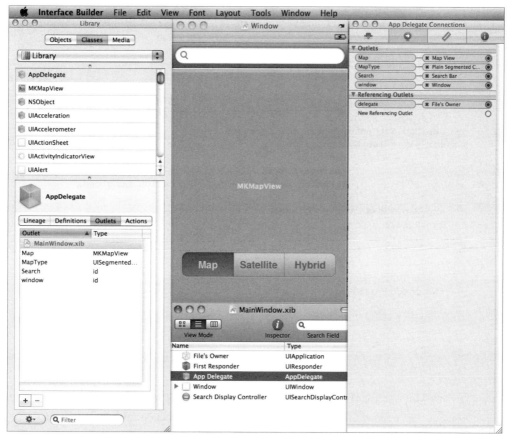

FIGURE 7-17

Like CLCoreLocationManager the search bar requires a delegate subclass to handle events that it generates. Listing 7-11 is not a complete implementation of the UISearchBarDelegate but it implements the necessary behavior to enable searching the map. It uses the custom Geocoder (Listing 7-10) to retrieve a latitude/longitude from Google's web service, and uses the MyAnnotation subclass from Listing 7-6 to add the location to the map. Once the Geocoder class returns a location you center the map on that location and add an annotation to mark the spot.

LISTING 7-11: Basic UISearchBarDelegate (Mapping06\Main.cs)

```
public class MySearchBarDelegate : UISearchBarDelegate
{
    private AppDelegate app;
    private MyAnnotation lastResult;
    public MySearchBarDelegate (AppDelegate a)
    {
        app = a;
    }
    public override void SearchButtonClicked (UISearchBar searchBar)
    {
        var g = new Geocoder(GoogleMapsKey);
        CLLocationCoordinate2D location;
        if (g.LocateGoogle(searchBar.Text, out location))
        {
            if (lastResult != null)
                app.Map.RemoveAnnotation(lastResult);
            app.Map.SetCenterCoordinate(location,true);
            var pin = new MyAnnotation(
                            location
                          , searchBar.Text
                          , location.Latitude + "," + location.Longitude
                          );
            app.Map.AddAnnotationObject(pin);
            lastResult = pin;
        }
        else
        {
            using (var alert = new UIAlertView("Not found",
            "No match found for " + searchBar.Text, null, "OK", null))
            {
                alert.Show();
            }
        }
    }
}
```

Type Listing 7-12 into Main.cs. Note that you must sign up for a Google Maps Key at http://code.google.com/apis/maps/signup.html to use this class. When you have received your Key, paste it into the relevant spot in the code.

LISTING 7-12: Geocoding (Mapping06\Main.cs)

```csharp
public partial class AppDelegate : UIApplicationDelegate
{
    // This method is required in iPhoneOS 3.0
    public override void OnActivated (UIApplication application) {}
    // http://code.google.com/apis/maps/signup.html
    public static string GoogleMapsKey  = "YOU_MUST_OBTAIN_A_KEY_TO_PASTE_HERE";
    public override bool FinishedLaunching (UIApplication a, NSDictionary o)
    {
        MapType.ValueChanged += delegate
        {
            if (MapType.SelectedSegment == 0)
                Map.MapType = MKMapType.Standard;
            else if (MapType.SelectedSegment == 1)
                Map.MapType = MKMapType.Satellite;
            else if (MapType.SelectedSegment == 2)
                Map.MapType = MKMapType.Hybrid;
        };
        Map.MapType = MonoTouch.MapKit.MKMapType.Standard; // Hybrid | Satellite
        Map.Region = new MKCoordinateRegion(
                            new CLLocationCoordinate2D(37.331689, -122.030731)
                            , new MKCoordinateSpan(0.5,0.5));
        Map.GetViewForAnnotation = delegate
                (MKMapView mapView, NSObject annotation)
        {
            if (annotation is MKUserLocation) return null;
            var mapAnnotation = (MyAnnotation)annotation;
            var pinView = mapView.DequeueReusableAnnotation ("search");
            if (pinView == null)
            {  // create new view
                pinView = new MKPinAnnotationView(mapAnnotation, "search");
            }
            else
            {  // re-use view, with new annotation
                annView.Annotation = annotation;
            }
            pinView.AnimatesDrop = true;
            pinView.PinColor = MKPinAnnotationColor.Red;
            pinView.CanShowCallout = true;
            return annView;
        };
        Search.Delegate = new MySearchBarDelegate(this);
        window.MakeKeyAndVisible ();
        return true;
    }
    // MKAnnotation from Listing 7-6
    // SearchBarDelegate from Listing 7-11...
}
```

Figure 7-18 shows the `Geocoder` at work. It should successfully locate any search string that you would otherwise type into Google Maps.

SUMMARY

In this chapter you have learned about the two different frameworks that provide location-based services and mapping functionality to iPhone OS devices: `CoreLocation` and `MapKit`.

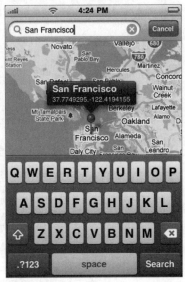

FIGURE 7-18

You have built samples to:

➤ Determine the current location of a device, the heading it is facing, and the nearest address to that location.

➤ Track movement with different levels of accuracy.

➤ Display a map and change the imagery from road to hybrid or satellite photography.

➤ Add pin markers to the map.

➤ Customize the pin markers to display informational text, images, and buttons and add functionality to those buttons.

➤ Use standard .NET Framework classes to build a simple geocoder using a Google web service and `MKMapKit`.

In the process you learned about some of the unique issues around MonoTouch's implementation of `MapKit` (such as the addition of .NET events to the `MKMapKit` class) and also the strategies for dealing with varying accuracy of location data in your applications.

8

Application Settings

WHAT'S IN THIS CHAPTER?

➤ Exploring the Info.plist

➤ Peeking in the settings bundle

➤ Reading and updating your settings

This chapter focuses on application settings, and looks at two aspects of settings for your MonoTouch app: the `Info.plist` and your settings bundle.

➤ The `Info.plist` contains some basic information about your app and how it should look and behave.

➤ Your settings bundle is where you would keep data that you need to persist from session to session.

This chapter looks at what settings you might want to set in your `Info.plist` and why, and then looks at what code it takes to read and use the settings that you save in the settings bundle.

This chapter also takes you through the building of the settings that you might have in a social media–type application. Going through each step, you will examine the `Root.plist` inside the Property List Editor and see the settings dialog that will result from it.

EXPLORING THE INFO.PLIST

`Info.plist` is short for information property list, and it is a structured text file that contains essential configuration information for your app. The file itself is encoded using the Unicode UTF-8 encoding and the contents are structured using XML. The root XML node is called "<plist>" and inside that you have the dictionary node "<dict>," whose contents are a set of keys and values describing different aspects of your app bundle. The iPhone OS uses these keys and values to obtain information about your application and how it is configured and how it will initially display your user interface by determining what XIB is loaded. The `Info.plist` name is case sensitive and must have an initial capital letter *I*. In iPhone applications, this file resides in the top level of the bundle directory.

The contents of a typical `Info.plist` file convey the following information to the system:

➤ The user-visible name to display for the app

➤ A unique identifier string (typically in the form com.*yourcompany.appname*) that can be used to locate the bundle at runtime

➤ Version information

➤ Information about how the application presents content initially

In most cases you won't really need to edit this file or manipulate the values. MonoDevelop handles these tasks in the iPhone Application Settings options dialog, shown in Figure 8-1, which can be found by right-clicking on your iPhone project and selecting Options and then iPhone Application Settings.

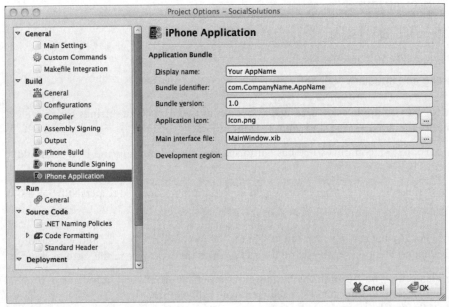

FIGURE 8-1

The following sections look at some of the values that you might need to edit and what they do.

UIStatusBarHidden

This is a Boolean value that, when set to `true`, launches the application with the status bar hidden. Another way to do this is under the `FinishedLaunching` event in the application delegate. In this method, you can add the line:

```
// Hide the StatusBar
UIApplication.SharedApplication.StatusBarHidden = true;
```

This hides the status bar, but only after the application has, well, finished launching. So your splash screen will come with a status bar for the majority of its appearance. However, if you use the `Info` `.plist` setting, your status bar will always be hidden.

UIInterfaceOrientation

This is a key with a string value. The available options are the orientation options for the iPhone. This is the key you need to set if you want the application to launch in landscape mode. The default value here is standard portrait.

If you want to launch the application in landscape mode, use `UIInterfaceOrientationLandscapeLeft` or `UIInterfaceOrientationLandscapeRight`.

You can also launch upside down using `UIInterfaceOrientationPortraitUpsideDown`.

These values are the available orientations for the phone throughout the application.

UIRequiresPersistentWiFi

This is a Boolean key that, when set to `true`, will operate a Wi-Fi connection when the application launches. Use this if your application doesn't work without Wi-Fi. This is especially helpful with displaying an error to users when no Wi-Fi is available.

 Apple wants you to notify your users if Wi-Fi isn't available (in other words, they'll reject your app if you're don't), and because this key opens the connection on launch, it takes care of user notification for you.

If this value is set to `false`, which is the default, the OS closes any active connection after 30 minutes.

UIPrerenderedIcon

When you put your 57×57 icon in the application, you'll notice that when it gets to the springboard, it has an added shine effect and looks glossy. Well, sometimes you don't want that. If you want your icon to show up how you designed it, without the shine and gloss, set this Boolean key to `true`, and it turns off the render effect.

PEEKING IN THE SETTINGS BUNDLE

Users are used to all the programs and web sites they have providing them with a preferences window where they can set application-specific options. The iPhone OS provides users with a dedicated application called Settings that allows users to control preferences for their iPhone and the individual apps installed on it. This section shows you how to add settings for your application to the Settings application and shows you how to access those settings from within your application.

The Settings Application

The Settings application lets the user enter and change preferences for any applications that have a settings bundle. A *settings bundle* is a group of files built into an application bundle that tells the Settings application what preferences the application wishes to collect from the user.

Figure 8-2 shows the Settings application open, where users can set preferences for their iPhone or for specific applications.

The Settings application acts as a common user interface for the iPhone's User Defaults mechanism. User Defaults is the part of Application Preferences that stores and retrieves preferences and is implemented by the NSUserDefaults class. Your applications use NSUserDefaults to read and store preference data using a key value, just as you would access keyed data from an NSDictionary. The difference is that NSUserDefaults data is persisted to the file system rather than stored in an object instance in memory.

If you use a settings bundle with your app, you get a UI for free from the Settings application. You create a property list defining your application's available settings, and the Settings application creates the interface for you.

There are limits to what you can do with the Settings application, however. Any preference that the user might need to change **FIGURE 8-2**
while your application is running should not be limited to the Settings application because your user would be forced to quit your application to change those values. If you have built an immersive application, you generally want to provide a preferences view from within your application so that the user doesn't have to quit in order to make a change. This is especially true in games; however, there are times that even utility and productivity applications might have preferences that a user should be able to change without leaving the application. Later in the chapter you learn to how to collect preferences from the user right in your application and store those in iPhone's User Defaults.

Adding Your App to the Settings Application

The first thing that you want to do is implement a settings bundle so that when the user launches the Settings application, he or she finds an entry for your application. Once inside the Settings application, if a user selects your application, he or she then drills down into a view that shows the preferences that are relevant only to your app. The Settings application can use lots of UI elements from the iPhone to gather input from your users.

Working with the Settings Bundle

The Settings application bases the display of preferences for a given application on the contents of the settings bundle inside that application. Each settings bundle must have a property list, called Root.plist, which defines the root-level preferences view. This property list must follow a very precise format. When the Settings application finds a settings bundle with an appropriate Root.plist file, the Settings application builds a settings view for your application based on the contents of the property list. If you want your preferences to include any sub-views, you have to add additional property lists to the bundle and add an entry to `Root.plist` for each child view. This is covered in detail later on in the chapter.

Adding a Settings Bundle to Your Project

Currently in MonoDevelop adding a settings bundle is a two-step process:

1. First you must create the `Settings.bundle` to do this you need to right-click Project ➪ Add ➪ New Folder then name this folder Settings.bundle

2. Then you right-click on the `Settings.bundle` and choose Add ➪ New File ➪ XML ➪ Empty XML File, which you name `Root.plist`.

Figure 8-3 shows the New XML file dialog on the iPhone home screen.

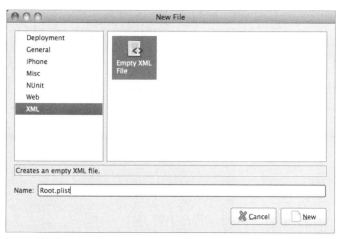

FIGURE 8-3

Setting Up Your Property List

If you double-click the `Root.plist`, you open up the Property List Editor. From here you can edit your file and make sure it's in the proper format for the Settings application to pick up. Before getting into the specifics about the format, it would be good to review some of the basics of the property lists. Property lists all have a root node that has a node type of `Dictionary`. This means that the node stores items using a key/value pair, just as an `NSDictionary` does. All of the children of a `Dictionary` node need to have both a key and a value. To be a valid property list, your `Root.plist` must have only one root node, and all additional nodes must come under it.

Several different types of nodes can be put into a property list. In addition to `Dictionary` nodes, which allow you to store child nodes, there are also `Array` nodes, which store an ordered list of other nodes similar to an `NSArray`. The `Dictionary` and `Array` types are the only property list node types that can contain other nodes. There are also a number of other node types designed to hold data. The data node types are `Boolean`, `Data` (Base64 encoded data, such as `NSData`), `Date`, `Number`, and `String`.

The first item under the root node needs to be `PreferenceSpecifiers`, and it's an array. This array node is designed to hold a set of dictionary nodes, each of which represents a single preference that the user can enter or a single child view that the user can drill down into.

Before you move on to editing the `Root.plist` with the Property List Editor, you must open this file in a Text Editor to get the basics in place. The code that follows shows all of what is required to have a valid `Root.plist`. After you have this code in place, you can save the file. When you double-click the `Root.plist`, as mentioned earlier, it opens up the Property List Editor, with the foundation of your application settings ready to go.

```xml
<?xml version="1.0" encoding="UTF-8"?>
<!DOCTYPE plist PUBLIC "-//Apple//DTD PLIST 1.0//EN" "http://www.apple.com/DTDs/
PropertyList-1.0.dtd">
<plist version="1.0">
<dict>
    <key>Title</key>
    <string>AppSettings</string>
    <key>StringsTable</key>
    <string>Root</string>
    <key>PreferenceSpecifiers</key>
    <array>
        <dict>
            <key>Type</key>
            <string>PSGroupSpecifier</string>
            <key>Title</key>
            <string>Optional Title</string>
        </dict>
    </array>
</dict>
</plist>
```

Figure 8-4 shows the Property List Editor with the foundation of your `Root.plist`.

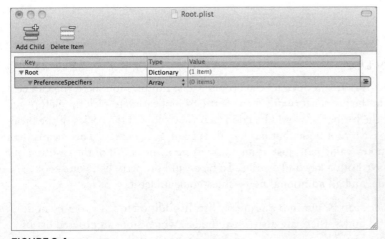

FIGURE 8-4

You now need to add a child item to your `PreferenceSpecifiers` node.

1. Highlight the `PreferenceSpecifiers` node and click the Add Child button in the top-left corner.

2. The Property List Editor will create an item for you named Item 0. You will want to make sure that it is of the type `Dictionary`.

3. You need to tell the Settings application what type of item this is going to be, so you need to highlight this newly created item and again click the Add Child button. The key for this item will be `Type`, the type will be `String`, and the value will be `PSGroupSpecifier`.

The `PSGroupSpecifier` is used to indicate the start of a new group. Each item that follows this item is part of the same group until the next `PSGroupSpecifier` is found. The Settings application uses the grouped `UITableView` to display the settings, and the `Title` key for the `PSGroupSpecifier` item is used as the `UITableView` section header text. The `Title` key is, however, optional and isn't required.

 You need to be sure that the very first item in your `PreferenceSpecifiers` *node is always a* `PSGroupSpecifier` *item because every valid Root.plist requires at least one* `PSGroupSpecifier` *item.*

Figure 8-5 shows the Property List Editor with the foundation of your `PSGroupSpecifier` item.

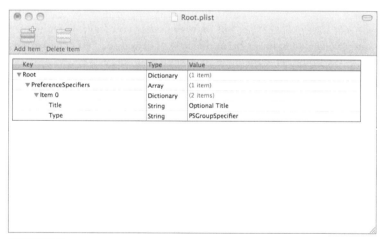

Key	Type	Value
▼ Root	Dictionary	(1 item)
▼ PreferenceSpecifiers	Array	(1 item)
▼ Item 0	Dictionary	(2 items)
Title	String	Optional Title
Type	String	PSGroupSpecifier

FIGURE 8-5

Adding a Text Field

Now that you have all the foundation of the `Root.plist` out of the way you can move on to adding some fields to gather input. You can start with the simplest and most frequently used item, the text field.

1. You need to add another child to the `PreferenceSpecifiers` node; however, you can't simply select the `PreferenceSpecifiers` node and click Add Child because this inserts the new item above your `PSGroupSpecifier` item, which makes your `Root.plist` invalid because the item has to be in a group. To take care of this you need to make sure that the `PSGroupSpecifier` item is closed. You can do this by clicking the disclosure indicator by the item. Highlight the item, and you should see a plus icon on the far right. Clicking this adds a new item in the proper place.

Figure 8-6 shows the Property List Editor with the `PSGroupSpecifier` item closed and highlighted so that you can add a new item in the proper place.

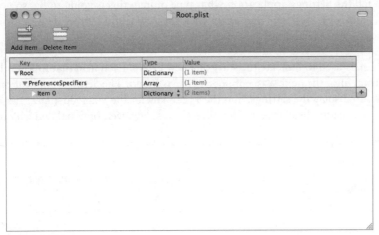

FIGURE 8-6

2. By default this new node has a type of `String`, but that isn't what you want. Each item within a `PreferenceSpecifiers` array must be of the type `Dictionary`. You change this type by clicking the word `String` under Type and changing it to `Dictionary`.

3. Now you need to expand this new item so that you can add the proper child nodes to it, letting the Settings application know how this field should look and act. Click the disclosure icon beside the item so that it is pointing down. It won't reveal anything yet because you don't have any child nodes, but this enables the Add Child Node button. Click that button, and a new node then appears underneath your item. This new node has a type of `String`, and this time that is exactly what you want. Change the key to `Type` and change the value to `PSTextFieldSpecifier`, which is the way you tell the Settings application how you want the user to edit the setting — with a text field.

4. You need to define the label to be displayed beside the text field. Click the button with the plus icon to the right of the row to add another item to your dictionary. The key for this node should be `Title`. You can leave the type for this item as `String`. Move on over to the Value column and set it to `Username`.

5. Now click the plus button at the end of the row to add yet another item to your dictionary. Again, the first thing you do is change the key for this new entry. The key for this entry is `key`. This is that key that you will use with the `NSUserDefaults` class to retrieve and set the value for this setting. So you also need to give the key a value; for this example go with `username`.

6. There are two more things that you will want to do with this text field. Because it is for user-names, turn off autocapitalization and autocorrection. As you know usernames are often case sensitive or words/phrases that the iPhone might try to autocorrect. You will want to keep both of these from happening to prevent frustrating your users.

➤ Add another child row to your `PSTextFieldSpecifier` item. This item needs a key of `AutocapitalizationType` and a value of `none`. This is the item that prevents the iPhone from trying to autocapitalize anything typed in this text field.

➤ Finally, the last item that you need for this field will need a key of `AutocorrectionType` and a value of `no`. This item prevents the iPhone from trying to auto-correct any words or phrases that may appear in this text field.

Figure 8-7 shows the Property List Editor with the `PSTextFieldSpecifier` that creates a text field within the Settings application with the label "Username." Figure 8-8 shows the visual result.

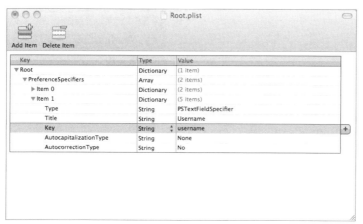

FIGURE 8-7

Adding a Secure Text Field

You have learned the basics that go into creating a text field for the Settings application. There is only one difference between a regular text field and a secure field, so luckily you can copy and paste the item you just created. Highlight the item and hit Command+C, then hit Command+V to paste it in. You then see a new item has been created that has all the child nodes of the text field item you just created. First you need to change the title value to `Password` and the key value to `password`.

To make this a secure text field you need to add one more child node to this field. It needs to have the key of `IsSecure`. You need to change its type from String to Boolean. Notice that instead of a string for the value you have a checkmark instead: Checked is for `true`, and unchecked is for `false`.

FIGURE 8-8

Figure 8-9 shows the Property List Editor with a
`PSTextFieldSpecifier` that will create a secure text field
within the Settings application with the label "Password."
Figure 8-10 shows the visual result.

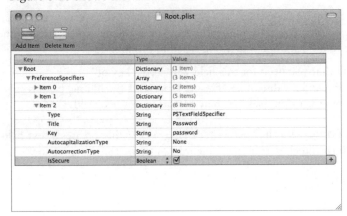

FIGURE 8-9

FIGURE 8-10

Adding a MultiValue Field

The MultiValue field allows your users to select from a set of predefined choices. It presents a row
with a disclosure indicator that leads to the available choices.

1. You start off like you did with the other elements by adding a child row to the
    `PreferenceSpecifiers` node. Click the disclosure button of the last item created so that it
    is closed and click the plus button on the end of the row. The newly created child row needs
    to have a key of `Type` and a value of `PSMultiValueSpecifier`.

2. Add a second row with a key of `Title` and a value of `Service`.

3. Create a third row with a key of `Key` and a value of `service`.

4. Now you come to the part where you actually establish the values that are going to be dis-
    played and stored. This is accomplished with two different arrays: one that has the value that is
    displayed to the user and one that has the value that is actually stored. This is so that you can
    provide the user with some very friendly text, while behind the scenes you are storing a number
    or an internal ID that might not be as friendly to display. The great thing is if you want the
    titles and the values to be the same, you can just create one array and copy and paste!

    Add another child item to your current item. This item needs to have a key of `Values` and
    a type of `Array`. Under this item you need to create the nodes to hold the actual values. For
    this example all the nodes are going to be `String`, and they are going to have the values
    `Twitter`, `Facebook`, and `Email`. Because you want to display to the user the same values
    that you are storing you can copy this item, paste it, and change its key name to `Titles`.

5. A MultiValue field has to have one and only one value, so the last thing you need to do for
    this field is to set a default value if no value has been selected. To do this you add a new child
    item to the `PSMultiValueSpecifier` item and you give it a key of `DefaultValue` and a
    value of `Twitter`. The value that you give in `DefaultValue` must be a valid value from the
    `Values` array (not the `Titles` array if they are different).

Figure 8-11 shows the Property List Editor with a `PSMultiValueFieldSpecifier` that creates a selection of sharing services (Twitter, Facebook, Email) that the user can choose from. Figures 8-12 and 8-13 show the visual result.

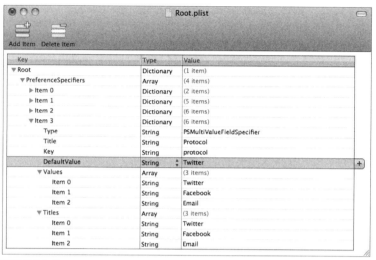

FIGURE 8-11

FIGURE 8-12

FIGURE 8-13

Adding a Toggle Switch

The next item you need to get from the user is a Boolean value that indicates whether the app shares with friends. To capture a Boolean value in your preferences, you are going to tell the Settings application to use a UISwitch by adding another item to your PreferenceSpecifiers array with a type of PSToggleSwitchSpecifier.

1. Create a new child item, and change its type to dictionary.

2. Then add a child item to your newly created item. Give the child row a key of Type with the value of PSToggleSwitchSpecifier.

3. Add another child row with the key of Title and the value of Share With Friends.

4. Next, add a child row with the key of Key and the value of share.

    By default, a toggle switch causes a Boolean true or false to get saved into the user defaults. You can override this behavior and assign a different value to the on and off positions by specifying the optional keys TrueValue and FalseValue. You can assign strings, dates, or numbers to either the on position (TrueValue) or the off position (FalseValue) so that the Settings application stores the string you specify instead of just storing true or false. Set the on position to save the string Enabled and the off position to store Disabled.

5. You need to add two more children to this item: one with a key of TrueValue and a value of Enabled, and a second one with a key of FalseValue and a value of Disabled.

6. You have one more required item in this dictionary, which is the default value. If you had not supplied the optional FalseValue and TrueValue items, you would create a new row with a key of DefaultValue and change the type from string to Boolean. However, because you did add those two items, the value you put in DefaultValue has to match either the value passed in TrueValue or the one passed in FalseValue.

7. Most iPhone users are social media junkies, so enable sharing by default. Create one last child and give it a key of DefaultValue and a value of Enabled. Note that the string Enabled is what is going to be stored in the User Defaults, but the UISwitch still displays On/Off.

Figure 8-14 shows the Property List Editor with a PSToggleSwitchSpecifier that allows the user to turn on or off sharing. Figure 8-15 shows the visual result.

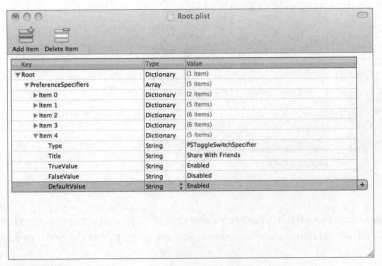

Key	Type	Value
▼ Root	Dictionary	(1 item)
▼ PreferenceSpecifiers	Array	(5 items)
▶ Item 0	Dictionary	(2 items)
▶ Item 1	Dictionary	(5 items)
▶ Item 2	Dictionary	(6 items)
▶ Item 3	Dictionary	(6 items)
▼ Item 4	Dictionary	(5 items)
Type	String	PSToggleSwitchSpecifier
Title	String	Share With Friends
TrueValue	String	Enabled
FalseValue	String	Disabled
DefaultValue	String	Enabled

FIGURE 8-14

Adding a Slider

Your last item type is the slider like the one for the iPod volume control.

1. The slider does allow you to place a small graphic at the beginning and end of the slider, but not a label, so generally it's a best practice to put a slider in its own `PSGroupSpecifier` with the Title key explaining to the users what setting they are changing. To save a little time you can just copy and paste the `PSGroupSpecifier` item that you created before. Now all you need to do is change the Title; for this example, change it to Refresh Rate.

2. You now need to add a sibling row to your newly created `PSGroupSpecifier`. Make sure that it is closed and click the plus button at the end of the row. Like with all items that hold your specifiers you need to change the type to a `Dictionary`.

FIGURE 8-15

3. Then add a child to this item, set its key to `Type`, and set the value to `PSSliderSpecifier`. This lets the Settings application know that it needs to use a `UISlider` to gather the input from the user for this setting.

4. You also need to add another child item with the key `Key` so that you can retrieve and update the value later. Set its value to `refreshRate`.

5. You can allow your user to select a value between a range of values you specify. For this instance, let the user select a value between 1 and 10. The `PSSliderSpecifier` also requires a default value. All of these values need to be stored as numbers instead of strings. So you need three more rows to handle all of these values. Give the first one a key of `DefaultValue` and a value of 6. Give the second one a key of `MinimumValue` and a value of 1, and give the final one a key of `MaximumValue` and a value of 10.

6. As mentioned earlier there is one more bit of customization that you can do to the `PSSliderSpecifier`: providing images for the `MinimumValue` and `MaximumValue`. You need two more child rows: one `MinimumValueImage` and another `MaximumValueImage`. For their keys you put the image name. You need to copy these image files into your `Settings.bundle` directory with your `Root.plist`.

Figure 8-16 shows the Property List Editor with a `PSGroupSpecifier` that displays the label "Refresh Rate" for the `PSSliderSpecifier`, which allows the users to select at what rate they want their data refreshed. Figure 8-17 shows the visual result.

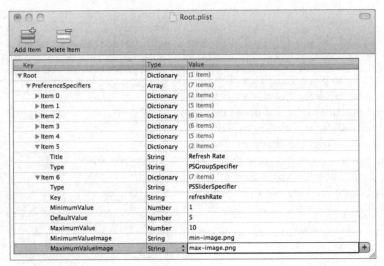

FIGURE 8-16

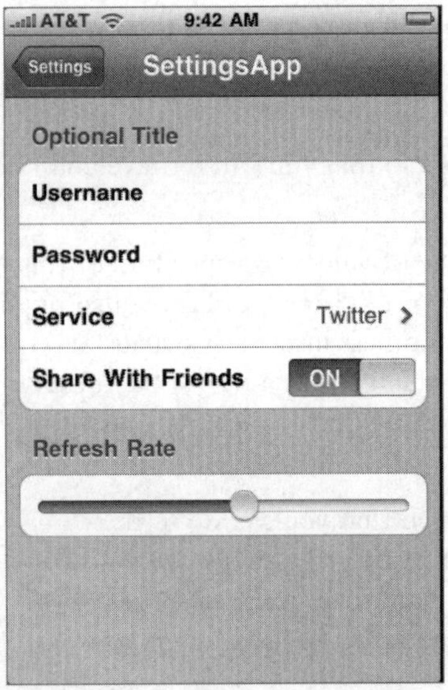

FIGURE 8-17

Now that you have gotten your settings all done, take a look at the final XML.

```xml
<?xml version="1.0" encoding="UTF-8"?>
<!DOCTYPE plist PUBLIC "-//Apple//DTD PLIST 1.0//EN" "http://www.apple.com/DTDs/
PropertyList-1.0.dtd">
<plist version="1.0">
<dict>
    <key>Title</key>
```

```
<string>AppSettings</string>
<key>StringsTable</key>
<string>Root</string>
<key>PreferenceSpecifiers</key>
<array>
    <dict>
        <key>Type</key>
        <string>PSGroupSpecifier</string>
        <key>Title</key>
        <string>Optional Title</string>
    </dict>
    <dict>
        <key>Type</key>
        <string>PSTextFieldSpecifier</string>
        <key>Title</key>
        <string>Username</string>
        <key>Key</key>
        <string>username</string>
        <key>AutocapitalizationType</key>
        <string>None</string>
        <key>AutocorrectionType</key>
        <string>No</string>
    </dict>
    <dict>
        <key>Type</key>
        <string>PSTextFieldSpecifier</string>
        <key>Title</key>
        <string>Password</string>
        <key>Key</key>
        <string>password</string>
        <key>AutocapitalizationType</key>
        <string>None</string>
        <key>AutocorrectionType</key>
        <string>No</string>
        <key>IsSecure</key>
        <true/>
    </dict>
    <dict>
        <key>Type</key>
        <string>PSMultiValueSpecifier</string>
        <key>Title</key>
        <string>Service</string>
        <key>Key</key>
        <string>service</string>
        <key>DefaultValue</key>
        <string>Twitter</string>
        <key>Values</key>
        <array>
            <string>Twitter</string>
            <string>Facebook</string>
            <string>Email</string>
        </array>
        <key>Titles</key>
        <array>
```

```
                    <string>Twitter</string>
                    <string>Facebook</string>
                    <string>Email</string>
                </array>
            </dict>
            <dict>
                <key>Type</key>
                <string>PSToggleSwitchSpecifier</string>
                <key>Title</key>
                <string>Share With Friends</string>
                <key>Key</key>
                <string>share</string>
                <key>TrueValue</key>
                <string>Enabled</string>
                <key>FalseValue</key>
                <string>Disabled</string>
                <key>DefaultValue</key>
                <string>Enabled</string>
            </dict>
            <dict>
                <key>Type</key>
                <string>PSGroupSpecifier</string>
                <key>Title</key>
                <string>Refresh Rate</string>
            </dict>
            <dict>
                <key>Type</key>
                <string>PSSliderSpecifier</string>
                <key>Key</key>
                <string>refreshRate</string>
                <key>DefaultValue</key>
                <integer>6</integer>
                <key>MinimumValue</key>
                <integer>1</integer>
                <key>MaximumValue</key>
                <integer>10</integer>
            </dict>
        </array>
    </dict>
</plist>
```

Reading Your Settings

Now that you have all of your specifiers set up and users can access your settings through the Settings application, you need a way to access those settings in your own application. Turns out this is really easy to do.

1.   First, you need to make sure that you have a reference to MonoTouch.Foundation. You do this just like you do with any other class:

```
using MonoTouch.Foundation;
```

2. (Optional) You are going to use the class NSUserDefaults to handle the communication with your saved preferences, so you need to create a reference to this class:

```
var prefs = NSUserDefaults.StandardUserDefaults;
```

3. After you have an instance of NSUserDefaults you can make some very simple calls to get the value for the key that you want. You will read in the settings that you created in the previous section of the chapter; notice there is a method for each type of variable that you may need: StringForKey, IntForKey, BooleanForKey, FloatForKey, DoubleForKey, DictionaryForKey, and ArrayForKey. You just need to use the method that corresponds to the variable type that you are expecting:

```
string username = prefs.StringForKey("username");
string password = prefs.StringForKey("password");
string sharingService = prefs.StringForKey("service");
string shareEnabled = prefs.StringForKey("share");
int refreshRate = prefs.IntForKey("refreshRate");
```

Updating Your Settings

You now know how to read your settings, but what if you need to make a change from inside of your app?

1. (Optional) Again, you need to make sure that you have a reference to MonoTouch.Foundation. This gives you access to the NSUserDefaults class that does all of the heavy lifting for you. Just as before, you need to create a reference to this class:

```
var prefs = NSUserDefaults.StandardUserDefaults;
```

2. After you have an instance of NSUserDefaults you simply use the key for the setting to set the value and call the Synchronize method as illustrated here:

```
prefs["username"] = new NSString(username.ToString());
prefs["password"] = new NSString(password.ToString());
prefs.["service"] = new NSString(sharingService.ToString());
prefs["share"] = new NSString(shareEnabled.ToString());
int refreshRate = prefs.IntForKey("refreshRate");
prefs.Synchronize();
```

You can take this knowledge along with the knowledge that you have learned about the screen controls in previous chapters and make an in-app settings view for settings that the user might need to adjust while in the application.

SUMMARY

This chapter introduced you to the NSUserDefaults class and the Settings.bundle so that you can allow your users to easily change the preferences for your application. You have also learned how easy it is to read and change these settings from inside your own app. Together with concepts and code you have learned in other chapters you can provide both an in-app settings view and also a settings view inside the Settings application.

Programming with Device Hardware

➤ Programming accelerometer, device orientation, and proximity detection support

➤ Supporting networking

➤ Developing with battery life in mind

The iPhone has a vast amount of exciting hardware within the device. Although this hardware in and of itself doesn't interest users, the excitement is when the application presents the users with information in a way that makes sense to them. This hardware is very interesting to developers building apps; it allows for applications to provide extraordinary features based on top of this hardware. This chapter looks at the accelerometer, device orientation, proximity detection, networking, and the battery. Some example uses of this hardware are as follows:

➤ A program can test that a network connection over any connection (WiFi, 3G, or EDGE) is available. If a connection does not exist, instead of displaying an error message when attempting to upload information, the user can be notified that there is no connection to a service.

➤ The accelerometer can be used to pull random data from a data source. When the device is shaken, the application can respond by reading random data from a data source.

➤ When the user changes the device from portrait to landscape, the application can change how it displays content to the user.

Most of this device support comes from the `MonoTouch.UIKit.UIDevice` class. The `UIDevice` class exposes the `CurrentDevice` instance, which represents the current device. `CurrentDevice` is a static, read-only member of the `UIDevice` class. The `UIDevice` class allows a developer to obtain information about the current device, such as its unique id (used for uniquely identifying an iPhone), assigned name, device model, operating system name, operating system version, and its physical device characteristics. These physical device characteristics include the device orientation, battery state, and the proximity sensor. Other pieces of the iPhone provide support, such as the networking stack that lets a program test whether an address is reachable, and the accelerometer, which lets a program know if a device is being shaken.

RESPONDING TO ACCELERATION

The accelerometer is one of the most interesting features of the iPhone. The UrbanSpoon.com iPhone app, one of the original native applications for the iPhone, is a great example of using acceleration to return random restaurant data. With that app, you just shake your iPhone and the app finds a good restaurant nearby for you. The accelerometer is commonly used along with user interface elements, such as the `UIPicker`, to randomly retrieve data. By programming the iPhone to respond to `Acceleration` events, you can refresh the data displayed to the user whenever they shake the iPhone.

Accelerometer

In general, an *accelerometer* measures the proper acceleration of the device relative to freefall. The accelerometer in the iPhone provides changes in the XYZ axis which allows for a program to detect the orientation of the device and the movement of the device. Because the changes are provided in the XYZ axis, the acceleration can be calculated in a vector.

The MonoTouch framework makes it easy to access the accelerometer via the `MonoTouch.UIKit` namespace, which exposes the `UIAccelerometer.SharedAccelerometer` member. Instances of the class are accessed as a static, read-only member of the `UIAccelerometer` class.

Using the XYZ Coordinate System

Understanding how the data is returned from the accelerometer is important. Multiple coordinate systems can be used. In the end, Apple has implemented the XYZ coordinate system for providing acceleration information. Figure 9-1 shows the iPhone within the coordinate system.

Assuming that the user is along the Z-axis, if the iPhone is moved toward or away from the user, acceleration occurs along the Z-axis. If the iPhone is moved left or right, acceleration occurs along the X-axis. If the iPhone is moved up or down, acceleration occurs along the Y-axis. The acceleration values can be determined along each axis. With each value known along an axis and the help of some math, the total magnitude of acceleration can be calculated as well as the direction of that acceleration at any given time.

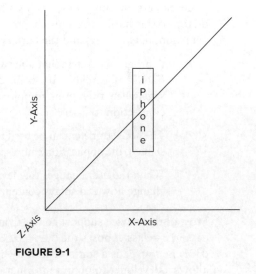

FIGURE 9-1

Coding with the Accelerometer

The accelerometer allows a program to read when the iPhone is moving and return data about the movement of the device. The iPhone OS and MonoTouch provide a software solution to integrating with the Accelerometer and handling acceleration events. The SharedAccelerometer is a shared C# object that provides access to the acceleration hardware on the device. Listing 9-1 shows how to handle acceleration events and to display that information to the user.

LISTING 9-1: Reading the accelerometer

```
// The name AppDelegate is referenced in the MainWindow.xib file.
public partial class AppDelegate : UIApplicationDelegate
{
// This method is invoked when the application has loaded its
// UI and is ready to run
public override bool FinishedLaunching (UIApplication app, NSDictionary options)
{
        // If you have defined a view, add it here:
        // window.AddSubview (navigationController.View);
        window.MakeKeyAndVisible ();
        //Acceleration does not work in the Simulator.
        UIAccelerometer.SharedAccelerometer.UpdateInterval = 1 / 10;
        dataLabel.Text = String.Empty;
        UIAccelerometer.SharedAccelerometer.Acceleration += delegate(object sender,
        UIAccelerometerEventArgs e) {
                UIAcceleration acc = e.Acceleration;
                double thresholdValue = 2.0;
                double Velocity = Math.Sqrt(Math.Pow(acc.X, 2) +
                    Math.Pow(acc.Y, 2) +
                    Math.Pow(acc.Z, 2));
                string strReturn = System.Environment.NewLine;
                if ( Velocity > thresholdValue ) {
                    dataLabel.Text = "Velocity: " +
                    Velocity.ToString() + strReturn +
                    " X: " + acc.X.ToString() + strReturn +
                    " Y: " + acc.Y.ToString() + strReturn +
                    " Z: " + acc.Z.ToString();
                }};
        return true;
    }
}
```

Found in the Accelerator\Main.cs file of the download

A couple of notes about programming with the accelerometer:

➤ The accelerometer returns changes in the X, Y, and Z directions. It is up to the developer to perform the math calculations to return the magnitude of the acceleration as well as the direction. The magnitude of the acceleration is calculated by adding the squares of the acceleration in the X, Y, and Z directions and then taking the square root of the sum.

➤ The Accelerometer is not available in the iPhone simulator. It can only be tested on an actual device.

➤ In this example, all that a user would have to do is shake the device and a result is displayed in the X, Y, Z, directions along with the magnitude of the acceleration.

➤ Setting the `UpdateInterval` directly affects the device. The more times that acceleration events are handled, the more the battery on the device is drained.

➤ The `UpdateInterval` can only be within the hardware resolution of the device. If there are more requested updates per second than the hardware supports, the maximum number of hardware updates is performed. No error occurs if the `UpdateInterval` is too quick for the hardware that the application is running on.

➤ Unless the iPhone is perfectly motionless, it is most likely undergoing some amount of acceleration. The acceleration measured may or may not be significant. It is a good idea to put some type of threshold value so that the acceleration is only used when it is actually needed.

➤ Acceleration is not the same as velocity. Technically, acceleration is the rate of change of velocity over a unit of time, so they are related. The accelerometer measures acceleration, and from the acceleration it is possible to determine velocity. (That discussion of mathematics is beyond this book.) Thanks to some basic calculus, it is fairly easy to take the acceleration values along with its initial location and to then figure out the location of the iPhone as it moves around, even if no wireless connection is available.

Using Acceleration for UI Input

As mentioned previously, the accelerometer can be used for user input. The UrbanSpoon app, which has a database of area restaurants, uses the accelerometer to perform a random search for restaurants in an area. When the iPhone is shaken, a random restaurant type is displayed. The user can then change the values and perform a search.

Listing 9-2 displays a `UIPicker` with the values rotating. These images are loaded and displayed in a `UIImagePicker`. In this example, nine images are displayed, and these images are loaded in through an array of `UIImages`.

LISTING 9-2: Using acceleration to create the UrbanSpoon UI effect

```
//setting the Animation duration smaller makes the animation tend
// to run quicker.
imageViewPicker.AnimationDuration = .1;
imageViewPicker.Hidden = true;
//load the images.
imageViewPicker.AnimationImages = new UIImage [] {
        UIImage.FromFile ("images/blur01.png"),
        UIImage.FromFile ("images/blur02.png"),
        UIImage.FromFile ("images/blur03.png"),
        UIImage.FromFile ("images/blur04.png"),
        UIImage.FromFile ("images/blur05.png"),
        UIImage.FromFile ("images/blur06.png"),
        UIImage.FromFile ("images/blur07.png"),
        UIImage.FromFile ("images/blur08.png"),
        UIImage.FromFile ("images/blur09.png")
};
UIAccelerometer.SharedAccelerometer.UpdateInterval = 1/10;
UIAccelerometer.SharedAccelerometer.Acceleration +=
```

```
delegate(object sender, UIAccelerometerEventArgs e) {
    double Threshold = 1.5;
    double magnitude;
    UIAcceleration acc = e.Acceleration;
    magnitude = Math.Sqrt(Math.Pow(acc.X, 2) + Math.Pow(acc.Y, 2) +
        Math.Pow(acc.Z, 2));
    if ( magnitude >= Threshold ) {
        if ( PreviousRun == false )
        {
        // Show the imageViewPicker & Start the Animation
        imageViewPicker.Hidden = false;
        imageViewPicker.StartAnimating ();
        PreviousRun = true;
        }
    }
    else{
        if (PreviousRun == true ){
        System.Threading.Thread.Sleep(150);
        // Hide the imageViewPicker & Stop the Animation
        imageViewPicker.Hidden = true;
        imageViewPicker.StopAnimating ();
        // Get a random value
        int n = _r.Next(pickerChoices.RowsInComponent(0));
        // Lets select our random index and set the animation
        // to true so that it looks "cool" :)
            pickerChoices.Select(n,0,true);
        }
        PreviousRun = false;
    }
};
```

Found in the UrbanSpoon\Main.cs file of the download

A few things to notice in the code include the following:

➤ A threshold is used to measure against the magnitude of the acceleration. By setting the value, small movements of the iPhone are discounted.

➤ There is a Boolean value called `PreviousRun`. This is used to determine the last state of the call for acceleration. Without this, an acceleration event would be occurring on the slightest movement of the iPhone, which would cause a different value to be displayed.

➤ The currently running thread is put to sleep for some milliseconds. By putting the UI thread to sleep for a short time, `UIPicker` appears to rotate for a short time after a user stops shaking the iPhone.

Figure 9-2 shows the spinning `UIPicker`.

FIGURE 9-2

 The `UIPicker` *spinning example was begun by Martin Bowling. The code was then modified to provide the accelerometer support.*

DETERMINING DEVICE ORIENTATION

When programming with a desktop application, very few situations exist where the screen rotates or moves in any perceivable way. This is not true with a mobile device, which has a number of orientations. The seven orientations (six plus Unknown) for an iPhone are:

➤ Unknown: The device's orientation is unknown.

➤ Portrait: The device's orientation is in portrait mode. The device is held upright and the home button is at the bottom.

➤ PortraitUpsideDown: The device's orientation is in portrait mode. The device is held upside down and the home button is at the top of the device.

➤ LandscapeLeft: The device is in landscape mode. The device is held upright and the home button is on the right-hand side of the device.

➤ LandscapeRight: The device is in landscape mode. The device is held upright and the home button is on the left-hand side of the device.

➤ FaceUp: The device has the screen facing up and is parallel to the ground.

➤ FaceDown: The device has the screen facing down and is parallel to the ground.

Beginning Notification

The first step to obtaining information regarding device orientation is to turn on the device notifications. You do this through a call to

```
UIDevice.CurrentDevice.BeginGeneratingDeviceOrientationNotifications();
```

Once this call is made, orientation notification information will be made available to a calling app. Along with turning this information on, it is important to turn the notifications off when they are not necessary. You can accomplish this by a call to

```
UIDevice.CurrentDevice.EndGeneratingDeviceOrientationNotifications();
```

Device orientation notifications are not immediately available after notification starts, but are available after a very short delay. BeginGenerationDeviceOrientationNotifications() *is not synchronous with respect to starting the notifications.*

Determining Static Device Orientation

Though not the most common scenario, there may be times when a developer needs to obtain the device orientation. It is simpler to learn the static case and then to learn the dynamic case. There are two steps in getting the device orientation. The first is to determine if the orientation notifications are on. If the orientations are not on, the value of Unknown is returned. See Listing 9-3.

Available for download on Wrox.com

LISTING 9-3: Determining device orientation

```
void HandleOrientationTouchUpInside (object sender, EventArgs e)
{
     if ( UIDevice.CurrentDevice.GeneratesDeviceOrientationNotifications == true )
     {
          OrientationLabel.Text = UIDevice.CurrentDevice.
                         GeneratesDeviceOrientationNotifications.ToString() +
          ": " + UIDevice.CurrentDevice.Orientation.ToString();
     }
}
```

Found in the DeviceSupport\Main.cs file of the download

Once it is determined that the device orientation notifications are on, the current device orientation is retrieved. In this case, it is displayed to the user.

Determining Event-Based Orientation

The more interesting situation is when the device's orientation change notification is turned on. Once the orientation change notification is turned on, an application can monitor for events through the `UIDeviceOrientationDidChangeNotification`. See Listing 9-4.

Available for download on Wrox.com

LISTING 9-4: Handling orientation change notifications

```
NSNotificationCenter.DefaultCenter.
     AddObserver ("UIDeviceOrientationDidChangeNotification",
          delegate {
               OrientationLabel.Text =
                    UIDevice.CurrentDevice.Orientation.ToString(); });
```

Found in the DeviceSupport\Main.cs file of the download

In this short code example, whenever a device orientation change occurs, a message is put on the label, so that the change can be communicated to the user. Figure 9-3 shows the output of event-based orientation.

LandscapeLeft
Orientation
FIGURE 9-3

The next step in this process is to actually do something with this change in the application. When the orientation of the iPhone changes, the application may need to change. This is done by overriding the `ShouldAutorotateToInterfaceOrientation` method to return `true`. This method is overridden on the view controller that is showing the current data.

```
public override bool ShouldAutorotateToInterfaceOrientation
          (UIInterfaceOrientation toInterfaceOrientation)
{
     return(true);
}
```

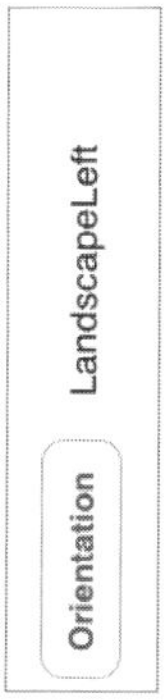

This code needs to be placed within a view controller. This code indicates if a view controller supports the specified orientation. By default, this method returns a true for the Portrait orientation. If the application needs to support other orientations, the method should be overridden.

READING THE PROXIMITY SENSOR

Users think of the iPhone as an iPod, web browser, app device, and sometimes a phone. The phone can be the least thought of feature of the iPhone for a software developer. The iPhone has a proximity sensor, which is used within the iPhone OS to deactivate the screen and the display when the iPhone is held up to the user's ear to make a phone call.

When an application is running, there may be situations when it needs to perform the same type of operation. The iPhone's proximity sensor is exposed to a developer through the `UIDevice` class. A notification can be set up on the proximity sensor as shown in Listing 9-5.

LISTING 9-5: Reading the proximity sensor

```
UIDevice.CurrentDevice.ProximityMonitoringEnabled = true;
NSNotificationCenter.DefaultCenter.AddObserver
    ("UIDeviceProximityStateDidChangeNotification",
    delegate {
        ProximityLabel.Text = UIDevice.CurrentDevice.ProximityState.ToString();
    });
```

Found in the DeviceSupport\Main.cs file of the download

The proximity sensor is not available in all iPhones. To test for it, the following code will enable the proximity sensor.

```
UIDevice.CurrentDevice.ProximityMonitoringEnabled = true;
if ( UIDevice.CurrentDevice.ProximityMonitoringEnabled == true ) {
// Place code here.
// This code will test for the proximity sensor.
// If the code detects the proximity sensor, the
// code within the if statement is executed.
}
```

If, after enabling the proximity sensor, the value of `ProximityState` is still `false`, the proximity sensor is not available on the device. Figure 9-4 shows the cropped output of the proximity sensor after it has moved away from a user's face.

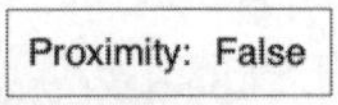

Proximity: False

FIGURE 9-4

The `ProximityState` returns a Boolean value. If the value is true, the device is near the user's face. If the value of `ProximityState` is false, the device is not near the user's face.

NETWORKING

While most of the work with integrating with the iPhone device is done through the UIDevice .CurrentDevice class, networking is done through the NetworkReachability class. The class checks for connectivity and returns a set of flags. See Listing 9-6. The flags for checking for network connectivity are not exclusive to each other.

LISTING 9-6: Determining the connection to a web site

```
void HandleNetworkingTouchUpInside (object sender, EventArgs e)
{
    NetworkReachability nr = new NetworkReachability("www.apple.com");
    NetworkReachabilityFlags flgs = new NetworkReachabilityFlags();
    nr.TryGetFlags(out flgs);
    NetworkingLabel.Text = String.Empty;
    if ( (flgs & NetworkReachabilityFlags.IsWWAN) == NetworkReachabilityFlags.IsWWAN )
    {
        NetworkingLabel.Text += "IsWWAN";
    }
    NetworkingLabel.Text += "Network Flag: " + flgs.ToString();
}
```

Found in the DeviceSupport\Main.cs file of the download

The flags for network reachability are:

➤   ConnectionAutomatic: The connection happens automatically. This value for the flag is an alias for ConnectionOnTraffic.

➤   ConnectionOnDemand: The connection happens when a connection is initiated. The connection will occur when a socket connection is made.

➤   ConnectionOnTraffic: The host is reachable. Once traffic is requested, a connection is made.

➤   ConnectionRequired: The host is reachable; however, a connection must be made.

➤   InterventionRequired: A connection to the host will require user intervention.

➤   IsDirect: The connection is direct and will not go through a gateway.

➤   IslocalAddress: The connection is to the local device.

➤   IsWWAN: The connection is made through a cellular connection, such as EDGE or 3G.

➤   Reachable: The host is reachable.

➤   TransientConnection: The host is reachable through a transient connection, such as PPP.

Testing the connections can be somewhat confusing. To assist with this, Miguel de Icaza has placed some code on the site http://github.com/migueldeicaza/monotouch-samples/tree/master/ reachability to assist. The code allows for easy testing as to whether a host is available over WiFi or a wireless phone network, which most developers need. Figure 9-5 shows output when checking for the host www.apple.com over a WiFi connection.

| Networking | www.apple.com: ReachableViaWiFi... |

FIGURE 9-5

TAKING BATTERY LIFE INTO ACCOUNT

The battery is an important part of mobile devices. Unlike a laptop, which is typically only disconnected from power for short periods of time (1–2 hours), mobile devices can be disconnected from power for several days in a row. Because of this, there are several important things to remember:

➤ Applications should not continually use features that will use the battery while providing no benefit back to the user. These features include networking, watching the accelerometer, device orientation, or any other device feature that uses extra power. A great question to ask is, "Does the user, or application, really need this feature all the time or just at this certain point?"

➤ It is important for applications to know what is happening with the battery at certain points.

Determining the Static Battery State

One way to determine the current status of the battery is to specifically ask for the information. This is done in a two-step process shown in the following code. In this code (Listing 9-7), the battery monitoring is turned on, and once the monitoring is turned on, the level and state of the battery can be determined.

The level of the battery is a floating-point number between 0.0, which is fully discharged, and 1.0, which is fully charged.

The state of the battery is one of four values from the BatteryState enum. These values are:

➤ Unknown: The state of the battery is unknown. This value typically occurs when UIDevice .CurrentDevice.BatteryMonitoringEnabled is set to false. The default state of BatteryMonitoringEnabled is false.

➤ Unplugged: This is the state when a user is actively using his or her iPhone and it is not attached to a charger.

➤ Charging: This is the battery's state when the iPhone is attached to the charger.

➤ Full: This is the battery's state when the iPhone is 100 percent charged.

LISTING 9-7: Reading battery levels

```
void HandleBatteryTouchUpInside (object sender, EventArgs e)
{
    try
    {
    UIDevice.CurrentDevice.BatteryMonitoringEnabled = true;
    BatteryLabel.Text = "Battery: " +
        UIDevice.CurrentDevice.BatteryLevel.ToString() + " " +
            "Battery Status: " +
        UIDevice.CurrentDevice.BatteryState.ToString();
    }
    finally
    {
```

```
            UIDevice.CurrentDevice.BatteryMonitoringEnabled = false;
        }
    }
```

Found in the DeviceSupport\Main.cs file of the download

Using Battery Change Events

Just like when dealing with other parts of the iPhone's hardware, some events are based on changes in the iPhone's battery. When the battery changes, an event is fired. Listing 9-8 shows how to listen for a battery state change event.

In this code, the `UIDeviceBatteryStateDidChangeEventNotification` is hooked up so that when a battery state change occurs, the developer can be notified of the change. The following code shows tracking the change in the battery state.

LISTING 9-8: Handling battery change notifications

```
NSNotificationCenter.DefaultCenter.AddObserver
    ("UIDeviceBatteryStateDidChangeNotification",
    delegate {
    BatteryLabel.Text = UIDevice.CurrentDevice.BatteryLevel.ToString() +
        ", " + UIDevice.CurrentDevice.BatteryState.ToString(); });
```

Found in the DeviceSupport\Main.cs file of the download

Figures 9-6 and 9-7 show the output of the battery state change notification while the iPhone is plugged in and unplugged, respectively.

FIGURE 9-6   **FIGURE 9-7**

ACCESSING SYSTEM INFORMATION

The `UIDevice` class provides access to information about the current device beyond the features in the device. The `UIDevice.CurrentDevice` class exposes a set of properties that allow for system-level information to be determined. These properties are:

➤ `LocalizedModel`: The localized model property is a localized string representing information about the specific model.

➤ `Model`: The model property returns a string with information about the specific model.

➤ `Name`: The name property returns a string with the name of the device. This is the value from the General ⇨ About settings.

➤ `SystemName`: The system name is the name of the operating system currently running on the iPhone.

➤ SystemVersion: The system name is the version of the operating system currently running on the iPhone.

➤ UniqueIdentifier: The unique identifier is a unique string based on hardware values.

Listing 9-9 shows getting the system information:

Available for
download on
Wrox.com

LISTING 9-9: Reading system information

```
string Output = String.Empty;
Output += "System Name: " + UIDevice.CurrentDevice.SystemName + Environment.NewLine;
Output += "System Version: " + UIDevice.CurrentDevice.SystemVersion +
    Environment.NewLine;
Output += "Unique ID: " + UIDevice.CurrentDevice.UniqueIdentifier +
    Environment.NewLine;
Output += "Localized Model: " + UIDevice.CurrentDevice.LocalizedModel +
    Environment.NewLine;
Output += "Name: " + UIDevice.CurrentDevice.Name + Environment.NewLine;
SystemInformationText.Text = Output;
```

Found in the DeviceSupport\Main.cs file of the download

Figure 9-8 shows the output of this code running in the simulator.

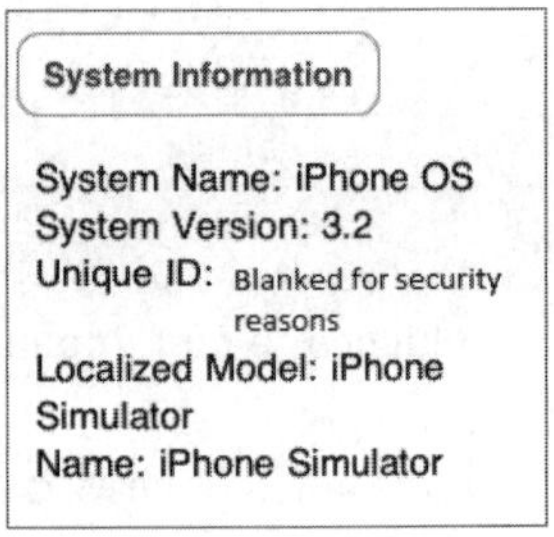

MOBILE DEVELOPMENT

There are a number of important points to remember when developing for the iPhone, or any other mobile devices:

➤ The iPhone is a mobile device and it has limited resources. Continually monitoring for notifications will use the battery.

➤ There is a tradeoff between notifications and using device resources that provide value to a user interface. Don't turn on features that are not needed.

➤ The iPhone simulator will allow developers to build applications; however, it does not have the complete featureset, such as the battery and device orientation.

> **System Information**
>
> System Name: iPhone OS
> System Version: 3.2
> Unique ID: Blanked for security reasons
> Localized Model: iPhone Simulator
> Name: iPhone Simulator

FIGURE 9-8

SUMMARY

The iPhone device has a number of interesting hardware features. These are exposed through the MonoTouch.UIKit.UIDevice.CurrentDevice and the NetworkReachability classes. These classes allow developers to interact with acceleration, device orientation, the battery, networking, and system information. Though a user is not interested in these features, they are important for developers. Developers can use these features to weave an exciting application for end users.

10

Programming with Multimedia

WHAT'S IN THIS CHAPTER?

➤   Integrating images and the image picker

➤   Watching and recording videos

➤   Playing and recording audio

➤   Using animation

Multimedia covers a broad range of items in the real world. Within the iPhone context, multimedia covers images, audio, video, and animation. The iPhone creates an innovative way of consuming multimedia, which hasn't gone unnoticed in the general media. The iPhone APIs provide an easy way of interacting with the multimedia functions of the device. We discuss each of the multimedia items throughout this chapter.

IMAGES

This section covers using images within your application, whether you want to display images, pick images, or even create your own.

Displaying Images

To use and display images within a view, you can use the `UIImageView` control. `UIImageView` is a simple control that allows two basic actions: the ability to view an image and the ability to view multiple images with animations.

To view images, you can either drag a `UIImageView` into the design view using Interface Builder or you can create a `UIImageView` in code. For this example, you create your `UIImageView` in code.

First you want to grab an image that you may have from your application. You can do this by using the static method `FromFile` on the `UIImage` class, passing in the path to the file.

 Make sure you have included your image in the project and set the image's build action to Content; otherwise the image will not show. You can do this by right-clicking on the image, going to Build Action, and then selecting Content.

You next pass the image into the `UIImageView` constructor. When you have created the new image view, you set the frame size for the image. You can use the actual width and height from your image to make sure it fits correctly. You can then simply add the image view as a sub-view of the main window to display it on the screen. Figure 10-1 shows the image in an image view on the screen, and Listing 10-1 shows the code.

LISTING 10-1: Adding a simple UIImageView in code

```
public override bool FinishedLaunching (UIApplication app, NSDictionary
                                                             options)
{
    var image = UIImage.FromFile("image.png");

    var imageView = new UIImageView(image);
    imageView.Frame = new RectangleF(0f, 20f, image.Size.Width,
                                            image.Size.Height);
    window.AddSubview(imageView);

    window.MakeKeyAndVisible ();

    return true;
}
```

As well as being able to display one image using the image view, you can allow the image view to animate through a series of images. To do this you pass in an array of `UIImage` objects and use the `StartAnimating` and `StopAnimating` methods to control when the images are animating. You can set additional properties to determine the length of the animation and the number of times the animation repeats. When the image is not animating, it just shows the default image. This default image is the one you pass into the constructor; you need to reuse the image object in the `UIImage` array if you want it to appear in the animation. Listing 10-2 shows how you would create a list of `UIImage` objects and start animating a `UIImageView`.

FIGURE 10-1

LISTING 10-2: Using UIImageView for Animations

```
public override bool FinishedLaunching (UIApplication app, NSDictionary
                                                               options)
{
    var image = UIImage.FromFile("image.png");
    var image2 = UIImage.FromFile("image2.png");
    var image3 = UIImage.FromFile("image3.png");

    var imageViewRectangle = new RectangleF(0f, 20f, image.Size.Width,
                                                     image.Size.Height);
    var imageView = new UIImageView(image);
    imageView.Frame = imageViewRectangle;
    imageView.AnimationImages = new [] {image, image2, image3};
    imageView.AnimationDuration = 4;
    imageView.AnimationRepeatCount = 2;

    imageView.StartAnimating();

    window.AddSubview(imageView);

    window.MakeKeyAndVisible ();

    return true;
}
```

The UIImageView class also provides a way of showing a highlighted image for a set image using the Highlighted property. You will normally want to provide a highlighted image when a user touches an image. To do this you can create your own UIImageView class and override the TouchesBegan and TouchesEnded methods to set the property to true and false, respectively. You must set the UserInteractionEnabled property to true so that it listens for touches. Listing 10-3 shows the initial setup of creating a new MyImageView using the MyImageView with a UIImageView base class.

LISTING 10-3: Overriding default UIImageView methods

```
public override bool FinishedLaunching (UIApplication app, NSDictionary options)
{
    var image = UIImage.FromFile("image.png");
    var imageHighlighted = UIImage.FromFile("image2.png");

    var imageView = new MyImageView(image, imageHighlighted);
    imageView.Frame = new RectangleF(0f, 20f, image.Size.Width, image.Size.Height);
    imageView.UserInteractionEnabled = true;

    window.AddSubview(imageView);

    window.MakeKeyAndVisible ();

    return true;
```

continues

LISTING 10-3 *(continued)*

```
    }

    ...

    public class MyImageView : UIImageView
    {
        public MyImageView(UIImage image, UIImage imageHighlighted) :
                        base(image, imageHighlighted)
        {
        }

        public override void TouchesBegan (NSSet touches, UIEvent evt)
        {
            Console.WriteLine ("Touches began");
            this.Highlighted = true;
        }

        public override void TouchesEnded (NSSet touches, UIEvent evt)
        {
            Console.WriteLine ("Touches ended");
            this.Highlighted = false;
        }
    }
```

Picking an Image

In a lot of applications, the ability to upload an image is often used. What you want is to allow a user to upload an existing photo they have in their photo album. The UIImagePickerController is used as a modal view; this means the user only has the option of selecting an image or canceling the image picker controller.

When you create the UIImagePickerController, you'll want to define your own delegate method, which will inherit the UIImagePickerControllerDelegate class. This enables you to override methods on the class as and when you need to override the default action for the methods. The UIImagePickerControllerDelegate provides two useful methods to override and one deprecated method.

The two methods you want to override are Canceled and FinishedPickingMedia. The Canceled method returns the picker that called the method. The FinishedPickingMedia method returns the picker that called the method as well as a dictionary of info. This dictionary contains key value pairs of information about the selected image, which you use later to handle this selected image. The FinishedPickingImage method is the deprecated method; the FinishedPickingMedia method has taken over the functionality for picking both images and video.

Listing 10-4 shows how you would use the UIImagePickerController and UIImagePickerControllerDelegate to display all photos from your album.

LISTING 10-4: Getting started with the UIImagePickerController

```
public partial class MainViewController : UIViewController
{
    public override void ViewDidLoad ()
```

```
    {
        base.ViewDidLoad ();

        UIButton button = UIButton.FromType(UIButtonType.RoundedRect);
        button.Frame = new RectangleF(0f, 30f, 320, 40f);
        button.SetTitle("Select Image", UIControlState.Normal);
        button.TouchUpInside += delegate(object sender, EventArgs e) {
        UIImagePickerController picker = new UIImagePickerController();
            picker.Delegate = new MyImagePickerDelegate(this);
            this.PresentModalViewController(picker, true);
        };
        this.View.AddSubview(button);
    }
}

public class MyImagePickerDelegate : UIImagePickerControllerDelegate
{
    MainViewController _mvc;
    public MyImagePickerDelegate(MainViewController mvc)
    {
        _mvc = mvc;
    }

    public override void Canceled (UIImagePickerController picker)
    {
        _mvc.DismissModalViewControllerAnimated(true);
        Console.WriteLine ("Cancelled picking an image");
    }

    public override void FinishedPickingMedia (UIImagePickerController
                                                picker, NSDictionary info)
    {
        _mvc.DismissModalViewControllerAnimated(true);
        foreach (var key in info.Keys)
          Console.WriteLine(key + " = " + info[key]);    }
}
```

Listing 10-4 uses a button to display the image picker; however, this could be attached to any type of control. You might notice that the custom image picker delegate passes the current view controller into the delegate constructor method. This is so that when the image picker is cancelled or an image is selected, you can modify the current view to reflect this, such as removing the image picker controller from the screen and displaying the selected image. To remove the image picker once an event has fired, you simply use the DismissModalViewControllerAnimated method on the view controller you passed in. Figure 10-2 shows what the default UIImagePickerController looks like.

FIGURE 10-2

IMAGE PICKING AND THE SIMULATOR

The simulator by default does not contain any images. This results in your inability to select an image from the image picker. To add images you can use the built-in Safari application to select an image and save it to the simulator. Your saved images then show up in the simulator.

Handling a Picked Image

Once an image has been picked, you want to grab the information from the `info` dictionary and handle what to do with the selected image. The dictionary uses the keys `UIImagePickerControllerMediaType`, `UIImagePickerControllerOriginalImage`, `UIImagePickerControllerEditedImage`, `UIImagePickerControllerCropRect`, and `UIImagePickerControllerMediaURL`. The dictionary does not include all the keys listed, so you need to check if they exist before using them. The keys exist depending on whether the image is edited and whether the image is actually a video.

For now you will only be using the `UIImagePickerControllerMediaType` and `UIImagePickerControllerOriginalImage` keys because this is all the information given when you select an image from a photo album. Using the `UIImagePickerControllerOriginalImage` key on the info dictionary gives you back an `NSObject`. You need to create the key as an Objective-C style object so you have to use `NSString` instead of just a `String` since you are interacting directly with the Objective-C bindings. Because you know this is a `UIImage` object you can cast it to that type. To show that this is the image picked, Listing 10-5 puts the newly picked image within an image view too.

LISTING 10-5: Handle a picked image

```
public override void FinishedPickingMedia (UIImagePickerController picker,
                                           NSDictionary info)
{
    var originalImage = new NSString("UIImagePickerControllerOriginalImage");
    UIImage image = (UIImage) info[originalImage];
    UIImageView imageView = new UIImageView(new RectangleF(0f, 0f,
                                                           320f, 460f));

    imageView.Image = image;
    _mvc.View.AddSubview(imageView);

    _mvc.DismissModalViewControllerAnimated(true);
    Console.WriteLine ("Did finish picking media");
}
```

Sometimes you may want to restrict what source the users get their images from when provided with an image picker. The three different source types are defined in the

`UIImagePickerControllerSourceType` enumeration as `SavedPhotosAlbum`, `PhotoLibrary`, and `Camera`.

➤ The `SavedPhotosAlbum` is a list of images that have been saved from an external source, such as Safari or through another application, and have not been created from the camera.

➤ The `PhotoLibrary` contains all the photos that are taken with the camera and also all the photos that may be synced to the device.

➤ The `Camera` source triggers that the source of the image will be a picture taken straight from the camera.

 Images taken with the camera through an application are not persisted in the other photo libraries, so it is a good idea to save the original image.

Creating an Image from the Camera

Using the camera to take images can be a great way of getting impromptu images from a user as and when necessary. Because iPod Touch devices do not include a camera, you need to check whether a user can use the camera functionality from within your application. The `UIImagePickerController` gives you the functionality to do this programmatically so you can handle the situation if it were to happen.

 The iPhone simulator does not support the camera feature; therefore, you need to do any testing with the camera on an actual device.

To check this functionality programmatically you use the static method `IsSourceTypeAvailable` and pass in the source type you want to determine is available. In this example you pass in the source type `Camera` from the `UIImagePickerControllerSourceType` enumeration. Once you have successfully found out that a camera exists, you simply set the `UIImagePickerController`'s source type to `Camera`. If a camera doesn't exist, you just show an error message. Listing 10-6 shows a way of validating the presence of a camera and displaying it.

Available for download on Wrox.com

LISTING 10-6: Picking an image from the camera

```
var cameraType = UIImagePickerControllerSourceType.Camera;
if(UIImagePickerController.IsSourceTypeAvailable(cameraType))
{
    UIImagePickerController picker = new UIImagePickerController();
    picker.SourceType = cameraType;
    picker.Delegate = new MyImagePickerDelegate(this);
    this.PresentModalViewController(picker, true);
}
else
{
    using (var alert = new UIAlertView("Whoops", "No Camera found",
```

continues

LISTING 10-6 *(continued)*

```
                                           null, "Ok!", null))
    {
        alert.Show();
    }
}
```

Figure 10-3 shows this code running on the simulator where the camera is not found.

Figure 10-4 shows the same code running on an actual device where the image picker with the camera will be showing.

Editing an Image

The image picker provides simple functionality to allow users to crop and edit an image after it has been picked. The image can be either a pre-existing image or an image taken from the camera. A rectangle shape is placed over the selected image within the image picker and provides the cut-off point for the cropped image. Despite the fact that users can crop their selected image, the original image is also kept for you to manipulate the way you would like.

To allow users to crop and edit their photos, you need to set the `AllowsEditing` property to `true`. There is also an `AllowsImageEditing` property; however, this has been superseded by the `AllowsEditing` property since the ability to edit and crop video was added. Editing and cropping videos are discussed further in the "Video" section later in this chapter.

As in Listing 10-5, you use the `info` dictionary and key to get the image reference from the `info` dictionary of the newly edited image and the size of the editing rectangle shape. The two additional keys that are added into the dictionary are `UIImagePickerControllerEditedImage` and `UIImagePickerControllerCropRect`. Even though the edited image is provided, the original image object is available, too. This allows you to manually update or store the original image as and when you need. The actual editing functions provided by the API are rather limited, but provide simple functionality for cropping and editing. Figure 10-5 shows the rectangle when editing is allowed.

FIGURE 10-3   **FIGURE 10-4**   **FIGURE 10-5**

Customizing the Camera

Using the camera on a device provides you with a few different options when it comes to customizing how the camera looks and how it works. This section explains what customization you can do when using the camera.

One of the things that you can customize with the camera is the camera "controls" that are displayed on screen by default. These controls are the same default controls that are used on the camera application on the iPhone. Most of the time the default controls are sufficient, but you also have support to override these and build up your own interface. The property ShowsCameraControls can be optionally set to false so that the controls are not visible.

Once the controls are not on the screen, notice that you cannot take a photo. To take a photo you need to overlay a control or two on the camera view to raise an event where you can programmatically take a photo. The CameraOverlayView allows you to provide a view to overlay over the top of the camera view. For this example you use a custom view shown in Listing 10-7.

Available for download on Wrox.com

LISTING 10-7: Overlaying a view in while using the camera

```
var cameraType = UIImagePickerControllerSourceType.Camera;
picker = new UIImagePickerController();
picker.SourceType = cameraType;
picker.ShowsCameraControls = false;
picker.CameraOverlayView = new MyOverlayView(this);
picker.Delegate = new MyImagePickerDelegate(this);
this.PresentModalViewController(picker, true);

...

public class MyOverlayView : UIView
{
    public MyOverlayView (MainViewController mvc)
    {
        this.Frame = new RectangleF(0f, 0f, 320f, 480f);
        UIButton button = UIButton.FromType(UIButtonType.RoundedRect);
        button.SetTitle("Take a Photo", UIControlState.Normal);
        button.Frame = new RectangleF(0f, 420f, 320f, 40f);
        button.TouchUpInside += delegate(object sender, EventArgs e) {
            mvc.picker.TakePicture();
            Console.WriteLine ("Took a picture!");
        };
        this.AddSubview(button);
    }
}
```

Listing 10-7 uses a simple custom view inheriting from the UIView base class. To set the custom view as the camera overlay, you create a new instance of your overlay view and pass it to the CameraOverlayView property. In the constructor you pass in the view that you are using the picker control within. This allows you to call into the current controller and programmatically take a picture using the TakePicture method. This is shown in the bold line in Listing 10-7. Figure 10-6 shows the overlaid button image.

The `UIImagePickerController` also provides the `CameraViewTransform` property. This allows you to pass in a transform using `CGAffineTransform` methods such as `MakeScale` and `MakeRotate`. You may have noticed that removing the camera controls leaves a black bar at the bottom the screen. This is because of the aspect ratio of the camera compared to the screen. You can optionally scale the camera view up with the `CameraViewTransform` property so the camera fits the whole screen using the code in the following snippet. However, it might skew the image slightly. The first parameter of the `MakeScale` method is the amount to scale the x coordinate by and the second parameter is the amount to scale the y coordinate by. To get the camera to fill the screen, you'll just scale the y coordinate by a ratio of 1.13.

```
picker.CameraViewTransform = CGAffineTransform.MakeScale(1f, 1.13f);
```

The result of using this transform is shown in Figure 10-7.

FIGURE 10-6

FIGURE 10-7

Saving an Image to the Photo Album

To save an image to your picture library, you first want to instantiate a new `UIImage` object. On the `UIImage` class there is a method called `SaveToPhotosAlbum`. The photo album has a special folder that is used for just images saved from external sources, such as Safari or through an application, and not taken from the built-in camera.

The `SaveToPhotosAlbum` method takes a delegate to allow it to pass back the saved image or an `NSError` object if an error occurs as trying to save the image. You can check to see if the `NSError` comes back as `null`; if this is the case, then you know the image was saved successfully. Listing 10-8 shows how you would save a static file from the project to the photos album.

 Make sure the image is included in the project and has its build action set to Content.

Figure 10-8 shows the image picker without any photos in it. After saving a photo with the code in Listing 10-8, you can see that Figure 10-9 shows the same image picker with the newly added photo.

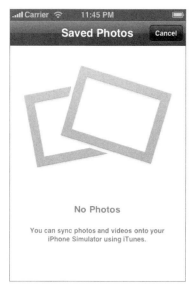

FIGURE 10-8

FIGURE 10-9

LISTING 10-8: Saving an image to the photo album

```
UIImage imageFile = UIImage.FromFile("image.png");
imageFile.SaveToPhotosAlbum(delegate (UIImage image, NSError error) {
   Console.WriteLine ("Saved to photo album");
});
```

VIDEO

The video functionality varies from device to device. All devices allow playback of video, but only the iPhone 3GS devices allow the ability to record video. The APIs allow you to detect what will or won't work for each device, enabling you to create a great experience for all users using video functionality. This section discusses how you can integrate video into your application and how you can use certain devices to record video as well.

Playing a Video

The iPhone SDK provides a simple controller to play videos within your application. Tucked away in the MonoTouch.MediaPlayer namespace, the MPMoviePlayerController class provides the functionality to play a movie, prepare to play a movie, and stop a movie. Listing 10-9 shows how to start playing a video. The first line shows the instantiation of a new movie player object, passing the video content file path in the constructor, and the second line simply calls the Play method, which displays the movie player and starts playing the video.

LISTING 10-9: Playing a video from a file

```
var player = new MPMoviePlayerController(NSUrl.FromFilename("video.mp4"));
player.Play();
```

If you would rather use an external video and progressively download the video than play one directly from the device, you use the NSUrl method FromString instead of FromFilename and pass in the URL location of the video. Of course, you need to replace the URL string with your own external video.

```
var videoUrl = NSUrl.FromString("http://example.com/video.mp4")
var player = new MPMoviePlayerController(videoUrl);
player.Play();
```

You might have noticed that there is a short buffering period before the video starts to play. This is known as the preload. You can set notifications on the video player, which fires off a message when the video has preloaded so you can first show a loading screen and then show the video when the preload finishes. You can also use notifications to get messages fired off when the video has finished playing and when the user has changed the scaling of the video.

You use the DefaultCenter property from the NSNotificationCenter class to add observers so that your messages fire off when a notification happens. You can think of an *observer* as a way of adding events on certain actions by using strings as a way of creating these events instead of using strongly typed events that you might be used to in C#. For this example, you just use the notifications MPMoviePlayerContentPreloadDidFinishNotification and MPMoviePlayerPlaybackDidFinishNotification. The other notification is named MPMoviePlayerScalingModeDidChangeNotification. You can add two class variables of type NSObject, which can be your preload and playback finished observers. Using the AddObserver method, you pass in an action method for each observer, which runs when the notifications are called. You can use a lambda expression to place this code inline. When the preload notification is fired, you just want to start playing the video so you call Play on your MPMoviePlayerController, and when the playback notification is fired, you want to remove the observers and clean up the movie player instance. You can use an activity indicator to make sure the user is aware that you are preloading the video when the application starts up. Listing 10-10 shows the example code to do this. Again, you need to make sure you change the URL on the eighth line to point to an external video of your choice.

LISTING 10-10: Using movie player observers

```
MPMoviePlayerController moviePlayer;
NSObject didFinishPreload, didFinishPlayback;

public override void ViewDidLoad()
{
```

```
        base.ViewDidLoad ();

        var videoUrl = NSUrl.FromString("http://example.com/video.mp4");
        moviePlayer = new MPMoviePlayerController(videoUrl);

        activityIndicator.StartAnimating();

        var centre = NSNotificationCenter.DefaultCenter;
        var preloadFinish = "MPMoviePlayerContentPreloadDidFinishNotification";
        didFinishPreload = centre.AddObserver(preloadFinish,
            (notify) => {
                Console.WriteLine ("Start playing movie");
                activityIndicator.StopAnimating();
                moviePlayer.Play();
            });

        var playbackFinished = "MPMoviePlayerPlaybackDidFinishNotification";
        didFinishPlayback = centre.AddObserver(playbackFinished,
            (notify) => {
                Console.WriteLine ("Movie finished, Clean up");

                centre.RemoveObserver(didFinishPreload);
                centre.RemoveObserver(didFinishPlayback);

                activityIndicator.Hidden = true;

                moviePlayer.Dispose();
                moviePlayer = null;
            }); }
    }
```

Customizing the Video Player

The functionality that the movie player provides is rather limited, allowing only two properties to be tweaked to your needs. These properties are ScalingMode and MovieControlMode.

Scaling mode sets the aspect ratio of the video playing. The options available for this are Fill, AspectFill, AspectFit, and None.

➤ Fill, as the name suggests, fills the screen with your video so both edges of the video fit on the screen, but the aspect ratio may not remain the same.

➤ AspectFill doesn't skew your video while filling the screen, but it does crop your video so that the video fits full on the screen leaving no gaps.

➤ AspectFit keeps the same aspect ratio for the video and fits it on the screen as best as possible for one edge of the video, but it might expose the background view if the video does not fit completely.

➤ None does not try to fit the video at all and plays it at its native size.

Using the MPMovieScalingMode enumeration, you can set the ScalingMode to any of the options in this list. See Figures 10-10 through 10-13 for examples of each scaling mode. The background of the player is set to blue (which shows as a lighter gray in the printed version of the figure you are looking at) so you can see the difference between the video size and the player size. Notice in this example that Aspect Fit and Fill video are the same. This is because the ratio of the video allows the edges of the video to fit on the screen without needing to change the aspect ratio.

FIGURE 10-10

FIGURE 10-11

FIGURE 10-12

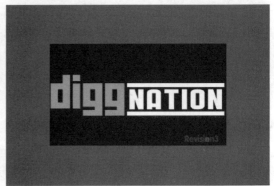

FIGURE 10-13

The other property that you can modify for a video player is the MovieControlMode property. Using the MPMovieControlMode enumeration, you can set the control mode to Default, Hidden, or VolumeOnly. Figures 10-14 and 10-15 show the Default and VolumeOnly control modes. Hidden hides all the default actions on the screen; this is useful if you want to provide your own user interface over the top of a video.

The movie player presents itself on the screen as a key window. To add a custom interface over the top of the movie player's key window, you can grab a reference of it from the list of windows that you have in your application. (A *key window* is essentially the topmost visible view available within the window frame.) You then can simply add a sub-view to the movie player key window. Because the movie player is presented in a landscape mode, you have to transform your overlay view to match. Listing 10-11 shows how you do everything just mentioned in this paragraph in code.

FIGURE 10-14

FIGURE 10-15

LISTING 10-11: Overlaying a view on a video player

```
public MPMoviePlayerController mPlayer;

public override void ViewDidLoad ()
{
    base.ViewDidLoad ();

    var button = UIButton.FromType(UIButtonType.RoundedRect);
    button.Frame = new RectangleF(0f, 20f, 320f, 40f);
    button.SetTitle("Play Video", UIControlState.Normal);
    button.TouchUpInside += delegate(object sender, EventArgs e)
    {
        PlayMovie ();

        var windows = UIApplication.SharedApplication.Windows;
        if(windows.Count() > 1)
        {
            var moviePlayerWindow = UIApplication.SharedApplication.KeyWindow;
            var customView = new MyOverlayView(this);
            moviePlayerWindow.AddSubview(customView);
        }
    };
    this.View.AddSubview(button);
}

void PlayMovie ()
{
    var url = NSUrl.FromFilename("video.mp4");
    mPlayer = new MPMoviePlayerController(url);
    mPlayer.Play();
}

...

public class MyOverlayView : UIView
{
    public MyOverlayView (MainViewController mvc)
```

continues

LISTING 10-11 *(continued)*

```
    {
        this.Frame = new RectangleF(0f, 0f, 320f, 480f);
        this.Transform = CGAffineTransform.MakeRotation((float)(Math.PI / 2));

        UIButton button = UIButton.FromType(UIButtonType.RoundedRect);
        button.SetTitle("Pause", UIControlState.Normal);
        button.Frame = new RectangleF(65f, 360f, 190f, 32f);
        button.TouchUpInside += delegate(object sender, EventArgs e) {
            Console.WriteLine ("Paused the video");
            mvc.mPlayer.Pause();
        };

        this.AddSubview(button);
    }
}
```

Figure 10-16 shows the overlay view created in
Listing 10-11.

Picking a Video

To allow a user to pick from a list of videos
that are stored on the device, you use the
UIImagePickerController you became
familiar with earlier in the chapter. Because
the video functionality for the iPhone is very
similar to the camera functionality, it's no
surprise to see that the video functionality is
part of the UIImagePickerController class.

FIGURE 10-16

In Listing 10-6 you used the method IsSourceTypeAvailable to determine if the device has a
camera. Because video functionality is limited to the iPhone 3GS model, simply finding out if
there is a camera is not enough. This is where the static method AvailableMediaTypes on the
UIImagePickerController class comes in handy.

The AvailableMediaTypes method accepts a source type and returns an array of media types
that the device has available. The media type of an image is public.image and the type of a video
is public.movie. If the method returns the public.movie type, you can set your instance of the
UIImagePickerController's MediaTypes property to only have the public.movie media type.
Listing 10-12 shows the picker being set in this way.

LISTING 10-12: Picking a video with an image picker controller

```
if (HasVideoSupport())
{
    UIImagePickerController picker = new UIImagePickerController();
    picker.SourceType = UIImagePickerControllerSourceType.PhotoLibrary;
    picker.MediaTypes = new [](){"public.movie"};
    picker.Delegate = new MyImagePickerDelegate(this);
```

```
      this.PresentModalViewController(picker, true);
   }
   else
   {
      using (var alert = new UIAlertView("Whoops", "No video support found",
                                         null, "Ok!", null))
      {
         alert.Show();
      }
   }

   ...

   bool HasVideoSupport()
   {
      var cameraType = UIImagePickerControllerSourceType.Camera;
      var cameraSupport =
                  UIImagePickerController.IsSourceTypeAvailable(cameraType);
      return (!cameraSupport) ? false :
              UIImagePickerController.AvailableMediaTypes(cameraType)
                                     .Contains("public.movie");
   }
```

When you display the picker, notice that you see only videos because they are the only type of media you can pick. Figure 10-17 shows how to display a video-only picker.

When a video is picked, it uses the same callback that the image picker uses: FinishedPickingMedia. The NSDictionary is populated with the two keys, UIImagePickerControllerMediaURL and UIImagePickerControllerMediaType. The media URL contains an NSUrl object that points to a temporary location for the selected video. This is where you can handle the video — either by moving it into the Documents directory or by using it another way. The temporary video is stored in the tmp directory of the application and is cleaned up by the OS at a time it thinks is appropriate.

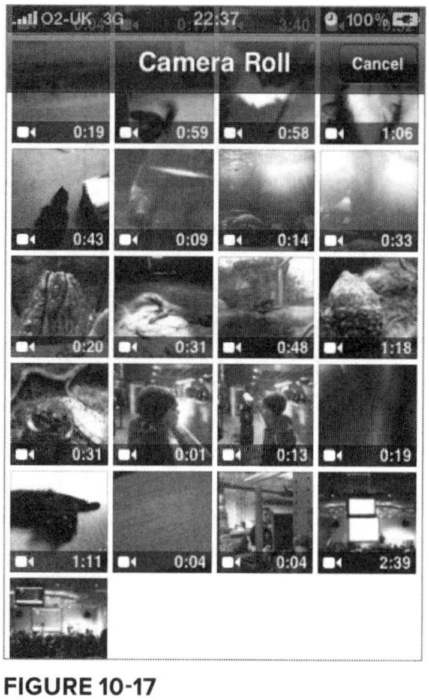

Recording Video

Recording a video with the iPhone is very similar to taking a

FIGURE 10-17

photo with the iPhone. From the previous example, you can just set the source type to the camera rather than the default of the photo library, and you are all set to record video instead of taking a photo. This is, of course, assuming that you have checked that the device can record video using the AvailableMediaTypes method. Notice that the camera controls change to reflect the fact that you are recording a video and not taking a photo. You can optionally choose to hide the camera controls by setting the ShowsCameraControls to false; however, at the time of this writing, there is no way of programmatically recording a video without using the default camera controls. Listing 10-13 is an example of setting up the UIImagePickerController to record video. Figure 10-18 shows the video recording screen.

LISTING 10-13: Recording a video

```
public override void ViewDidLoad ()
{
    base.ViewDidLoad ();

    UIButton button = UIButton.FromType(UIButtonType.RoundedRect);
    button.Frame = new RectangleF(0f, 30f, 320, 40f);
    button.SetTitle("Record Video", UIControlState.Normal);
    button.TouchUpInside += delegate(object sender, EventArgs e) {

        var cameraType = UIImagePickerControllerSourceType.Camera;
        if(HasVideoSupport())
        {
            UIImagePickerController picker = new UIImagePickerController();
            picker.SourceType = cameraType;
            picker.MediaTypes = new [] {"public.movie"};
            picker.Delegate = new MyImagePickerDelegate(this);
            this.PresentModalViewController(picker, true);
        }
        else
        {
            using (var alert = new UIAlertView("Whoops",
                          "No video support found", null, "Ok!", null))
            {
                alert.Show();
            }
        }
    };
    this.View.AddSubview(button);
}

...

bool HasVideoSupport()
{
    var cameraType = UIImagePickerControllerSourceType.Camera;
    var cameraSupport =
              UIImagePickerController.IsSourceTypeAvailable(cameraType);
    return (!cameraSupport) ? false :
           UIImagePickerController.AvailableMediaTypes(cameraType)
                                  .Contains("public.movie");
}
```

When recording a video, you can also set the quality of the video recording. The lower the quality, the smaller the file size of the resulting video. You can set the VideoQuality property on the image picker using the UIImagePickerControllerQualityType enumeration like so:

```
picker.VideoQuality = UIImagePickerControllerQualityType.Low;
```

The enumeration provides three options for quality: High, Medium, and Low. The default setting used in video recording is Medium. The other property you can use while recording a video is the VideoMaximumDuration property. As you would gather from the property name, this is where you can set the maximum duration for a recorded video in seconds. The longest a video can be is 10 minutes, and the default value for recording a video is 10 minutes, too.

Editing a Video

In the same way that you can allow the editing of images through the UIImagePickerController, you can also set the AllowEditing property to true for when you are recording or picking a video. This provides you with an interface to trim a video when you have picked a video from the image picker. Unlike when you are editing an image, when the editing has finished, you only get back a temporary trimmed or edited video with the UIImagePickerControllerMediaURL key in the NSDictionary available after a video is selected or recorded — and not the original video. The video, which is temporarily created, is eventually cleaned up automatically by the device, so you want to save the video out to a different place. The UIImagePickerControllerMediaURL object is of type NSUrl, and you need to cast the object to NSUrl to extract the Path property needed to locate the file. Figure 10-19 shows what the image picker video editor looks like.

FIGURE 10-18

However, the video picker is not the most recommended way of editing the video. For editing, you are better off using the specialized class UIVideoEditorController instead. The video editor controller presents you with an editing window that is similar to the one used with the image picker. However, notice that there are two options for the user to select: Cancel and Save. You are exposed to three different events on the UIVideoEditorController class:

➤   UserCancelled: Handles when the user clicks Cancel.

➤   Saved: Handles when a user clicks Save.

FIGURE 10-19

➤   Failed: Fired off when an unexpected error happens, such as the video was in the wrong format to be edited.

The Saved event returns the path to the edited video file, the Failed event returns an NSError object, and the UserCancelled event does not return any extra information. If you need to get back the original file path, you can always cast the sender to a UIVideoEditorController object and use the VideoPath property.

The video editor can be used only in portrait mode.

With the video editor you can set the edited video to be of lower quality and force the edited video to be of a set maximum length by setting the `VideoQuality` and `VideoMaximumDuration`, respectively.

Creating a video edit screen is pretty straightforward. You instantiate a new `UIVideoEditorController`, set the `VideoPath` property to the path of the video you want to edit, and then present the video editor as a modal view. Because you won't know if the iPhone that is running the application has support for editing video, you want to use the video editor static method `CanEditVideoAtPath`. Passing in the video path returns `true` if the video can be edited. Listing 10-14 shows an example of creating a dedicated video editing screen and Figure 10-20 shows what the `UIVideoEditorController` screen looks like.

FIGURE 10-20

 LISTING 10-14: Using a dedicated video editor screen

```
if(UIVideoEditorController.CanEditVideoAtPath(ChosenVideoPath))
{
    var videoEditor = new UIVideoEditorController();
    videoEditor.VideoPath = ChosenVideoPath;
    videoEditor.Saved += delegate(object sender, UIPathEventArgs e) {
        this.DismissModalViewControllerAnimated(true);
        // Handle edited video with e.Path
    };
    videoEditor.Failed += delegate(object sender, NSErrorEventArgs e) {
        this.DismissModalViewControllerAnimated(true);
        // Handle error here with e.Error
    };
    videoEditor.UserCancelled += delegate(object sender, EventArgs e) {
        this.DismissModalViewControllerAnimated(true);
        // Handle cancel
    };
    this.PresentModalViewController(videoEditor, true);
}
```

Saving a Video to the Saved Photo Album

When saving an image to the saved photo album, you use a static method on the `UIImage` class to save the file. Because all references to a video file are using a path and not the object in memory, the UIVideo static class provides the methods you need to save the video to a photo album. As you know, video functionality is limited to only certain devices, so before you save the video to the photo album, you need to check if the device can actually save a video to its photo album. The static method IsCompatibleWithSavedPhotosAlbum provides this functionality and returns true if you pass in a path of a video that can be saved to the photo album.

To save the video to the photo album, once you have checked that the device can actually save a video, you use the SaveToPhotosAlbum static method on the UIVideo class. You pass in the path to the video you want to save and a callback that triggers when the video has been saved. Listing 10-15 shows the code to do this.

Available for download on Wrox.com

LISTING 10-15: Saving a video to the photo album

```
var videoPath = videoSavePath;
if(UIVideo.IsCompatibleWithSavedPhotosAlbum(videoPath))
{
    UIVideo.SaveToPhotosAlbum(videoPath, delegate (string path,
                                            NSError errors)
    {
        using (var alert = new UIAlertView("Success", "Video saved!",
                                        null, "Ok!", null))
        {
            alert.Show();
        }
    });
}
```

AUDIO

The iPhone provides many different ways of playing audio on the device, whether it is a short sound clip or a full-length podcast show. This section discusses the different ways that you can play audio through the iPhone, how to handle listening to audio, and also how to record audio.

Playing Audio

Using audio in an application allows you either to play a short system sound, which offers a quick and limited audio experience, or to play a much longer sound making use of the AVAudioPlayer class. The next few sections describe how to use audio in both these ways.

Short Audio

Using the SystemSound functionality in the AudioToolbox is the best way to play short audio clips. You can only use the SystemSound method for playing audio that is shorter than 30 seconds in duration. This is because the SystemSound class uses a low-level C interface to play short system sounds. I discuss playing audio for a longer amount of time later in this chapter.

To use `SystemSound`, you need to instantiate a new `SystemSound` object, passing in to the constructor an `NSUrl` containing the file path to the audio you want to play. The `SystemSound` object then exposes two methods to play the sounds.

➤ You can play an alert sound with the `PlayAlertSound` method. The alert sound behaves differently depending on the user settings on the device (such as vibrate when the sound is played) and the type of device (for example, an iPod Touch versus an iPhone).

➤ The other method exposed to you is the `PlaySystemSound`, and this is likely to be the method you would use most for playing short sound clips.

Listing 10-16 shows how to create the `SystemSound` object and play the audio file. The `PlaySystemSound` and `PlayAlertSound` methods are asynchronous, so they do not block the thread and therefore do not block the UI thread.

 Remember the audio file needs to be included in your project and have the build action set to Content for it to work. Compressed audio files such as MP3 files are not supported, so you either need to use the AVAudioPlayer class (discussed later in the chapter) to play compressed audio files or use an uncompressed file type such as CAF (Core Audio Format).

LISTING 10-16: Playing uncompressed audio

```
using MonoTouch.AudioToolbox;

...

var audioFile = NSUrl.FromFilename("audio.caf");
SystemSound sound = SystemSound.FromFile(audioFile);
sound.PlaySystemSound();
```

Vibration

You're probably thinking this is in the wrong place; vibration is not a sound or audio. However, to make the device vibrate, you use the `PlaySystemSound` method on a special field on the class called `Vibrate`. You can directly call the play method on this field to make the device vibrate. You should note that the vibration works only on a device and nothing happens in the simulator.

```
SystemSound.Vibrate.PlaySystemSound();
```

Long Audio

Chances are you are going to want to either play compressed audio in your application or play audio that lasts longer than 30 seconds. The `AVAudioPlayer` class provides functionality to play different types of files and much longer audio files.

The methods available on the AVAudioPlayer are shown in Table 10-1.

TABLE 10-1: AVAudioPlayer Methods

METHOD	DESCRIPTION
AveragePower(uint channel)	The average power, in decibels, for the channel passed in. UpdateMeters() must be run before calling this method.
Pause()	Pauses the audio playback.
PeakPower(uint channel)	The peak power, in decibels, for the channel passed in. UpdateMeters() must be run before calling this method.
Play()	Starts the audio playback. If it was previously paused, it continues from the place where it was paused.
PrepareToPlay()	Prepares the audio to play. The Play() method calls this method if it isn't explicitly called.
Stop()	Stops the audio playback and requires PrepareToPlay() to be called again.
UpdateMeters()	Updates the values for AveragePower and PeakPower .MeteringEnabled needs to be set to true.

To get a simple track to play, you can instantiate a new AVAudioPlayer from the static method FromUrl. Using this method you pass in the location of the audio file you want to play, similar to the way you used the SystemSound class. You can optionally use the FromData method to pass in an NSData object of audio data. Once the class is instantiated, you can just call the Play method, which in turn first calls the PrepareToPlay method to start the audio playing. You use the FinishedPlaying delegate to clean up the audio player after the audio file has finished playing. Listing 10-17 shows the way to play a long audio file.

LISTING 10-17: Playing longer audio

```
var audioFile = NSUrl.FromFilename("audio.caf");
var audioPlayer = AVAudioPlayer.FromUrl(audioFile);
audioPlayer.Play();
audioPlayer.FinishedPlaying += delegate(object sender, AVStatusEventArgs e)
    {
        audioPlayer.Dispose();
    };
```

Recording Audio

To allow recording functionality within your application, you need to use the AVAudioRecorder class. To create a new audio recorder, you use the static method ToUrl, which is expecting the path location to save the recorded audio to, an `NSDictionary` containing recording settings, and an `NSError` object.

First you construct two `NSObject` arrays. The first object array contains `NSNumber` objects representing the settings values, and the second represents the settings keys. Using the `NSDictionary` static method `FromObjectsAndKeys`, you pass in the two arrays, which populate the settings `NSDictionary`.

Now that the settings dictionary is set, you want to set up a location for the audio file to be recorded to. Because the Documents folder is saved when an iPhone backup happens, you save it in there for this example. You can use the `Environment.GetFolderPath` method to get the Documents folder, and then you simply use the `Path.Combine` method to concatenate the Documents folder with the name of the audio file you want to save.

Once you have the `AVAudioRecorder` set up, you can call `Record` to start recording and then `Stop` to stop recording, or you can use the `RecordFor` method and pass in the amount of seconds you want to record. You use the `FinishedRecording` event to tell you when recording has finished so you can clean up the `AVAudioRecorder` you created. You can also check whether the audio file you just recorded exists and create a button that allows you to play the recorded file. Listing 10-18 shows how to record audio for 5 seconds.

LISTING 10-18: Recording audio in code

```
var values = new NSObject[]
            {
                NSNumber.FromFloat(44100.0f),
                NSNumber.FromInt32((int)AudioFileType.WAVE),
                NSNumber.FromInt32(1),
                NSNumber.FromInt32((int)AVAudioQuality.Max)
            };

var keys = new NSObject[]
            {
                AVAudioSettings.AVSampleRateKey,
                AVAudioSettings.AVFormatKey,
                AVAudioSettings.AVNumberOfChannelsKey,
                AVAudioSettings.AVEncoderAudioQualityKey
            };

var settings = NSDictionary.FromObjectsAndKeys(values, keys);

var documentsFolder =
        Environment.GetFolderPath(Environment.SpecialFolder.Personal);
var audioUrl =
        NSUrl.FromFilename(Path.Combine(documentsFolder, "audio.wav"));

var error = new NSError();

var recorder = AVAudioRecorder.ToUrl(audioUrl, settings, out error);
recorder.FinishedRecording += delegate
    {
```

```
using (var alert = new UIAlertView("Success", "Finished recording!",
                                    null,"Ok!", null))
{
   alert.Show();
}

if(File.Exists(audioUrl.Path))
{
   var button = UIButton.FromType(UIButtonType.RoundedRect);
   button.Frame = new RectangleF(0f, 30f, 320f, 32f);
   button.SetTitle("Play recorded audio", UIControlState.Normal);
   button.TouchUpInside += delegate(object s, EventArgs events) {
      var audioPlayer = AVAudioPlayer.FromUrl(audioUrl);
      audioPlayer.Play();
      audioPlayer.FinishedPlaying += delegate(object sender,
                                              AVStatusEventArgs e)
      {
         audioPlayer.Dispose();
      };
   };
   this.View.AddSubview(button);
}

recorder.Dispose();
};
recorder.RecordFor(5f);
```

ANIMATION

Animation with the iPhone is a big topic and could quite easily be a book on its own. This chapter touches on a few of the key points on animation to get you on your way. The following examples show how to animate individual controls as well as how to animate with views.

Creating Basic Animation

As a simple animation example, you are going to create a new text label and animate it to move from the top of the screen to the bottom.

To perform a basic animation like this one you need to be familiar with some important concepts:

➤ **Key path:** A path mapping to a layers property on a control. You can think of this like accessing properties with a string path rather than strongly typed properties.

➤ **CALayer:** The layer contains generic properties on an object such as the position, frame and opacity. This allows you to change the properties (such as setting the opacity) on a view through the layer properties.

➤ **CABasicAnimation:** A class that you use to animate a property on an object, like a text label's opacity or its Y position.

To get started, you want to create a `CABasicAnimation` object from a specific key path. The key path is a string that represents a `CALayer` property (when creating the animation, you are actually animating the `Layer` property of your object). A few examples of key paths would be `position.y`, `transform.translation.x`, and `opacity`. The following is a list of the possible properties that you can animate from a `CALayer`.

- `anchorPoint`
- `backgroundColor`
- `borderColor`
- `borderWidth`
- `bounds`
- `contents`
- `contentsRect`
- `cornerRadius`
- `doubleSided`

- `hidden`
- `masksToBounds`
- `opacity`
- `position`
- `sublayers`
- `sublayerTransform`
- `transform`
- `zPosition`

When you animate your layer, you use the key path and use `From`, `To`, and `By` properties to set up the animation.

Because you want to animate a label from the top of the screen to the bottom, you first should create the label and place it on the view. To animate the label going from the top of the view to the bottom of the view, you want to translate the label on the Y-axis to 420 (which is near the bottom of the iPhone). When creating the `CABasicAnimation` object, you use the static method `FromKeyPath` passing in `transform.translation.y` as the key path you will use. Setting the `To` property to 420 allows you to transform the label 420 pixels on the Y-axis (move the label 420 pixels down on the device). Because the `From` property is expecting an `NSNumber`, you can use a float with the `NSNumber.FromFloat` method to get this for you.

All animations last an explicit amount of time, so you want to set the `Duration` property. For this example it will be 3 seconds. You probably don't want the label left at the bottom of the screen so you can set the `AutoReverses` property to `true` so that when the animation finishes, it returns back to the top.

Now that the animation has been created, you can apply it to your label that you created first. Every `UIView` object has a `Layer` property that allows you to animate any `UIView` object you want. For this example, you will use the method `AddAnimation` on the `Layer` property and pass in your newly created animation and a unique key for the animation. Adding the animation to the layer starts the animation straight away.

You might want to trigger an event when an animation starts or finishes. You can do this by creating your own `CAAnimationDelegate` class and using this as the delegate for the animation you created. You override both the `AnimationStarted` and `AnimationStopped` methods to update the label's text to reflect the animation status.

Listing 10-19 shows the code for a simple animation of the label animating from the top of the screen to the bottom of the screen and back again.

LISTING 10-19: A simple animation

```
public override void ViewDidLoad ()
{
    base.ViewDidLoad ();

    var label = new UILabel (new RectangleF (0f, 20f, 320f, 40f));
    label.TextAlignment = UITextAlignment.Center;
    label.Text = "Example Label";
    this.View.AddSubview (label);

    var animation = CABasicAnimation.FromKeyPath ("transform.translation.y");
    animation.To = NSNumber.FromFloat (420f);
    animation.Duration = 3;
    animation.AutoReverses = true;
    animation.Delegate = new MyAnimationDelegate (label);
    label.Layer.AddAnimation (animation, "moveToBottomAndBack");
}

...

public class MyAnimationDelegate : CAAnimationDelegate
{

    public UILabel Label { get; set; }

    public MyAnimationDelegate (UILabel label)
    {
        Label = label;
    }

    public override void AnimationStarted (CAAnimation anim)
    {
        Console.WriteLine ("Animation Started");
        Label.Text = "Animation Started";
    }

    public override void AnimationStopped (CAAnimation anim, bool finished)
    {
        Console.WriteLine ("Animation stopped.");
        Label.Text = "Animation Stopped";
    }

}
```

Using UIView Animations

Using the basic animation class is a good way of providing simple animations to properties on a
UIView. However, creating an individual animation for each property you want to modify can be
quite verbose. Using static methods on the UIView class, you can animate a group of controls and
properties in one animation.

In Listing 10-19 you animated a label going to the bottom of the screen and back up to the top. For this example, you animate the label you had previously spinning and fading out while revealing a button that was previously hidden. Listing 10-20 shows an example of how to achieve this in code.

LISTING 10-20: Animation with UIViews

```
UILabel label;
UIButton hiddenButton;

public override void ViewDidLoad ()
{
    base.ViewDidLoad ();

    label = new UILabel (new RectangleF (0f, 20f, 320f, 40f));
    label.TextAlignment = UITextAlignment.Center;
    label.Text = "Example Label";
    this.View.AddSubview (label);

    hiddenButton = UIButton.FromType (UIButtonType.RoundedRect);
    hiddenButton.Frame = new RectangleF (0f, 60f, 320f, 50f);
    hiddenButton.SetTitle ("Surprise!", UIControlState.Normal);
    hiddenButton.Layer.Opacity = 0;
    this.View.AddSubview (hiddenButton);

    UIView.BeginAnimations ("AnimateLabel");
    UIView.SetAnimationDuration (1);
    UIView.SetAnimationDidStopSelector (new Selector
                                        ("didFinishAnimation:"));
    UIView.SetAnimationDelegate(this);

    label.Layer.Opacity = 0;
    hiddenButton.Layer.Opacity = 1;
    label.Transform = CGAffineTransform.MakeRotation ((float)(Math.PI));

    UIView.CommitAnimations ();
}

[Export("didFinishAnimation:")]
void DidFinishAnimation ()
{
    label.Dispose();
    Console.WriteLine ("Did finish animation");
}
```

Listing 10-20 starts off by creating a UILabel and a UIButton; you initialize the controls in the ViewDidLoad method. Notice that you set the hiddenButton's opacity to 0. This allows you to animate the opacity later to reveal the button. To create an animation, you use the static method BeginAnimations on UIView to start an animation block. Once you have finished animating your objects, you then use CommitAnimations to commit the block of animations and to start the animation.

Within your animation block, you do two things. The first is to set up additional parameters on the animation block. In this example you're setting the animation duration to last one second, creating a new selector to fire when your animation has finished, and you're setting the delegate to the class you're in so that the selector will be found. Because the selector needs to be fired off from Objective-C, you use the Export method on your DidFinishAnimation method to expose this. (A *selector* is simply the name of a method within Objective-C.) When the animation is complete, your label's opacity will be set to 0 and will not be visible. In your DidFinishAnimation method, you can dispose of the label.

The second thing you do within your animation block is to animate the actual objects. You set the final properties on your objects to how you want them to appear after the animation happens, and CoreAnimation takes care of the transformation between the two states. By default, the label's opacity is set to 1. Because you want this to be hidden, you set the opacity to 0 so it animates a fade out. You want the hiddenButton to appear so you do the inverse of the label and set the opacity to 1, and to create the rotation effect, you put a transform on the label to rotate it upside down.

SUMMARY

As you have seen from this chapter, you have a plethora of possibilities with the multimedia side of the iPhone; however, it's wise to check whether the device supports rich features such as video recording or even whether it has a camera. The ability to add in this functionality allows your application not just to consume multimedia, but also to create multimedia.

Talking to Other Applications

WHAT'S IN THIS CHAPTER?

➤ Making MonoTouch talk with other applications with the OpenURL method

➤ Having your applications integrate with third-party applications

➤ Accessing the iPhone Address Book or the iPod music library

➤ Integrating with third-party libraries with Objective-C and .NET

This chapter discusses the ways you can use MonoTouch to talk to other applications on the iPhone, both Apple-built applications and those downloaded from the App Store. It also provides helpful ways of accessing the iPhone's Address Book and the iPod music library.

The secret behind interfacing with any application on the device is the OpenUrl method on the current UIApplication, which can be accessed via UIApplication.SharedApplication. This method handles where and what to open when you pass in an NSUrl object for it to parse. When the method is called, the app closes in its normal fashion by calling the WillTerminate method as it closes and carries out the appropriate action based on the URL passed in.

INTEGRATING APPLE APPLICATIONS

This section shows how you can integrate Apple-built applications into your own application.

Opening Up Safari

Opening up Safari is a pretty straightforward place to start. The most likely reason for you to close down your app and open up Safari is because you would like a web site to be displayed. The web site URL is the NSUrl object that you pass into the OpenUrl method:

```
var url = NSUrl.FromString("http://wrox.com");
UIApplication.SharedApplication.OpenUrl(url);
```

You may notice we are using `NSUrl.FromString()` *here and not just simply* new `NSUrl()`. *This is because using the constructor would throw an exception if there were an error, whereas* `FromString` *will return null.*

You can achieve a similar solution by using the `UIWebView` to include web sites directly within your application without the need for the app to close down. This is covered earlier in this book in Chapter 4.

Opening Up E-Mail

Opening e-mail is very similar to how you'd expect it to work with the `mailto:` protocol:

```
var url = NSUrl.FromString("mailto:chris@example.com");
UIApplication.SharedApplication.OpenUrl(url)
```

 Whoops. This code won't run in the simulator. The simulator does not have the Mail capability, so you need to test this code on the device. You'll notice this is the same for making phone calls, sending text messages, and working with other applications, which might not be installed on the device, including third-party apps.

The `OpenUrl` *method returns a Boolean telling you whether or not the method was run successfully. You should use this information when it doesn't run successfully to show an appropriate error message.*

As the `mailto:` protocol states, you can also pass in these other commands: `bcc`, `cc`, `subject`, and `body`. This populates the necessary fields in the standard mail template. The `from` command normally used with the `mailto:` protocol is ignored by the iPhone SDK, so it will not work. Here's an example of the extra commands being used:

```
var url = NSUrl.FromString("mailto:chris@example.com?cc=other@example.com
                           &subject=Wrox&body=Monotouch");
UIApplication.SharedApplication.OpenUrl(url);
```

Making a Telephone Call

Using the `tel:` protocol, you can use the built-in telephone functionality of the iPhone by using the following `NSUrl` example. This example shows hyphens within the number, which are automatically stripped out as necessary.

```
var url = NSUrl.FromString("tel:+1-408-867-5309");
UIApplication.SharedApplication.OpenUrl(url);
```

Sending a Text/SMS Message

The `sms:` protocol enables you to open the Messages application and open a new message to a specified number. There is no option to pass a predefined message into a new text message. This first code example shows how to just open up a list of texts on the device:

```
var url = NSUrl.FromString("sms:");
UIApplication.SharedApplication.OpenUrl(url);
```

This next example shows how to open up a new text message with the passed-in number:

```
var url = NSUrl.FromString("sms:1-408-537-6309");
UIApplication.SharedApplication.OpenUrl(url);
```

Opening a Location in the Maps Application

To load up the Maps application from within a native iPhone app, you simply use a normal web site link to Google Maps. A few query string parameters are available to use when creating a Google Maps URL, such as `q` for a search query and `saddr` and `daddr` for source and destination address, respectively. This example loads up a map of Manchester, United Kingdom:

```
var url = NSUrl.FromString("http://maps.google.com/maps?q=Manchester,UK");
UIApplication.SharedApplication.OpenUrl(url);
```

 If you are running this in the simulator, since the simulator does not have the Google Maps application, the map loads up in Safari. On the device, the link loads up in the Google Maps application.

The ability to have web sites within your own application without closing your application down is also available with the MapKit API. You can see how to use this in Chapter 7.

Opening a YouTube Video

As you saw previously with the Maps example, you just use a normal URL to open up the Maps application; this principle is the same when you want to play a YouTube video. You can use either of the two YouTube URLs in the following example code. You need to use the video identifier to play the video. The two variables in the code snippet below — `youTubeUrl1` and `youTubeUrl2` — show examples of the two different types of URLs that can open up a YouTube video.

```
var videoId = "QHy0nBYwIKM";
var youTubeUrl1 =
        String.Format("http://youtube.com/watch?v={0}", videoId);
var youTubeUrl2 =
        String.Format("http://youtube.com/v/{0}", videoId);
var url = NSUrl.FromString(youTubeUrl2)
UIApplication.SharedApplication.OpenUrl(url);
```

Just as was the case with the Google Maps example in the previous section, in the simulator the link in this example opens up Safari and plays the video through there, whereas on the device it opens the YouTube application.

Opening Up the iTunes Store and the App Store

To open up the iTunes store and the App Store in an application you use the same URLs you would expect to use with iTunes or the App Store on the desktop. With this code, you don't need to tell your application which store to open; the device decides this based on the URL that it is using.

```
// This appStoreUrl will open up the AppStore.
var appStoreString =
        "http://itunes.apple.com/gb/app/linked-app/id342467961?mt=8";
var appStoreUrl = NSUrl.FromString(appStoreString);

// This iTunesUrl will open up the iTunes Store.
var iTunesString = "http://itunes.apple.com/gb/album/effloresce/id27518899";
var iTunesUrl = NSUrl.FromString(iTunesString);
UIApplication.SharedApplication.OpenUrl(iTunesUrl);
```

THIRD-PARTY APPLICATION INTEGRATION

In addition to opening up native Apple applications from your own app, you can also open up applications written by third-party companies. These third-party applications need to optionally expose a protocol for them to allow this interaction with other applications (this method is explained in the next section). Because applications can pick and choose how they go about implementing a protocol, they also need to provide documentation on how to use their protocols.

Finding a particular application's web site and then additionally how to implement its protocol can be very difficult. Luckily, a web site called www.handleopenurl.com provides a great resource for this. It's a community-driven site where you can easily search for an application you may want to interact with. The following examples show you how to interact with two free applications available from the AppStore.

Simple Integration with Google Earth

Google Earth on the iPhone is a version of the desktop program of Google Earth you may already be familiar with. Using the information found on www.handleopenurl.com, you can see that to open up the Google Earth application, you have to use the comgoogleearth: protocol. Because you can't rely on the user having the application installed, or even having a version that allows you to call it, you can use the CanOpenUrl method to determine this. This static method, on the current

`UIApplication` instance, can be useful when you want to contextually show a link to open up an application but only when you know that it exists on the device. The following code shows how you would use this:

```
var application = UIApplication.SharedApplication;
var url = NSUrl.FromString("comgoogleearth:");
if(application.CanOpenUrl(url))
{
    // Show button to open Google Earth app.
}
```

Since you've already gone through the Apple application protocols earlier in this chapter, loading Google Earth works as you might expect, and you can call it using the following example:

```
var url = NSUrl.FromString("comgoogleearth:");
UIApplication.SharedApplication.OpenUrl(url);
```

Further Integration with Skype

Unlike the Google Earth application, the Skype application allows a few different options to choose from when you want to open up the application on the iPhone. The Skype developer zone publishes a list of URLs that the Windows version of Skype will handle (see `http://bit.ly/skypeopenurl` for the full list), but it doesn't mention anything about the URLs handled on the iPhone. With a bit of trial and error, the URLs from that list that will complete the correct actions in the iPhone app are displayed in Table 11-1. Any URL starting with `skype:` will open the app regardless.

TABLE 11-1: Skype iPhone URLs

URL	ACTION
`skype:`	Opens Skype application
`skype:echo123?call`	Calls the user echo123
`skype:echo123?chat`	Starts a chat with the user echo123

Because there is no official word on what the Skype iPhone app supports in the way of URL structure, this could change at any point with no notice. Extra URLs could be added that support more features, so it's best not to rely on these existing too much.

ACCEPTING CALLS FROM OTHER APPLICATIONS

Having your application be able to open up other applications can be very useful; however, enabling your application to be opened by other applications can create many other useful situations.

Configuring Your Info.plist File

To enable your application to be opened by others, you need to update your `Info.plist` file. The `plist` file is essentially an XML file made up of key-value pairs describing information about your application. This is covered in more detail in Chapter 8. MonoDevelop generates this file for you when you build and run your application, but if you want to add in custom settings, you need to create this from scratch. To do this, right-click your project and go to Add ⇨ New File as shown in Figure 11-1.

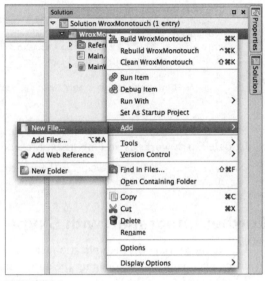

FIGURE 11-1

From here the New File template dialog box appears. Select the iPhone Application Manifest Template icon (see Figure 11-2). You'll notice that it is already named `Info.plist`.

Double-clicking the `Info.plist` file causes Apple's Property List Editor to pop up. This program helps in adding parent and child XML nodes to the `plist` file. To make sure your app responds correctly to incoming calls from other applications, you need to add in a parent node of URL types to the `plist` file. You also need to add a URL identifier string. This value is sent to an application when you call its open URL schema — this will become clearer further in the chapter. Normally you would use a reverse domain to keep the URL identifier value unique (for example, `com.chrisntr.myapp`). In addition to adding a URL identifier, you need to add in a node within URL Schemes. The URL Schemes are the protocol that another app calls when addressing your app, such as `skype` or `comgoogleearth`. For this example, the scheme is `myapp:`. Because `myapp` probably is not a very unique scheme, it's a good idea to also use your URL identifier as an additional scheme to use in case of a conflict. Figure 11-3 shows how your `plist` file should look.

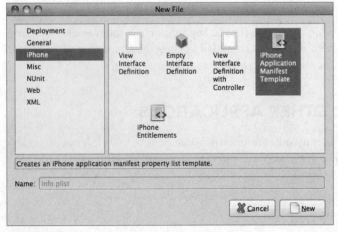

FIGURE 11-2

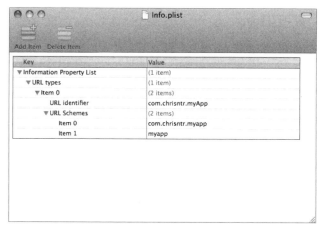

FIGURE 11-3

I often find the Property List Editor to be a little fiddly and quite difficult to make it do exactly as I want. Luckily, `plist` files are just simple XML files — if you open up the file in a normal text editor you can easily modify the file this way. Listing 11-1 is the raw text example of the `Info.plist` file shown previously.

LISTING 11-1: Raw Info.plist file

```
<?xml version="1.0" encoding="UTF-8"?>
<!DOCTYPE plist PUBLIC "-//Apple//DTD PLIST 1.0//EN"
 "http://www.apple.com/DTDs/PropertyList-1.0.dtd">
<plist version="1.0">
<dict>
        <key>CFBundleURLTypes</key>
        <array>
              <dict>
                    <key>CFBundleURLName</key>
                    <string>com.chrisntr.myApp</string>
                    <key>CFBundleURLSchemes</key>
                    <array>
                          <string>com.chrisntr.myapp</string>
                          <string>myapp</string>
                    </array>
              </dict>
        </array>
</dict>
</plist>
```

You can find this Info.plist file as part of the files in the Listing 11-2 folder of the download.

You can see in the XML that you can define keys, dictionaries, and arrays. In this sample you can see the two keys, `CFBundleURLName` and `CFBundleURLSchemes`, are wrapped in a `CFBundleURLTypes` array. This sets the application up to listen out for requests to the URL schemes provided, and since the `CFBundleURLSchemes` value is an array, you can set up multiple URL schemes for the application to listen out for. Once this has been set up, save the file and then you're ready to listen for it in your code.

Implementing an OpenURL Schema

If you have already played around with the UIApplication.SharedApplication object, you may have noticed the event HandleOpenURL is exposed. In the second version of the iPhone SDK, this method was the recommended way of handling incoming requests with the open URL Schemes. In the latest version of the iPhone SDK (Version 3.1.3 at the time of writing), the HandleOpenURL method has been superseded by the method FinishedLaunching that has the NSDictionary parameter options. This method was introduced to be the de facto standard of handling the application starting up, handling opening URLs, and handling Apple Push Notification Service (APNS) requests. This method is the default FinishedLaunching method used in the MonoDevelop iPhone templates, so you shouldn't need to change any code to add this in.

When an application calls into your app, the options dictionary contains two key-value pairs: UIApplicationLaunchOptionsURLKey and UIApplicationLaunchOptionsSourceApplicationKey. Listing 11-2 shows how to extract the URL used to call into your application and how to work out the source of the call.

LISTING 11-2: Extract open URL information

```
public override bool FinishedLaunching (UIApplication app, NSDictionary options)
{
    if(options != null)
    {
        var urlOptionKey = new NSString("UIApplicationLaunchOptionsURLKey");
        var urlSourceKey = new
                NSString("UIApplicationLaunchOptionsSourceApplicationKey");
        var url = (NSUrl) options[urlOptionKey];
        var source = options[urlSourceKey].ToString();

        // Grab information from NSUrl object.
        Console.WriteLine ("Url = " + url.AbsoluteString);
        // The URL Identifier from the app that called this app.
        Console.WriteLine ("Source = " + source);
    }
    ...
```

The URL that you receive back can be parsed to enable deep linking into your app by extracting the relevant information. To test that this works and that your app opens up as it should, you can use Safari on the simulator as a way to call the URL. To do this, you want to enter the URL in the address bar of the Safari app, which then closes Safari and opens up your application. This works for all the previously mentioned URLs and protocols.

INTEGRATING WITH THE ADDRESS BOOK

The Address Book is a key part of the existing iPhone functionality. This is where all the contacts users might have on their phone live. Accessing this information can be very useful within your application. You may want to allow users to see a list of their friends so they can send a link to your application, for example.

To get access to the Address Book you need to create a new ABAddressBook object. This object type exposes a few different methods to gather data from the Address Book. These methods are shown in bold in Listing 11-3.

LISTING 11-3: Accessing the Address Book object

```
using MonoTouch.AddressBook;

...

        ABAddressBook adBook = new ABAddressBook();

        // Groups can define a section of contacts
        // Used if you've synced contacts from another machine.
        ABGroup[] allGroups = adBook.GetGroups();
        Console.WriteLine ("Group Count: " + allGroups.Count());

        // Gets an array of ABPerson objects
        ABPerson[] allPeople = adBook.GetPeople();
        Console.WriteLine ("People Count: " + allPeople.Count());

        // Gets People with First or Last Name "Fred"
        ABPerson[] allFreds = adBook.GetPeopleWithName("Fred");
        Console.WriteLine ("Fred Count: " + allFreds.Count());

        // If you already know the Id, you can get an individual person
        int personRecordId = 57;
        ABPerson person = adBook.GetPerson(personRecordId);
```

When you are starting out with iPhone development, the iPhone simulator's address book will be empty. To make sure the code in Listing 11-3 works, you want to add someone called "Fred" as a contact. Chances are you will not have an ID for an individual person so you may also want to comment this code out too.

If you look at the person object created, you see many properties you would expect such as FirstName, LastName, and Birthday; however, also notice there is no TelephoneNo property. This is because the data for properties such as e-mail addresses, phone numbers, and URLs comes in a typed ABMultiValue object. There are a few methods you call to extract this information as needed. Listing 11-4 shows an example of getting back a list of phone numbers and e-mail addresses when you already have an array of people.

LISTING 11-4: Accessing phone and e-mail information

```
foreach(var person in allPeople)
{
    var phones = person.GetPhones();
```

continues

LISTING 11-4 *(continued)*

```
    if(phones.Count > 0)
    {
        foreach(var phone in phones)
        {
            Console.WriteLine("Phone Type " + phone.Label);
            Console.WriteLine("Phone Number " + phone.Value);
        }
    }

    var emails = person.GetEmails();
    if(emails.Count > 0)
    {
        foreach(var email in emails)
        {
            Console.WriteLine("E-mail Type " + email.Label);
            Console.WriteLine("E-mail Address " + email.Value);
        }
    }
}
```

You may have noticed while running through the example that labels come back as "_$!<Mobile>!$_" or "_$!<Home>!$_", and this happens for all labels except for custom labels or the iPhone label. This is because the labels can be localized to the device's current locale. To programmatically access this, you use the static method `LocalizedLabel` on `ABAddressBook`. By passing in the label that you get from the original label, you are returned the localized string label.

Accessing the Address Book programmatically can be useful for the most part, but to hand crank UI components on top of this takes a long time when you really just want the default behavior users expect from their iPhones. Fortunately `Monotouch.AddressBookUI` has this covered and provides a few helpful view controllers to make this interaction easier.

The four classes that provide this functionality are `ABPersonViewController`, `ABPeoplePickerNavigationController`, `ABNewPersonViewController`, and `ABUnknownPersonViewController`.

 All the views but the `ABPeoplePickerNavigationController` *need to be used with a navigation controller; otherwise they do not work properly.*

ABPersonViewController

The `ABPersonViewController` is a view controller that provides the ability to display and edit a single Address Book contact. Figure 11-4 shows how a default person view would look, and Figure 11-5 shows the edit view. By default, editing is not enabled, but you can enable it by setting `AllowEditing` to true. The `DisplayedPerson` property requires an `ABPerson` variable and sets the view controller to display this person. Listing 11-5 shows how you would use this view controller. Make sure you have a person with "Example" in their name for the sample to work.

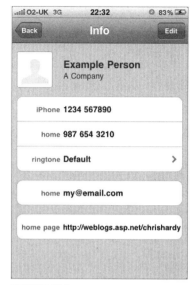

FIGURE 11-4

FIGURE 11-5

Available for download on Wrox.com

LISTING 11-5: Adding a person view controller

```
var adBook = new ABAddressBook();
var personvc = new ABPersonViewController();
personvc.DisplayedPerson = adBook.GetPeopleWithName("Example")[0];
personvc.AllowsEditing = true;
navigationController.PushViewController(personvc, true);
```

The Address Book object is only used to populate the displayed person and not needed to use the person view controller. Make sure you add in a contact with the name "Example" for the example to work.

ABPeoplePickerNavigationController

To allow users to select a particular person from a list of all their contacts, you use the `ABPeoplePickerNavigationController`. The picker is generally used as a modal view and not pushed onto a navigation controller. When the view is loaded, you are presented with a list of all users, similar to that list shown in the Contacts applications (see Figure 11-6). With the picker, you have two options when handling the user selecting a contact.

➤ If you want to handle the picker the automated way and continue to a person view controller, you set the event argument `Continue` to `true` in the `SelectPerson` event callback.

➤ By default, `Continue` is set to `false` and it will leave you to handle the action once a person is selected.

The `Person` event argument is populated with the selected person. If the user selects Cancel, a `Cancelled` event will be fired. See Listing 11-6 for an example on how to instantiate the picker controller and how to handle the events just mentioned.

LISTING 11-6: Using the people picker navigation controller

```
var ppvc = new ABPeoplePickerNavigationController();

ppvc.Cancelled += delegate(object sender, EventArgs e) {
   Console.WriteLine("Picker cancelled");
   navigationController.DismissModalViewControllerAnimated(true);
};

ppvc.SelectPerson += delegate(object sender,
                              ABPeoplePickerSelectPersonEventArgs e) {
   // Uncomment to allow Picker to show Person View Controller
   // e.Continue = true;
   Console.WriteLine("Selected " + e.Person.FirstName);
   if(!e.Continue)
      navigationController.DismissModalViewControllerAnimated(true);
};

navigationController.PresentModalViewController(ppvc, true);
```

In Listing 11-6, you first create a new instance of the `ABPeoplePickerNavigationController`. This creates your view controller that you can then present using the navigation controller (see the last line). Since you want to handle how a cancelled event or a select person event happens, you create delegate methods on the events. The cancelled event simply uses the navigation controller and dismisses the view controller you originally passed to it. This acts as if the picker was closed. The select person event will want to handle the selected person before it closes the picker, so again you create a delegate method for it to handle this event.

ABNewPersonViewController

As you would expect from the view controller name, the `ABNewPersonViewController` is what you would use if you want the user to create a new person to add into the Address Book. The view controller provides the same view that you would see in the Contacts app (see Figure 11-7).

Because all you can do with the new person view controller is add a new person, there is only one event named `NewPersonComplete`. In the event arguments, it returns whether or not a person was added through the `Completed` property. If `Completed` is true, the `Person` property is filled with the person who was just added to the Address Book. An example of how to use the new person view controller is shown in Listing 11-7.

LISTING 11-7: Using the new person view controller

```
var pvc = new ABNewPersonViewController();

pvc.NewPersonComplete += delegate(object sender,
                                  ABNewPersonCompleteEventArgs e) {
   if(e.Completed)
```

```
            Console.WriteLine ("Added new person " + e.Person.ToString());
        else
            Console.WriteLine ("Cancelled View");
        navigationController.PopViewControllerAnimated(true);
    };

    navigationController.PushViewController(pvc, true);
```

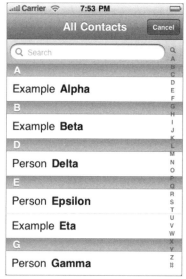

FIGURE 11-6

FIGURE 11-7

ABUnknownPersonViewController

The `ABUnknownPersonViewController` is used when a person may exist but you do not retrieve the information from your Address Book. For example, this unknown person view controller is used when you receive a telephone call from an unknown number but you may want to create a new contact with the number or add the number to an existing contact. You want to create a new `ABPerson` object to fill what information you do know about a person. If you don't have a name for the person, the `AlternativeName` property shows up as a name placeholder but is not used if you create a new contact or add to an existing contact. If you have only one property, this is best used as the alternative title. Listing 11-8 shows how you would instantiate and use the unknown person view controller.

Available for download on Wrox.com

LISTING 11-8: Using the unknown person view controller

```
var upvc = new ABUnknownPersonViewController();

// Create a new person
upvc.DisplayedPerson = new ABPerson();

// Set the phone number as Alternate name and
// the pre-defined person property.
var phoneNumber = "0123456789";
upvc.AlternateName = phoneNumber;
var numberProperty = new ABMutableStringMultiValue();
```

continues

LISTING 11-8 *(continued)*

```
numberProperty.Add(phoneNumber, ABLabel.Home);
upvc.DisplayedPerson.SetPhones(numberProperty);

// Allow Actions and Adding to Address Book
upvc.AllowsActions = true;
upvc.AllowsAddingToAddressBook = true;

// Handle Person Created Event Callback
upvc.PersonCreated += delegate(object sender,
                           ABUnknownPersonCreatedEventArgs e) {

    if(e.Person != null)
    {
        Console.WriteLine("Person Created");
        upvc.ModalViewController.DismissModalViewControllerAnimated(true);
        // Optionally close view controller after creating a person
        //
    }
    else
    {
        Console.WriteLine("Cancelled");
        upvc.ModalViewController.DismissModalViewControllerAnimated(true);
    }
};

this.NavigationController.PushViewController(upvc, true);
```

In Listing 11-8 you first instantiate a new unknown person view controller. This view controller will be used to display what known details of a person that are available. To display a person, you need to first create a new person object to set values on; this person will be the `DisplayedPerson`. To start with you create a new `ABPerson` object and assign this to the `DisplayedPerson` property. In a real-life situation, you may have a telephone number and no other information. For this example, you just use the telephone number as the known information. Since the device does not know what the person's name is, you can set an alternative name to show. To do this you set the `AlternativeName` property to the known telephone number. To set the telephone number for this person, you first create an empty `ABMutableStringMultiValue` object. This allows you to enter multiple telephone numbers, but you are just adding on for this example. You simply add the telephone number with the label property into the new `ABMutableStringMultiValue` object and then pass this object into the `SetPhones` method on the `DisplayedPerson` property.

FIGURE 11-8

Setting `AllowsActions` and `AllowsAddingToAddressBook` to `true` enables the context buttons at the bottom of the view controller (see Figure 11-8) to be visible. By default these are both set to `false`. Since creating a person or cancelling the creation of a person presents a modal view controller, when the user decides to either cancel the creation or does go through and create a person, after you have dealt with their choice, you want to dismiss the modal view controller so it returns back to the unknown person view controller.

Handling the Selection of Properties

On most of the views in the last few code samples, notice some of the properties (such as telephone number or e-mail address) are selectable, but when they are selected, nothing happens. This is because you need to decide whether or not the default action for the property (such as selecting a phone number would start dialing it) should happen. On the view controllers that allow you to handle this, you see a `PerformDefaultAction` event. The event arguments for this event include a property called `ShouldPerformDefaultAction`. To allow the default action to happen, you simply set the property to `true`. Along with a few other properties in the event arguments, the property that was selected is also passed in. This means you can optionally let only certain types of properties perform their default action. This is useful, for example, if you don't want your application quitting from someone clicking a telephone number but you want to provide the in-app mail functionality. Listing 11-9 shows an example of achieving this.

LISTING 11-9: Handling default actions

```
// Example for ABPersonViewController
personvc.PerformDefaultAction += delegate(object sender,
                          ABPersonViewPerformDefaultActionEventArgs e) {

    // Only allow E-mails to be clickable
    if(e.Property == ABPersonProperty.Email)
    {
        if (MFMailComposeViewController.CanSendMail)
        {
            var email = e.Person.GetEmails()[e.Identifier.Value];
            var mail = new MFMailComposeViewController();
            mail.SetToRecipients(new []{ email.Value });
            mail.Finished += delegate {
                personvc.DismissModalViewControllerAnimated(true);
            };
            personvc.PresentModalViewController(mail, true);
        }
        else
            e.ShouldPerformDefaultAction = true;
    }
};
```

Make sure you have a contact with the name "Example" in your address book that also has an e-mail address so that this example works.

Listing 11-9 shows how you would go about creating a default action when tapping a property on a person view controller. The `ABPersonViewPerformDefaultActionEventArgs` event argument has a property named `Property`. This is of `ABPersonProperty` type so you can check the type before you handle the default action. In this example, notice that it handles the action when an e-mail property is tapped. Using the `CanSendMail` method on `MFMailComposeViewController`, you can check if the device can send e-mail, and if this is the case, you can provide the `MFMailComposeViewController` to allow the user to send an e-mail inside your application. If the user cannot send an e-mail inside the application, you want to set `ShouldPerformDefaultAction` to `true`. This means the device handles the tap how it thinks is necessary — for an e-mail field this means that the application closes and the e-mail application opens.

INTEGRATING WITH IPOD MUSIC COLLECTIONS

Using the user's iPod music within your application is a great way of providing extra functionality, especially when you could potentially add it in as a paid feature. Similar to the way the Address Book allows you to programmatically code against the data stored within it, the iPod music collection provides the same sort of ability and also provides two different ways to play this content. You also have access to the methods you would normally expect from a music player such as `Play`, `Pause`, `Stop`, `SkipToBeginning`, `SkipToPreviousItem`, `SkipToNextItem`, `BeginSeekingForward`, and `BeginSeekingBackward`, as well as the property `CurrentPlaybackTime`, which you can set so that it skips to that time on the current track or read the value so you can use this information to set the value on a slider to indicate the current track position.

The iPod integration only allows you to play audio content and will not play video content.

The `MPMusicPlayerController` has two Music Player properties: `ApplicationMusicPlayer` and `iPodMusicPlayer`.

➤ The application music player is self-contained in your application. This means that if you quit your app, the music stops as well.

➤ The iPod music player, however, starts playing with the built-in iPod functionality and when your application quits, the music continues playing.

Listings 11-10 and 11-11 show how to create both types of music player and start playing a queue of all the songs on the device.

Because the simulator does not have iPod functionality or any music on it, you will only be able to test and develop applications with iPod integration functionality on the device. You will need to have the full version of MonoTouch installed and the correct certificates from Apple to do so. You will also need at least one song on the device.

LISTING 11-10: Creating an application music player

```
var musicPlayer = MPMusicPlayerController.ApplicationMusicPlayer;
musicPlayer.SetQueue(MPMediaQuery.songsQuery);
musicPlayer.Play();
```

LISTING 11-11: Creating an iPod music player

```
var musicPlayer = MPMusicPlayerController.iPodMusicPlayer;
musicPlayer.SetQueue(MPMediaQuery.songsQuery);
musicPlayer.Play();
```

The NowPlayingItem property provides information on the current item that is playing. You can use this property to show information on the screen. To do this, you use the ValueForProperty method and pass in an MPMediaItemProperty property:

```
MusicPlayer.NowPlayingItem.ValueForProperty(MPMediaItemProperty.Title);
```

This returns an NSObject, so you may need to cast it to the appropriate type such as an NSString for an album title or an MPMediaItemArtwork for artwork from an album. To display the artwork for the currently playing item, you need to create a UIImageView for the artwork to sit in. For this example my UIImageView is called albumArtworkView. This can be created either within Interface Builder or in code. Once the image view is in place, you can pull the image from the artwork media item in the NowPlayingItem and set the Image property on your UIImageView to the newly created artwork. Listing 11-12 shows setting the album artwork in code.

LISTING 11-12: Setting the album artwork image

```
var albumArtwork = (MPMediaItemArtwork)
MusicPlayer.NowPlayingItem.ValueForProperty(MPMediaItemProperty.Artwork);

if(albumArtwork != null)
{
    var imageSize = new PointF(albumArtworkView.Frame.Width,
                               albumArtworkView.Frame.Height);
    UIImage albumArtworkImage = albumArtwork.ImageWithSize(imageSize);
    albumArtworkView.Image = albumArtworkImage;
}
else
{
    // No artwork so use a placeholder image.
    // Make sure the file is included in the project and
    // the build action is set to "Content"
    albumArtworkView.Image = UIImage.FromFile("emptyArtwork.png");
}
```

You may realize that when a new song starts playing, the UI still shows the old track information and doesn't get updated. To address this issue, you can use notifications to provide information to you when the player state changes (such as going from Play to Pause) as well as when a new song is playing so you can update the track information. This allows you to update the UI as and when it is needed. You can declare your NSObject observers (these listen for certain notifications sent from the music player) as class variables; this makes them easier to add and remove so you don't listen multiple times for notifications. Listing 11-13 shows how to add observers to listen for these notifications.

LISTING 11-13: Using notifications with the music player

```
NSObject NowPlayingItemChanged, PlaybackStateChanged;
MPMusicPlayerController MusicPlayer;

public override void ViewDidLoad()
{
    base.ViewDidLoad();

    var center = NSNotificationCenter.DefaultCenter;

    var nowPlayingNotification =
        "MPMusicPlayerControllerNowPlayingItemDidChangeNotification";
    NowPlayingItemChanged = center.AddObserver(nowPlayingNotification,
        (notification) => {
        Console.WriteLine("Update UI with Now Playing Info");
    });

    var playbackStateNotification =
        "MPMusicPlayerControllerPlaybackStateDidChangeNotification";
    PlaybackStateChanged = center.AddObserver(playbackStateNotification,
        (notification) => {
        Console.WriteLine("Update UI with Playback State: " +
                        MusicPlayer.PlaybackState);
    });

    MusicPlayer = MPMusicPlayerController.iPodMusicPlayer;
    MusicPlayer.SetQueue(MPMediaQuery.songsQuery);
    MusicPlayer.BeginGeneratingPlaybackNotifications();
    MusicPlayer.Play();

}

public override void ViewWillDisappear (bool animated)
{
    base.ViewWillDisappear(animated);

    NSNotificationCenter.DefaultCenter.RemoveObserver(NowPlayingItemChanged);
    NSNotificationCenter.DefaultCenter.RemoveObserver(PlaybackStateChanged);

    MusicPlayer.EndGeneratingPlaybackNotifications();
    MusicPlayer.Dispose();
}
```

Hopefully you will be familiar with using notifications by now and using notifications with the `MPMusicPlayerController` is very similar to the way other notifications work. One difference you may notice in the preceding listing is that you need to explicitly begin and end notifications whereas other notifications start automatically when you add and remove an observer. Line 27 shows `BeginGeneratingPlaybackNotifications` being called and line 39 shows `EndGeneratingPlaybackNotifications` being called to stop observers from being called.

At the moment you're still just playing all the songs on the device. This isn't really useful, so you'll want to programmatically filter down the music that's playing. You should note that there are other convenient predefined media queries to use aside from the `songsQuery`. To do this you'll create your own `MPMediaQuery` using the `MPMediaPropertyPredicate` filters. Because not all media item properties are allowed as a filter, you also should check whether or not the media item you are filtering against can actually be filtered. For example, you cannot filter against the artwork media item property. Listing 11-14 shows how to filter the iPod music collection by a media item property.

LISTING 11-14: Creating a media query

```
var musicPlayer = MPMusicPlayerController.iPodMusicPlayer;
var mediaQuery = new MPMediaQuery();

if(MPMediaItem.CanFilterByProperty(MPMediaItemProperty.Artist))
{
    var artistFilter = MPMediaPropertyPredicate.PredicateWithValue
                        (new NSString("Mew"), MPMediaItemProperty.Artist);
    mediaQuery.AddFilterPredicate(artistFilter);
}

if(MPMediaItem.CanFilterByProperty(MPMediaItemProperty.AlbumTitle))
{
    var albumFilter = MPMediaPropertyPredicate.PredicateWithValue
                (new NSString("Frengers"), MPMediaItemProperty.AlbumTitle);
    mediaQuery.AddFilterPredicate(albumFilter);
}

musicPlayer.SetQueue(mediaQuery);
musicPlayer.Play();
```

Listing 11-14 shows how you would use the `AddFilterPredicate` method to filter down the `MediaQuery` of all the songs in your iTunes library. You may want to change the artist `"Mew"` and the album name `"Frengers"` to an artist and album that you have in your iTunes collection. To filter the `MediaQuery` you first create a `MPMediaPropertyPredicate` by providing the value you want to filter down on (in the first predicate the example uses `"Mew"`) and the property type of the media (in this case `MPMediaItemProperty` is `Artist`). After the `MPMediaPropertyPredicate` is populated, you then add the predicate to the `MediaQuery` with `AddFilterPredicate` and continue to use `MediaQuery` as you have done previously. This then gets you back the filtered list of media items.

As you saw with the Address Book functionality, there was a useful picker control to allow the easy selection of a person using a familiar interface. With the iPod functionality there is a media picker, which allows you to provide the default user interface for iPod audio picking. Listing 11-15 shows how to create the picker.

LISTING 11-15: Using the iPod media picker view controller

```
using(MPMediaPickerController mediaPicker = new MPMediaPickerController())
{
    mediaPicker.AllowsPickingMultipleItems = true;
    mediaPicker.ItemsPicked += delegate(object sender,
                                    ItemsPickedEventArgs e)
    {
        if(e.MediaItemCollection != null)
        {
            foreach(var item in e.MediaItemCollection.Items)
            {
                Console.WriteLine ("Title: " +
                        item.ValueForProperty(MPMediaItemProperty.Title));
            }
        }
        mPlayer.SetQueue(MPMediaQuery.songsQuery);
        mPlayer.Play();
        Console.WriteLine ("Hiding media picker.");
        this.NavigationController.DismissModalViewControllerAnimated(true);
    };
    Console.WriteLine ("Presenting media picker");
    this.NavigationController.PresentModalViewController(mediaPicker, true);
}
```

Using the `ItemsPicked` callback allows you to get a list of the collection of picked songs from the user. Here you are able to send it straight to the music player to play; however, you could also store this information and re-use it again later.

INTERFACING WITH OBJECTIVE-C

Even though you can use C# and .NET to write iPhone applications with MonoTouch, there are a lot of Objective-C third party libraries that you may want to utilize in your application. To get a better understanding of Objective-C and using MonoTouch, read Chapter 14, which should help you out for this section. Before you jump right into how you go about using the Objective-C library in your application, however, you need to take a look at the namespaces that enable you to do this. The example in this section will be using the analytics library "Flurry™ ("Flurry")."

MonoTouch.Foundation

The `MonoTouch.Foundation` namespace contains all the important bindings to the core Objective-C types in the Cocoa API. The most familiar type would be the `NSObject` type, which almost all of the non-.NET objects use as their base class. Another example that was used heavily in this chapter would be the `NSUrl` class. These classes and types work by using the classes that are found in the `MonoTouch .ObjCRuntime` namespace, and this is what actually communicates with the Objective-C runtime.

MonoTouch.ObjCRuntime

When you want to communicate with any Objective-C code, the `MonoTouch.ObjCRuntime` namespace and the classes within it are the place to start. The key classes that you are most likely to use are `Runtime`, `Selector`, and `Messaging`.

➤ The `Runtime` class allows you to gather information back from the Objective-C world such as `NSObjects`.

➤ The `Selector` class allows you to work with selectors (remember selectors are essentially methods in Objective-C) from C#.

➤ `Messaging` is the glue between these two classes allowing them to communicate and work together.

In the next section you can see a very simple binding to the Flurry analytics using a tool called `btouch`, which is created by the MonoTouch team to enable an easy automated way of creating the Objective-C binding. This saves having to manually create a binding yourself.

Automatic Binding to Objective-C with btouch

Using btouch is a great way of using third-party Objective-C libraries within your MonoTouch application. To allow this to happen, first you must download the third-party library you want to bind to. The example uses the analytics library "Flurry." This example uses the 1.4 version of Flurry, so using a different version may vary. With this library, the downloaded files consist of a few different files.

➤ **FlurryLib:** Flurry library folder without location functionality.

➤ **FlurryLib.h:** Header file for the Flurry library.

➤ **libFlurry.a:** A statically compiled library file.

➤ **FlurryLibWithLocation**

➤ **FlurryLib.h:** Header file for the Flurry library with added location specific methods.

➤ **libFlurryWithLocation.a:** A statically compiled library file with location functionality.

➤ **ProjectApiKey.txt:** This text file contains the API key you need to use with the library.

➤ **README.txt:** ReadMe file on how to use the library; this won't be needed since it focuses on Objective-C code.

➤ **RELEASE_NOTES.txt:** Release notes explaining what has changed since previous versions.

Since this example is rather straightforward, it uses the first "FlurryLib" folder, which does not include the location functionality.

Next, you want to create a C# interface, which is used by btouch to automatically generate the Objective-C bindings. To allow btouch to know what to bind, you need to decorate the interface with different attributes that define the bindings. You need to look at the header file included with the statically compiled library to understand how you want to translate that into C#. A header file in Objective-C is essentially a way of allowing you to code against a static library so this is useful when trying to bind against it, too. Listing 11-16 shows the Flurry header file in the Flurry 1.4 SDK.

LISTING 11-16: Flurry Objective-C header file

```
//
//  FlurryAPI.h
//  Flurry iPhone Analytics Agent
//
//  Copyright 2009 Flurry, Inc. All rights reserved.
//
#import <UIKit/UIKit.h>

@class CLLocationManager;
@class CLLocation;

@interface FlurryAPI : NSObject {
}

+ (void)startSession:(NSString *)apiKey;
+ (void)logEvent:(NSString *)eventName;
+ (void)logEvent:(NSString *)
    eventName withParameters:(NSDictionary *)parameters;
+ (void)logError:(NSString *)
    errorID message:(NSString *)message exception:(NSException *)exception;

+ (void)setUserID:(NSString *)userID;
+ (void)setEventLoggingEnabled:(BOOL)value;
+ (void)setServerURL:(NSString *)url;
+ (void)setSessionReportsOnCloseEnabled:(BOOL)sendSessionReportsOnClose;

@end
```

There are a few things to note about this header file and things you need to take into consideration when creating the C# interface file for it. These are:

➤ The UIKit namespace is used.

➤ @class CLLocationManager and CLLocation don't actually get used, so you won't need these.

➤ The base class of the FlurryAPI is NSObject.

➤ All the methods are static.

*One more thing to note is the method name; if the method has no parameters, then the method name will look like "*methodName*." If the method has one parameter, then you simply attach a semicolon to the end, and the method name is "*methodName:*." Finally, if the method has more than one parameter, then the method name would be "*methodName:secondParameter:*." You need to correct exported Objective-C method names to C# methods, so it's good to remember this.*

Now that you have looked through the header file, you can go and create the C# interface. Listing 11-17 shows the finished interface file that we will use with btouch.

LISTING 11-17: Flurry C# interface

```
///
// Binding to the FlurryAPI Analytics SDK from Flurry
//
// MIT X11 licensed
//
// Copyright 2009 ChrisNTR
//
using System;
using MonoTouch.Foundation;
using MonoTouch.UIKit;

namespace MonoTouch.Binding
{

    [Static][BaseType (typeof (NSObject))]
    interface FlurryAPI
    {

        [Static][Export ("startSession:")]
        void StartSession(string apiKey);

        [Static][Export ("logEvent:")]
        void LogEvent(string eventName);

        [Static][Export ("logEvent:withParameters:")]
        void LogEvent(string eventName, NSDictionary parameters);

        [Static][Export ("logEvent:message:")]
        void LogEvent(string errorId, string message);

        [Static][Export ("setUserID:")]
        void SetUserId(string userId);

        [Static][Export ("setEventLoggingEnabled:")]
        void SetEventLoggingEnabled(bool enabled);

        [Static][Export ("setServerURL:")]
```

continues

LISTING 11-17 *(continued)*

```
        void SetServerUrl(string url);

        [Static][Export ("setSessionReportsOnCloseEnabled:")]
        void SetSessionReportsOnCloseEnabled(bool enabled);
    }
}
```

There are a few things you should notice from the interface file. Most of what you see should make sense following on from the Objective-C header file. Since Objective-C doesn't have namespaces, you can see that one has been added in. Since the Flurry API is a completely static class, all the methods have been decorated with the `[Static]` attribute so that when btouch runs through the interface creating the bindings, it create this class and corresponding methods as static. Since the API also has the base type of `NSObject`, you simply add the `[BaseType()]` attribute and pass in the `NSObject` type. The only other attribute that needed to be added was the `[Export ()]` attribute. Following from the note mentioned earlier in this section on method names, you can see in Listing 11-17 how these are translated for each method.

Now that the C# interface file has been created, you want to run the btouch tool against it. To do this you need to use the terminal, which is similar to the command-line window on Windows. Navigate to where you saved the interface file; the interface file is simply called `Flurry.cs` in these examples. The line you need to run looks like this

```
/Developer/MonoTouch/usr/bin/btouch Flurry.cs
```

where `Flurry.cs` is the C# interface file and `/Developer/MonoTouch/usr/bin/btouch` is the location to the btouch application to run. You won't see a confirmation, but if you have a look in the directory, you should see a dll named Flurry.dll. This will be the assembly of the Objective-C bindings of the API.

You can now go ahead and reference the new dll in a project to enable coding against the library in C#. In addition to adding the reference, you need to add in the static library libFlurry.a from the Flurry 1.4 SDK into the same folder as your project, but you will not need to include it into the project. It will be used when extra arguments are added to the project. The extra arguments you need to add to the project enable MonoTouch to build the project to allow bindings to third-party libraries. These extra arguments look like this:

```
-gcc_flags "-L${ProjectDir} -lFlurry -ObjC"
```

and this needs to be added in the iPhone Build section of the project settings. You should notice that you don't need to include the full name of the library libFlurry.a. You just need to add in a hyphen and lower case `l` followed straightaway with the library name stripped of its extension and the pre-appended "lib".

To code against the new Objective-C binding, since the namespace is `MonoTouch.Binding`, you can type in `MonoTouch.Binding.FlurryAPI.StartSession("YourAPIKey")` to start using analytics on the iPhone. The best way to take this all in is to use the API with a real iPhone project. Listing 11-18 shows the API being used and the download material contains the extra arguments in the project added in with the static library.

LISTING 11-18: Using the created Flurry API in a project

```
using MonoTouch.Binding;
using MonoTouch.Foundation;
using MonoTouch.UIKit;

...

public override bool FinishedLaunching (UIApplication app,
                                        NSDictionary options)
{
    // API Key from ProjectAPIKey.txt
    var apiKey = "Your API Key here";

    // Call the Flurry API to start the session.
    FlurryAPI.StartSession(apiKey);

    window.MakeKeyAndVisible ();

    return true;
}
```

Although this shows how to bind to a third-party Objective-C library with btouch, there is still a lot that cannot be covered in this book, which you can find on the MonoTouch web site here, http://bit.ly/objc-binding. Hopefully this example is useful in getting you started with converting third-party libraries for use with MonoTouch.

SUMMARY

Allowing applications to talk to each other is great way of allowing communication between the native Apple applications to keep a consistent and intuitive user experience. Allowing access to the user's address book and music collection can enable unique application experiences and allow your application to make a much more personal connection with the user.

12

Localizing for an International Audience

WHAT'S IN THIS CHAPTER?

➤ Defining internationalization and localization

➤ Displaying translated text and images

➤ Formatting dates, times, and numbers

➤ Extracting text for translation

Localization and internationalization sound similar; however, they describe different parts of the multilingual software development process.

Internationalization describes the writing of software that supports multiple languages and display formatting. It is a task generally undertaken by software architects and developers and influences the way that applications store and represent their user interface and data. Attributes of internationalized code include:

➤ All display text is stored separately from the code, so that it is easy to update.

➤ Images, videos, colors, and icons are easily updatable.

➤ Sorting of lists is language-sensitive.

➤ Date and time formatting (and measurement) and time calculations take the current user's settings into account.

➤ Number and currency formats (symbols, commas, and points) are flexible and appropriate for the user.

➤ Measurements (temperature, weight, distance) can be represented in different units.

➤ Appropriate input and display of addresses, telephone numbers, and government identification numbers.

It should be possible to release an internationalized application in many different countries/languages, once it has been *localized*.

Localization is the process of translating the text into a target language, updating images and other cultural references. It is a task usually performed by translators and/or native speakers of the target locale. Important aspects of localization include:

➤ Translating the text into the target language.

➤ Using appropriate cultural references (colors, imagery, writing style).

➤ Providing parameters/guidance for localized requirements such as tax rates and applicability (assuming the internationalization process for the application made it flexible enough to cope with such localized business rules).

Globalization is another term that is sometimes used to describe both internationalization and localization. In the .NET Framework the `System.Globalization` namespace contains the classes used to create multilingual applications.

Figure 12-1 shows some of the built-in applications with different language and region settings. This chapter shows you how to achieve similar results for your applications, vastly expanding the market for your iPhone OS applications!

FIGURE 12-1

 The terms internationalization and localization are often shortened to i18n and L10n, respectively — the numbers refer to the number of characters between the first and last letter of each word.

INTERNATIONALIZING AN APPLICATION

To internationalize an application you must be able to:

➤ Detect what language the user wants to view.

➤ Detect what regional settings (also known as locale) the user has selected.

➤ Display all text, numbers, dates, imagery, colors, and so on according to those settings.

➤ Accept and validate user input in their preferred language.

The iPhone OS *and* the .NET SDK provide frameworks that will assist you with all of these tasks, as long as you structure your code to take advantage of them. This chapter focuses on the built-in iPhone OS internationalization and localization features that are exposed/supported by MonoTouch, mentioning the .NET `System.Globalization` classes where relevant.

CHANGING LANGUAGE AND REGION SETTINGS

You configure iPhone language and region information via the Settings ➪ General ➪ International screen.

Changing the Language on your iPhone causes the operating system to display the Home screen with all the text translated into the selected language. Applications that support that language will also display content in that language.

 Choosing a language does not imply any particular region/locale settings.

Enabling Keyboards on your iPhone allows different languages (and their corresponding characters) to be entered.

Changing the Region Format on your iPhone affects the formatting of dates, numbers, and the calendar.

Before writing code that uses these settings, Figure 12-2 shows you how to change them on the simulator (many more unrelated options exist on a real device). It is easier to set the Region Format first before changing languages, because a language change causes the operating system to reload the Home screen (which takes a second or two).

Remember *where* these options are before you change your phone or simulator to a language you can't read, otherwise it might be tricky to change them back to your native language. If you do forget, you can always use the Reset Content and Settings menu option in the simulator.

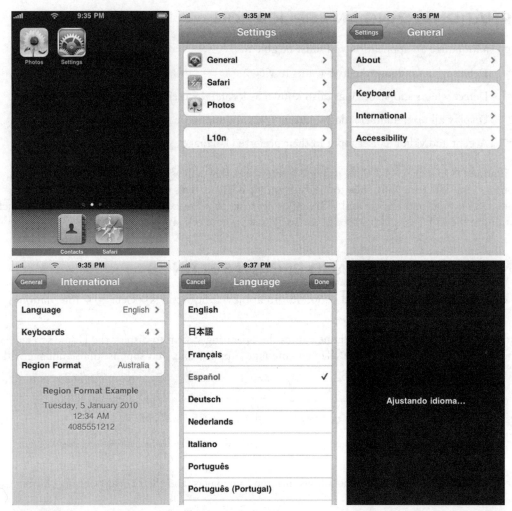

FIGURE 12-2

The choices you make on those screens affect the way content is displayed by iPhone native classes and by .NET, which both use the same standard to identify language and region. The standard consists of two parts:

➤ **Language code:** The two-letter ISO 639-1 code is the preferred method to identify languages. Common examples are en for English, ja for Japanese, es for Spanish, fr for French, and de for German.

➤ **Region code:** The two-character ISO 3166-1 code that identifies a region or locale that speaks a particular language (for example, US for the United States, FR for France, and ES for Spain).

These two values combined make a *locale*. Sometimes the region code is the same as the language code, for example fr-FR indicates French spoken in France and es-ES indicates Spanish spoken in

Spain. By contrast, some iPhone users will use `fr-CA` (French spoken in Canada) or `es-US` (Spanish spoken in the United States). Common region codes for English include `en-US`, `en-GB`, `en-CA`, `en-AU`, and `en-NZ` (for the United States, Great Britain, Canada, Australia, and New Zealand, respectively).

In addition to locales defined by a language and region code are some custom locale tags such as `zh-Hans` (simplified Chinese script) and `zh-Hant` (traditional Chinese script) that aren't linked to a specific region.

> *The locale identifiers in the preceding text used the .NET formatting with a dash (-) separating the language and region. iPhone OS methods use an underscore (_) instead.*
>
> *Both formats are used in this chapter because some examples use MonoTouch methods calling into the iPhone framework and others use the .NET class libraries (in the* `System.Globalization` *namespace).*
>
> *Both follow the convention of lowercase for the language code and uppercase for the region code.*

DISPLAYING MULTIPLE LANGUAGES

Developers building applications without considering other languages frequently "hardcode" text into the application — in the case of the iPhone the text could be in constants or variables, directly assigned to `UIKit` objects

```
var greeting = "Hello world";
MyLabel.Text = "First name:";
```

or even embedded in the XIB files that define your views. Images, audio, and video resources may be similarly "hardcoded." Such an application has *not* been internationalized and therefore cannot be localized (unless the developer was to go into the code and replace every language-specific piece with the equivalent in another language).

The process of internationalizing requires the separation of text, images, and so on from the code so that you can create different versions of that content for each locale. Once you have separated the content you just need to load the correct values based on the user's language and locale settings.

The iPhone OS facilitates internationalization with these features:

➤ **Language-specific (.lproj) folders:** You can place certain content, such as images and `.strings` files (more on them later) in these folders and the operating system will know where to look for them when the following two methods are called. The folders are named with the two-character language code for their contents, such as `en.lproj`, `fr.lproj`, and `es.lproj`.

➤ **.strings files:** Specially formatted text files that contain translations for individual pieces of strings. The default file in each language-specific folder is called `Localizable.strings`.

➤ **LocalizedString() method:** Loads a localized string from a `.strings` file.

➤ **PathForResource() method:** Resolves a path to a localized image or other file type in a language-specific folder.

Figure 12-3 shows how the language-specific folders and `.strings` files are structured. The following sections describe how they work.

FIGURE 12-3

The `.strings` file format is a collection of key-value pairs that allows comments. An example of the "standard" format is shown in Listing 12-1 — notice the keys and values are quoted and the line is terminated with a semicolon. C-style comments are allowed in the file to provide directions or explanations to the translator, who should only edit the bolded text. Apple recommends saving these files in the UTF-16 encoding (although the UTF-8 encoding works).

LISTING 12-1: .strings standard file format

```
/* comment to aid translation */
"text to translate (key)" = "translation (value)";
/* this text has a newline */
"text with escaped\nnewline" = "translation with escaped\nnewline";
/* this text has quotes */
"text with escaped \"quotes\"" = "translation with escaped \"quotes\"";
/* this text has greaterthan and lessthan */
"text with angles" = "this text has < angle brackets >";
```

The `.strings` file may also use a Property List (`.plist`) format although it should still have the same `.strings` file extension. Listing 12-2 shows the same data in Property List XML format — note that different characters require "escaping" with this format: Quotes and newlines are allowed, but greater-than/less-than must be XML entity encoded. This type of file is saved with UTF-8 encoding (as specified in the XML).

LISTING 12-2: .strings file using XML plist format

```
<?xml version="1.0" encoding="UTF-8"?>
<!DOCTYPE plist PUBLIC "-//Apple//DTD PLIST 1.0//EN"
"http://www.apple.com/DTDs/PropertyList-1.0.dtd">
<plist version="1.0">
    <dict>
        <!-- comment to aid translation -->
        <key>text to translate (key)</key>
        <string>translation (value)</string>
        <!-- this text has a newline -->
        <key>text with escaped
newline</key>
        <string>translation with escaped
newline</string>
```

```
        <!-- this text has quotes -->
        <key>text with escaped "quotes"</key>
        <string>translation with escaped "quotes"</string>
        <!-- this text has greaterthan and lessthan -->
        <key>text with angles</key>
        <string>this text has &lt; angle brackets &gt; </string>
    </dict>
</plist>
```

Most Apple-supplied examples use the standard format, however both formats work fine in MonoTouch/MonoDevelop. Remember when using the Property List Editor application to Save As the correct File Type (XML in this case).

> *Apple's SDK Reference specifically states "In iPhone OS, the bundle interfaces do not take dialect or script information into account when looking for localized resources; only the language designator code is considered. Therefore if your project includes language-specific project directories with both a language and region designator, those directories are ignored."*
>
> *This means you should create language-specific directories only for the two-character language codes (such as en, es, fr, ja, and so on). Whereas MacOS does support region-specific .lproj folders (such as fr-CA), the iPhone OS does not.*

Showing Translated Text

The first example in the chapter download — Localization01 — displays some simple strings in a different language depending on the user settings.

First add two labels to a new iPhone MonoTouch project's MainWindow and add the following two lines to set their Text property:

Available for
download on
Wrox.com

```
LocaleLabel.Text = NSLocale.CurrentLocale.LocaleIdentifier;
LanguageLabel.Text = NSLocale.PreferredLanguages[0];
```

Localization01\Main.cs

These methods allow your code to retrieve the user's settings:

➤ NSLocale: Class that provides information about the current language and locale settings on the device.

➤ CurrentLocale: Provides information about the region that the user has selected. The LocaleIdentifier returns the code in the format discussed previously, such as en_US.

➤ PreferredLanguages: Provides a list of language codes in the order in which they will be searched. It is an array of two-letter language codes, with the first element reflecting the user's language choice.

Figure 12-4 shows these two fields populated with data for English, Spanish, and French settings.

FIGURE 12-4

Now place some more labels and a segment control (with three segments) on the view.

Second, in `FinishedLoading` set the display properties using the `LocalizedString` as shown here:

```
HelloLabel.Text =
    NSBundle.MainBundle.LocalizedString("Hello","A greeting");
GoodbyeLabel.Text =
    NSBundle.MainBundle.LocalizedString("Goodbye","Say bye bye");
Segments.SetTitle(
    NSBundle.MainBundle.LocalizedString("One","Number one"), 0);
Segments.SetTitle(
    NSBundle.MainBundle.LocalizedString("Two","Number two"), 1);
Segments.SetTitle(
    NSBundle.MainBundle.LocalizedString("Three","Number three"), 2);
```

Localization01\Main.cs

The parameters for `LocalizedString` are:

➤ `key`: The string used to lookup the translation in the default `.strings` file (and is also used as the fallback display value). This string should *not* contain extended ASCII characters such as accented letters (like é).

➤ `comment`: Comment describing the text to aid translators. It is useful to store this in the code where the string is used. The `comment` is not displayed in the application.

And the method works like this:

1. Look for a matching key in the language-specific directory's default `Localizable.strings` file.

2. If no match is found, use the key passed to the `LocalizedString` method as the display text.

Because the operating system looks in multiple places and then defaults to the `key` string passed to the method, when the application is run without any `.strings` files it is still usable. Apple's development documentation recommends always using displayable text as the key for this reason — if no suitable translation can be found, at least proper English will be displayed.

There are two more overloads of the `LocalizedString` method:

When three parameters are passed, they are:

➤ `key`: The string used to lookup a translation in the default `.strings` file.

➤ `value`: The fallback value to use if no translation is found in any `.strings` file. When this overload is used, the `key` is never displayed to the user. Extended ASCII (including accented characters like é) are allowed in this parameter.

➤ `table`: Allows you to specify a different `.strings` file to use or to pass an empty string to indicate this item is in the default `Localizable.strings` file. You should specify the file-name without the `.strings` extension. For example, if you called

```
HelloLabel.Text =
    NSBundle.MainBundle.LocalizedString("Hello","Hi there","More");
```

the operating system will search in `More.strings` instead of `Localizable.strings` for the translation of `"Hello"`, and if nothing is found, `"Hi there"` will be displayed by `HelloLabel`. This enables you to create multiple smaller files to help manage your translations.

When four parameters are passed, they are:

➤ `key`: The string used to lookup a translation in the default `.strings` file.

➤ `value`: The fallback value to use if no translation is found in any `.strings` file. When this overload is used, the `key` is never displayed to the user. Extended ASCII (including accented characters like é) are allowed in this parameter.

➤ `table`: Allows you to specify a different `.strings` file to use. You should specify the file-name without the `.strings` extension.

➤ `comment`: Comment describing the text to aid translators.

 Note that the `key` *and* `table` *parameters of* `LocalizedString` *are case-sensitive. You should also use the* `comment` *parameter wherever possible to provide context for the translator, to ensure it chooses the most appropriate words or phrases for your application.*

To provide translations for the example create language-specific folders `es.lproj` and `fr.lproj`, then in each folder create a new text file called `Localizable.strings` (the folder structure was shown in Figure 12-3). Provide translations for these strings as shown in Table 12-1.

TABLE 12-1: Localized strings Files

ES.LPROJ/LOCALIZABLE.STRINGS	FR.LPROJ/LOCALIZABLE.STRINGS
`"Hello" = "Hola";`	`"Hello" = "Bonjour";`
`"Goodbye" = "Adiós";`	`"Goodbye" = "Au revoir";`
`"OK" = "Si";`	`"OK" = "Oui";`
`"Cancel" = "Cancelar";`	`"Cancel" = "Annuler";`
`"One" = "Uno";`	`"One" = "Un";`
`"Two" = "Dos";`	`"Two" = "Deux";`
`"Three" = "Tres";`	`"Three" = "Trois";`

Figure 12-5 shows the application running in English, Spanish, and French. Notice how `"Bonjour"` has been resized — element sizing is an important part of internationalizing software because the amount of space required for equivalent text can vary widely. A word in English (such as `"Hello"`) may translate into a longer word in another language (such as `"Bonjour"` in French), and if you have sized your `UILabel` to exactly fit the English text, other languages may be resized or even truncated. There is no "magic rule" to fix this problem; you need to be aware of text sizing issues and try to design your view layout to accommodate all the languages you intend to support.

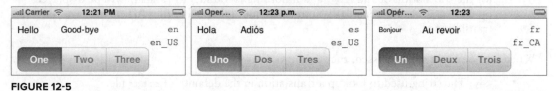

FIGURE 12-5

Translating Buttons

Translating `UIButtons` is slightly different than you might expect, because a common way for setting a button's Title property doesn't work as you'd expect — it only sets the text value for one possible display state of the button. If you internationalize a button's text like this

```
OkButton.TitleLabel.Text =
    NSBundle.MainBundle.LocalizedString("OK","Affirmative");
```

the translation will be displayed at first but will revert to English (or whatever the base language is) when it is touched/enabled/disabled or any other state-change is applied.

Buttons have six states (defined by the `UIControlState` enum: `Normal`, `Disabled`, `Highlighted`, `Selected`, `Application`, and `Reserved`) and each state can have its own text. To localize the button properly use the `SetTitle()` method so that all states will reflect the localized text:

```
OkButton.SetTitle(
    NSBundle.MainBundle.LocalizedString("OK","Affirmative button"),
    UIControlState.Normal);
CancelButton.SetTitle(
    NSBundle.MainBundle.LocalizedString("Cancel","Negative button"),
    UIControlState.Normal);
```

Alternatively, you could set the title for the other states explicitly, potentially using different text on each state (although be careful not to make your user interface more confusing by doing so):

```
OkButton.SetTitle(
    NSBundle.MainBundle.LocalizedString(
        "OK","Affirmative button"),
    UIControlState.Normal);
OkButton.SetTitle(
    NSBundle.MainBundle.LocalizedString(
        "OK (unavailable)","Affirmative button disabled"),
    UIControlState.Disabled);
```

Localization01\Main.cs

Figure 12-6 shows the example complete with labels, segments, and buttons.

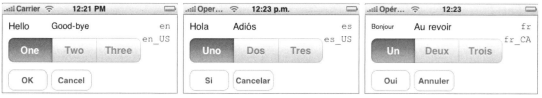

FIGURE 12-6

Sometimes you will need to display text that is partially generated in code (for example, a message about how many e-mails have arrived). In non-internationalized code developers often write code like this:

```
var message = "You have " + count + " new emails";
```

However, that is both difficult to localize and has poor usability. A better approach is to provide three different strings for all possible cases and select the correct message at runtime:

```
var message0 = NSBundle.MainBundle.LocalizedString
              ("You have no new messages","no messages");
var message1 = NSBundle.MainBundle.LocalizedString
              ("You have 1 new message","1 message");
var messageN = NSBundle.MainBundle.LocalizedString
              ("You have {0} new messages","{0} placeholder messages");
// choose the correct message to show, if the last one, apply format
messageN = String.Format (messageN, count);
```

These types of messages are much easier to translate accurately and provide the best user experience in all languages.

 Always use placeholders in preference to concatenating strings together.

If you include placeholders (such as {0} or {1}) in your Localizable.strings *files, be sure to instruct the translator how to deal with them. Be aware that the translator may need to change the order that placeholders appear in the translated string.*

Displaying Images

The second code sample in the chapter download — Localization02 — shows how images are handled. Images are normally loaded by path so to internationalize image references you obtain a localized image path using the PathForResource method.

In the following example we have created three images (one each for English, Spanish, and French) and placed them in the respective language folders (en.lproj, es.lproj, fr.lproj), all with the same name: `MyImage.jpg`. We then use the `PathForResource()` method to provide a path to the correct localized image to be displayed.

```
var imageName = NSBundle.MainBundle.PathForResource("MyImage","jpg");
UIImage image = UIImage.FromFile(imageName);
MyImage.Image = image;
```

Localization02\Main.cs

Figure 12-7 shows the result.

FIGURE 12-7

The downside of this approach is that you *must* provide a localized image in *every* language-specific directory — otherwise an `ArgumentNullException` reference will result. `PathForResource` only determines the correct path based on the language settings; it doesn't verify that the image exists.

If a particular image requires localization only for a small number of your supported languages, you might consider using the image's path as a localizable string; for example, place the image in your `en.lproj` folder and reference its full path in `Localizable.strings`

```
/* Path to image that isn't usually localized */
"en.lproj/CommonImage.jpg" = "en.lproj/CommonImage.jpg";
```

then in your code create the image like this

```
var imageName = NSBundle.MainBundle.LocalizedString
    ("en.lproj/CommonImage.jpg",
      "Path to image that isn't usually localized",);
UIImage image = UIImage.FromFileUncached(imageName);
MyImage.Image = image;
```

which means that any language for which that key hasn't been given a value, the English image will automatically be shown. For the languages that do require a custom image (such as Japanese, in this example), place the localized `CommonImage.jpg` in the `ja.lproj` folder and add this key-value pair to `ja.lproj/Localizable.strings`:

```
/* Path to image that isn't usually localized */
"en.lproj/CommonImage.jpg" = "ja.lproj/CommonImage.jpg";
```

If you include image paths in your Localizable.strings *files, be sure to instruct the translator how to deal with them so they do not attempt to translate the string as a phrase. If your translator is also translating and supplying updated images, be sure to agree in advance on the correct dimensions, file format, fonts, styles and colors to ensure translated images fit seamlessly into your application.*

Localizing App Icon and Name

Localizing your application's icon won't always be necessary — icons rarely include text due to the size when rendered on the iPhone — however, you may still want to display a different icon depending on the language of your user.

Simply place the localized application icons in the relevant language-specific directory named icon .png. Localized icons have been added to the Localization02 example in the chapter download.

The application name is typically set in the MonoDevelop Project Properties or in a manually added Info.plist file (as discussed in Chapter 8). It is possible to localize entries in the Info.plist file by adding a specially named InfoPlist.strings file to the language-specific directories.

Table 12-2 shows the two additional files added to your project to provide a localized application name.

TABLE 12-2: Localized strings Files

ES.LPROJ/INFOPLIST.STRINGS	FR.LPROJ/INFOPLIST.STRINGS
"CFBundleDisplayName" = "L10n-es";	"CFBundleDisplayName" = "L10n-fr";

Figure 12-8 shows the directory structure with InfoPlist and icon files as well as the final result of a localized icon and application name. The iPhone OS caches icon images so if you don't always see the updated image when you switch back and forth during testing, delete the application completely and re-install.

Displaying "Double Byte" Characters

The term "double byte character-set" is often used to refer to scripts such as Chinese, Japanese, and Korean because historically they required two bytes to store most characters whereas most Western languages required only one byte. With the broad acceptance of Unicode and its various encodings (UTF-8 being the most common) the "double byte" distinction is irrelevant — the iPhone supports a number of complex scripts including Japanese, Korean, and Chinese.

Unfortunately, MonoDevelop (version 2.2) doesn't seem to like editing .strings files containing some of these characters. The

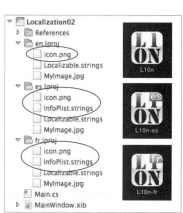

FIGURE 12-8

solution is to use Xcode — Figure 12-9 shows the `ja.lproj/Localizable.strings` file from the code download in Xcode and the resulting output on the iPhone simulator.

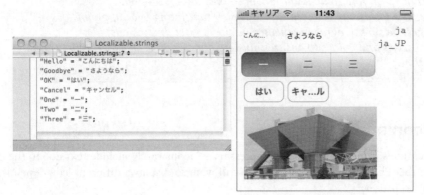

FIGURE 12-9

Formatting Dates, Times, Numbers, and Currency

The other thing that is important to customize to a user's preference is the format used for display dates, times, and numbers. This is especially critical when the data can have a totally different meaning based on its format; for example, a date shown as 3/12 means March 12th in the United States but the 3rd of December in many other countries.

Because MonoTouch C# code will usually be using the .NET Framework classes for string and date/time handling, these methods need to respect the preferences set by the user. The `CultureInfo` class in the `System.Globalization` is the .NET "equivalent" of `NSLocale`. The two properties `CurrentCulture` and `CurrentUICulture` tell us which region the .NET Framework will use when formatting output.

The third example in the code download — Localization03 — adds more display labels to show how the localized formatting works. First it uses two labels to display the current `CultureInfo` settings being used. These values will often (but not always) be the same as the `LocaleIdentifier` you learned about earlier — the set of locales supported by .NET and the iPhone OS isn't the same, which is why they sometimes differ (for example, `es-US` can be selected on the iPhone but is not supported by .NET).

```
MonoCultureLabel.Text =
    System.Globalization.CultureInfo.CurrentCulture.ToString();
MonoUICultureLabel.Text =
    System.Globalization.CultureInfo.CurrentUICulture.ToString();
```

Having verified that the .NET Framework does reflect the iPhone's region settings, the following lines of code show the easiest way to output locale-aware dates and times:

```
DateLabel.Text  = "LongDate  " + DateTime.Now.ToLongDateString();
DateLabel2.Text = "ShortDate " + DateTime.Now.ToShortDateString();
```

```
DateLabel3.Text = "LongTime   " + DateTime.Now.ToLongTimeString();
DateLabel4.Text = "ShortTime  " + DateTime.Now.ToShortTimeString();
```

Localization03\Main.cs

Many non-internationalized applications use custom format strings to achieve a specific output (such as `ToString("dd-MMM-yyyy")`, which outputs 03-Mar-2010). Even though that output might be desirable in English, it may not match the expectations of users in other languages. Using the locale-aware built-in formats is the best way to achieve a user interface that all users can understand.

The same consideration applies to displaying currency and numbers. Non-internationalized code might use `"$" + someValue` to show a price, however many countries have a different currency symbol and it is customary in some places to put the symbol at the end of the price (rather than before it). The decimal point and thousands separator also differ across cultures — sometimes the point is a comma and the separator is a space, for example. These two lines show syntax for displaying currency and a formatted number:

```
NumberLabel.Text  = "Currency " + String.Format("{0:c}", 5432.11);
NumberLabel2.Text = "Thousands " + String.Format("{0:n}", 123456789.01);
```

Localization03\Main.cs

The localized output of these examples is shown in Figure 12-10.

 When displaying different currencies, remember that it is your code's responsibility to do any conversions to ensure the correct amount is being displayed.

FIGURE 12-10

MANAGING LOCALIZABLE.STRINGS IN REAL-WORLD APPLICATIONS

In a sample application like in the chapter download, you find only a handful of calls to `LocalizedString`, making it relatively easy to keep the `Localizable.strings` files up-to-date with all the `keys` you have used.

However, in a large application keeping track of all the strings you need translated will be more difficult as the calls to `LocalizedString` will be spread across your entire codebase. Every time you add, delete, or alter a localizable string, you need to remember to update the `.strings` files to reflect the changes in your code. It could become a very time-consuming manual task to extract all the keys and comments to create the base `.strings` files to send off for translation.

genstrings

To help Objective-C programmers extract all the localizable strings from their code Apple provides a tool called `genstrings`. Developers use `genstrings` to parse their source code to find calls to `LocalizedString` methods, extract the parameters and create a `Localizable.strings` file (or files) to be translated.

Unfortunately the `genstrings` tool can only parse C, Objective-C, and Java code so it cannot be used with MonoTouch.

ngenstrings

The download for this chapter contains a project `ngenstrings` that performs the same function as Apple's tool but for MonoTouch projects. It works slightly differently — instead of parsing the source code, it parses the .NET assembly compiled by MonoDevelop — but the output is the same: `.strings` files that you can translate and then include in your application.

`ngenstrings` not only extracts the keys and default values from your code, but also any comments you've included in certain `LocalizedString()` method overloads. This helps translators to understand the context of each piece of text (assuming your comments are good) and ultimately improves the quality of their translation and therefore your localized application.

Using ngenstrings

Find `ngenstrings.exe` and `lib.dll` in the chapter download and save to the Applications folder on your Mac. You can then automatically generate `.strings` files from your internationalized application with the following steps:

1. Compile your application for the iPhone simulator in Debug mode. (Release mode will also work but the folder specified in step 3 will be different.)

2. Use the MonoDevelop context menu to find where your application files are as shown in Figure 12-11. This directory will contain a `/bin/` folder; the .NET assembly is located in `/bin/iPhoneSimulator/Debug/`.

FIGURE 12-11

3. Copy the .NET assembly to the Applications folder where you saved `ngenstrings.exe`.

4. Open the MacOS Terminal application from the Utilities folder (the icons are shown in Figure 12-12).

5. Navigate to the `ngenstrings` Applications folder in the Terminal application.

6. Use Mono to execute `ngenstrings` passing your .NET assembly as a parameter like this:

FIGURE 12-12

```
mono ngenstrings.exe <yourapplication>.exe
```

or to use an example from this chapter:

```
mono ngenstrings.exe Localization03.exe
```

The Terminal output will look similar Figure 12-13 (each string is written to the Terminal as it is processed) and the resulting `Localizable.strings` file is shown in Figure 12-14.

FIGURE 12-13

FIGURE 12-14

You can then supply the `.strings` files to translators for each language you wish to support. When they supply the finished translations, simply place the files in the correct `.lproj` folders within your MonoDevelop project and rebuild your application.

 The content of the `.strings` *files is sorted alphabetically by the key, so you can easily see changes, additions, and deletions over time with a file-comparison tool.*

Limitations of ngenstrings

`ngenstrings` works by examining your compiled code for calls to the `LocalizedString` method, it then extracts the parameters from the method to build the `.strings` output files.

Because of this you should always embed the actual strings in the method call, like this:

```
NSBundle.MainBundle.LocalizedString ("First name:","Label for firstname");
NSBundle.MainBundle.LocalizedString ("Greeting","Hi {0}","");
NSBundle.MainBundle.LocalizedString ("One","1","Nums","The number one");
```

You should *not* pass variables into this method as the `ngenstrings` tool cannot parse them. The following localizable strings will not be extracted successfully:

```
var key = "Firstname";
var product = "iPad";
NSBundle.MainBundle.LocalizedString (key,"Label for firstname");
NSBundle.MainBundle.LocalizedString ("Product","The " + product,"");
```

The `genstrings` tool from Apple has the same limitation.

 `ngenstrings` *is an open source tool written in C# with Mono. You are free to modify the source code provided in the download or get the latest release online from* `http://github.com/conceptdev/ngenstrings`.

SUMMARY

The App Store is available in more than 70 countries, which means there is a large market for applications in native languages. If you take the time to internationalize your code from the start — using `.strings` files and retrieving text and images using the methods on `MainBundle` — it will be much easier for translators to localize it.

You also learned about the open-source tool `ngenstrings` that can help you manage the localized strings regardless of the size of your project and the amount of translation required.

Releasing a translated application that makes careful use of localized formatting and culturally aware images and concepts will give you the maximum chance of success. Ideally, foreign-language users will not be able to distinguish your localized application from something that was created specifically for their market. Achieving that level of familiarity can be difficult across a large number of languages, but the iPhone with MonoTouch provides you with the tools to do it.

13

Programming the iPad

WHAT'S IN THIS CHAPTER?

➤ Short history of the iPad

➤ Learning how iPad differs from iPhone

➤ Using some of the new controls

➤ Building a Universal Application

On January 27, 2010, Apple announced the eagerly anticipated iPad tablet computer running the iPhone OS, and on April 3 the device first went on sale. The iPad falls into a category between a laptop and a mobile phone. It is the first large-screen device from Apple that runs the iPhone Operating System, with roughly four times the screen area of the iPhone and iPod Touch.

In this chapter you learn what the capabilities of the device are, what new APIs and controls have been introduced that you can use in iPad-specific applications, and how to build applications that can work on both iPad and iPhone devices.

THE IPAD DEVICE

The iPad is a tablet computer running the iPhone Operating System. It has a 9.7-inch LED backlit multi-touch display and is powered by a 1-gigahertz ARM processor designed by Apple and referred to as the A4. Connectivity is supported via a 30-pin standard iPhone connector, Bluetooth 2.1 support, and 802.11n Wi-Fi networking. A separate model adds support for 3G network connectivity. Figure 13-1 shows the iPad next to an iPhone, demonstrating the difference in the size of the screen and the on-screen keyboard.

FIGURE 13-1

The biggest change with the iPad is its screen resolution of 1024×768. This is an increase from the iPhone and iPod Touch's 480×320 screen resolution. The question for a developer is "What should I do with the additional screen real estate?" For a game application, the strategy will most likely involve providing more visual detail in the application, more control presented to the user, and more status information within the game. For productivity applications, you can take advantage of some new controls and APIs.

The iPad brings a variety of new hardware and user interface capabilities to the iPhone OS platform, such as:

➤ Split views allow two custom views to be presented side-by-side. These can be used along with master detail views and navigation-based interfaces.

➤ Popovers allow for data to be presented on top of existing views in a temporary fashion. Popovers are useful for menus and palettes.

➤ New presentation styles are available for modally presented views.

➤ Toolbars can now be placed at the top and bottom of a view and can contain more information due to the increased screen size.

➤ Gesture recognition is now part of the UIKit framework, making it easy to support pinch, pan, tap, rotate, and the long press in your applications.

➤ Custom input views are now supported. The custom input view slides up from the bottom of the screen when the view becomes the first responder (as the on-screen keyboard does). Previously, text fields and text views supported *only* the keyboard as the input view, but on the iPad you can provide your own custom input methods.

➤ Custom input accessory views are also available. An input accessory view is a view that is attached to the top of an input view (such as the Previous and Next buttons attached to the keyboard when entering data on a web form in Safari). It slides in with the input view when the object becomes the first responder. This allows you to add a custom toolbar to the top of the virtual keyboard.

➤ There is new support for text display and input:

    ➤ Sophisticated text display and layout has been added in the Core Text framework.

    ➤ The UIKit framework includes enhancements to support custom views, a new UITextChecker class for spell checking, and support for new custom commands in editing menus.

➤ External displays and projectors can be detected and content can be displayed on the second screen.

➤ There is support for files and documents. This is needed for productivity style applications.

➤ The UIKit framework has been enhanced to support creating PDF content from an application.

WHAT MAKES AN IPAD APPLICATION?

An iPhone OS application identifies itself as an iPad application via the UIDeviceFamily entry in the Info.plist configuration file. The number "1" indicates iPhone/iPod Touch support, the number "2" indicates iPad support, and supplying both means the application runs on all iPhone OS devices.

```
<key>UIDeviceFamily</key>
<array>
    <string>1</string>
    <string>2</string>
</array>
```

When you create an iPad application in MonoTouch, this file and entry is created for you automatically. You can choose to support iPhone, iPad, or both via the Project Options as shown in Figure 13-2, and the Info.plist entry is automatically adjusted. Unless otherwise specified, the examples in the chapter download all target the iPad only.

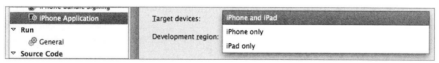

FIGURE 13-2

If you change this setting in a well-written existing iPhone application (that already has a flexible user interface layout) it should run at the full iPad resolution without further changes. This configuration entry is the smallest possible difference between an iPhone and iPad application.

Of course you want your iPad application to be optimized for the device — and the rest of this chapter shows you how to do that.

Device Orientation Support

One important feature of the *iPad Human Interface Guidelines* is that all iPad applications must operate in any device orientation. Although some iPhone applications already support portrait and landscape orientations (the built-in applications such as Mail and Safari are good examples), even they support only three views: Portrait, LandscapeRight, and LandscapeLeft. To conform to Apple's guidelines, iPad applications are expected to work in the PortraitUpsideDown position as well.

When your application rotates you must then ensure your views will resize appropriately, which can be simple or complex depending on how you build your user interface. When developing iPhone applications, you can often create and use a UIViewController object directly; however, to override the autorotation behavior for an iPad application you always need to create a subclass as shown in Listing 13-1.

Available for download on Wrox.com

LISTING 13-1: Overriding ShouldAutorotateToInterfaceOrientation (iPad01\MyViewController.cs)

```
[Register("MyViewController")]
public class MyViewController : UIViewController
{
    public MyViewController () {}

    public override bool ShouldAutorotateToInterfaceOrientation
        (UIInterfaceOrientation toInterfaceOrientation)
    {
        return true;
    }
}
```

To see this work you need to place some controls on this UIViewController and add it to your window. On each control you need to set the AutoresizingMask property to indicate how the control's shape and position should change when the device is rotated. Listing 13-2 contains two autoresizing examples:

➤ A UITextView that has flexible Left, Top, Right, and Bottom margins. This means the control keeps the same Height and Width but the position changes in proportion to its original place in the window.

➤ A UIScrollView that has flexible Height and Width, which implies that the margins are "fixed" and will remain "anchored" to the edges of the window regardless of orientation.

Available for download on Wrox.com

LISTING 13-2: FinishedLaunching (iPad01\Main.cs)

```
text = new UITextView();
text.Text = "Golden Gate Bridge,\nSan Francisco";
text.Font = UIFont.FromName("Helvetica", 36f);
text.Frame = new System.Drawing.RectangleF(200,40,400,100);
text.AutoresizingMask = UIViewAutoresizing.FlexibleLeftMargin
    | UIViewAutoresizing.FlexibleTopMargin
```

```
    | UIViewAutoresizing.FlexibleRightMargin
    | UIViewAutoresizing.FlexibleBottomMargin;
text.ScrollEnabled = false;
text.Editable = false;
// create image
UIImage image = UIImage.FromFile("GoldenGate.jpg");
UIImageView imageView = new UIImageView(image);
// assign to scrollview
customScrollView = new UIScrollView(this.window.Bounds);
customScrollView.AutoresizingMask = UIViewAutoresizing.FlexibleHeight
    | UIViewAutoresizing.FlexibleWidth;
customScrollView.AddSubview(imageView);
customScrollView.ContentSize = imageView.Frame.Size;
customScrollView.ViewForZoomingInScrollView = delegate (UIScrollView sender)
{
    return imageView;
};
customViewController = new MyViewController();
customViewController.Add(customScrollView);
customViewController.Add(text);
window.AddSubview (customViewController.View);
```

Figure 13-3 shows the image and text rotating and re-centering to match the device orientation.

FIGURE 13-3

You can use any combination of UIViewAutoresizing values to create the layout behavior you need, and if that does not provide sufficient control you can subscribe to notifications about orientation change events and write custom code to resize and re-layout your classes manually.

Your `FinishedLaunching` *code should* not *attempt to determine the device's orientation before building the original layout. Instead you should construct your user interface (either in code or in your* `MainWindow.xib` *file) for a single orientation — once the application has finished loading, the operating system will notify your app of the device's current orientation and cause the layout to change appropriately before it is displayed for the first time.*

Startup Images

Now that your application supports all available orientations, you should ensure your launch image similarly adapts to the screen. The image should fill the screen, leaving 20 pixels along the top for the status bar.

Two elements are required to provide this support: First, use the `Info.plist` file to advise the operating system which orientations your application supports and then add specially named images to your project to be displayed for each orientation.

Your `Info.plist` file should contain the following key and value array:

```
<key>UISupportedInterfaceOrientations</key>
<array>
    <string>UIInterfaceOrientationPortrait</string>
    <string>UIInterfaceOrientationLandscapeLeft</string>
    <string>UIInterfaceOrientationLandscapeRight</string>
    <string>UIInterfaceOrientationPortraitUpsideDown</string>
</array>
```

and your MonoDevelop project should include specially named images described in Table 13-1 (with their `Build Action` set to `Content`).

TABLE 13-1: Orientation-Specific Startup Images

KEY	DESCRIPTION
`Default.png`	The filename used in the iPhone OS to identify the startup image prior to the release of the iPad. You should *not* use this filename for iPad applications, but provide a 320x460-pixel image if you have built a Universal Application that runs on both types of device; this image will be used on the iPhone and iPod Touch. For iPad applications you should provide at least two images: `Default-Portrait.png` and `Default-Landscape.png` as described next.

KEY	DESCRIPTION
`Default-Portrait.png`	A 768x1004-pixel image that is displayed if the device is vertical (that is, the Home button is at the top or bottom), unless `Default-PortraitUpsideDown.png` has also been supplied, in which case that image will be used when the Home button is at the top.
`Default-PortraitUpsideDown.png`	A 768x1004-pixel image that is displayed if the device is upside down (that is, the Home button is at the top). This image supersedes the `Default-Portrait.png` that has also been supplied and is used when the Home button is at the top.
`Default-Landscape.png`	A 1024x748-pixel image that is displayed if the device is on either side. You can choose to supply this single image or create the following two images depending on whether the Home button is to the left or right of the device.
`Default-LandscapeLeft.png`	A 1024x748-pixel image that supersedes `Default-Landscape.png`.
`Default-LandscapeRight.png`	A 1024x748 pixel image that supersedes `Default-Landscape.png`.

Example iPad02 in the chapter download uses the orientation-specific filenames to demonstrate how these work. Figure 13-4 shows two of the four possible orientations using `Default-Portrait.png` and `Default-Landscape.png` images.

FIGURE 13-4

NEW IPAD FEATURES

In addition to the controls covered in Chapters 3 and 4, the iPad supports some new user interface controls that take advantage of the larger screen and the "any orientation" user interface. Figure 13-5 shows the iPad Mail application using the new orientation-aware *split view* control. On an iPhone you must switch back and forth between your Inbox and messages; however, the iPad allows you to see both. The Inbox and message appear side-by-side in landscape mode, whereas in portrait mode the Inbox is available in a new *popover view* control.

FIGURE 13-5

Using UISplitViewController

A split view manages two other view controllers and displays one or both of them depending on the orientation of the device. In landscape mode the first view has a fixed width of 320 pixels (the width of the iPhone's screen) and the second view uses up the rest of the display. In portrait mode the 320-pixel-wide view is hidden by default but is accessible via a popover control.

To use the UISplitViewController class you simply need to tell it which view controllers to use; it then detects the device's orientation and shows or hides the first view as required. Listing 13-3 shows how easy it is to set up a split view (the UISplitViewController was dragged onto the window in Interface Builder and outlets were created to the other controls).

The only requirement for the other two view controllers is that they support any orientation as shown in Listing 13-1.

LISTING 13-3: Creating a split view (iPad03\Main.cs)

```
public override void FinishedLaunching (UIApplication app, NSDictionary options)
{
    DetailViewController = new MyDetailViewController();
    MasterViewController = new MyMasterViewController(this);
    SplitViewController  = new UISplitViewController();
    SplitViewController.ViewControllers =
        new UIViewController[] {MasterViewController, DetailViewController};

    window.AddSubview(SplitViewController.View);
    window.MakeKeyAndVisible ();
    return true;
}
```

You can find the complete code for the two view controllers in the chapter download iPad03 files `MyMasterViewController.cs` and `MyDetailViewController.cs`. Neither contains anything new: The detail view controller uses the code from Listings 13-1 and 13-2 combined into a single class, and the master view controller contains a simple `UITableView` covered in Chapter 6.

The example is shown in Figure 13-6 with the table showing in landscape mode but hidden in portrait mode. Notice that in portrait mode there is currently no way to access the popover containing the list of photos.

FIGURE 13-6

Although it is not implemented by default, it is recommended that when the first view controller is hidden (in portrait mode) you provide a button on the remaining view that displays the hidden view controller in a popover (for example, the Mail application as shown in Figure 13-4).

Example iPad04 in the code download shows how to implement the button and take advantage of the automatic popover support.

1. First, you must add a toolbar to the view containing the scrolling image (a navigation bar can also be used) so that you have somewhere to place the button.

2. Second, you must implement and assign a UISplitViewControllerDelegate to manage the showing and hiding of the button. Place this line of code in your FinishedLaunching method and then implement the delegate:

    ```
    SplitViewController.Delegate = new MySplitViewDelegate(this);
    ```

Listing 13-4 shows how to implement the delegate class. You do not have to know anything about the UIPopover control to make this work; simply place the button passed into the WillHideViewContoller method on your toolbar and everything else is wired up automatically.

LISTING 13-4: UISplitViewDelegate (iPad04\Main.cs)

```
class MySplitViewDelegate : UISplitViewControllerDelegate
{
    AppDelegate appd;
    public MySplitViewDelegate(AppDelegate app)
    {
        appd = app; // passed in so we can access the toolbar
    }
    public override void WillHideViewController (UISplitViewController svc,
        UIViewController aViewController,
        UIBarButtonItem barButtonItem,
        UIPopoverController pc)
    { // show the button when the view is otherwise hidden
        appd.Toolbar.SetItems (new UIBarButtonItem[]{barButtonItem},false);
    }
    public override void WillShowViewController (UISplitViewController svc,
        UIViewController aViewController,
        UIBarButtonItem button)
    { // remove ALL buttons with empty array when the view is being shown
        // you could use the passed in one to remove from array
        appd.Toolbar.SetItems(new UIBarButtonItem[0],false);
    }}
```

Figure 13-7 shows the UISplitView in action: In landscape orientation the toolbar is empty, and both the table and image are visible. In portrait mode the table view is hidden and accessed via the button added to the toolbar (popovers default to 1100 pixels tall which just fills the screen).

You can get more control of the popover by implementing the WillPresentViewController method on the split view delegate class. In Listing 13-5 that method is used to set the size of the popover to 140 pixels high. However, you can perform any other actions that you might need before the view is displayed in the popover.

FIGURE 13-7

LISTING 13-5: UISplitViewDelegate (iPad05\Main.cs)

```
class MySplitViewDelegate : UISplitViewControllerDelegate
{
    AppDelegate appd;
    public MySplitViewDelegate(AppDelegate app)
    {
        appd = app;
    }
    // ...WillHideViewController implementation...
    // ...WillShowViewController implementation...
    public override void WillPresentViewController (
        UISplitViewController svc,
        UIPopoverController pc,
        UIViewController aViewController)
    {
        // Set the size, otherwise it defaults to 320x1100;
        pc.SetPopoverContentSize(new System.Drawing.SizeF(320,140),true);
    }}
```

Creating a Custom UIPopover

The `UISplitViewController` automatically creates a popover for one of its views, but the `UIPopover` control is used throughout the iPad's built-in applications for a variety of other purposes (some of which are shown in Figure 13-8):

➤   To display information about an item on the screen by showing the popover when the object is touched (similar to the annotations in the Maps application)

➤   To present actions that can be taken on a particular object (similar to a context-sensitive menu)

➤   To act as an input helper (such as the birthday field in the Contacts application, which presents a `UIDatePicker` in a `UIPopover`)

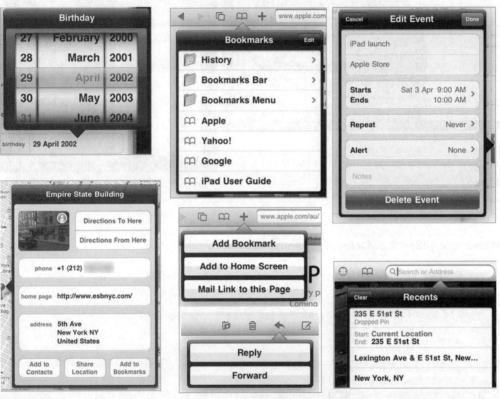

FIGURE 13-8

Chapter download example iPad05 adds a button to the toolbar that displays a custom popover. Listing 13-5 shows how to create the button, add it to the toolbar, and assign a delegate that displays the popover (defined later). The delegate assigns the popover to a public field on the `AppDelegate` class declared like this:

```
public UIPopoverController CustomPopover;
```

so that other code can reference it (to dismiss it, for example).

The highlighted code in Listing 13-6 works as follows:

➤ Create an instance of a `UIViewController` that you want to display in a popover. This view controller can be as simple as a few buttons (such as the Mail reply/forward popover), or it could contain a complex `UINavigationController` hierarchy (such as the Mail inbox).

➤ Create an instance of `UIPopover`, passing it the view controller to display.

➤ Call the `PresentFromBarButtonItem` method, passing the button and direction so that the popover knows where to draw itself. You should normally leave the direction as `Any` and let the popover decide how to best render.

LISTING 13-6: Creating a popover (iPad05\Main.cs)

Available for download on Wrox.com

```
barButton = new UIBarButtonItem();
barButton.Title = "Popover";
barButton.Style = UIBarButtonItemStyle.Bordered;
barButton.Clicked += delegate(object sender, EventArgs e)
{
    MyCustomPopoverViewController content =
        new MyCustomPopoverViewController (this);
    CustomPopover = new UIPopoverController (content);
    CustomPopover.PresentFromBarButtonItem (
        (UIBarButtonItem)sender,
        UIPopoverArrowDirection.Any, true);
};
ToolbarItems = new UIBarButtonItem[]{barButton};
customToolbar.Items = ToolbarItems;
```

Listing 13-7 shows the implementation for the popover view controller. In most respects it is a regular view controller — in this case containing three buttons — with the addition of the `ContentSizeForViewInPopover` property being set to control the size of the popover. The buttons reference the `customPopover` field on `AppDelegate` to call the `Dismiss()` method and hide the popover.

LISTING 13-7: iPad05\MyCustomPopoverViewController.cs

Available for download on Wrox.com

```
[Register("MyCustomPopoverViewController")]
public partial class MyCustomPopoverViewController : UIViewController
{
    AppDelegate appd;
    public MyCustomPopoverViewController(AppDelegate app)
    {
        appd = app;
    }
    readonly UIButton button1 = UIButton.FromType(UIButtonType.RoundedRect);
    readonly UIButton button2 = UIButton.FromType(UIButtonType.RoundedRect);
    readonly UIButton button3 = UIButton.FromType(UIButtonType.RoundedRect);
    public override void ViewDidLoad ()
    {
```

continues

LISTING 13-7 *(continued)*

```
        ContentSizeForViewInPopover = new SizeF(320, 110);
        button1.SetTitle("PageSheet",UIControlState.Normal);
        button1.Frame = new RectangleF(10,10,144,40);
        button1.TouchUpInside += delegate
        {
            Console.WriteLine("Button1 touched");
            appd.CustomPopover.Dismiss(true);
        };
// ...repeat for two more buttons: button2 and button3...
        View.AddSubview(button1);
        View.AddSubview(button2);
        View.AddSubview(button3);
    }
}
```

Note that your code does not have to dismiss the popover if it makes sense to stay open (such as if the user is entering multiple pieces of data or can make multiple choices within the popover). If the user touches outside the popover, it is automatically dismissed. Figure 13-9 shows how the popover looks on the screen.

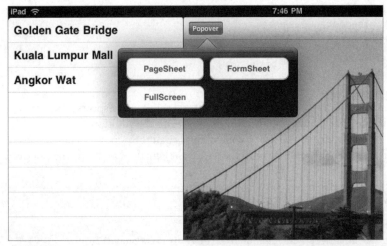

FIGURE 13-9

Popovers can also be triggered by other controls than `UIBarButtonItem` (in response to tapping an image or other view, for example). Instead of the `UIPopover.PresentFromBarButtonItem()` method you would call `PresentFromRect` with the following parameters:

- ➤ `rect`: The `RectangleF` area in the view where the popover will originate
- ➤ `view`: The view containing the `rect` specified
- ➤ `arrowDirections`: The arrow directions the popover can use to display itself
- ➤ `animated`: Whether to animate the display of the popover or just display immediately

Displaying Modal Views

In earlier versions of the iPhone OS a modal view took up the entire visible area of the window. `UIViewController` now has a `ModalPresentationStyle` property that allows you choose whether to fill all or only part of the screen. Visible parts of the underlying view are dimmed when a modal view is being displayed. Table 13-2 lists the available styles.

TABLE 13-2: ModalPresentationStyle Options

STYLE	DESCRIPTION
PageSheet	Full height and width of portrait (therefore appears fullscreen in portrait mode but in landscape mode the background view is visible on either side)
FormSheet	Small centered view
FullScreen	Fullscreen (same as earlier iPhone OS versions)
CurrentContext	Inherits the same style used by the parent view controller

You can also choose from four different animation styles to use when displaying a modal view, shown in Table 13-3.

TABLE 13-3: ModalTransitionStyle Options

STYLE	DESCRIPTION
CoverVertical	Slides up from the bottom of the screen then slides back down when done.
FlipHorizontal	Horizontal right-to-left flip to show the modal view on the "back" of the previous view. Animation is reversed when done.
CrossDissolve	Old view fades out as the modal view fades in.
PartialCurl	One corner of the current view curls up to reveal the modal view underneath. You can only use this transition when the parent view controller is fullscreen, and you cannot present any additional modal views when using this style.

Listing 13-8 contains two new methods for your `AppDelegate` to show and hide a modal view using different transition styles with the `PresentModalViewController()` and `DismissModalViewController()` methods on `UIViewController`.

LISTING 13-8: Showing a modal view (iPad05\Main.cs)

```
public void ShowModal(int buttonId)
{
    switch (buttonId)
```

continues

LISTING 13-8 *(continued)*

```
    {
    case 1:
    modalView = new MyModalViewController(this, "PageSheet", 0);
    modalView.ModalTransitionStyle = UIModalTransitionStyle.CrossDissolve;
    modalView.ModalPresentationStyle = UIModalPresentationStyle.PageSheet;
    break;
    case 2:
    modalView = new MyModalViewController(this, "FormSheet", 0);
    modalView.ModalTransitionStyle = UIModalTransitionStyle.CoverVertical;
    modalView.ModalPresentationStyle = UIModalPresentationStyle.FormSheet;
    break;
    case 3:
    modalView = new MyModalViewController(this,"FullScreen",500);
    modalView.ModalTransitionStyle = UIModalTransitionStyle.PartialCurl;
    modalView.ModalPresentationStyle = UIModalPresentationStyle.FullScreen;
    break;
    }
    this.SplitViewController.PresentModalViewController(modalView, true);
}
public void HideModal()
{
    this.SplitViewController.DismissModalViewControllerAnimated(true);
}
```

Then add the following line to each button `TouchUpInside` delegate (in Listing 13-6) to test each modal style:

```
_appd.ShowModal(1); // or 2 or 3
```

Figure 13-10 shows the resulting `PageSheet`, `FormSheet`, and `FullScreen` modal presentation styles.

FIGURE 13-10

Recognizing Gestures

Touch gestures are an important part of the iPhone and iPad user interface; however, previous versions of the iPhone OS required some programming to react to gestures. iPhone OS 3.2 introduced the six gestures shown in Table 13-4 to simplify the code required to respond to these types of user interactions.

TABLE 13-4: Types of UIGestureRecognizer

CLASS	GESTURE
UITapGestureRecognizer	Tapping a configurable number of times
UIPinchGestureRecognizer	Pinching fingers together or apart (for zooming)
UIPanGestureRecognizer	Panning by dragging a finger across the screen
UISwipeGestureRecognizer	Swiping in any direction
UIRotationGestureRecognizer	Rotating using fingers moving in opposite directions
UILongPressGestureRecognizer	Holding down a finger

Listing 13-9 shows how to use the UITapGestureRecognizer to detect and respond to a double-tap. The important lines are as follows:

➤ Create an instance of UITapGestureRecognizer to watch for this type of gesture.

➤ Set the NumberOfTapsRequired property to 2 to detect double-taps. You can choose to respond to "triple-taps" or "quadruple-taps" as well.

➤ Call the AddTarget() method to inform the recognizer which method to call when the gesture is detected. Generally you will specify this as the class and create a new Selector to indicate which method.

➤ "Register" the gesture recognizer with the UIView that you want to be double-tappable using the AddGestureRecognizer() method. Note that the UIImageView also requires UserInteractionEnabled=true.

➤ Declare the method to handle your double-tap and mark it with an export attribute using the same Selector string you passed to AddTarget(). The C# method name is not important as long as the export and selector strings match.

➤ Within the method you can capture details about the double-tap event from the UIGestureRecognizer sender, such as the location the tap occurred. You must pass in the UIView that you want the coordinates relative to — in most cases that will be the view that detected the event (which in the example code is a UIImageView). Your code can then respond to the double-tap using those coordinates.

LISTING 13-9: DoubleTap Gesture (iPad06\MyViewController.cs)

```
[Register("MyViewController")]
public class MyViewController : UIViewController
{
    AppDelegate appd;
    UIImage image;
    public MyViewController (AppDelegate app)
```

continues

LISTING 13-9 *(continued)*

```
        {
            appd=app;
            image = UIImage.FromFile("GoldenGate.jpg");
            appd.Image.Image = image;
            appd.Image.UserInteractionEnabled = true;

            UITapGestureRecognizer doubletap = new UITapGestureRecognizer();
            doubletap.NumberOfTapsRequired = 2;
            doubletap.AddTarget(this,
                new MonoTouch.ObjCRuntime.Selector("DoubleTapSelector"));
            appd.Image.AddGestureRecognizer(doubletap);
        }
        [Export("DoubleTapSelector")]
        public void DoubleTap (UIGestureRecognizer sender)
        {
            var locInView = sender.LocationInView(sender.View);
            appd.Text.Text += "\n[DoubleTap] " + sender.State +
                " Location: " + locInView.X + "," + locInView.Y;
        }
        public override bool ShouldAutorotateToInterfaceOrientation
                (UIInterfaceOrientation toInterfaceOrientation)
        {
            return true;
        }
    }
```

When you double-tap anywhere in the image, the `DoubleTap()` method is called once and the coordinates will be added to the scrolling text area. This is called a *discrete gesture*. The `UILongPressGestureRecognizer` also represents a discrete gesture that generates only one message to the `Selector`.

Similar code can be used to react to other gestures such as pinch and pan. Listings 13-10 and 13-11 show how to respond to pinch and pan, respectively. There is a very important difference between the `UITapGestureRecognizer` and the `UIPinchGestureRecognizer` and `UIPanGestureRecognizer`: these latter gestures take place over time and multiple action messages are sent to the `Selector` as the gesture is taking place. These are called *continuous gestures* and they require more complex `Selector` code that checks the `State` property to help decide what to do with each message and to detect when the gesture has completed (either successfully or if it fails).

LISTING 13-10: Pinch gesture (iPad06\MyViewController.cs)

```
public Initialize ()
{
    // ... image setup code ...
    UIPinchGestureRecognizer pinch = new UIPinchGestureRecognizer();
    pinch.AddTarget(this, new MonoTouch.ObjCRuntime.Selector("PinchSelector"));
    appd.Image.AddGestureRecognizer(pinch);
}
[Export("PinchSelector")]
public void Pinch (UIGestureRecognizer sender)
```

```
{
    UIPinchGestureRecognizer pgr = (UIPinchGestureRecognizer)sender;
    var locInView = sender.LocationInView(sender.View);
    switch (sender.State)
    {
        case UIGestureRecognizerState.Began:
            appd.Text.Text += "\n[Pinch] Began-store the start value";
            break;
        case UIGestureRecognizerState.Changed:
            appd.Text.Text += "\n[Pinch] "+sender.State +
                        " Scale: " + pgr.Scale +
                        "\t\tLocation: " + locInView.X + "," + locInView.Y;
            break;
        case UIGestureRecognizerState.Cancelled:
            // revert
            break;
        case UIGestureRecognizerState.Recognized:
            appd.Text.Text += "\n[Pinch] Recognized";
            break;
    }
}
```

The UIGestureRecognizerState values are listed in Table 13-5. All gestures start in the Possible state. Discrete gestures then send a message only with Recognized state (or else no message if they Failed). Continuous gestures go through a number of states and generate multiple messages.

TABLE 13-5: UIGestureRecognizerStates

STATE	GESTURE
Possible	Default state — gesture has not been recognized.
Began	Indicates that the gesture has been recognized. You should capture starting values of the properties your gesture affects in this state.
Changed	Message contains updated gesture data (such as location, scale, translation, velocity) depending on the type of gesture. This data is not sent as a delta value since the last message but rather the change since the gesture Began.
Ended	Take any final actions related to the gesture, such as performing a page animation once a swipe gesture has Ended.
Recognized	Synonymous with Ended for multi-touch gestures (for example, generated by pinch but not pan).
Failed	Recognition failed. No action message is sent for this state.
Cancelled	Recognition cancelled. Your code should discard any property changes applied during the gesture (for example, snap an updated visual object back to its previous size/location).

The pan gesture code in Listing 13-11 is slightly different again: It has Translation and Velocity properties in addition to the location.

LISTING 13-11: Pan gesture (iPad06\MyViewController.cs)

```
public Initialize ()
{
    // ... image setup code ...
    UIPanGestureRecognizer pan = new UIPanGestureRecognizer();
    pan.AddTarget(this, new MonoTouch.ObjCRuntime.Selector("PanSelector"));
    appd.Image.AddGestureRecognizer(pan);
}
[Export("PanSelector")]
public void Pan (UIGestureRecognizer sender)
{
    UIPanGestureRecognizer pan = (UIPanGestureRecognizer)sender;
    var locInView = sender.LocationInView(sender.View);
    System.Drawing.PointF translate = pan.Translation;
    switch (sender.State)
    {
        case UIGestureRecognizerState.Began:
        appd.Text.Text += "\n[Pinch] Began-store the start value";
            break;
        case UIGestureRecognizerState.Changed:
            appd.Text.Text += "\n[Pan] "+sender.State +
                "\t\tTranslate: " + translate.X + "," +  translate.Y +
                "\t\tVelocity: " + pan.Velocity +
                "\t\tLocation: " + locInView.X + "," + locInView.Y;
            break;
        case UIGestureRecognizerState.Cancelled:
            // revert
            break;
         case UIGestureRecognizerState.Recognized:
            appd.Text.Text += "\n[Pinch] Recognized-now do pan content ";
            break;
    }
}
```

The output of these gesture recognizers is shown in Figure 13-11. Your code would take some action in response to each gesture rather than just emitting the changing property values to the screen.

BUILDING A UNIVERSAL APP

A Universal App runs on both the iPad and iPhone class devices. The key elements of a Universal App are:

➤ Inform the App Store and operating system that both platforms are supported in the Info.plist file (using the MonoDevelop Project Options windows to choose "iPhone and iPad," as shown in Figure 13-2).

➤ Specify what orientations are supported for each platform (recalling that Portrait is the default if none are specified).

➤ Provide auto-resizing views that will work on both platforms *or* use different view layouts after checking which device is being used.

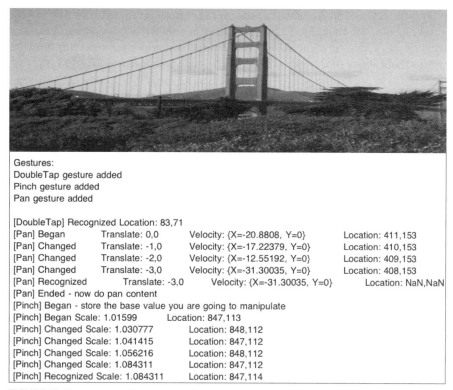

FIGURE 13-11

You should also provide at least three startup images from the options listed in Table 13-1:

➤ `Default.png`, which will be displayed on the iPhone and iPod Touch devices

➤ `Default-Portrait.png` and `Default-Landscape.png`, which will be used by the iPad (depending on its orientation)

You can also set the application icon in the `Info.plist`. The `CFBundleIconFiles` key can contain an array of icon filenames so that a different icon appears on the iPhone and the iPad. Simply create two icon images and add them to your MonoDevelop project: a 57×57 pixel image for the iPhone and a 72×72 pixel image for the iPad. Then add both filenames in the `CFBundleIconFiles` array (as shown in Listing 13-12). The iPhone OS will automatically choose the correct image based on its dimensions.

LISTING 13-12: iPhone and iPad icon settings (iPad07\Info.plist)

```
<key>CFBundleIconFiles</key>
<array>
   <string>Icon.png</string>
   <string>IconiPad.png</string>
</array>
```

Using `AutoresizingMask` and `ShouldAutorotateToInterfaceOrientation` ensures that the controls fill the screen on each device. To make chapter download example iPad07 work on iPhones *and* iPads, it presents the same two view controllers as the other examples in this chapter but with a `UINavigationController` in place of the `UISplitView`. The code is shown in Listing 13-13.

LISTING 13-13: Universal FinishedLaunching (iPad07\AppDelegate.cs)

```
public override bool FinishedLaunching (UIApplication app, NSDictionary options)
{
    tv = new UITableView();
    tv.Source = new MyTableViewSource(this);
    TableViewController = new MyTableViewController();
    TableViewController.TableView = tv;

    navigationController = new UINavigationController();
    navigationController.PushViewController(TableViewController, false);
    navigationController.TopViewController.Title ="My Photos";

    window = new UIWindow (UIScreen.MainScreen.Bounds);
    window.AddSubview(navigationController.View);
    window.MakeKeyAndVisible ();
}
```

To test a Universal App on multiple device types you need to target the correct SDK version (that is, the SDK that runs on all of those devices). At the time of writing, the latest release for the iPhone is 3.1.3, and the iPad is running 3.2. So, in the Project Options you should choose 3.1.3 as shown in Figure 13-12.

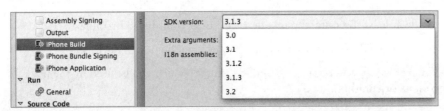

FIGURE 13-12

Once you have selected a particular SDK, the Run menu in MonoDevelop presents simulator options for you to test. Choose both iPhone Simulator 3.1.3 and iPad Simulator 3.2 (shown in Figure 13-13) to test your code on both device types.

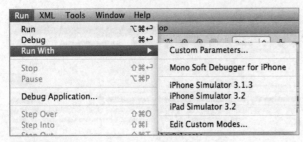

FIGURE 13-13

Figures 13-14 and 13-15 show the application (example iPad07 from the chapter download) running on the iPhone and iPad, respectively.

The iPad version obviously wastes a lot of screen space — while you have the same code running on both devices, it does not take full advantage of the iPad's larger screen.

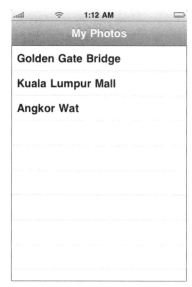

FIGURE 13-14

FIGURE 13-15

A "true" Universal App should adapt to the iPad's capabilities where appropriate. If you want to build customized layouts for each platform, either of these lines of code can help you determine whether or not the device is an iPad so you can optimize your user interface:

```
bool IsIPad = UIDevice.CurrentDevice.Model.ToLower().Contains("ipad");
```

or

```
bool IsIPad = (UIScreen.MainScreen.Bounds == new RectangleF(0,0,768,1024));
```

Example iPad08 in the chapter download performs a device check in order to provide an iPad-specific user interface while continuing to work on the iPhone. The code in Listing 13-14 shows how it works:

➤ First, the table view and controller are created regardless of the device type. On the iPhone the table is the only view initially displayed, and on the iPad the table is incorporated into a split view.

➤ Then the device type is detected by comparing the `MainScreen.Bounds` property. 768x1024 means the device is an iPad.

➤ If the device is an iPhone (or iPod Touch), then a `UINavigationController` is created and added to the `window`. This then presents the table and images as a regular iPhone application.

➤ If the device is an iPad, the code creates a `Toolbar` to add to the `DetailViewController`, then it creates and assigns the `DetailViewController` and the `SplitViewController` before adding the split view to the `window`.

LISTING 13-14: Optimized FinishedLaunching (iPad08\AppDelegate.cs)

```
public override bool FinishedLaunching (UIApplication app, NSDictionary options)
{
    window = new UIWindow (UIScreen.MainScreen.Bounds);
    // the table view is used regardless of which device is targetted
    tv = new UITableView ();
    tvs = new MyTableViewSource (this);
    tv.Source = tvs;
    TableViewController = new MyTableViewController (tv);
    TableViewController.Title = "My Photos";
    IsIPad = (UIScreen.MainScreen.Bounds == new RectangleF (0, 0, 768, 1024));
    if (!IsIPad)
    { // iPhone - use a navigation controller
        navigationController = new UINavigationController ();
        navigationController.PushViewController (TableViewController, false);
        navigationController.TopViewController.Title = "My Photos";
        window.AddSubview (navigationController.View);
    }
    else
    { // iPad - use a splitview, and add a toolbar to the image view controller
```

```
            Toolbar = new UIToolbar ();
            Toolbar.Frame = new RectangleF(0,0,UIScreen.MainScreen.Bounds.Width,40);
            DetailViewController = new MyDetailViewController (Toolbar);
            ViewPort = DetailViewController.ViewPort; // for RowSelected
            SplitViewController = new UISplitViewController ();
            SplitViewController.Delegate = new MySplitViewDelegate (this);
            SplitViewController.ViewControllers = new UIViewController[]
                { TableViewController, DetailViewController };
            window.AddSubview (SplitViewController.View);
        }
        window.MakeKeyAndVisible ();
        return true;
    }
```

The `RowSelected` method for the table is the only other method that requires customization depending on the device. On the iPhone, when a row is selected, you need to push a new image view onto the navigation controller stack (refer to Chapters 4 and 6 for more information about navigating with tables). For an iPad the image view is already created in the other half of the split view, so you simply need to reset the image file each time a row is selected.

Listing 13-15 demonstrates the two different approaches. The iPad-specific code uses the `ViewPort` public field on the `AppDelegate` to allow the other half of the split view to be accessed from this method.

LISTING 13-15: RowSelected (iPad08\AppDelegate.cs)

```
public override void RowSelected (UITableView tableView, NSIndexPath indexPath)
{
    if (!appd.IsIPad)
    { // iPhone, need to create and push new view controller
        var ivc = new MyDetailViewController (imagePath[indexPath.Row]);
        appd.navigationController.PushViewController (ivc, true);
    }
    else
    { // just create and set the image in the Split View
        image = UIImage.FromFile (imagePath[indexPath.Row]);
        imageView = (UIImageView)appd.ViewPort.Subviews[0];
        imageView.Image = image;
    }
    tableView.DeselectRow (indexPath, true);
}
```

The optimized Universal App looks just like Figure 13-14 when used on an iPhone; however, the addition of the split view (as shown in Figure 13-16) makes a much better iPad user interface than Figure 13-15.

FIGURE 13-16

With careful planning you can often reuse views for both iPhone and iPad display in a Universal App. UISplitViewController and UIPopover both help to present iPhone-formatted (that is, 320 pixel wide) views on the larger iPad screen in a usable way while allowing them to be functional on the iPhone as well.

SUMMARY

This chapter introduced you to the iPad and some of the new iPhone OS features that have been introduced in version 3.2 to take advantage of the device's large screen. The chapter covered:

➤ An overview of the iPad hardware

➤ A list of the new features of iPhone OS 3.2

➤ Examples of the main new user interface elements: UISplitView and UIPopover

➤ How to take advantage of the new UIGestureRecognizer

➤ An example Universal Application that can run on both iPhone and iPad platforms from the one binary

The launch of the iPad has introduced a lot of new features to iPhone OS, and this chapter has provided working examples of the most important elements to build compelling iPad applications using MonoTouch.

14

Just Enough Objective-C

WHAT'S IN THIS CHAPTER?

➤ Looking at Objective-C and Cocoa

➤ Using an academic approach versus a pragmatic approach

➤ Learning basic syntax and concepts

➤ Helpful cheat sheets

MonoTouch is appealing for many reasons. If you're already a .NET developer, the utility is obvious. If you're accustomed to writing managed code (Java, Python, and so on), MonoTouch is a sensible choice regardless of your level of experience with .NET. Whether you're a Java dev, a Python dev, or a VB dev, you're used to working with tools and languages that do a lot of the heavy lifting for you.

As far as object-oriented versions of C go, Objective-C is a fairly simple, straightforward implementation. However, compared to other, more modern C-style languages, Objective-C can seem arcane, verbose, and cumbersome. It isn't a bad language by any means, but there's a reason you chose MonoTouch.

Why, then, is there a chapter on Objective-C in a MonoTouch book? Especially considering that you likely chose MonoTouch in part to *avoid* learning Objective-C?

It would be nice if those of us who choose MonoTouch over the native dev stack could spend all our time in the comfort of C#, the MonoTouch bindings, and the subset of the .NET Framework it ships with, but the reality is that, the deeper you go with iPhone MonoTouch development, the more likely it is you're going to run up against a question or problem that can only be addressed if you have at least a rudimentary understanding of Objective-C.

Novell did such a good job of creating a .NET development platform for the iPhone that it's easy to forget MonoTouch apps ultimately compile down to native binaries. When you do finally encounter an issue that exists in the Objective-C runtime rather than in MonoTouch, you're going to find yourself digging through Apple's documentation rather than Novell's. Obviously, that documentation isn't going to be presented in terms of MonoTouch and C#. At that point, everything will be in Objective-C.

Although MonoTouch is growing in popularity, Apple's dev tools are, and will remain, the standard for iPhone app development. As such, if you want to take advantage of the majority of iPhone app example code, whether to learn from it or incorporate it into your own work, an ability to mentally parse Objective-C and translate it into C# is a useful skill to have even if you never intend to write a line of Objective-C yourself.

Many third-party iPhone libraries will be provided exclusively in Objective-C. It's easy to find MonoTouch bindings for the most popular of these libraries, but it's inevitable that, if you do end up needing to use a third-party library, you will eventually find at least one for which Objective-C will be the exclusive language in the documentation and sample code.

An ability to comprehend Objective-C is something that will come in very handy. The goal of this chapter is to provide you with a reference and introduction to Objective-C that will help you acquire that comprehension.

HOW TO USE THIS CHAPTER

You don't need to learn Objective-C inside-out to be able to read and make sense of it. If you're comfortable with OOP concepts and C-style languages, which you likely are if you're using MonoTouch, the amount of time you need to invest is surprisingly small. That said, it's also important to be realistic when learning new things. Setting expectations accordingly helps you not to become discouraged.

Being realistic, here are a few things to keep in mind as well as directions on how you might best make use of the information here.

Many Objective-C tutorials and books go on and on about how simple Objective-C is. There's some truth to this if:

1. You already know C. Not just a C-like language, but C itself.
2. You're familiar with Smalltalk (Objective-C was influenced by Smalltalk and has Smalltalk-style messaging).

For the developer coming from C#, Objective-C does look a bit odd. Some of the terminology used to describe the language will be foreign. Aspects of the Objective-C runtime, Objective-C conventions, and so on, might temporarily make you feel like you're learning to code all over again.

If you were to spend your life working in Objective-C, there *are* very real differences between how it and, say, C#, work that you would benefit from learning. However, the syntax, jargon, runtime, and so on, have, for the most part, analogs in C#. In the same way a Spanish speaker can get by with reading Portuguese, a C# developer can, with a little help, get by with reading Objective-C.

If you're interested in learning more about Objective-C than just how to read it, you can go through this chapter from start to finish.

If you're in a hurry and trying to meet a deadline, and if part of meeting that deadline involves making sense of Objective-C, your first stop should be the "cheat sheets" at the end of this chapter. There you'll find "translation tables" organized by keywords, syntax, concepts, and so on. The information in those tables might be sufficient to get you through. If you need more information, each table has a corresponding section in this chapter that goes into more detail.

Ultimately, whatever route you choose, don't be too intimidated by the thought of learning about a language that's new to you and likely different from what you're accustomed to. Expect to be challenged. But, you're a coder, and what coders do for a living is work with tools most people will never see or understand. You absolutely can wrap your head around foreign syntax and conventions. C# was strange to you once (if not C#, then whatever other language you began with).

Remember: you don't need to be able to write Objective-C; you only need to be able to *read* it. Armed with a decent phrasebook and multilingual dictionary, you can make your way through a foreign country well enough. If you were moving to another country, it would pay to become fluent in the language. But, when you're only visiting, there's no need to take it any further.

Use this chapter, then, as you might a travel guide.

A BRIEF LOOK AT OBJECTIVE-C AND COCOA

Before learning to read/understand Objective-C and Cocoa, it helps to know what they are. It's clear enough from its name that Objective-C is an object-oriented version of C.

To clarify, Objective-C *is* C, but with an object-oriented layer built on top of it. You might expect, then, that Objective-C will look and behave much like C itself. Though a reasonable assumption, when you dig in a little, it will initially surprise you to learn all the ways in which they're *dissimilar.*

C is a simple, if cumbersome, language. It can feel stiff, curmudgeonly, and stubborn; it can be relentless and unforgiving. Someone's first dip into C will introduce him or her to C's cleanliness, but also the fact that it's like a house that's been designed to be dangerous to newborns. Power outlets are well within reach, stove burners are left on, and you occasionally come across a gun with which to shoot yourself in the foot. It teaches you to code well by being your drill instructor and giving you little leeway.

Objective-C, as is covered in more detail later in this chapter, is powerful and, for most developers, a much faster and easier way to write applications than straight C. You can still shoot yourself in the foot and accidentally burn yourself from time to time, but it was designed in part to achieve that increased productivity by being more forgiving. It comes with the potential dangers of C, and some APIs for the iPhone are strictly C (no corresponding Objective-C framework), but most of a typical iPhone app's source will be a combination of C and Objective-C that borrows from the former to provide a foundation to build on (basic data types like integers, if/for blocks, and so on), whereas the latter creates a more developer-friendly way to take advantage of that foundation.

Compared to C, and even C#, Objective-C is also much looser when it comes to how certain things are done. In C#, much functionality is enforced by the compiler. In Objective-C, many things, rather than being subject to hard and fast rules, are done by *convention*. Constructors are a great illustration of the difference. In C#, there is a single, formal way to create constructors. In Objective-C, by convention, one implements equivalent functionality in *initializers*. Rather than creating an object by invoking the process through a constructor, an Objective-C object, with a little help from the developer (memory-management is simple in Objective-C, but not automatic), is created, and *then* the developer explicitly calls a method on the newly created object — one of its initializers — that carries out the duties a C# developer would usually place in a proper constructor.

The fact that so much is done by convention is one of the trickier aspects of Objective-C if you're used to a world that is run according to rules. That kind of flexibility can give you more power over your code, but comes with a lot of responsibility. It puts developers in charge of things that, in more formal environments, are governed by syntax and compilers.

As for Cocoa, it's not so clear from its name what it is. The one thing you might already know is that, wherever you go in the world of Objective-C, you're all but certain to encounter Cocoa as well. The two are linked in a way that could easily lead you to confuse one with the other.

Why is this? If Objective-C is the language, what's Cocoa?

Fortunately, having already learned C# (or a similar language like Java), you're familiar with the separation of a language (C#) from its framework (.NET). Outsiders to C# tend to assume that C# and the .NET Framework are the same thing. Of course, the .NET Framework is the set of libraries that does the heavy lifting for your applications, and C# is one of the languages you can use to code against that framework.

Objective-C and Cocoa have a similar relationship. Objective-C is the language, and Cocoa is basically the framework against which Objective-C developers write their applications.

Cocoa is to Objective-C what the .NET Framework is to C#.

In Objective-C terms, frameworks are called *kits*. As you explore the various iPhone frameworks (UIKit, Game Kit, Map Kit), you'll quickly learn and remember this.

The name Cocoa is also used as an umbrella term to refer to the core frameworks as well as frameworks that provide additional functionality. Just as a C# developer might refer to an ASP.NET project simply as a .NET project, an Objective-C developer might refer to Cocoa rather than the specific kit he or she is using.

To make matters a little confusing, Cocoa for the iPhone is actually called *Cocoa Touch*. Cocoa Touch is a version of Cocoa that has been designed specifically around the form-factor and capabilities of the iPhone, iPod, and, more recently, the iPad. Much of the core functionality remains the same, but there are differences in design that shift dependencies around, and the desktop versions of Cocoa's various kits have iPhone equivalents that have very different names (AppKit, for example, which provides much of the core support for application development on the desktop, has an equivalent on the iPhone called UIKit).

Differences aside, it's perfectly acceptable to refer to Cocoa Touch simply as Cocoa. The context of the conversation makes it clear that it isn't the desktop version of Cocoa being discussed.

Purists might not care for using certain terms in ways that are technically incorrect, and that brings us to the next section of this chapter.

ACADEMIC VERSUS PRAGMATIC APPROACHES

MonoTouch is an interesting place to be.

Although Objective-C is built on top of plain old C, what sets it apart is that it's a layer of object-orientation implemented in a message-passing, dynamic paradigm. With Objective-C, you can basically pick up the phone, call an object, say whatever you'd like to it, and it'll either answer or it won't.

C#, on the other hand, began its life as a statically typed language. You couldn't pick up the phone and call a C# object at runtime, tell it whatever you wanted to, and then expect it to behave. For the most part, if you could place a call to a C# object, you would have to "Press 1 to place an order, press 2 to check the status of an order, press 3 to cancel and order, and, if you'd like to do anything else, please call another object." Functionality is baked in at compile time.

Objective-C, being built on top of C, isn't purely dynamic. C#, which has been acquiring dynamic features over the years, is no longer purely static. Each is an amalgam of methodologies, incorporating a little of this, and a little of that.

In the middle is MonoTouch.

You can now write statically typed code that gives you the benefits of compile-time error checking. Some developers consider this a hindrance, whereas others like the idea of catching simple errors due to typos *before* their apps are in the hands of customers.

Although MonoTouch isn't nearly as widely known as Apple's native developer stack, there's a tendency for Objective-C developers to butt heads with C#/MonoTouch developers in forums, at talks, in letters to the editor, and anywhere else you might find the two worlds overlapping.

When the emotions and brand loyalties are stripped from the arguments, there's usually nothing left. However, in the cases where the stacks and their actual technical details are being discussed, they can be pared down even further.

Ultimately, die-hard Objective-C developers tend to dislike it when Objective-C is talked about in terms that don't belong to the domain of languages based on messaging (Smalltalk, the inspiration for Objective-C, being one such language). This is perfectly fair. There *are* significant differences in how Objective-C works as opposed to how C# works.

A common example of a dispute-causing difference is when a C# developer says something like, "I have an NSString object, and I'm trying to call its intValue method, but I'm getting an error..."

In Objective-C, one doesn't "call methods." Rather, "messages" are "sent" to an object. At runtime, if the class the object is an instance of has a method implementation that can be reached by the message being sent, the object instance will handle it and do its job. If an object, or "receiver," doesn't "respond" to a message, meaning that it doesn't have a corresponding method implementation, that message could be ignored.

If you're accustomed to languages like C#, and if that paragraph didn't make much sense to you, you aren't alone. Developers might argue about the advantages of either paradigm, but developers are also known for presenting their opinions as facts.

Whether one system is better than the other doesn't ultimately matter. Presumably, you're a C# developer, and you want to write apps for the iPhone using C#. With that in mind, the goal here isn't to teach you to code in Objective-C, but to teach you just enough that you'll be able to mentally parse Objective-C code and "translate" the associated jargon into terms you're familiar with when reading documentation.

The approach here, then, is pragmatic rather than academic. You have a job to do. The philosophy and deeper explanations behind Objective-C are available should you choose to go on and learn about the language for reasons beyond those presented here.

An aspect of the pragmatic method in this case is trying to map the *closest* concepts and terms between the two languages, their runtimes, and frameworks. To return to an earlier example, as different as it might be to send a message as opposed to calling a method, sending messages and calling methods are, to an app developer, basically the same thing.

BASIC SYNTAX AND CONCEPTS

As discussed earlier, Objective-C is a set of object-oriented functionality built *on top of* C. As such, much of the code in an Objective-C app, despite how different it can look, *is* C.

In those cases, C#, Java, Python, or any other number of languages, will have already familiarized you with variable creation, flow-control, and other core details of coding. An if block in Objective-C will be instantly recognizable.

The aspects of Objective-C most likely to trip you up are:

➤ Initializers versus constructors

➤ Sending messages versus calling methods

➤ Reference-counting versus garbage-collection

What's great about MonoTouch is that it, for the most part, lets you write C# as you normally would, abstracting away the unfamiliar and presenting it to you in a manner so natural that you might never have realized how differently things are done in Objective-C:

➤ Initializers are implemented as constructors.

➤ You call methods like you always would, not having to worry about what it means to "send a message" (for more information, see Chapter 11).

➤ Reference-counting is hidden from you.

To read Objective-C, you still need to know a little about what this all means and how to parse it in your head.

At this point, code is the easiest way to demonstrate the differences and how Objective-C concepts map to C#.

Listing 14-1 shows a block of Objective-C. Take a look at it, allow yourself to be confused, and let questions form in your mind. This will prime you for quickly learning how to see this code as C#.

LISTING 14-1: Object Creation and Initialization in Objective-C

```
// Create and initialize our objects
NSString *aString = @"Hello, World";
UILabel *aLabel = [[UILabel alloc] init];

// "Send a message", accompanied by an argument, to "aLabel"
[aLabel setTextAlignment:UITextAlignmentLeft];

// Assign a string value to the label's "text" property
aLabel.text = aString;

// Print formatted output to the console consisting of
// the string we assigned to the label's "text" property
NSLog(@"The label's text: %@", aLabel.text);
```

As is sometimes the case with example code, this code doesn't *do* much, but it does introduce some of Objective-C's idiosyncrasies.

Before I explain what's going on here, take a look at the equivalent code in C# (using MonoTouch) in Listing 14-2.

LISTING 14-2: Object Creation and Initialization in C#

```
// Create our objects using constructors
string aString = "Hello, World";
UILabel aLabel = new UILabel();

// Assign a value to a property that wraps
// the Objective-C "message"
aLabel.TextAlignment = UITextAlignment.Left;

// Assign a string value to the label's "text" property
aLabel.Text = aString;

// Print formatted output to the console consisting of
// the string we assigned to the label's "text" property
Console.WriteLine("The label's text: {0}", aLabel.Text);
```

These examples are extremely simple and don't show off many of the benefits of MonoTouch, but they're more than enough to give you a base off of which to conduct your mental parsing of Objective-C.

Initialization

This line from Listing 14-1 is the string initialization in Objective-C:

```
NSString *aString = @"Hello, World";
```

Here is the C# version from Listing 14-2:

```
string aString = "Hello, World";
```

The data types NSString and string ("string" being a C# shortcut to refer to System.String) are functionally equivalent. They also both get special treatment as far as object construction goes, due to the frequency with which strings are used in apps.

In the Objective-C version, you declare your variable's type (NSString) and then assign it a string value. There's no manual allocation of memory, nor do you have to call a constructor, just like C#.

In Objective-C, a string literal always takes the format @"String value goes here." The @ symbol indicates that this is a *compiler directive*, all of which begin with the @ symbol. The purpose of these directives is to notify the compiler that it has to do some work for you. In this case, that work is to process the string literal's convenience shortcut. The @ symbol isn't used *exclusively* for this purpose, as you'll see in the string formatting section of the line that outputs the string value to the console, but, outside a string literal, the @ symbol before a word indicates that the compiler has to step in and help out. Mostly, it's to handle drudgework for you (nobody wants to have to manually create string objects again and again).

The * indicates that the variable you're creating is a pointer to the location in memory where the object is stored. Functionally, you can think of this as an everyday object in C#. Developers who have never worked with pointers tend to fear them, but because you're *reading* this code rather than writing it, don't let the * scare you.

In the C# version, the quotes alone act as the shortcut. The C# compiler "knows" what to do here. You also don't need to add a * because you don't need to tell C# that your variable is ultimately a reference to memory where your object is stored. It's just understood.

The next line, repeated in the following code snippet, gets you right into the differences between constructors and initializers. It also shows the syntactical differences between "sending messages" and "calling methods."

```
UILabel *aLabel = [[UILabel alloc] init];
```

Code like this is everywhere in Objective-C.

You declare your variable, along with its type, much as you would in C#. Where it's dramatically different is the code on the *other* side of the assignment operator ("=").

You aren't using new to create your object. The allocation of memory and object creation takes place when you "send" the alloc "message" to the UILabel class. Somewhere up the food chain, the Objective-C runtime sets aside memory for your object and returns a pointer to that object space.

It's confusing for the moment on account of Objective-C's syntax (which is addressed momentarily), but, after you've received a pointer to your newly created object, you send it the init message. As noted earlier, init is an Objective-C convention that performs the duties you would usually handle in a C# constructor. An Objective-C class may have many initializers, and they're named differently depending on what special set each may contain. In C#, you would create multiple constructors, each containing a different set of parameters to accomplish the same job. An example of this may look like the following.

If you have a C# constructor that you define like this:

```
public MyClass(string theString)
```

then in Objective-C it would look like:

```
-(id)initWithString: (NSString *)theString;
```

For a constructor with an extra variable in C# it would look like this:

```
public MyClass(string theString, DateTime theDate)
```

In Objective-C, it would look like:

```
-(id)initWithStringAndDate: (NSString *)theString date:(NSDate *)theDate;
```

Messages and Methods

To return to the part of Objective-C's syntax that will probably look the most foreign to you, take a look at the square brackets ("[...]").

Because Objective-C is built on top of C, and because dot-notation (which is used in C# for various purposes, including accessing an object's members) is already used by C for accessing the values of a struct, something needed to be done to tell the compiler that you're using an Objective-C object and that you need it to *do something*.

The square brackets are what distinguish that code. The general format is
`[variableName messageToSend];`.

When the compiler sees the square brackets, it knows that you're entering Objective-C territory; specifically, that you're sending a message to an object instance.

Before continuing, let's discuss what "message sending" is.

Pragmatically speaking (see "Academic versus Pragmatic Approaches," earlier in this chapter), "sending a message" to an object is basically the same thing as calling a method on a C# object. Yes, the purists will want to point out how different the technical underpinnings are, but for your purposes, it's perfectly fine to say that sending messages is analogous to calling methods.

While reading documentation, books, posts, and so on, you might also run into the term "receiver." Again, pragmatically speaking, you can simply think of the "receiver" as being your object instance.

All together, when discussing Objective-C, if it's written or said that, for example, "You're sending the `init` message to its receiver," you can read it as, "You're calling the object's `init` method." If you say it out loud, you'll get kicked out of the Objective-C club, but at least you'll understand in C# terms what's being said.

Now, you also likely noticed that the line contained nested square brackets. In C#, this would be similar to chaining methods together using dot-notation.

To translate, you'd take this snippet of Objective-C:

```
[[variableName messageToSend] anotherMessageToSend];
```

and translate it into C# like so:

```
someVariable.SomeMethod().AnotherMethod();
```

The first few times you look at the Objective-C syntax, you might feel like your head is going to explode. It's certainly different from C#, but concerns about head explosions will be allayed over time as you grow more familiar with Objective-C.

Something that will take a little more getting used to is the way arguments are passed in Objective-C. Consider the following code from the Listing 14-1 example:

```
// "Send a message", accompanied by an argument, to "aLabel"
[aLabel setTextAlignment:UITextAlignmentLeft];
```

Once again, you're looking at the square brackets that indicate you're sending a message to a receiver (from here on out, to familiarize you with it, Objective-C terms are used when discussing Objective-C, provided the terms has already been explained).

What's different is that you're passing an argument along with the message you're sending.

You've established that messages can be thought of as C# methods. In this code snippet, the message you're sending to the receiver (aLabel) is setTextAlignment:. Note the colon at the end of the message. The colon indicates that what follows is an argument. In C#, you would call the equivalent method and then, rather than appending a colon followed by your argument, you'd place the argument inside parentheses.

In this example, the argument you're passing is a value that tells your label you want all text to be left-justified.

The following is the equivalent code in C# (although the MonoTouch binding wraps the setTextAlignment: message in a property, for the sake of this example, you're going to pretend it was bound instead as a method).

```
// Call the SetTextAlignment method on the "aLabel" object with an argument
aLabel.SetTextAlignment(UITextAlignment.Left);
```

An important distinction is that, in Objective-C, the colon that precedes the argument is *part of the message name*. If an Objective-C message can take an argument, when typing out the message name, the colon *must* be included. Some of the dynamic functionality of Objective-C allows you to choose messages at runtime to send to a receiver. If the means by which you're taking advantage of this dynamic feature requires that you first notify the runtime of the message name (usually as a string value), if the message takes an argument, you *must* append the colon. The colon, then, is part of the signature.

> The Objective-C runtime wouldn't know that the message you're calling takes an argument without the colon, and the result would usually be an error that's difficult to track down. It's easy to forget this rule, so do your best to burn it into your mind.

Moving on, the syntax for assigning and retrieving values to/from properties in Objective-C is similar enough to C# that it doesn't require explanation. It's the one place in Objective-C where dot-notation is used, so it's easy to spot. The only thing to watch out for is whether the operation in question is on an Objective-C object or a C struct. Typically, this doesn't represent much of a problem, because it's clear from context which it is. If you're accessing the `text` property of a label, for example, you're clearly working with an Objective-C object. C structs act strictly as data models; they do *not* have methods. In the example code, `aLabel` is sent a message, so you can see that it is not a struct. In Objective-C 2.0, dot notation for property values were added so instead of

```
[label setText:aString];
```

you can now just write

```
label.Text = aString;
```

Another clue is that, because labels are common UI components, and because most iPhone app UIs are created using members of the Objective-C based UIKit, you can infer that `aLabel` is an Objective-C object.

The last line of the Objective-C example shows where C and Objective-C can mix. `NSLog` takes its arguments within parentheses, so it's a plain old C function. But, because it's a function written specifically for Objective-C, it "knows" what to do with the Objective-C objects and values it's passed. As a MonoTouch developer learning to read Objective-C, you don't need to worry about *how* this is done. Still, it doesn't hurt to have some idea of how Objective-C and C can coexist like this. Simply put, the Objective-C runtime is a library written in C. Anything you can do with Objective-C syntax, you can also accomplish by coding directly against the Objective-C runtime library. It's tedious and cumbersome and something few app developers will ever have to do, but that's how they would do it.

Memory Management

The last aspect of Objective-C that's most likely to confuse you at first is its memory-management.

Based on reference-counting, Objective-C's method of managing memory leaves the developer with a lot of control and responsibility over when an object should be created and when it should be destroyed. On the desktop, Objective-C supports garbage collection (as of Objective-C 2.0). It is not, however, available on the iPhone. This is one of the many things MonoTouch does for us. And although reference-counting is trivially simple compared to other methods of non-GC memory-management, it still requires that a developer be cautious and extremely methodical while writing iPhone apps in Objective-C.

If you've ever used an iPhone app for a few minutes and then had it crash on you, it's likely that the developer wasn't paying enough attention to managing memory, and a leak resulted in depletion of system resources. That scenario prompts the OS to shut the app down before it takes *everything* and brings the device to a halt, likely requiring a reboot. Hence, the crash.

As a MonoTouch developer, you're fortunate in that you can generally safely ignore any reference-counting you find in the Objective-C source you're reading.

Here's a list of messages involved in reference-counting:

➤ retain

➤ release

➤ autorelease

When you see these messages, feel free to discard them when mentally translating to C#.

In terms of implementation, reference-counting doesn't go away just because of MonoTouch, but because MonoTouch handles it for you, you can skip over those three messages and continue mentally parsing without concern.

It isn't inconceivable that there will be times when you *do* need to be aware of how memory is being handled in a particular block of Objective-C, but, for now, be happy that the burden has all but been taken off your shoulders.

Incidentally, the number of bugs in your apps, and, in turn, the number of crashes your users are likely to encounter, decreases tremendously because of what MonoTouch does for you. Even seasoned, expert Objective-C developers routinely make mistakes where memory-management is concerned.

When you belong to a demographic that's known for staying up for several days straight, drinking gallons of caffeinated beverages to remain alert, becoming sloppier by the minute, and constantly being "*almost* done with this feature," the benefits of having a tool like MonoTouch cannot be overstated.

Once you've become comfortable with the syntactical and conceptual issues you looked at in this section, you should have just enough of an understanding of Objective-C to be able to determine well enough what's going on.

For the rest, the "cheat sheets" in the following section should help you with the smaller-picture issues you'll encounter along the way (terminology, compiler directives, and so on).

CHEAT SHEETS

This section consists of a series of quick-reference translation tables organized by aspects of Objective-C and their corresponding C# analogs:

- ➤ Terminology
- ➤ Compiler Directives
- ➤ Data Types

The tables are organized by these categories and then in alphabetical order for the term/data type and so on.

Sometimes there isn't a C# equivalent for an item. In those cases, an explanation of the closest concept will be given, as well as whether or not it's something you need to worry about. There are a few things that can simply be ignored.

It's important to remember that these tables are meant to be a quick way to find the *closest* C# version of an aspect of Objective-C. The technical underpinnings may vary widely, but for getting the gist of what's going on, these tables will help.

Terminology

In French, "sensitive" has the same meaning as the English word "sensible," and the word "sensible" has the same meaning as the English word "sensitive." The two languages have many things in common, and that often helps, but sometimes those commonalities are the source of confusion.

The same is true for any true programming languages, but even more so in this case. Objective-C and C# are both object-oriented languages, but *how* they're implemented differs enough that to properly speak about one or the other requires independent sets of jargon.

Table 14-1 contains terms you're likely to encounter in documentation or publications on Objective-C, and how to translate those terms into what you would likely find in C# documentation when analogous concepts are being discussed.

TABLE 14-1: Terminology in Objective-C and C#

IN OBJECTIVE-C...	IN C#...	NOTES
Attributes	N/A	In C#, attributes are used to provide metadata about a class. In Objective-C, attributes apply specifically to properties. They give the compiler information on how to generate a property (whether it should be treated as a value type, a reference type, and so on).
Categories	Extension Methods	Almost identical in use. You also might encounter the term "category method." The word "categories" in Objective-C typically refers to a group of "category methods." Also note that the convention is for categories to be defined in files that follow the naming convention `ExtendedType+CategoryName.h/.m`. So, for `NSString`, you might see `NSString+JSONParsing.h/.m`. What follows the "+" is a short name that describes what the category methods are for. In this case, you should expect the category to add methods to `NSString` for parsing JSON. It isn't always so clear, though, because some developers are better at descriptive naming than others.
"Conforms to..."	"Implements interface..."	In C#, we say that a class *implements* an interface. In Objective-C, interfaces are called protocols, and classes are said to "conform" to a protocol. So, if an Objective-C class "conforms to the XYZ protocol," it's basically the same as saying that a C# sharp class "implements the XYZ interface."
Delegates	Events	Many Objective-C types have a property called "delegate" to which a protocol (an interface in C#) implementation is assigned. The implementation can exist in the current class (`someObject.delegate = self`) or in another object entirely. Functionally, Objective-C delegates implement methods that would be events in C#. Where it makes sense, some Objective-C delegates have been bound as C# events in MonoTouch, making the experience feel much more natural to C# developers.

continues

TABLE 14-1 *(continued)*

IN OBJECTIVE-C...	IN C#...	NOTES
Interfaces	Class definition	In Objective-C, an interface (see `@interface` in Table 14-2) specifies the class name, superclass, which protocols (interfaces in C#) it implements, its local instance variables, method definitions, and properties. It goes in the class's header file. In C#, the class definition and its implementation are the same.
Messages	Methods	Wherever "messages" are discussed, it's safe to think of them as C# methods. Though there are differences, for the purposes of reading Objective-C, you can usually get away without having to consider these differences.
Properties	Properties	Though properties are similar between Objective-C and C#, their purposes can be quite different. In Objective-C, properties don't just generate getters and setters for local instance variables, but can also handle some of the repetitive drudgework of Objective-C, such as reference-counting. Because C# is garbage-collected, and because MonoTouch takes care of reference-counting for us, the particulars of Objective-C's property implementation don't matter much to the C# developer. One thing to remember is that Objective-C properties are always accessed via "self" (the equivalent of C#'s "this"). It's also the only place Objective-C makes use of dot-notation (`self.propertyName = someVariable`).
Protocols	Interfaces	An Objective-C protocol is very similar to a C# interface, but with one important exception: Objective-C protocols can be partially implemented. With Objective-C 2.0, developers can now specify that a method is required (see `@optional` and `@required` in Table 14-2). However, traditionally, Objective-C protocols don't require full implementation.
Receivers	Object instances	In Objective-C, you "send messages," and those messages go to a "receiver." In C#, you "call methods" on an "object."
Selectors	Methods	Like messages, the C# developer can safely think of selectors as methods. The distinction becomes important when working with the Objective-C runtime. For more information, see Chapter 11 on creating MonoTouch bindings.

Compiler Directives

As discussed in the "Basic Syntax and Concepts" section, compiler directives, which are preceded by the "@" symbol, tell the compiler that there's work for it to do.

Sometimes, a compiler directive is intended to replace code that, were it written by the developer, would be more or less identical regardless of the app being written. The first directive listed — that for string literals — is a good example. Strings are used often in app development, and developers shouldn't have to write the code to manually instantiate a string (unless there's a specific reason to do so, which, with strings, is often *not* the case). So, the `@""` directive frees the developer from having to write that repetitive code.

In other cases, compiler directives can provide metadata. They can represent code that would be tedious to write that the compiler can safely generate for you.

Whatever function they perform, they're instructions that serve a purpose at compile time. Table 14-2 contains these compiler directives.

TABLE 14-2: Compiler Directives in Objective-C and C#

OBJECTIVE-C	APPLIES TO...	C#	DESCRIPTION
`@"string"`	Data Types	`"string"`	The only significant difference between string literals in Objective-C and string literals in C# is the "@" symbol that precedes the literal in Objective-C. Otherwise, the two maybe be treated equally.
`@catch()`	Exception Handling	`catch`	Functionally equivalent.
`@class`	Data Types	`using`	`@class` is used in Objective-C when referencing a data type that hasn't been defined in any of the header files referenced by the current class. It's a way of telling the compiler that the data type exists, but to resolve it at runtime.
`@dynamic`	Properties	None	When properties are declared in Objective-C, the compiler expects to find a corresponding implementation in the class body. Sometimes a property implementation is created at runtime. `@dynamic` tells the compiler not to look for implementations for the specified properties.
`@end`	Classes/ Interfaces/ Extension Methods	`}`	`@end` allows the compiler to recognize the end of an Objective-C definition. Translating to C# is as simple as substituting a closing curly-brace
`@finally`	Exception Handling	`finally`	Functionally equivalent.

continues

TABLE 14-2 *(continued)*

OBJECTIVE-C	APPLIES TO...	C#	DESCRIPTION
@implementation	Classes	Class definition	Objective-C splits a class definition and its implementation between two files (".h" and ".m"). C# combines these in the same file. The C# equivalent is the beginning of a class definition.
@interface	Classes	None	Not to be confused with C#'s interface keyword, @interface begins an Objective-C class definition (found in a class implementation's header file). C# basically combines @interface and @implementation in one line (public class ClassName...).
@optional	Interfaces	None	Indicates that the specified methods in an Objective-C protocol (analogous to a C# interface) don't have to be implemented. There is no equivalent in C#.
@private	Scope	private	Functionally equivalent.
@property	Properties	property	An Objective-C property consists of a definition and implementation. The @property directive goes in a class's header file. It specifies the property's attributes (in parentheses), data type, and name. Its implementation is either generated automatically (see: @synthesize) or at runtime (see: @dynamic).
@protected	Scope	protected	Functionally equivalent.
@protocol	Interfaces	interface	An Objective-C protocol is roughly the same as a C# interface, and may be treated as such. The primary difference is that Objective-C has support for interfaces
@public	Scope	public	Functionally equivalent.
@required	Interfaces	None	Indicates that the specified methods in an Objective-C protocol (analogous to a C# interface) must be implemented. There is no equivalent in C#.

OBJECTIVE-C	APPLIES TO...	C#	DESCRIPTION
`@synthesize`	Properties	None	Found in the class implementation file, `@synthesize` tells the compiler to automatically generate the getters and setters for a property. In C#, this is done on a case-by-case basis (`property PropertyName { get; set; }`).
`@throw`	Exception Handling	`throw`	Functionally equivalent.
`@try`	Exception Handling	`try`	Functionally equivalent.

Data Types

For the most part, the C# equivalent to a data type in an Objective-C application will be obvious either by name or context. Objective-C actually adds very little on top of C. Most of the differences are in Cocoa, and it's fairly easy to determine the C# equivalents of those types as well (NSArray can be represented as a List, an NSDictionary as a Dictionary, and so on).

Where things get confusing is when you encounter an Objective-C type that has no C# counterpart or for which C already seemed to have a perfectly good data type.

Table 14-3 is for those times.

TABLE 14-3: Unknown Data Types in Objective-C and C#

OBJECTIVE-C	C#	EXPLANATION (IF NEEDED)
`BOOL`	`bool`	
`IBAction`	None	Used by Interface Builder to connect UI component "events" to Objective-C methods.
`IBOutlet`	None	Used by Interface Builder to connect UI components to local instance variables in Objective-C classes.
`id`	`var/object`	The go-anywhere-and-do-anything generic pointer.
`nil`	`null`	
`NO`	`false`	
`YES`	`true`	

SUMMARY

Objective-C comes in handy for both reading and learning from various Objective-C articles and books. Although it is not necessary to learn Objective-C at all, it's key to understanding the Objective-C-based iPhone SDK and all the documentation provided by Apple on the SDK. This enables you to quickly figure out how to convert Objective-C sample code into C# in no time at all.

15

The App Store: Submitting and Marketing Your App

WHAT'S IN THIS CHAPTER?

➤ Getting your app ready to submit

➤ Submitting your app

➤ Promoting and profiting from your app

After hours of wire framing, designing, developing, and testing, you are finally ready to share your app with the world. This chapter discusses all things App Store. First, it talks about the process that you need to go through before you are ready to submit — this includes final testing with Ad-Hoc builds and a presubmission checklist. Next it addresses actually submitting to the App Store, and then finally what to do with your app after it's in the App Store. This chapter also touches on alternative monetization strategies such as ads or in app purchases.

USING AN AD-HOC BUILD FOR PRESUBMISSION TESTING

Before you jump right into submitting and marketing in the App Store, you need to make sure a few items are covered. Apple has a notoriously stringent review process where it tests your app on a variety of hardware in a variety of conditions. So before I submit my apps, I like to run them through a similar process.

Now, most people don't have the whole family of iDevices laying around. This is where the Ad-Hoc build comes in. Doing an Ad-Hoc build allows you to send your app to up to 100 people and have them install it on their device. If you can, try to find a variety of devices to test your app on, at the minimum at least test on iPhone and iPod Touch; but if you have access to additional people try to get at least one from each generation of currently released iDevices.

When I am trying to find users to test my Ad-Hoc builds, the first place I look is my Twitter or Facebook friends. If you have a decent size network on either of these services, chances are you can find several types of iDevices among those people. So I usually send out a message asking for volunteers to help me test. People are generally very eager to help; they like the idea of having the software before it's in the App Store, and it gives them a sense of being special. Additionally, head over to some of the iPhone Developer forums, my favorite happens to be `http://iphonedevsdk.com/forum/`. Lots of these forums have specialized sections where people can ask for or volunteer to be an Ad-Hoc tester. If you are looking for someone local who you can meet with face-to-face and give some feedback, try Craigslist. Another great resource for finding local testers is Tweetups. These are Meetups that are organized over Twitter. They are usually filled with tech-savvy people who would be more than willing to jump in and help on a project.

However, before you can have someone test your app you need their UDID (Unique Device Identifier). Every iPhone or iPod Touch has a sequence of letters and numbers that is unique to each device. An example UDID might look like this: 7bkls09tqep3674lp0747hxzp4d9k301nf523jh7. I am sure you are wondering why you need the UDID to install your program — this is because Apple requires only App Store-approved applications be installed on the iPhone/iPod Touch. By providing the UDID, Apple can then grant permission for the app to be run on specific devices. This is Apple's way of allowing beta testing without having to approve each version of your application.

Getting a UDID from Your Testers

You can easily get the UDID from your testers in two ways.

The easiest way is to point them to Erica Sudan's free Ad Hoc Helper App (`http://appsto.re/adhochelper`). Your testers can install this, and as soon as they run it, a Compose Mail Dialog is presented with their UDID in the body of the message. Provide them with an e-mail address to send their UDID to and they are done.

The other way to get the UDID involves using iTunes.

1. Instruct your testers to open iTunes and connect their phone (see Figure 15-1).

2. Direct them to the Summary tab in the right pane. This is the tab that contains the information about their phone such as name, capacity, software version, serial number, and phone number.

3. When they click the serial number, it reveals their device's UDID (see Figure 15-2).

4. They can now copy the UDID to their clipboard by selecting Edit ➪ Copy (see Figure 15-3).

5. Now they can paste that in an e-mail or use a contact form to get you their UDID.

FIGURE 15-1

FIGURE 15-2

FIGURE 15-3

Making Ad-Hoc Provisioning Profiles

Now that you have gathered the UDID from your users, you need to log in to the iPhone Dev Center (http://developer.apple.com/iphone). Once you are there, navigate to Devices and select Add Device. See Figure 15-4.

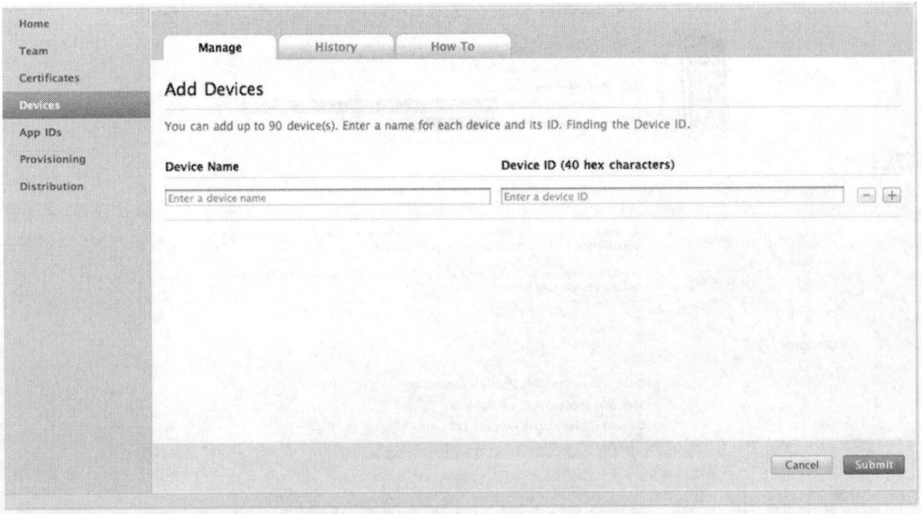

FIGURE 15-4

Under Device Name add your tester's name (this is only for your own personal reference). Under Device ID input the UDID for that user. If you need to add additional users click the green plus sign; otherwise, you can hit Submit if you are done.

The last step in making an Ad-Hoc build that can be installed on your testers' devices is creating a provisioning profile. In the iPhone Developer Program Portal navigate to Provisioning ⇨ Distribution, click New Profile, and then select Ad-Hoc for the Distribution Method. In the Profile Name type your application name (that is, **monotouchapp**). In the App Id select the name of your app. Select all of the devices that you would like this code to run on, and click Submit when you are done. You need to hit Refresh at least once (sometimes Apple's server might be behind and you may need to hit it multiple times); you will then see the download button. Now download the provisioning profile. I save this in my MonoTouch app's /bin directory, so that I can keep all of my files together; but you can put this anywhere that you want. Keeping the provisioning file in your /bin directory will make it easier for you later when you package your Ad-Hoc builds.

Building an Ad-Hoc Version of Your App

You need to make a special build of your app that can be used along with the Ad-Hoc provisioning profile that you created so that your testers can use your app on their devices.

Adding a New Configuration for Ad-Hoc

Before you can make an Ad-Hoc build you need to add a new configuration to MonoDevelop for distribution. You must do this for the solution and for each project in the solution.

Select Project ⇨ Solution Options from the menu, and you will be presented with the Solution Options dialog box. Select the Configurations panel and click the Add button. In the New Configuration dialog pick a name for the configuration, such as *AdHoc*, and make sure that the Platform field is set to iPhone.

 To save you the step of having to perform this action for each project in your solution, simply check the box Create configurations for all solution items.

Changing the Signing Options for the Configuration

In the Project Options dialog, select the iPhone Bundle Signing panel, and using the drop-downs at the top of the panel, select the configuration for which you wish to edit signing settings. This should be the configuration you created in your previous step, in this case *AdHoc*. You will need to repeat this process for each of the projects that are in your solution.

Pick an identity for signing your application. This should be the distribution identity that you obtained from Apple's iPhone Developer portal when you created your distribution certificate. Choose Distribution (Automatic) if you want MonoDevelop to select the correct identity automatically.

Pick the Ad-Hoc provisioning profile that you have created for your application that you obtained from Apple's iPhone Developer portal. MonoDevelop only lists the provisioning profiles that are associated with the identity you have selected.

Custom Entitlements.plist

One way that an Ad-Hoc build differs from a build for the App Store is the need for an `Entitlements.plist` file. Add a new `Entitlements.plist` file to your project by choosing File ⇨ New ⇨ File ⇨ iPhone ⇨ iPhone Entitlements. You will then need to open `Entitlements.plist` and disable the get-tasks-allow entitlement. This prevents the debugger from attaching to your application, which is required for Ad-Hoc distribution.

Reviewing Bundle Settings

Before you actually build the app you need to review the bundle settings to ensure that they are correct for this app. To do this:

1. Select the iPhone Application pane.

2. While you are here you want to ensure that you have set a display name and version number, and that the bundle identifier matches the bundle identifier that is part of the provisioning profile. You also specify your 57x57 app icon on this screen.

3. Now you need to switch over to the iPhone Build Signing pane and add the `Entitlements` `.plist` file that you created in the previous step to the Custom Entitlements field in the code signing options. Make sure that you do this only for the Ad-Hoc distribution configuration.

Building the Project

After completing the preceding steps you can now proceed to making your Ad-Hoc build. Before starting the build process in MonoDevelop, switch your active build configuration to the new profile you set up earlier (*AdHoc*).

Then build the project. You can then find the build bundle by going to the project folder /bin (the default location) or where you have pointed the output for your Ad-Hoc configuration. This will be shown in the Output pane of MonoDevelop. You will need to send both the app and the Ad-Hoc provisioning profile that you created to anyone that you want to test this app.

Packaging Your Ad-Hoc Build

You have your Ad-Hoc build ready to go; now you need to actually get it to your testers. Your testers will need both the app and your Ad-Hoc provisioning profile. You have two options: You can make an `.ipa` of your app, where iTunes will handle the unzipping, or you can make a `.zip` of your app.

 If you have testers that are on Windows machines, including an `.ipa` *is the preferred method because iTunes handles the decompression.*

The .zip Method

If you have selected the `.zip` method, you will need to send your testers the following: `YourApp .app` compressed in a `.zip` file along with the file `YourApp_AdHoc_Provisioning_Profile .mobileprovision`.

I usually send these two files to testers via e-mail. Note, however, that some e-mail providers may not let you send the `AppName.zip` because it contains a binary file. If this is the case, upload your files to an FTP server and send your testers a link. Installing an Ad-Hoc build is much like installing a normal iPhone app.

1. If you have the `.zip` and `.mobileprovision` files in an e-mail, save them to a convenient location, such as your desktop.

2. Drag and drop the `.mobileprovision` file onto Library ➪ Applications in iTunes. On the Mac, you can just drag it to the iTunes icon in your dock (Figure 15-5 shows this in Windows).

3. Extract the `.zip` file. To do this, right-click the `.zip` file and select Extract All... (see Figure 15-6). Step through the wizard and accept the defaults by clicking Next. Windows Vista Users: The built-in Extract All... command corrupts the application so that it cannot be installed. You should try using a different zip program like WinZip or WinRar to extract the zip file.

4. Find the `.app` folder (usually `AppName.app`) (see Figure 15-7).

FIGURE 15-5   **FIGURE 15-6**   **FIGURE 15-7**

5. Drag and drop the whole `.app` folder onto Library ➪ Applications in iTunes. On the Mac, you can just drag it onto the iTunes icon in the dock (refer back to Figure 15-5).

6. Verify that the application shows up in Library ➪ Applications. Note that it will not have its normal icon (see Figure 15-8).

FIGURE 15-8

7. In iTunes, select your device under Devices, choose the Application tab, and make sure that the new application is checked (see Figure 15-9).

FIGURE 15-9

8. Now sync your iPhone/iPod Touch as you normally would. After the sync is complete, the new Ad-Hoc app will appear as a regular application on your device.

The .ipa Method

To create an .ipa, move your AppName.app directory into a new directory called Payload and then zip the Payload folder and change the file extension to .ipa.

1. If you have the .ipa and .mobileprovision files in an e-mail, save them to a convenient location, such as your desktop.

2. Drag and drop the .ipa and .mobileprovision files onto Library ⇨ Applications in iTunes (see Figure 15-5). On the Mac, you can just drag them to the iTunes icon in your dock.

3. Verify that the application shows up in Library ⇨ Applications. Note that it will not have its normal icon (see Figure 15-8).

4. In iTunes, select your device under Devices, choose the Application tab, and make sure that the new application is checked (see Figure 15-9).

5. Sync your device and try out the new app!

PREPPING FOR SUBMISSION

Before you can release a paid app to the App Store, there are several steps you must take. First, you must agree to all of the paid app contracts, and submit your tax and bank routing info. For best results you should do this before you even begin working on your apps. These contracts have an approval process that they must go through and can sometimes take several weeks to be approved by Apple.

Building a Distribution Version of Your App

The MonoTouch team has done a great job on making the process of building for distribution in MonoDevelop mimic closely the process in Xcode to make it possible for you to follow Apple's instructions for building for distribution.

 Note that you can also export your project to Xcode using the Run ⇨ Debug in Xcode command, and follow Apple's instructions for code signing for distribution in Xcode.

Adding a New Configuration for Distribution

Before you can make a distribution build you need to add a new configuration to MonoDevelop for distribution. You must do this for the solution and for each project in the solution.

Select Project ⇨ Solution Options from the menu, and you are presented with the Solution Options dialog box.

Select the Configurations panel and click the Add button. In the New Configuration dialog pick a name for the configuration, such as *Distribution*, and make sure that the Platform field is set to iPhone.

 Again, to save you the step of having to perform this action for each project in your solution, simply check the box Create configurations for all solution items.

As with your solution you would then select the Configurations panel and click the Add button. In the New Configuration dialog use the same name for the configuration that you used in your solution, such as *Distribution*, and make sure that the Platform field is set to iPhone, just as it was in your solution.

Changing the Signing Options for the Configuration

In the Project Options dialog, select the iPhone Bundle Signing panel, and using the drop-downs at the top of the panel, select the configuration for which you wish to edit signing settings. This should be the configuration you created in your previous step, in this case *Distribution*.

Pick an identity for signing your application. This should be the Distribution identity that you obtained from Apple's iPhone Developer portal when you created your distribution certificate. Choose Distribution (Automatic) if you want MonoDevelop to select the correct identity automatically.

Pick the distribution provisioning profile that you have created for your application that you obtained from Apple's iPhone Developer portal. MonoDevelop only lists the provisioning profiles that are associated with the identity you have selected.

Reviewing Bundle Settings

Before you actually build the app you need to review the bundle settings to ensure that they are correct for this app. To do this, select the iPhone Application pane. While you are here, ensure that you have set a display name and version number, and that the bundle identifier matches the bundle identifier that is part of the provisioning profile. You also need to specify your 57x57 app icon on this screen.

Building the Project

After completing the preceding steps you can now proceed to making your distribution build. Before starting the build process in MonoDevelop, switch your active build configuration to the new profile you set up earlier (*Distribution*).

Then build the project. You can then find the build bundle by going to the project folder /bin. All that you need to submit to Apple is the app compressed in a `.zip` file.

Once again, the app could be somewhere other than the /bin folder: It will be wherever you decided to put it, shown on the Output pane in the project options.

Presubmission Checklist

The following checklist covers the basic steps you need to address prior to submitting your app.

1. Complete all Ad-Hoc testing.

2. In an Xcode app, this is where you need to make sure that you update the `Info.plist` file in your app. Luckily MonoDevelop handles all of this for you, with the information that you fill out in the Application Bundle and Application Signing Panes.

3. Set the bundle identifier (if you haven't already) to YourAppName. The identifier should not contain spaces or special characters — alphanumeric characters and dashes are okay.

4. If you want your app to be named something different on the actual device than its name in MonoDevelop, change the Bundle Display Name as well.

5. Update the bundle version. If this is your first time submitting this app, the version number should probably be 1.0.

6. Be sure the icon file is set (this should be a 57x57 .png file).

7. Write a description for your app for the App Store. The app upload page says the description should be 700 characters or less, but that limit doesn't seem to be enforced.

8. Choose a numeric SKU for your app. This can't be left blank, and it has to be a unique number for each of your apps. (I usually use YYMM, like 0902, but you can use whatever you want as long as it's a number.)

9. Assemble your screenshots. You'll need at least one primary screenshot, and up to four more secondary screenshots. Be sure they're the right size (320x480 for portrait or 320x460 for landscape).

10. Prepare your iTunes artwork. This is a 512x512 pixel, 72dpi JPEG. It should match your icon artwork as closely as possible — apps are sometimes rejected if these two images are dissimilar.

Submitting via iTunes Connect

Now that you have run through your pre-submission checklist and gotten all those items out of the way, you are ready to submit the app via iTunes Connect. When you log in to `developer.apple .com/iphone`, there's a link to iTunes Connect on the right. Once you're logged in to iTunes Connect, click Manage Your Applications and then Add New Application.

The app info page asks for your app name, description, copyright info, version number, SKU, application URL and support URL, and support e-mail address (all of these are required). The URLs you enter translate as follows:

ITUNES CONNECT CALLS IT:	WHAT IT SHOWS ON YOUR APP'S PAGE IN ITUNES:
Application URL	Company Name Web Site
Support URL	Appname Support

If this is your first time uploading an app to the App Store, and you enrolled as an individual developer, you'll be asked if you want to set a Company Name. Think carefully about this — once you set it, you *cannot* change it without calling Apple and going through its phone support line. If you set a company name, all of your apps will show it.

The app upload page is where you upload the goods: your app (the `.zip` file of the compiled binary), the iTunes artwork JPG, and your primary and secondary screenshots. When uploading your secondary screenshots, you should upload them in *reverse* of the order you want them to appear in the App Store. For example, if you have screenshots named ss1.jpg, ss2.jpg, ss3.jpg, and ss4.jpg, you'll enter ss1.jpg as the primary screenshot, then add (one at a time) ss4.jpg, ss3.jpg, and ss2.jpg to the secondary screenshots fields.

You also need to provide the following information on the upload page:

➤ **Ratings:** You'll be asked to rate your app by indicating whether it includes any offensive material.

➤ **Pricing and availability:** This is where you set the price and release date for your app. You'll get a chance to review this after you select a pricing tier. The page should show a link to the pricing tiers, but if it doesn't show one initially, just set the price to anything and let it refresh. The link should show up then. The pricing tiers as offered by Apple are as follows:

  ➤ Free

  ➤ Tier1 — 0.99

  ➤ Tier 2 — 1.99

  ➤ Tier 3 — 2.99

  ➤ Tier 4 — 3.99

  ➤ Tier 5 — 4.99

  ➤ Tier 6 — 5.99

  ➤ And so on.

➤ **Release date:** This defaults to the present day, but you can set it to a date in the future if you like.

When your app gets approved, log back into iTunes Connect and reset the release date to the approval date; that way the app shows up at the top of the new releases section of its category. If you fail to do this, when your app gets approved, it shows up buried several pages down — not very desirable.

If you're submitting an app update, however, you shouldn't touch the release date until you get word that your update has been approved. If you change the release date of an update to sometime in the future, your current app vanishes from the App Store!

Finally you get to the summary page, where you can review all the info on your app before submitting it for review. Check to be sure everything looks okay, and then click Submit.

Now you just have to wait. Apple's approval process can be a mystery; your app might get approved in a week, a month, or never. They will usually e-mail you to let you know when your app is ready for sale. (They'll also e-mail you the dreaded "your app is taking longer to review," which means your app might be in review for several more weeks or months.)

PROMOTING YOUR APP

Wow, after all that, your app is finally in the App Store, but your work is only half done. Even great apps generally won't sell themselves. Getting noticed in the App Store is a job all in itself. This section reviews some ways that you can help your app stand out from all of the rest.

Supporting Your App Promotion

When you roll out your app you need a few support items right away:

- ➤ A web site and blog
- ➤ A Twitter account
- ➤ A Facebook fan page
- ➤ A YouTube channel

The next sections briefly discuss how to set up these supports in the most effective ways to give you the best platform from which to manage the promotion of your app.

Your Web Site and Blog

Even though you have a description in the App Store, having at least a one-page web site for each of your apps can really help your perception among potential buyers.

If this will be an ongoing project for which you plan to add new features or continue development, I would also encourage you to blog about it. Not only will this help get more content about your app into search engines, but will also give users and potential buyers a little insight into you and your app, making them feel a part of the process.

Your web site should include not only screenshots that appear in your App Store description but any additional screens that are important to the app but didn't make the cut. The look and feel of an iPhone app is a big selling point so highlight anything that sets your app apart from the competition.

Use the great SimFinger utility from Atebites (`http://bit.ly/SimFinger`*) to create a screencast showing your app in use. Not only can you post this on your web site, but you can also syndicate it out on video sharing sites. This can increase your exposure and also help with search engine rankings.*

Your Twitter Account

Being accessible to your users can be key to getting good reviews and also word of mouth referrals. The weapon of choice for mass communication these days seems to be Twitter, so make sure that you have your Twitter account prominently displayed on your site. Use your Twitter account to gather user feedback, keep users updated, run contests, and to just have fun. You don't want your Twitter account to merely be a feed of your blog; you need to engage users and take part in the conversation. If you don't have anything to share about yourself, your app, or what might be coming next, look for content items that might relate to your app or that fit in the same niche that your app focuses on. By providing this content you are likely to pick up new followers who could turn into new customers. You should try to read and if possible answer any tweets that pertain to your apps. Do this by not only looking in the mentions tab on Twitter, but also utilize the Twitter search to look for your app name, your own name, your company, or anything that might relate to your app.

> *You might run into some negative comments as well as some constructive criticism. If this happens don't lose your cool; try to defuse the situation, and do whatever you can to rectify the issue for the naysayer. This might seem like overkill, but one unhappy customer can quickly turn into a few tweets, a blog post, several YouTube videos, bad App Store reviews, and before you know it, these things can impact your sales and ultimately your brand.*

Your App's Facebook Page

In addition to Twitter, Facebook is another wildly popular social media platform that many people not only use to communicate with friends and family, but also their favorite brands. Set up a Facebook fan page for your app. Encourage your Twitter followers to also become a fan. You will find that you will use the fan page much like you will use your Twitter account. Remember, it's not just about pushing your content — use this platform to open up the lines of communications with your users and potential customers.

YouTube Channel

Continuing down the path of social media musts for your app, head over to YouTube and set up an official YouTube channel for your app. Use this for how-to videos, feature demos, and sneak peeks of upcoming versions. Your YouTube channel won't be as much about the two-way communication with your users as Facebook and Twitter, but it will be equally important because it can serve as a living sales page for your app. As Google and other search engines have adapted to the increasing amount of video that is consumed by Internet users, they have started to incorporate video as part of their search engine result pages, so having a video with your app name and other relevant keywords are likely to rank high for those search queries. Users are also very likely to head to YouTube to try and find a video on how something works. Making how-to's for your app can help reduce support e-mails, tweets, calls, or forum posts.

Key App Promotion Techniques

Now that you've gone over the basics that you need to have for getting the support structure in place for your app, this section discusses some specific app promotion techniques.

Running a Contest

With each version of your app you will receive 50 promo codes. This will allow whomever you have given the promo code to redeem it on the App Store for a free copy of your app. So the first thing I suggest is to set aside five promo codes and run a contest on Twitter, a simple contest where all the user has to do is follow you and retweet a message promoting the contest. At the end of the contest you award the promo codes to either a random follower or a random retweeter. The web site twitRand (`http://twitrand.com`) is a great and easy way to select either a follower or a retweeter. You can also adapt this to a contest for getting more Facebook fans.

Before you give away all 50 of your promo codes you need to set aside a few and submit them to App Review sites:

> ➤ `http://gizmodo.com`

> ➤ `http://arstechnica.com/apple/iphone/apps/`

> ➤ `http://www.macworld.com/appguide/index.html`

> ➤ `http://toucharcade.com`

> ➤ `http://appsafari.com`

> ➤ `http://148apps.com`

> ➤ `http://appadvice.com`

> ➤ `http://appcraver.com`

> ➤ `http://iphoneapplicationlist.com`

> ➤ `http://iphonealley.com/reviews/apps/`

> ➤ `http://appleiphoneschool.com/`

> ➤ `http://appvee.com`

> ➤ `http://apptism.com`

> ➤ `http://appstoreapps.com`

> ➤ `http://whatsoniphone.com/`

> ➤ `http://krapps.com/`

> ➤ `http://iphoneappreviews.net/`

> ➤ `http://dailyappshow.com`

> ➤ `http://freshapps.com/`

> ➤ `http://theiphoneappreview.com/`

> ➤ `http://reviewmyiphoneapp.com/`

➤ http://appshouter.com/

➤ http://nativeiphoneapps.com

➤ http://slapapp.com/

➤ http://www.imedicalapps.com/

➤ http://apptheater.com

➤ http://tapcritic.com/

➤ http://iphoneblog.de

➤ http://alliphoneappsreview.com

➤ http://app-reciationreviews.blogspot.com

➤ http://ifanzine.blogspot.com/

➤ http://www.iusethisapp.com/

➤ http://www.applesauceblog.com/

➤ http://www.macworld.com/appguide/index.html

Starting a PR Campaign

Something many developers overlook is a good PR campaign around their app. There are several PR sites where you can write a press release and push it out to hundreds or thousands of sites in one click. Blogs, magazines, papers — they all need content to write about to try and entice readers to visit their site, so make it easy for them to feature a piece about your app. In your PR include links to your web site and also a direct link to a media kit, where you can have web and print ready art of your app's logo and screenshots. Don't overlook your local media outlets. Local news organizations might cover your story; it might not drive lots of downloads, but could increase exposure and also give you something to quote on your web site.

Using In App Ads

In App ads can be a great way to promote your app as well. Lots of the mobile ad networks provide pinpoint audience targeting that includes age, gender, geography, category, carrier, device, and handset. Pricing models include bid per-click and per-engagement. Conversion tracking and reporting are standard offerings. By using the audience targeting you can be sure that you are reaching someone who is more likely to take a look at your app. You can choose a cost per click or cost per engagement with most providers as well. Do some research and find the network that will reach your demographic and fit your budget.

Marketing through the Social Media Sites

Not only can you use social media yourself to promote your app, but you can also use it to crowd source marketing and promotion of your app. A Tell-A-Friend feature on your about or settings view can be the best selling tool there is. When someone recommends a product to a friend or family member they are more likely to purchase that item than if they saw a commercial or ad for it. I like to provide several ways for users to share this information. First, I implement an E-mail and SMS share with friends; this allows me to leverage their contacts to instantly share their new favorite app. The easier you make it for them, the more likely they are to use it. Next up: the social media big dogs — yup, you guessed it — Facebook and Twitter. Include a few prewritten blurbs and a shortened link to your app in the App Store, or have a space for them to write their own.

SUMMARY

This chapter explored the final process to get your app running on end-users' phones. Remember the importance of testing on a variety of real devices; this will help you avoid any technical rejections. Apple will be quick to reject your app if it doesn't behave properly on a real device.

Promotion is key with your app, make sure you use social media and review sites to maximize your exposure. Include ways for users to reach out from inside your app; the easier it is for them to tell their friends, the more likely they are to do it. Free apps can be monetized too; ads or even sponsorships are a great way to monetize free apps.

INDEX

W

WCF. *See* Windows Communication Foundation
web services, MonoTouch, 14
Web Services Description Language (WSDL), 94
Web View, 20
WhereButton.TouchUpInside, 148
Window, IB Library, 21
Window, 50–52
window, UINavigationController, 300
Windows Communication Foundation (WCF), 14, 96–98
Windows, Views, & Bars, IB Library, 21
WSDL. *See* Web Services Description Language

X

XBOX, 2
Xcode, 8, 272

XDocument.Load(), 101
XElement, 100
XIB. *See* XML-based Interface Builder
.xib, 19
XML. *See* eXtensible Markup Language
XML-based Interface Builder (XIB), 18
XYZ coordinate system, Acceleration, 192

Y

YES, Objective-C, 319
YouTube, 235–236, 334

Z

.zip, 327–328
zoom level, mapping, 162–163
ZoomEnabled, 156
ZoomScale, 59